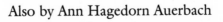

Also by Ann Hagedorn Auerbach

Wild Ride:
The Rise and Tragic Fall of Calumet Farm, Inc.

Ransom

Ransom

The Untold Story of International Kidnapping

ANN HAGEDORN AUERBACH

Henry Holt and Company • New York

Henry Holt and Company, Inc.
Publishers since 1866
115 West 18th Street
New York, New York 10011

Henry Holt® is a registered trademark of
Henry Holt and Company, Inc.
Copyright © 1998 by Ann Hagedorn Auerbach

Library of Congress Cataloging-in-Publication Data

Auerbach, Ann Hagedorn.
Ransom : the untold story of international kidnapping / Ann
Hagedorn Auerbach.—1st ed.
p.   cm.
Includes bibliographical references and index.
ISBN 0-8050-4078-1 (hardcover : alk. paper)
1. Kidnapping.   2. Travelers—Crimes against.   3. Ransom.
4. Hostages.   5. International offenses.   I. Title.
HV6595.A93   1998
364.15'4—DC21   97-51625

Henry Holt books are available for special promotions
and premiums. For details contact: Director, Special Markets.

First Edition 1998

DESIGNED BY KELLY SOONG

Printed in the United States of America
All first editions are printed on acid-free paper.
1   3   5   7   9   10   8   6   4   2

In memory of

Hans Christian Ostro,
Frank Pescatori, Jr.,
Sidney Reso,

and the countless other hostages
who have died in captivity

Contents

PART I

Stolen Lives

Ever since I was caught, I have been walking through mountains and passes and I am tired. I appeal to the Government of India and the Norwegian Government to do anything they can to release us because we don't know when we will be killed. I appeal especially to the tourist office because everybody there told me that this place was safe. An officer even gave me his card and said I could call him if there was a problem. Well I am calling [him] now.

—Hans Christian Ostro
July [17,] 1995

1

AUGUST 13, 1995
EARLY MORNING
KASHMIR

The mountains seemed as high as the sky was deep, challenging even the sun as it climbed the peaks each dawn to deliver a new day to the villages below. And as the sun rose higher, hanging ribbons of light across the Himalayan terrain, women in the village of Prazmulla carried machetes to a grove of trees to crop limbs for firewood, as the women of the village had done every morning for generations. But today was different. This August morning in 1995 would break the peaceful spell of the ages, ushering in the curse of the violent present. The terror began as the women crossed a dirt road at the grove's edge.

Near the road beneath the chopped branches of a willow tree was the headless body of a man. The first woman saw it and gasped. Two others hid their faces in their hands. The head lay some forty yards away, its curly flaxen hair speckled with dirt. The women did not know the man. He was not from their village, nor was he from their country. He was a tourist, an innocent, a well-meaning man slain by strangers in a land he passionately loved, far away from his home.

Other villagers quickly gathered round the corpse, staring at the feet and hands bound tight with hemp. Tucked between the folds of the dead man's clothing were scraps of paper, on which he had written poems, and a strip of birch bark on which he had secretly jotted notes about his feelings and beliefs. The handwriting was sometimes hard to decipher; perhaps his hands had been bound as he wrote. Or maybe he was scribbling in the darkness of a mountain night. Some poems described his fascination and love for Indian culture; others revealed an emotional landscape of despair, a hopeful plan to escape, and a valiant effort to face an unspeakable fate.

"If I die now," he wrote, "then I will not die poor. I have within me many worlds as this one with all its richness, beauties and contrasts."

Police from the nearest town soon came to examine what the villagers had discovered that day. They returned the head to the body and carefully set it down upon the long, once-sturdy legs. Kneeling at its side, they examined carvings on the chest that later would be identified as the initials *A-L-F-A-R-A-N,* a militant group apparently named for a mountain in Saudi Arabia near the birthplace of the prophet Muhammad, founder of Islam. They saw too a note pinned to the dead man's shirt. Written in Urdu, a language of Pakistan spoken in Kashmir, it read: "We have killed the hostage because the government has failed to accept our demands. In 48 hours, if our demands are not met, the other hostages will meet the same fate."

2

Jane Schelly looked down the long, white-clothed table, wondering if anyone else had noticed the subtle shift in mood. She and the other wives, girlfriends, and families of the five tourists now in captivity in Kashmir had been invited to the German embassy for what was meant to be a social luncheon, a time to mingle and to relax. But something was amiss. During lunch, the diplomats, at various times, had placed their fine, embroidered napkins on their velvet-cushioned seats and quietly left the room. Upon returning several minutes later, they seemed withdrawn and even solemn, wearing the strained, anxious looks of sailors who had just been informed of a menacing storm ahead. In the hallway outside, there was an unusual stir and bustle in the air. Doors opened and closed amid the foreboding sound of hushed voices. And as the guests began the last course, an irresistible serving of strawberry crepes with vanilla ice cream, Jane observed that the German ambassador, Frank Elbe, who had just returned to the seat next to hers, was unable to eat.

By then Jane had grown eerily familiar with the ups and downs of her new life as a hostage wife. Her husband, Donald Hutchings, a highly respected neuropsychologist from Spokane, Washington, had been in captivity in the Himalayas for forty days, since July 4. With him were two Brits, Keith Mangan and Paul Wells; a Norwegian, Hans Christian Ostro; and a German, Dirk Hasert. Another American, Connecticut businessman John Childs, had escaped on the fifth day of captivity. Although Jane believed Don and the others would be released soon—any day now—there had been moments of heart-stopping doubt that they would ever be seen alive again. Death threats and deadlines had brought endless worries to her wakeful nights and a clinging sense of terror to her days. At times it seemed she could not breathe until the deadlines had passed and she had heard the news that Don was still alive somewhere in the mountains. No man had ever been more alive for Jane than Don Hutchings, whose charismatic smile and cheery, witty demeanor had brightened her life for the better part of eleven years. But during the past forty days, in her imagination, Don had been killed and resurrected and killed again a dozen times or more.

The first big scare had occurred three weeks earlier, on July 21, the day the rebels had announced to the local press that two of the hostages had been wounded in a bloody skirmish between Kashmiri rebels and the Indian troops. At 9 P.M., the hostage families gathered at the British High Commission in New Delhi and were told the news. Jane wrote in her journal later that night: "We were absolutely silent and aghast. It just didn't seem possible. Our thoughts were: What sorts of wounds do pistols, machine guns and hand grenades cause? How would you get them to a safe place on horseback, or on a litter [stretcher]? Would they be in shock? Would there be risk of infection or amputation? Would Don be critically injured and perhaps be handi-capped? If they were injured, would the [militants] allow them to be helicopter rescued? So many thoughts and concerns that I actually felt physically ill, a feeling I hadn't had to such a degree since the night and the morning that Don was actually taken."

The next morning relief had swept through the New Delhi embassies of four governments when the U.S. State Department informed Jane and the others that the Indian government adamantly denied the occurrence of any skirmish.

And now, at the German embassy, Jane hoped her fears for Don's safety would once again prove groundless. But the look on Ambassador Elbe's face was unmistakably grim. He would later tell the father of one of the hostages that the toughest job he ever had faced in his long career as a diplomat was playing the role of luncheon host that day, a role that required him to deliver the tragic news that he and officials of four other governments had learned just before the strawberry crepes were served. After adjourning the group to a sitting room for coffee, the ambassador dolefully asked for the attention of the guests he had hoped to entertain and to console that day. "The body of a white-skinned male has been found in the area where we believe the hostages have been held," he said. "The body will be taken to Srinagar [Kashmir's capital] for identification."

At that instant, as Jane looked at the other hostage families, it felt as though a cold wind had gusted through the elegant, high-ceilinged room. One of the women began to sob; another said she wanted to go "home" immediately, back to her embassy. Jane comforted both by saying that it did not appear to be certain that the body was indeed one of "theirs." What was going through her mind was that, considering the presence of other tourists in the area, there was likely only a 50 percent chance it was one of the five men, and a one-fifth chance that of those it would be Don. Jane tried to calm herself with the notion that there was only a 10 percent chance that Don was dead.

"There was this feeling that you did not want it to be your loved one and yet you looked around that room and thought with horror that you could not wish this on anyone," Jane recalled. "I asked if it was certain that the killed one was one of our five and Mr. Elbe looked at me as if he did not understand my English and said absolutely nothing."

A British official then announced that the car was ready to take the guests back to their embassies. As Jane walked out, the tall, formal ambassador put his arm gently around her and very softly said, "It's not your husband."

Leaning into Elbe, she began to sob.

3

AUGUST 13, 1995
MORNING
LONDON

As the sun mounted its midday post above northern India, glaring like a spotlight on the tragedy below, it had barely burned off the first layer of fog over the Thames. In East London, Roy Ramm's day was about to begin in a way he had not anticipated: with a call from the British Foreign Office.

The stocky, blue-eyed commander—Scotland Yard's number-three man—had planned a rather unprecedented Sunday in his life, a day without a schedule. Indeed, it was a day with only one goal, to spend time with his family. He might visit his eighty-five-year-old mother or take his wife Janet for a country drive in his favorite car, the 1970 MG, or join Janet and his son James for an afternoon movie. Sundays were meant for such things, the commander firmly believed, though he rarely had time to indulge in leisure. Janet, of all people, knew such a day was as unlikely as a Sunday afternoon visit from the queen. Once asked what it was like to live with Commander Ramm, his wife smiled and said, "Who?"

Although he kept a low profile in the British press, Ramm played a leading role at Scotland Yard. "RR," as his colleagues called him, was a veritable combination of Eliot Ness, Indiana Jones, and Tom Clancy's hero, Jack Ryan. He even looked the part with his Hollywood good looks—a British Nick Nolte with a cockney accent. His boss was the assistant commissioner, and his boss's boss was the commissioner. And with his post came a prodigious list of responsibilities. He was head of the Organized Crime group, which meant he supervised the undercover unit, known by its code name SO10 and considered one of Scotland Yard's most effective weapons. It also meant he directed the extradition unit, the witness protection program, the international extortion unit, and the nearly 600 men and women in the Flying Squad, a group that handled bank robberies. He headed up the Fraud Squad, at 200 strong, and the Firearms Unit, the 200 or so bobbies who carried guns. And he was lauded by his colleagues as one of Britain's greatest detectives ever.

For the past five years, too, the commander had been the director of hostage negotiation, which meant exactly what it suggested—and more. As director, not only did Ramm supervise Scotland Yard's negotiator-training school—an internationally renowned program— but he also was in charge of handling hostage crises in Britain. Moreover, during the past two years, he and his team of twelve crisis negotiators had begun to work with the British Foreign Office on cases abroad. The squad was dispatched to investigate murders and drug trafficking, and they advised governments on ways to gain the release of hostages taken by terrorists, rebel tribesmen, or common criminals. Abductions of Brits in foreign lands, especially developing nations, were on the rise.

The image of Scotland Yard's finest getting calls from the Foreign Office at every odd hour—with cars routinely picking them up before dawn and secretly depositing them on planes to exotic lands, from Sierra Leone to Indonesia—was, like the commander himself, the stuff of movies. Visions of globe-trotting cops indulging in lavish travel during the bleak months of a London winter provoked jealousy among colleagues, who dubbed the team "the suntan squad," and criticism in the local press, which questioned the practicality of such endeavors. To be sure, the budget was filled with highly unusual—and at first glance, very indulgent—items for London cops, including business-class airline tickets to sunny climes overseas. The missions, however, were anything but lavish junkets on the warm, white beaches of the world.

To the contrary, they were often rigorous, demanding expeditions involving long, sometimes treacherous plane trips; the need for inoculations against every disease and virus for which an antidote existed; bumpy rides through battle-torn landscapes often stitched with land mines and marked by haunting scenes (like the display of human heads impaled on wooden poles that Ramm had witnessed in Cambodia); hikes through hot, hostile jungles and periodic bouts with illnesses contracted by ingesting contaminated food and water; many weeks away from home; and many, many interrupted Sundays. Accommodations were typically austere.

On one case in South Asia, Ramm and fellow negotiators decided they must relax for a few hours at the end of a grueling day and watch a movie. A government official had given them some pirated videos and an old TV with a VCR. There was only one problem: insufficient electrical power. After gathering enough car batteries to rev up their rugged entertainment center, they settled back to watch Sharon Stone in *Basic Instinct,* which for a while provided a much-needed escape. But halfway through the movie, a new problem yanked them back to reality: rats perched atop the TV.

Then there was the work itself. In a foreign culture, every challenge of negotiating a kidnapping was doubly difficult.

That Sunday morning in August marked the middle of what had already been a frantic first year for the Yard's international cops. In early July, when the Kashmir incident began, Ramm had just returned from Bosnia, where he had advised the United Nations on gaining the release of the 120 British peacekeepers held hostage by the Bosnian Serbs. The Bosnia assignment had begun shortly after the resolution of a five-month case in Africa, where Ramm had secured the release of six Britons held by guerrillas, and this had followed several grueling cases in Cambodia. But for the commander and his team of negotiators, what was about to transpire in the year ahead was the scheduling equivalent of a Gatling gun. By spring the so-called suntan squad had little hope of ever seeing the light of day again. The group—much like kidnap experts worldwide that year—would be hurriedly trying to keep up with a rapid-fire caseload. With calls coming in from negotiators in time zones all over the world and urgent flights to its remotest regions, the notion of a free Sunday for Ramm would seem like a chapter from another person's life.

But on this particular Sunday, India was uppermost on the commander's mind. Kidnapping was a common weapon in the struggle for independence in India's northernmost region, Kashmir, but rarely had foreigners been abducted. Now there were five tourists who had been held in mountain hideaways for nearly six weeks. Ramm and others on his staff had been especially concerned because Scotland Yard had not been invited to the front lines of the incident. That was up in Srinagar, where daily contact with the kidnappers was occurring. Both Scotland Yard and the U.S. Federal Bureau of Investigation had representatives in New Delhi who were permitted to submit written suggestions *only* to the governments of the four affected countries— the United States, Britain, Germany, and Norway—referred to as the "G4." But none of the professional negotiators was allowed to set up what was called a "cell"—an entity through which they systematically organize and analyze information and messages, script communications to kidnappers, consult with local police, and advise the head communicator. They were not where they wanted to be, but Ramm knew that pushing his way to "the front" would not be diplomatic and might compromise his position if the negotiators were eventually invited. The commander was a gentleman, and when it came to diplomacy, he was a master. He understood that there had been so much optimism among the diplomats in New Delhi regarding the imminent release of the hostages that any intrusion by Scotland Yard or the FBI would likely have been frowned upon. In fact, such interference could have been insulting to the diplomats who had successfully dodged a minefield of death threats, demands, and deadlines, and who had pridefully managed the case without the daily direction of professional negotiators.

Ramm would not remember much about that Sunday, after he got the call. He was accustomed to receiving calls at odd hours regarding abductions and other crises, but he had never gotten one about the decapitation of a hostage. His heart sank as he listened to the somber official from the Foreign Office who told him about the body that was found in the willow grove. The authorities believed it was a Norwegian tourist, the official said, by the name of Hans Christian Ostro.

Although he wore more hats than any commander in Scotland Yard's history, including a new one as a United Nations adviser on hostage negotiation, the commander's capacity for empathy was far greater than any sense he had of self-importance. Good negotiators, whether they admit to it or not, live with a case in their minds and hearts every waking hour until it is resolved and the hostages are safely released. And the commander was clearly one of the best.

As he listened to the government official, Ramm knew that the death of Ostro, a twenty-seven-year-old actor, director, and writer from Oslo, would transform the case in India, both strategically and emotionally. It would be the catalyst to force open the gates to outside negotiators from Scotland Yard and elsewhere, who had been in New Delhi since July. India's intransigent pride—one of many issues affecting the search for a resolution—would diminish as the former colony and the "G4" sought an end to the crisis.

The stakes were much greater now. The rebels had killed one hostage; it would be easier for them to kill again.

4

August 15 was the forty-eighth anniversary of India's independence from Great Britain. As marches and speeches replaced the usual clamor of India's swarming cities, five time zones away Roy Ramm was fastening his seat belt and settling in for a long plane ride east. He would arrive in New Delhi at about dawn and, despite the hour, be whisked away to meetings that would consume his day. Typically, on such long flights, the commander divided his time between briefing himself on the myriad details of the case at hand and reading a novel, often by John Le Carré, his favorite living writer. Coming back from Sierra Leone the previous spring, he had read *The Dark of the Sun* by Wilbur Smith, a British novelist and another Ramm favorite. But today he would sleep, if possible, and as he forced himself to relax he would mull over the imposing task ahead, perhaps even jot down a few thoughts.

His job was to move delicately, diplomatically, and as smoothly as possible to position his negotiators—and those from the FBI—onto the center stage at Srinagar. Among other things (such as keeping the hostages alive and delaying any further violence by the rebels), he and his team must try to prevent, or at least stall, a military invasion, the typically knee-jerk governmental response to the killing of a hostage. Although a rescue might be necessary eventually, now was not the time, and because of the rugged, vast terrain, there might never be a moment when military action would not endanger the lives of the hostages. It was worrisome that dozens of Delta Force agents from the United States, as well as Special Air Services (SAS) operatives from Britain and members of India's Black Cats commando division—created after the assassination of Prime Minister Indira Gandhi—were already planning their maneuvers through the craggy passes of the Kashmir Valley, though they had not dared to venture yet to northern India. It wasn't that they weren't competent; it was simply that the timing was wrong. They did not yet have enough information to conduct a successful raid.

As he tilted back his seat and closed his eyes, he thought of the hostages in Kashmir. Ostro was killed on the fortieth day of their captivity, and Ramm, like everyone else in the case, hoped the remaining hostages did not know of his death. The commander well understood the comments of Charlie Mangan, the father of one of the British hostages, who told a local reporter that, although he was confident his son was strong enough to "ride things out and to adapt to situations quite quickly," he was deeply worried that "if Keith knows what happened to Hans Ostro . . . well, I shudder to think what he's thinking about."

As a parent as well as a hostage negotiator, the commander could almost feel the father's concerns. It seemed abundantly clear now that, unlike previous incidents in India, this one might not be so quickly resolved. The psychological and physical ability of the hostages to endure a long captivity depended, in large part, on hope. And the enduring source of hope for captives was the belief that they were more valuable to their captors alive than dead. The hostages' knowledge of Ostro's savage demise could smother that hope as quickly as a mountain avalanche could kill them.

As the plane roared toward the Mediterranean, the commander, as if playing solitaire with his memories, drifted in his thoughts, flipping back through his past cases. There was Bosnia and the satisfaction of seeing so many hostages set free, and the incident in Sierra Leone, which ended with the safe release of two young engineers. But then, like shadows suddenly closing in, the images of Cambodia invaded his thoughts, reminding him of the pain of the previous year.

In November 1994, the Khmer Rouge had admitted to killing three Western tourists whose freedom Ramm's team had been trying to obtain since their abduction the previous summer. The captors' intent was to scare away foreign investors whose money would strengthen Cambodia's new government. In April that same year, the Khmer Rouge had abducted three other foreigners who were traveling the 135 miles from Sihanoukville to Phnom Penh. After four or five days in captivity, they beat the captives to death with clubs and rifle butts. But no one knew of the murders for months. Among the tragic details of the case was the fact that the guerrillas continued to ask for money, a $150,000 ransom and a $5,000 fee for proof-of-life information, long after the two young women and the man, all in their midtwenties, were dead. "Madness without a full moon," Chris Newman, a Scotland Yard negotiator, called it.

Ramm, who faced death threats throughout the ordeal, could still hear the words of one victim's father, who kept believing—until the day the bones were found—that his twenty-four-year-old daughter was alive. The father even wanted to sell everything he owned to pay the costly ransom and to buy the proof-of-life details. "I feel she's alive; I feel she's alive," he kept repeating. It was stunningly cruel when the rebels asked the grieving families for money for the remains of the bodies. Shortly afterward, the father, whom the commander believed to be "one of the finest people" he had ever met, died of a heart attack. Although the commander had been teaching hostage negotiation for some time, his ability to deal with the intense emotional needs of a family was acquired only through experience. And the horrors of Cambodia had been one of his most intense classrooms.

When he found himself trying to erase the images, he kept thinking of the hostage families and then of his own son who had been amply warned about potential dangers abroad. He thought for a moment about the Khmer Rouge and their heinous acts through the years. They were perhaps the bloodiest of all rebel groups, certainly among the century's most vicious. Yet in the years after the fall of communism and the installation of a new regime—and despite the 8.5 million land mines still buried in its war-wracked earth—the "new Cambodia" was touted in travel brochures and articles. "Cambodia: Journey of a Lifetime" was the title of one glossy brochure. And a Cambodian tourism official had recently told the press, "We want to promote nature-based tourism. We want people to discover our virgin provinces, such as Rattanakiri and Mondulkiri."

But the old problem, the Khmer Rouge, was still there, roaming the hills and jungles outside Phnom Penh. In 1994—a record year for Cambodian tourism, up 50 percent from the year before—guerrillas were taking Western hostages. "Serial kidnappings," the locals were calling them; foreigners taken for the ransom income or for manual labor, or both. First an American woman from North Carolina, who was released after forty-two days, and then the others, in two separate cases: three Brits, two Australians, and a Frenchman. All of them had been killed.

Ramm was not a religious man, but as he slipped into a light, fitful sleep, his thoughts were forming what seemed almost a prayer, hoping that what had happened in Cambodia would not happen in Kashmir, that it was not too late for the negotiators to step in, that the hostages and their families had the strength to endure the time it would take to resolve the case, and that the four nations drawn to this maelstrom of emotions and issues would somehow work together toward the goal of gaining the hostages' release.

Despite his experience and the skills of the people he would meet in India, the commander knew how many factors could spin out of the control of the negotiators, even after they were allowed to operate at the front lines. Governments and kidnap experts, no matter how dedicated, could do only so much. Kidnap negotiation, as Ramm had told students and friends through the years, was the most sensitive and delicate operation in counterterrorism. And this case would be exceptionally delicate, one that would linger in his mind long after its bedeviling conclusion.

Five innocent pawns in someone else's war. And now one was dead. Ramm slept barely an hour during the eight-hour flight.

PART II

Madness without a Full Moon

⟨≈×≈⟩

The crime of kidnap is, after murder, the vilest and foulest crime known to English criminal law.

—Judge Simon Goldstein,
England, March 27, 1997

5

August 13, the 40th day of captivity for the hostages in Kashmir, was the second day for Briton Timothy Cowley, snatched by rebels while bird-watching on a Saturday afternoon in Colombia. He would endure 111 more days as a hostage, many spent at altitudes as high as 18,000 feet. For Raymond Rising, an American from Minnesota, it was the 500th day in captivity somewhere in the misty mountains of Colombia, where at least 800 hostages were held. John Emberly, who worked for General Electric out of Peterborough, Canada, and his wife, Gina, marked their 240th day as the hostages of Colombian guerrillas. And it was hoped that Americans Mark Rich, Rick Tenenoff, and Dave Mankins, missionaries abducted in Panama in 1993, were still alive and well enough to mark another day with their Colombian captors.

Kidnap negotiator Robert Dwyer spent part of the day at his Florida office brushing up on his Portuguese in anticipation of his next big case in Rio, where abductions were occurring at a rate of one every forty-eight hours.

In China that day, the wife of a Hong Kong executive paid a $2 million ransom for her husband's return, while businessmen in several provinces demanded a greater police presence to help boost investor confidence in the face of rising crime—one of the threats, a kidnapping wave.

The London office of a private counterinsurgency group, Control Risks Group, was more active than most Victoria Street businesses on a Sunday afternoon, with a staff monitoring colleagues' efforts to resolve nine kidnapping cases: in Guatemala, Colombia, Brazil, and Panama.

And Thomas Hargrove, a Texan abducted in Colombia in 1994, wrote in his makeshift diary on this, the 325th day of his captivity—and the day, unbeknownst to him, that his family had paid a second ransom for his release: "Kidnapping. The deliberate creation and marketing of human grief, anguish and despair."

⊲⊜⊳

Kidnapping, an ancient weapon whose immense power was described as early as the writings of the Old Testament, has been employed for centuries by the greedy, the disenfranchised, the poor, the angry, and the alienated. Of all crimes and terrorist acts, none has so cruelly played upon the primal human fears of torture and death. Families have sacrificed fortunes to obtain the release of loved ones; governments have broken laws, covertly or indirectly, to free hostages; corporations have spent millions of dollars in ransoms, in security, and in lawsuits related to kidnappings; individuals have risked and sometimes lost their lives trying to rescue captives. And the captives themselves—whether pushed along perilous mountain paths twelve hours a day, tied to tree trunks, crammed into closets for months on end, or locked in iron boxes beneath the ground—have glimpsed a dark and demonic side of human behavior that few others have ever known.

Now, on the eve of a new millennium, as the world is shrinking and distant lands draw near, seemingly far-off threats grow closer, too. The power of kidnapping increasingly threatens the free-trade entrepreneurs, the corporate managers and workers, and the ambitious travelers whose ventures lure them across the globe, as far as the ragged edges of the post–Cold War world. This is a crime that has always thrived on chaos, flourishing in periods of societal transition when countries suffer from ever-widening gaps between rich and poor, from weak and corrupt law enforcement, or from the constant turmoil of civil war. It becomes more prevalent when nations evolve from agrarian systems to industrial societies and from industrialism into an age of information systems. And so it is that the international frontier of the late twentieth century, with its multitude of ethnic, religious, and tribal conflicts, its economic inequities, and its continual reordering of political and social relationships, has become a veritable breeding ground for the act of taking hostages to gain money and power.

Worse still, whether it is a hostage-taking incident, in which the location of the hostages is known and contained, or a kidnapping, in which a voice on the phone or a messenger through the jungle is the only link to the hostages' remote, unknown locale, no government, corporation, or individual, despite immense efforts, knows exactly how to deal with and abate the peril, much less how to eliminate it. Some governments, in facing kidnappers abroad, have upheld no-concessions policies, while others, recognizing that perpetrators are often criminal gangs as well as terrorist bands, have begun to rethink such policies. In the United States, for the first time since the federal government established a no-ransom policy regarding terrorists in 1971, agencies have revisited the critical issues of negotiations, ransoms, concessions, and the ways to achieve the release of hostages.

While motives for the crime and its intensity vary from country to country—from bankrolling terrorist activities to protesting foreign investment—the causes seem to be universally the same: stepped-up globalization in combination with the social and economic effects of the end of the Cold War. Today, there are fewer barriers to doing business globally than ever before. Bountiful resources, untapped markets, free-trade agreements, and the privatization of state-owned industries entice entrepreneurs to invest and multinational corporations to expand. For the tourism industry in many countries and for the eager traveler, too, the emergence of a borderless world has unearthed a treasure trove of opportunities.

But like those who invaded the American West in the nineteenth century, the post–Cold War trailblazers pay a price. The beckoning landscape is aglow with menace. Like the Old West, it's a land in transition—a wild, untamed world where crime and violence are common and law enforcement is often slow, inept, and deficient. Just as business executives see opportunity in the unregulated lands of plenty, all varieties of bandits, political terrorists, and criminal gangs see diamonds in the chaotic rough—especially in the unprecedented numbers of foreigners, who are welcome prey for roving kidnappers.

It's a boom-town world. And for the postindustrial nations, expansion into new frontiers is an inevitable step, necessary for developing new ways to create wealth and for competing in a global economy. It is imperative and utterly irresistible to explore, invade, and even at times to conquer less-developed nations, many of which were once inaccessible to such forays or accessible only to the very richest individuals and the most powerful corporations. Now it is possible for anyone, from executives of small and midsize companies to the ordinary, middle-class tourist, to stake a claim on the new frontier.

But the hell-bent rush, whether to exploit consumer markets or to take adventuresome treks through exotic mountain ranges, periodically conflicts with the visions and agendas of the inhabitants of the coveted lands. When the champagne corks popped to toast the end of the Cold War, generations of pent-up passion were released. Across the globe, nationalist campaigns and ethnic crusades were no longer suppressed by the Soviet structure. The world became a tangle of countries at different stages in their evolutions. Some, like the United States, were expanding their influence, while others were seeking a long-desired sovereignty in struggles left over from the era of colonization—shards from the broken promises of past empires. Some wanted to embrace the world, while others wished to shut it out. Not every indigenous tribe or freedom fighter or religious group welcomed the West and its companies and its brand of modernization. In some lands, the invading investors and corporations—and even the tourists—have been accused of spoiling valuable farmland, dissipating natural resources, and crippling traditional industries. And kidnapping, with its power to scare and intimidate, has become a weapon of choice. Rarely before, in times of world peace, have there been so many chances for innocent civilians, especially foreigners, to be pawns in someone else's struggle.

In earlier eras, kidnapping was used to politically blackmail governments. Now it has emerged as a popular tactic for groups independent of governments to raise money, to publicize causes, and to discourage, if not wholly deter, the intrusive presence of foreigners. In the 1970s and 1980s, numerous high-profile abductions brought the crime to the media's attention. Today, the targets are typically unknown individuals attracting few, if any, media spotlights. Yet the incidence is insidiously higher.

Gone are the days when high-profile statesmen such as Italy's ex–prime minister Aldo Moro or top-flight military officials such as U.S. Brigadier General James Dozier were the targets. Kidnapping, 1990s-style, has forced ordinary people into extraordinary circumstances.

Between 1968 and 1982, one government study reported, 951 hostages were taken in seventy-three countries. In 1995, at least 6,500 kidnappings took place in Latin America alone. Worldwide the annual kidnap total during the 1990s has been as high as 20,000 to 30,000, counting both political and criminal cases, according to studies by private industry and government groups. By 1997, most experts agreed that the countries most afflicted, starting with the worst, were: Colombia, Philippines, Brazil, Mexico, Pakistan, Guatemala, the United States, Venezuela, India, and Ecuador.

Still, as kidnap and terrorism expert Brian Jenkins wrote in a 1994 report for Kroll Associates, "There are no reliable international statistics on kidnappings. Fear of retribution, incompetent or corrupt police, or laws that prohibit the payment of ransom, provide powerful disincentives to reporting an abduction, and governments themselves, seeking foreign investment or tourism, have little incentive to broadcast a kidnapping problem. As a result, there may be great disparities between official statistics and informed estimates. The numbers are useful only in identifying high-risk areas and spotting long-term trends."

Some experts warn that politically motivated kidnappings, in which insurgents often try to gain the release of jailed compatriots or in which tribesmen protest foreign exploration, are a constant, looming threat. While incidents of political violence overall were declining by the mid-1990s and political terrorists seemed to prefer bombings above all other tactics, kidnappings, in absolute terms and proportionately, were on the rise.

Other experts, who claim the profit motive has overtaken ideology in the world of kidnapping, point to a troubling surge in ransom incidents—to epidemic levels in some countries.

Still others assert that to identify exact motives has become difficult. The lines are often blurred. Political terrorists sometimes employ common criminals to conduct kidnappings for ransoms, thus filling their war chests with much-needed cash to undertake larger projects, such as bombings or the purchase of high-tech weaponry. And conversely, because the image of a terrorist can be more daunting than that of a common criminal, bandit kidnappers have been known to maximize their demands by brazenly waving the banners of fervent causes, thus extracting maximum profits from maximum terror. After all, unlike the garden-variety street thug, political terrorists are often willing to die for their causes. Criminal gangs also occasionally make money by selling their captives to the guerrilla groups, which then use the hostages to garner political booty or ransoms.

Some countries, such as the Philippines and Colombia, seem to be plagued with gangs of both political *and* criminal kidnappers. In the Philippines, former Muslim rebels, now bandits without a cause, routinely snatch wealthy business executives for sizable ransoms, while political separatists kidnap to buy up weapons from the Middle East.

But whatever the motive and whatever the known statistics, it is clear that a confluence of events has compelled a staggering number of groups and individuals worldwide to turn to the grim act of taking hostages as a way to get what they want—especially money.

At the end of the Cold War, what could best be described as a labor problem boosted the rosters of ransom seekers across the globe. There was literally a financial crisis for Marxist rebels as well as the anti-Communist soldiers they had so long been fighting. The fall of the Soviet Union stopped the flow of money and equipment out of the USSR and Cuba to gangs of leftist rebels, and out of the United States to contra rebels, all of whom suddenly needed alternative sources of money. For some, kidnap ransoms became a bountiful and unburied treasure.

The loss of funding caused some gangs to disband or at the very least to downsize by laying off gang members. Indeed, the loss of state sponsorship, the end of wars against the Soviet Union and its surrogates, and the shrinking armies of many countries caused a dearth of jobs for some of the world's most vicious and sophisticated cold warriors, many with deft, finely tuned kidnapping skills. Failed insurgencies had left a large class of young men without work and had caused a glut of high-powered weapons in the marketplace as well. To survive, many of them, equipped with sophisticated weapons, resorted to what they knew best: kidnapping, robbery, and extortion.

In Colombia, for example, the two principal rebel gangs stepped up their drug trafficking as well as kidnapping—both more lucrative than robbing banks—to compensate for the lost funding. And with the crackdown on Colombian cartels and cocoa farmers in the 1990s, kidnapping became more crucial than ever to the survival of such gangs. In the 1970s in Colombia, there had been only a few dozen kidnappings, at most, a year, and the targets were typically politicians and bureaucrats. The motive clearly was political. By the mid-1990s, kidnapping was a $120-million-a-year industry, at least, in that country, where the National Liberation Army (ELN) and the leftist Revolutionary Armed Forces (FARC) utilized it as a fund-raising strategy.

Colombia, among other countries, experienced the phenomenon of "double displacement," with the crackdown on drugs causing layoffs of drug operatives, including cartel security agents, who were well trained in the use of high-tech weaponry, evasion tactics, and kidnapping. Some subcontracted their services to political terrorist groups looking to upgrade and expand their teams of kidnappers. Others were recruited by criminal gangs.

In Nicaragua, former contra rebels resurfaced as marauders credited with numerous abductions in the region, including even seemingly idyllic Costa Rica. At the same time, when 85,000 soldiers in the 100,000-strong Sandinista army—the former opponents of the contras—were demobilized throughout the first half of the 1990s, some turned to kidnapping as a livelihood. Nicaragua, as well as El Salvador, also experienced the sudden influx of unemployed refugees returning home from the United States—mainly Los Angeles—at the end of the civil wars. Unable to find work, they frequently resorted to crime.

To be sure, the immediate effect of a peace treaty was rarely peace. In Guatemala, where at least four abductions a week were reported in 1995, the kidnap boom stemmed in part from an influx of unemployed military and police officers as well as demobilized rebels from neighboring countries whose wars had ended. So successful were the gangs—many of which targeted tourists—that Guatemala's political parties, in the spring of 1995, had allegedly raised money for their upcoming election campaigns through kidnapping. And after the peace treaty in Guatemala was signed in late 1996, a new wave of kidnappings overtook parts of the nation. There was much speculation that the culprits were Guatemala's own displaced government and guerrilla fighters from the thirty-six-year civil war.

In Africa, soldiers unable to find work after returning home from peacekeeping duties in places such as Liberia, as well as former rebels in several countries, were joining the ranks of the criminals. In Mozambique, for example, former rebels of the Mozambican National Resistance, demanding money and food, took 300 hostages in 1994, including several senior United Nations officials and at least one Brit.

When Muslim zealots in Afghanistan, funded and armed for more than a decade by the United States, Britain, and various Arab states, stopped fighting the Soviet army, they sought new outlets to exploit their superb military skills and to deploy their heavy artillery. By the summer of 1994—in a development that few tourists could have known about—hundreds of fighters from Afghanistan, as well as Tajikistan and the Sudan, were slipping into Kashmir and fighting alongside local Muslim insurgents to free Kashmir from Indian rule. Beyond the Kashmir crusade, some were driven by the goal to wipe out the Indian security forces, which they believed were trying to annihilate Islam. Whatever their motives, these mujahideen warriors were tougher, better trained, far better equipped, and reputedly more ruthless than the local rebels, many of whom were Muslims in the moderate Sufi tradition. The mujahideen migrations turned up the heat of the conflict, placing foreigners at greater risk.

In Russia, there was a shocking twist to the displacement story. Criminal gangs, including kidnappers whose activities were on the rise, recruited the obvious "laid-off" members of the former Soviet structure: former KGB, former police, and former military personnel. But the gangs' rosters also included the onetime jewels of the Soviet system: sports figures. Some former weight lifters, wrestlers, and other world-class athletes now worked as low-level operatives—basically thugs—in gangs that, among other crimes, were kidnapping in St. Petersburg, Moscow, and outlying rural areas. An integral part of the business culture of Russia, kidnapping, as an intimidation tactic, was useful in getting bills paid and deals done. In 1995, about 320 kidnappings occurred in Russia; at least fifty of the victims were businessmen from the United States, Britain, or Germany. By the end of 1996, some intelligence reports issued by private research agencies were placing the total number of kidnappings in Russia for that year at 1,000 and were warning of an increasing risk to foreigners.

The displacement phenomenon was even evident on the high seas, where by 1996 pirates were pillaging and kidnapping with a boldness not seen since the eighteenth century. By most accounts, the pirates were former soldiers, many of whom spoke English, though their origins varied. Albanian pirates had abducted and robbed tourists as their yachts cruised through the Aegean in the summer of 1996. And according to one account, from the *Economist* magazine: "Captain Peter Newton from Derby, who was held hostage by Indonesian pirates, said that the leader who put a sword to his throat spoke perfect English and 'was obviously a military officer.' " With the International Maritime Bureau, which monitors seagoing crimes, reporting incidents of piracy rising from 90 in 1994 to 226 in 1996, the British Foreign Office has lobbied for a United Nations task force to study the threat.

In addition to paying former warriors' wages, ransoms are the venture capital used to jump-start new drug trafficking enterprises and to lay the foundation for new terrorist gangs. In Mexico, kidnappings more than doubled from 1994 to 1995—when, according to nongovernmental analysts, the tally ranged from 1,200 to 2,000. In the summer of 1996, a new rebel group, the Popular Revolutionary Army (EPR), suddenly surfaced with a hefty war chest. While government sources told members of the press that its source of funding was a Euroterrorist group—thus shifting the focus and the fear away from Mexico—kidnap experts and terrorism analysts claimed the EPR had been raising funds largely through kidnappings in Mexico during the previous two years. Incidents blamed on the gang included two kidnappings that yielded a total of nearly $20 million. Experts speculated that the EPR was created on the Colombian model. At the very least, its members had been trained in Colombia and its purpose was to provide another branch—much like an overseas subsidiary of a corporation—for Colombian guerrillas who needed not only new supplies of cash but also new routes for drug trafficking.

In Baja California, roving bands of kidnappers began to surface during 1993, when there were nearly twenty abductions, compared with only three reported abductions in 1992. These kidnappers were mostly professionals who thus far had singled out wealthy businessmen and members of their families and who by the mid-1990s had collected several million dollars in ransoms. The problem was so worrisome in Baja that the state attorney general formed a special antikidnap squad made up of thirty-eight agents.

The surge in ransom kidnaps in some countries was a wrenching sign that globalization—the worldwide spread of free trade, open markets, and foreign investments—was expanding the gap between the richest people and the poorest, dividing populations more than any political boundary or doctrine ever had in history. Globalization in the 1990s was effectively a pipeline facilitating the flow of money from the richest nations to the developing world. And, to be sure, during the first half of the decade, an infusion of at least $170 billion had raised the quality of living for many of the Third World's poorest inhabitants. But at the same time, in some developing nations, foreign money was causing a sudden surge in wealth among the upper classes—or, as in the case of China, the creation of a new wealthy class—with minimal benefit to the poorest classes.

"Unfortunately we are living in a world that has become more polarized economically, both between countries and within them," a

United Nations study reported. "Today we live on a planet which increasingly represents not 'one world' but 'two worlds.' Far from narrowing, the gap [in average individual income] between the industrial and developing worlds tripled between 1960 and 1993, from $5,700 to $15,400. Today, the net worth of the world's 358 richest people is equal to the combined income of the poorest 45 percent of the world's population—2.3 billion people. If current trends continue and are not quickly corrected, economic disparities will move from inequitable to inhuman, from unacceptable to intolerable."

Meanwhile, kidnapping, like an uncontrollable, poisonous weed, flourishes in the crime-fertile gap between rich and poor—in Brazil, in Mexico, in India, in China, and in the Philippines, where the number of kidnapping cases during 1996 rose by nearly 40 percent over the previous year. In India that year, ransoms—ranging from $1,000 to $1.5 million—were redistributing the wealth of the nation faster than any bureaucratic or legal move by the government could ever accomplish. In Mexico and in other countries, a risk analyst at Pinkerton's wrote in 1996, it was ironic that "the same circumstances attracting foreign firms to its low-wage work force also create conditions which make kidnapping for ransom an attractive activity."

Why criminals choose kidnappings over bank robberies and other crimes is partly a matter of security. It's the same reason that carjackings have been on the rise. With the development of more and more sophisticated alarm and security systems, criminals are forced to steal the cars with the owners *in* them. "As we make crimes against property more difficult in all societies, it forces crimes against people. The criminals must confront the people. And kidnapping is the ultimate crime against persons," said Mike Ackerman, a professional kidnap negotiator based in Miami.

But perhaps the primary factor feeding the crime of kidnapping has been the alluring image of its success. Although only 10 to 30 percent of kidnappings are reported in many countries, the big cases—with big names or big ransom demands—typically are headline news. By the mid-1990s, it was clear that in many countries kidnapping had indeed become a profitable endeavor, an industry worth the risk for anyone willing to traffic in human misery. One study of kidnappings, covering only those perpetrated by political groups, showed that the groups had taken in more than $200 million in ransoms worldwide in 1994. But of course this figure fell far short of the total because so many incidents were unreported and many that were reported did not include the ransom amounts.

The 1994 kidnappings of billionaire Alfredo Harp Helu, the chairman of Mexico's largest financial group, Banamex, and of supermarket tycoon Angel Losada Moreno seemed to unleash a stampede of kidnappers to Mexico. The ransom demand was $100 million in the Harp Helu affair, with the publicized payment at about $30 million. The Losada ransom was reportedly in the range of $50 million, although it was neither officially announced nor confirmed. Part of the problem in these cases was that the reported amounts far exceeded the actual ransoms paid. At most, four individuals knew the exact amounts, according to one source familiar with the cases, and none of them informed the press. Meanwhile, the speculation was that the press got the wrong amounts from government officials, who were too embarrassed to admit they did not know the figures and so provided estimates based on their knowledge of the cases. The two ransoms totaled at most $20 million, sources said. Although this figure was far less than the reported ransoms, it was still an incentive for more kidnappings. By the end of 1994, the tally of reported kidnappings in Mexico—where the annual average from 1990 through 1992 had been 500—had soared to 1,400.

In Colombia, rebels had obtained $328.9 million from kidnappings between 1991 and 1994, according to a 1995 Colombian government report. In 1994, two guerrilla groups announced they would kidnap all U.S. citizens working for their government or for multinational companies and ask multimillion-dollar ransoms to pay the operating expenses in their "war on imperialism." They would seek these giant sums, they told the press, to compensate for the plundering of their national resources by the carpetbagging foreign governments. One rebel leader called kidnapping a "war tax" on the wealthy. By 1996, there was an average of four abductions a day in Colombia, and only 2 percent of the captors were ever prosecuted. In one case a baby, barely a day old, was abducted.

Success might have been the motivating factor in Ireland, where authorities began to see a steady rise in kidnappings around 1992. A decade before, the Provisional IRA was the culprit as it used ransom monies to build up a sizable war chest. But the IRA had plenty of other funding by the early 1990s. The perpetrators now are ex-terrorists and common criminals, and their targets are typically low-profile, moderately wealthy businessmen.

State-of-the-art kidnapping is bold, both in style and in what is demanded. In some countries, kidnappers ask for property in addition to ransoms, demanding that a deed be signed over to a front for the kidnappers. In Colombia, as in the case Commander Ramm had encountered in Cambodia, gangs occasionally have demanded money in exchange for the corpse of a hostage. In parts of Latin America and Asia, it has not been uncommon for more than one member of a family to be kidnapped within the same year, or for one person to be abducted two times or more. Paying an agreed-upon ransom also no longer guarantees the captive's release. The kidnappers might pick up the ransom and then send a message asking for more money, or release the victims only after they promised that more would be paid. Experts call this the "double-tap" technique, or the "double-dip."

Kidnappers in Brazil—where many targets have been wealthy Jewish families whose relatives fled Nazi Europe—have successfully extorted money, much like Mafia protection money, just by whispering a threat in the ear of one of their targets. To prevent the crime, the potential victim might have to pay a sort of "advance ransom." In a Rio case in 1995, a father was abducted, and while he was in captivity, four members of his family received letters saying that if they paid a fee now, they could prevent what was happening to their loved one from happening to them. In the end, they paid the ransom for the father's release and four additional amounts to prevent their own abductions.

In the Philippines, kidnappers sometimes avoid what is typically the riskiest stage of the crime for them, the ransom dropoff, by accepting their victims' personal checks made out to "cash" and by threatening another abduction with a higher demand if any stop payments are placed on the checks. "Logo hunting," meaning the "sport" of searching for wealthy targets, particularly employees of big-time multinational companies, has become increasingly common as more and more former terrorists and drug operatives have taken up kidnapping as a livelihood. Like lawyers with client lists, they come to their new positions with target lists. Occasionally, such lists, resembling invitation lists for charity fund-raisers, have turned up in the rubble of a bombing or in the briefcases of slain informants.

In 1993, a list of more than 100 individuals and businesses in Brazil, Mexico, Ecuador, Venezuela, and Bolivia was discovered after a bomb exploded in a secret arsenal beneath an automobile repair shop in Managua. Investigators found a cache of explosives, antiaircraft missiles, and rifles apparently belonging to a Salvadoran guerrilla group, the People's Liberation Forces. They also excavated a computer printout and files exposing the existence of an international kidnapping ring based in Nicaragua with ties in Spain, Chile, and Argentina, among others. The document contained kidnapping plans and the list of targets with their addresses, itemized lists of their assets and net worth, and a suggested feasible ransom for each target. Handwritten in the margins of the list were notes about the targets' personal habits and daily routines.

Whether in India, where Afghan-trained terrorists marched their captives along rugged Himalayan passes; in Colombia, where exorbitant ransoms funded the training of new recruits; or in the Philippines, where kidnapping syndicates were developing foreign "moles," the sophistication of some kidnappers appeared to be growing and spreading by the 1990s. The so-called moles of the Filipino syndicates were positioned in places such as Hong Kong and Taiwan to trace funds that their targets had transferred out of the country to shield from the kidnappers' grasp. The syndicates were also subcontracting the work of kidnapping to three types of specialists: one to supervise the abduction, one to arrange the hideouts and food supplies, and one to pull off the abduction.

With the complexity of a corporation, kidnapping operations in parts of Latin America were often divided into teams of a more complex variety than in the Philippines or in India. For example: One team might focus on researching the targets, another on analyzing the wealth of the potential prey. A third team then scrutinized the selected target's habitual comings and goings and daily regimen. As one team devised a strategy for the snatch, a completely different group orchestrated it, diverting the victim and driving the getaway vehicle. Another unit was responsible for selecting hideouts and guarding and feeding the captives. Yet another negotiated with authorities for their demands in exchange for the victim. And finally, a separate team was responsible for collecting the ransom and releasing or delivering the victim. These duties were often subcontracted to highly specialized groups by the professional kidnappers, in part to ensure that members of one team would never know the identities of members of another. In Rio, there were even what some kidnap experts call "hostage hotels"— houses stocked with food and medicine and operated just for the lodging of hostages.

In parts of Latin America (mainly Colombia), an intriguing new development had emerged as the kidnap industry grew: individuals operating as "ransom brokers" and collecting a percentage of the ransoms they delivered. The problem was that such services were upping the market price for the safe return of a hostage and adding to the appeal of the crime. There were allegations, too, that one of these so-called brokers had helped kidnappers target wealthy foreign nationals. A professional negotiator, called by the family of the hostage or the company, would be in the midst of negotiation talks, discussing ransoms in the $500,000 to $1 million range perhaps, when suddenly the rebels would cut their contact. Word would get back to the negotiators that someone else was talking with the kidnappers, someone offering to get a higher ransom, someone the rebels now preferred, and someone who would allegedly get a healthy chunk, or "commission," from the $3 million or $4 million ransom.

In the United States, where strong local law enforcement and the FBI seemed to control the problem, there was nevertheless a slight rise each year. Kidnap experts surmised it reflected changes in American society, such as corporate downsizing, which had provoked disgruntled former employees to kidnap, and the slowly widening gap between rich and poor, which could encourage the crime in the years ahead. A new trend emerged in 1996 in California: abductions of employees on their way to or from work, to extort high-tech information about computer chips. "Doorbell abductions" were on the rise by the mid-1990s. In these incidents, the kidnappers literally rang the doorbell, forced their way into a home, and held a family captive until a ransom was extracted out of a local ATM machine or bank account. Sometimes security officers with access to company vaults were targeted.

What was clearly helping to lure rebels and criminals to kidnapping in so many cultures—and what added a new angle to an old crime—was the sheer abundance of targets: tourists, entrepreneurs, corporate managers, wealthy landowners, engineers, missionaries. Beyond the elite corps of high-level diplomats or affluent executives, kidnappers were beginning to aim at the rank and file of the world.

Over time, the preferential targets had changed. Two centuries ago, the most common hostage targets were merchantmen and traders from the wealthiest and most powerful nations—the men who were exploring and conquering the remotest corners of the world. Pirates and bandits preyed upon the early explorers, sailors, and mapmakers, using kidnapping as a way to get money or to discourage further invasions of their own lands. During colonization, as embassies were added to the international landscape, diplomats became major targets, a trend that lasted many years, occasionally resurfacing in the 1990s. But with the expansion of multinational corporations, diplomats began to lose some of their appeal, at least for the purposes of ransom seekers. Governments, after all, didn't always pay ransoms, and corporations almost always did. Hence the business executive emerged as the preferred prey.

The snatching of oil and mining executives was common in the 1970s and 1980s in developing nations, but by the early 1990s the target group had widened to include any executive at any level from any company anywhere. Midlevel executives were often just as vulnerable, if not more so, than their wealthier bosses, who protected themselves with high walls around their homes, bodyguards—as many as ten in some Latin American families—and very expensive armored cars. Middle managers familiar with a company's security system had become popular prey in both the United States and abroad. Throughout the 1990s, kidnappers seemed to be moving down the corporate ladder seeking "softer," less-protected targets.

The threat to foreigners has varied greatly from region to region, with Latin America ranking the highest. Worldwide estimates for kidnapping in the 1990s ranged from 200 per year—a number that some claim includes only Americans—to 3,000 per year. One five-year study, beginning in 1992, showed that of the foreign nationals kidnapped, 66 percent were eventually released after some sort of negotiation, 20 percent were rescued, 9 percent were killed or died in captivity, and 5 percent escaped. Roughly half of the captives were held from 1 to 10 days, a quarter were held from 11 to 50 days, and the rest from 50 to over 100 days. And the definition of a ransom—whatever was given to gain the release of the hostages—ranged from millions of dollars to new roads and schoolhouses to even basketball uniforms, courts, and balls.

In some countries, such as Mexico, foreigners were relatively secure because Mexican executives were wealthier, far pricier victims. No wonder: despite its poverty, Mexico, by 1994, had at least two dozen multibillionaires as well as hundreds of millionaire tycoons. Halfway through the decade, many wealthy Mexicans, as well as Brazilians and Colombians, had been kidnapped at least once. As the wealthiest were busily spending their money on security measures—buying up armored cars, such as the Mercedes Supercar, erecting fifteen-foot walls around their homes, and hiring firms to teach them prevention techniques—the kidnappers found themselves in need of new quarry. By late 1994, foreigners in residence or long-term visitors were increasingly at risk. That year, behind the scenes in the U.S. government, there was enough concern about the welfare and safety of Americans in Mexico that the State Department formed a new branch of the Overseas Security Advisory Council specifically for U.S. business executives on extended stays in Mexico.

Soon the expatriate was at risk in Brazil, Colombia, Ecuador, India, Guatemala, Honduras, Venezuela, Russia, China, and the Philippines. In Russia, where targets were still mostly local businessmen, there were no official kidnapping statistics for foreigners, except a tally put together by the embassies in 1995: fifty Americans, Brits, and Germans. What was clearly on the rise in Russia, and predicted to continue to increase, were abductions of the resident employees of big foreign companies. With the deep pockets of their employers, these targets offered opportunities for big ransoms but without the involvement of Scotland Yard, the FBI, or any other foreign investigative agency. The perfect target group—the one that kidnap analysts were watching very carefully for signs of trouble—was the Russian employee of an American company. Still, despite predictions that foreigners and employees of American firms were increasingly at risk, Russia had a built-in protection for foreigners, especially business executives. Kidnappers were sometimes hesitant to abduct businessmen because they could be working for companies that were in partnership with the kidnappers' own employers.

The high-profile 1996 abduction of the Japanese head of a U.S. subsidiary of the Sanyo Electric Company—after he had attended a company baseball game in Mexico near the U.S. border—set off a screeching alarm to foreign targets, especially businessmen. Not only was the $2 million ransom demand met, but the company's payment was publicly announced. This was the equivalent of advertising honey to bears.

By the mid-1990s, the ever-shrinking world and the ever-enthusiastic tourism industry was increasing the supply of a long-favored target: the tourist. And among the most tempting of prey of the new era was the trekker. No doors, no phones, no one near to hear a scream of alarm or the warning shots of a submachine gun. Sleeping in a tent on an isolated "away-from-it-all" hillside, trekkers had become a sweet nectar to kidnappers.

6

A man and a woman, both Americans, are sitting innocently on the banks of a white-capped river in northern India. Their guides are cooking rice and lentils for dinner. The man is washing shirts and socks in the clear, cold mountain water. And the woman is writing in her journal, as she so often has done in their travels together. It is a moment in two busy lives when tranquillity seems as endless as the river's flow—but only a moment.

As she writes, the rushing water muffles the cries of the nearby mynah birds and the creaking of the limbs of towering pines touched by the breeze of a Himalayan dusk. The water, thrusting loudly through narrow passes between river rocks, drowns out the sounds of the twelve armed men moving toward them.

In her journal, the woman notes the date, July 4, in part because of its significance back home—and not because of what this date would soon mean to her and to the man rinsing socks in the river. She writes in a precise, confident manner, neatly fitting as many words to a line as possible and recalling details such as the names, colors, and heights of wildflowers on ridges and riverbanks, the exact time the couple began hiking that day, and the degree of the fever of a shepherd's child brought to their campsite the previous day. They are sitting along this particular river on this day because the guides told them the night before that there was too much snow to travel through the Sonamous Pass, as they had planned to do. The guides informed them the pass was closed, the woman writes, "so we agreed to come back the same way we had come." And that is where the entry ends, at the moment when the heavily armed men, horse blankets slung over their shoulders and belts of ammunition crisscrossing their chests, fell upon them on the river trail.

The couple is from Spokane, Washington, where until that moment, they had led a well-ordered, nearly idyllic existence. The man, Donald Hutchings, is a forty-two-year-old neuropsychologist, highly respected in the Spokane medical community for his work with head-injury victims. And the woman, his forty-year-old wife, Jane Schelly, a seasoned trekker and intrepid traveler, is equally regarded for her leadership in the regional outdoors club, the Spokane Mountaineers, and her work as a physical education teacher at Spokane's Arlington Elementary School.

Richly esteemed in the culture in which he lives and moves, Donald Hutchings is a man known for his strict moral code—the kind of person who never drives over the speed limit and would never think of dodging jury duty, which he considers a civic responsibility. If a patient overpays by even fifty cents, Hutchings will send a reimbursement check. Some patients, unable to pay at all and without adequate insurance, have yet to receive a bill. Friends talk also of Hutchings' sense of humor and his zest for life.

"Don is this unbeatable combination, a moral fiber that is absolute high carbon steel," says Buddy McManus, a pediatrician in Spokane. "I don't think there is anyone I've ever met who is as moral as Don. With that comes this excellent sense of humor and an infectious smile. You don't meet people like this; he's different, unique."

Former patients quickly credit Hutchings for their abilities to live without daily care, to be employed, and to accept without fear diminished capabilities from brain tumors, Alzheimer's, gunshot wounds, and from brain injuries suffered in car collisions and other accidents. Only a decade ago, many of those injured in accidents would have died at the scene, but today, because of high-speed helicopter rescues and new medical technologies, they survive—albeit to live with severe impairments. Partly because of Hutchings and his concern for the rising numbers of such victims, hospitals in Spokane have opened special head-injury clinics.

When he isn't helping, treating, or inspiring, Hutchings is trekking, biking, climbing, skiing, or teaching. Revered as a leader of the Spokane Mountaineers, a club of 800 or so outdoors enthusiasts founded in 1915, he teaches climbers and trekkers to scale frozen waterfalls and rocky precipices, leading arduous expeditions to peaks 20,000 feet or higher. Practiced in the use of picks, pulleys, and ropes, he knows the physical and psychological perils inherent to high-altitude ascents, the dangers of frostbite and altitude sickness. Although Hutchings is a cautious man, well prepared, he also has a reputation as a hard-driving motivator who encourages climbers to reach heights as challenging as Mount McKinley and Mount Rainier. His slight, lean body belies his physical strength and his unyielding determination. He has always reveled in a good challenge, indulging a hunger for adventure, though he is neither foolish nor impulsive and no one ever describes him as a risk taker. This is the man who is now joining his wife along the Lidder River as she looks up from her journal to greet him for the few peaceful seconds before their lives are changed forever.

In Don and Jane's house in Spokane, on a hill covered with Ponderosa pines, high above the Spokane River, there are two walls of photos: among them, Don atop Mount McKinley, Jane on Annapurna in Nepal, Jane conquering Rainier, Don and Jane on Mount Huayna Potosi (a 21,000-foot peak in the Bolivian Andes), and Don and Jane in helmets and sunglasses on the summit of Shuksan, high in the Cascade Mountains. Don took the pictures, and Jane matted and framed them, a skill she learned when she realized Don had taken an interest in photography. In a yard they landscaped themselves, Don's beloved herbs, his carefully planted rosemary, thyme, sage, lemon mint, and parsley, gently mingle with Jane's lilies and violets, billowing rosebushes, and clusters of hot-pink azaleas.

Their travels, too, have been well-organized, shared projects, often fueled by her adventuresome spirit and abetted by his boundless energy. In 1987, they trekked through the Swiss Alps and, in 1988, the Himalayas in Nepal. In 1991, they spent a month in Ladakh, adjacent to Kashmir and one of the most remote regions of India. The next year, they climbed rocks and hiked in Czechoslovakia after backpacking in Germany. In 1993, they spent a month or so in Bolivia, mostly scaling two peaks—each over 20,000 feet high—in the Bolivian Andes. They toured both urban and rural landscapes of Turkey in 1994. And now, in 1995, they have returned to India to explore the mystique of Kashmir.

Like her husband, Jane seems rather unremarkable from a distance, with her small, trim figure moving swiftly from one destination and commitment to another, her thick black hair worn in efficient short, tight curls. But one conversation, one glance at her animated eyes and her lasting smile, and the image transforms to a vibrant, luminous presence that is most definitely remarkable.

Seemingly quiet and unassuming, Jane is, according to her friends, one of the most fearless people—if not the most fearless—that they have ever known. She is strong, bold, curious, doggedly determined, resourceful, and lucky. "Jane is the type who always lands on her feet," said Jacki McManus, wife of Buddy and longtime friend of both Don and Jane. "She's always said that she's lucky, and she is. But she's also really positive, so she sees things as lucky when other people might not see the same things. She has a really good attitude."

It was Jane, a past president of the Mountaineers, who first inspired Don to travel. She had traveled frequently during the years before they met (in 1984). But Don's dedication to his doctorate and his subsequent hospital work prohibited vacations until 1988 when he launched his private practice. Even then, he often could only get away for a month during the summers, while Jane's schoolteacher schedule allowed her much longer summer excursions. Because of this, Jane would sometimes begin their annual summer trip several weeks earlier than Don, intrepidly yet cautiously traveling to some of the world's most exotic lands.

In 1991, for example, she spent two weeks touring Thailand, then two weeks in India before Don joined her in Manali, a town known to locals as a honeymoon resort and to Westerners as a gateway to the Himalayas.

The last half of her trip began in New Delhi, where she arrived from Bangkok at about 1 A.M. Jane had read all about the dangers of riding in cabs out of the New Delhi airport—an escalated danger for a woman alone. As she stood in line at the customs gate, she chatted with a college student from Canada who was ahead of her, and who said he had read the same warnings. His plan was to spend the night at the airport and then at dawn to find transportation. It would be safer in the morning, he thought. Jane had a better idea. She began to work the airport crowd, as if it were a social gathering, inquiring about others' plans to find safe passage and shelter that night. Soon she had a group of seven people willing to share taxis and to stay as a group at the local YMCA, which was considered a reputable place.

After several days in New Delhi, Jane took the train three hours south to the town of Agra and eventually moved north to Manali. What Jane and Don knew of Manali they had read in the *Lonely Planet Guide* for the Himalayan regions, which reported that the town had a post office and an Indian government tourism office. Considering the immense potential for delays in traveling across South Asia, Don and Jane established a window of three days during which Don would likely arrive in Manali. On each of those days, Jane was to be at the tourist bureau at 10 A.M. and the post office at 3 P.M. to wait for Don. As expected, he was delayed coming out of Thailand (because of a problem in getting his baggage). On the third day, as Jane waited anxiously on the front stoop of the post office, she saw Don, with that irresistible, boyish smile of his, approaching the building, under the sweaty glare of India's summer sun.

Jane and Don first met on a Mountaineers club outing in Lolo Hot Springs, Montana, in the Bitterroot Range of the Rocky Mountains, near the area depicted in the film and book *A River Runs Through It*. It was early morning and they were the only two people sitting in a roomlike cavern etched out of the side of a mountain where the hot springs flow. Immersed in the soothing mineral waters, they chatted about the beauty of Montana and why they were each there that particular weekend in 1984. Later, Don would tell Jane that he had had a strong instinct that morning that she would be the woman with whom he would spend the rest of his life. Over the next year or so, they skiied together, ran races together, took backpacking trips, and then started climbing peaks—together, of course. "When you are tied to someone with a rope," Jane would say later, "you get to know them very well and you learn quickly about trust." When they were married in 1991—both for the second time—they tied a knot, literally, by each holding two pieces of rope to symbolize the trust in their relationship. Don spoke that day about the trust between climbing partners, how lives become so interdependent on mountain walls, and he likened it to a lifelong relationship between husband and wife.

Don was the romantic and philosophical one, while Jane always handled the logistics. She was the practical type. Don remembered special occasions with flowers, though he wasn't one to shop and so rarely bought presents. Many a weekend he would tell Jane to pack her overnight bag with various items that he listed and be ready to leave Friday after work, then sweep her away to a surprise destination. One time, it was San Francisco, a bed-and-breakfast on the bay. Another time, they flew into Portland, rented a car, and drove to North Beach Peninsula at the southwestern tip of the Washington coast. Once they went to Point No Point on Vancouver Island in Canada, and once, after getting rained out of a climbing trip on Mount Hood, they salvaged the weekend by staying at a beautiful inn overlooking the Columbia River. One time when Don could only get Saturday night off, he took Jane to the honeymoon suite at the Coeur d'Alene resort just twenty or so minutes away from their front door. And often after trips Don would spend hours upon hours putting together slide shows in which he would share the couple's adventures, mixing in the history and culture of the area, and then showing the documentary-like film to a roomful of Mountaineers.

A few nights before they left for India in late June 1995, Don and Jane invited Buddy and Jacki McManus and other friends to dinner at their home. As a man who enjoyed listening to Indian music, had read the words of Buddha, and had named one of his two golden retrievers Bodhi Satva—Bodhi for short—which means "enlightened being" in Hindi, Donald Hutchings saw the upcoming excursion to the Himalayas as nothing less than a trek to heaven. But as conversations inevitably turned to their plans for the trip, one friend asked if either of them had any reservations about traveling in Kashmir, and if the ongoing civil conflict over Kashmir's independence was a concern. Don, recalled one friend, was well aware of the problem and was not completely committed to going to Kashmir. If they could go there, Don had told his friends, it would be nice, but the plan wasn't set in stone. "We're going to look into it, of course," he assured them, "and we'll ask the authorities there, including the Indian government tourism bureau and the American embassy, and we'll see what they have to say. And if they say it's not safe, then we'll go to another area. We have several alternative plans."

On June 25, after a brief stop in Bangkok, Jane and Don landed in New Delhi. Later Jane would recall: "We did a lot of preparation before we left. We knew we wanted to go to India. We also knew there was some turmoil in Kashmir, but we had been in northern India in 1991 and what we had heard consistently about the Kashmir area from various people was that as long as you stayed out of the central part of Srinagar, the summer capital, out of the old part of the city where there would be gatherings of people, that there were typically no problems. Especially there were no problems trekking in the areas where we were most interested, such as Pahalgam. But, with the possibility that we might hear a negative, we went with our research and maps in hand so we could change plans easily and go to the Valley of the Flowers, in a different region, or back to the Ladakh area where we had been before. Don had some other areas he had researched and was thinking about, if we were told Kashmir was unsafe.

"Before we left, Don called the Indian consulate in San Francisco several times but was never able to get through. Then we decided to get the most up-to-date information once we had arrived in India. It only seemed logical that the Indians would know best what was safe or unsafe. It would be the latest information. [The State Department's most recent advisory on the region was dated November 25, 1994.] So our plan was to check with the government tourism office in New Delhi and the American embassy.

"When we arrived and inquired at the airport about our hotel, we were told the rooms were air-cooled, though when I had called before our arrival and had spoken with the hotel, they assured me of air-conditioning. This was something I had stressed because of the very high temperatures, and, if you look at the newspapers from that time, people were dying from the extreme heat in India. So, at the airport, we arranged for another hotel, and I guess that was when we told them [the hotel employees] that we were in the process of organizing a trip, that we would be going to the Indian government's tourism agency in the morning. Then, the next morning, to our surprise, a car arrived at our hotel—which we had never asked for—to take us to a private tourism agency from which I'm sure the hotel was getting kickbacks.

"We knew there was some sort of scam going on here, but the car was there and so we said to ourselves, OK, we will go and listen, but we will be watchful. We did and we were. We listened and things sounded attractive, but we knew the prices were high. There was no mention of kidnappings. So next we went to the Indian government tourism office. Again no one mentioned anything about kidnappings, though they didn't deny there were problems when we asked about safety. The advice was to stay out of areas in the downtown section where you might have gatherings of people, and we did ask about backpacking and trekking, and they did say that was all right. After that we talked to people on the street who had just come back from trekking trips in the areas where we wanted to go. They seemed to love it and gave glowing reports of the beauty. We couldn't help but remember our experience in La Paz, Bolivia, in 1993, where we were warned about Machu Picchu [in Peru], the place we really wanted to go to but didn't go, although people were coming back and saying 'no problem' and how great it was. But we didn't go. This time, in Kashmir, we thought we'll go if the information from the people returning from Kashmir and from the tourism offices in that country is positive. And it was.

"After arriving in Srinagar, we went to the Kashmir state tourism office, where the fellow tried to give us many reasons why we shouldn't go on our own, why we should hire someone to go with us, the ponyman, etc. Nothing about kidnapping. And, lo and behold, standing by his side was one of those people—to be hired. Why would you have an independent person, a solicitor, who has no connection to the government, standing right there while we were asking questions? I don't blame him really because in Kashmir it is common practice to do anything to get business. But it was inappropriate, and as we left he followed us out and tried to sell us his services. After standing on the corner and talking to him quite a bit, however, we were persuaded that it might not be significantly more expensive to hire him and that it would definitely be easier. The guide then hired the ponymen."

Because Jane had strained her back shortly before the trip, the couple had decided to follow a trail that could accommodate horses, allowing the animals to bear the weight of gear and supplies. And because the reports on Kashmir out of New Delhi and Srinagar were encouraging, they chose to take the Pahalgam tour instead of trekking in the Valley of the Flowers, their alternative route, which was a backpacking trail inaccessible to horses in a region south of Kashmir. Satisfied with the information they had accumulated from the government tourism office in New Delhi as well as the private tourism agency, the Kashmir tourism office, and reports from people who had already returned from trips to the Pahalgam area that June, Jane and Don did not call the American embassy. "We thought we had gathered enough information telling us that it was safe, as long as we avoided urban centers," Jane said months later. "If there had been a red flag at any point, then we would have researched further."

What they did not know and were not told was that Muslim militants controlled parts of the Kashmir Valley, including areas near Pahalgam, about forty miles south of Srinagar. And the militants often followed paths along the rivers to traverse the region.

The itinerary Jane and Don arranged was as popular and as well-worn in India as the trails up and down the Grand Canyon in the United States. They first followed the route to the Amarnath Cave, a large, legend-filled cavern that is among the most sacred sites in the Himalayas. But due to heavy snows that year, the passes they had chosen to exit the cave, toward the northwest, were still closed, even in early July. And so they traveled south and then west for several days along a path leading them to the vast and scenic Kolahoi Glacier. Their most spectacular day was July 3, when they hiked along steep and rocky ridges that overlooked ice-covered lakes, traversed fast-running streams and rivers, and waded through fields of wildflowers just emerging from the melting snow. By July 4, Jane and Don were pleased with their decision to come to Kashmir, where the only obstacles had been the snow-blocked passes and the only scary moments had come in facing nature's own startling, precipitous landscapes.

Later, Jane would worry about whether the guides had known what was about to happen, whether she and Don had been lured to this particular site along the Lidder River—cornered like the unsuspecting prey of a cunning predator. The guides could have been part of a conspiracy. She and Don hadn't seen the blocked, snowbound pass; the story about the snow could have been a lie. And for no reason, when their small caravan of ponies and people turned around and headed back from the Sonamous Pass, the guides led them an hour or so beyond the spot where they had agreed to stop for the night of July 4.

"Maybe they thought the area would be too crowded," Jane would later say. "Or maybe they were told to do this. If they were told by militants, did they even have a choice?" Perhaps the guides too were pawns in someone else's game, as Don and Jane were soon to be. In Jane's mind, the guides did not act or seem suspicious, and she and her husband had no reason not to trust them as they led the way. Later, the guides would ask Jane to write a statement saying that they were not in collusion with the terrorists and that they had tried to protect Don and Jane. The guides and ponymen feared that the Indian troops, known to abuse Kashmiris, might interrogate or torture them. Jane harbored no suspicions strong enough to allow that, so she provided the statement. She would later learn that one of the men was incarcerated for thirty days because of the incident.

7

JULY 4–5, 1995
KASHMIR

At first, Don and Jane were not afraid; they were startled and unnerved, slightly suspicious and curious, but not afraid. One minute they were sitting on the banks of the river looking in the direction of the guides who were cooking their dinner; next minute, they saw, walking toward them, a grim-looking group of men whose chests were draped in belts of ammunition. The men were speaking Urdu, a Pakistani tongue, and Pashto, a language of Afghanistan. The American couple knew nothing about the kidnappings that had occurred in Kashmir, and so they didn't fear abduction; nor did they sense they were in danger. For a short time, they believed the armed men, none of whom once pointed a gun directly at them, were simply passing through in an effort to evade Indian troops. The men appeared to be looking for someone and perhaps that was why the militants told the guides to fetch the Americans' passports. It never occurred to the Spokane couple that the men standing before them were terrorists sizing up the value of hostages by determining national identities. In such a contest, Americans were nearly always the winners, though in some parts of the world Japanese business executives had become desirable prey.

The men were neither rough nor aggressive. As the sun was setting, a villager walked through the campsite peddling chipatis (flour tortillas), and one of the militants approached him. What Jane would always remember was that the militant paid for the chipatis; this, she believed, was an encouraging sign. With all his weaponry, he could have taken anything he wanted. But he didn't. And when ten of the militants marched out of the camp, the two who remained told the guides to proceed with dinner; when it began to grow chilly, they told Don and Jane to get warmer clothes; and finally, when it began to drizzle, they told the couple to go to their tent, not to talk, and to sit at the front where they could be seen at all times. As the Americans walked to the tent, the guide whispered to them, "Your money," as a warning to them to hide their cash and other valuables. But there was no opportunity to conceal the contents of the tent, and so they sat in the tent for nearly an hour, unaware of the cards that fate was dealing them, all the while nervously watching their visitors' every move and whispering their observations, as discreetly as possible, sharing suspicions.

While the two Muslim militants took turns unraveling their turbans, washing their hands in the river, neatly spreading the turbans on the ground, and praying, the other ten were pillaging the tents of trekkers camping farther up the narrow river valley: a Swiss woman and her daughter, an American woman, a Japanese man, and a Japanese woman, all traveling separately. Stuffing binoculars, cameras, loose cash, and flashlights into nylon bags, they herded the hikers up the Lidder River Valley to another campsite, roughly a mile and a half from the camp of Jane and Don.

It was about 6:30 P.M., and Julie and Keith Mangan, two Brits, were relaxing on a hillside meadow above the turbulent Lidder. Nearby, at the same site, were two other Brits, Paul Wells and Catherine Moseley, Canadian Bart Imler, and several guides—all trekking companions who had hiked to the Kolahoi Glacier the day before. About fifty yards away, along the river, twenty or so Kashmiri schoolboys, mostly fifteen to seventeen years old, were on an expedition. And farther up the hill, a few hundred yards, was an American businessman, John Childs, and his guide.

Julie and Keith, who had been in Kashmir for only three days, were waiting for dinner and talking about feet: why hers were so sore and his were not. After an all-day hike the day before, Julie had chosen to stay near the campsite on July 4, while Keith, full of energy and without a sore bone in his lanky body, didn't want to miss a day of exploring the spectacular alpine landscape. And so he journeyed alone up a hill trail that afternoon. Julie, who normally worked as a cake decorator, and Keith, an electrician, had been making plans and saving money for the past two years for their eighteen-month trip around the world. They were planning to celebrate their tenth wedding anniversary, on August 3, by visiting the Taj Mahal in Agra. Their previous stop had been Sri Lanka, where they had checked with the Indian consulate on the safety of hiking in the western Himalayas, especially in Kashmir, before proceeding to that stage of their trip. When they arrived in Srinagar and met up with Cath and Paul, the four Brits spoke with a Kashmir tourism official, who told them that trekking near Pahalgam was quite popular. It was, indeed, a trekkers' Shangri-la—and safe, too, they were told.

During his hike alone, Keith told Julie, he had met an American couple—Jane and Don—who were coming back from the direction he was heading. "Yes, I know," Julie said. "They stopped here this afternoon and said, 'We met your husband.' And I asked them if you were OK, and they said yeah, they were glad to have met you." Then as the couple chatted more about the Americans, where they had been and where they were bound, Julie suddenly sensed motion behind them. They both turned their heads to see several gun-toting men in baggy trousers and sashes of bullets. Some wore turbans, and others donned small flat-rimmed hats common in Afghanistan. There were six or seven of these men surrounding them, while two others held guns on the students. Another guarded the guides.

Julie whispered to Keith, "They must be mountain police." Their guide, who spoke the language of the encircling men, quickly approached their hillside perch and told them to hand over their passports. A few militants paraded in front of the tourists, back and forth, turning the passports upside down and rightside up, over and over, in an awkward display suggesting that they were unable to read them. (This performance would later be exposed as a ruse.) When the guide told Julie and Keith that they must not say a word from now on—no whispering, no gesturing to the other tourists— both of them, without saying a word to each other, suspected the men might be bandits, at the very least.

As Keith grabbed Julie's hand, the anxious couple watched one of the militants point his gun at Bart Imler's tent. Using the barrel to lift the flap, he gruffly asked the guide, "Who is the man inside, and why is he there?" The guide said it was a Canadian who was suffering from severe altitude sickness. This was only the third day in the mountains for this group, the guide explained, and the Canadian, with his dysentery and fatigue, had not yet adjusted. The militant then opened his jacket, the one stuffed with the passports, and threw some pills into Imler's tent, telling the guide to tell Imler, "Take them." The guide explained that the Canadian had been taking pills and was still too ill to be moved. The militant then nodded and walked away. For the tourists, this was the last hopeful gesture.

It was nearly 7 P.M. when the sun disappeared. The fading light of a mountain dusk had lost its appeal, and the constant sounds of the rushing river and the barking dogs of nearby shepherds were no longer reassuring. Silence, like a stifling, slow-moving fog, was spreading through the river valley, a terrain just recently filled with the laughter of schoolboys and the idle banter of tourists.

Julie would later recall: "There were two huts, shepherd's huts, at the campsite, a small one and a large one. I presume that one could take in about four people and the other about ten. So they told us to stand behind the hut, the small hut. I suddenly thought I was going to die. This time I thought, this is a firing line. We're going to be lined up behind that hut and killed. I tightened the grip on Keith's hand, squeezing the life out of it. We—there were the four of us—silently walked behind the hut. We were told not to talk under any circumstances, and I just held on to my husband's hand. It was a great shock to me when the man, the rebel, told us to sit down. It really was a shock and a relief. He was always talking to the guide and using the guns like a finger, motioning us to do this or that.

"While we were sitting, we could see the schoolboys being taken to the hut, the larger hut, all the boys pushed into the hut, no one saying a word, like a silent movie. But this was real. Our cook was sent in there with them, our pony guide too, and our guide's nephew who was about fifteen or sixteen years old. Bashir, our guide, stayed with us because they were using him for translation. We sat in a semicircle as two militants watched us, their guns relaxed. But I knew if we made a move, they would not be so relaxed.

"Then after a few minutes, one of the militants left and went up the hill and came back with John Childs, the American, and sat him down with us. Then they started asking questions. 'Any of you in the army? Do you work for the government? What's your job? Who is your husband, your wife?' Silly questions. They were doing this to distract us while they were raiding the tents, taking cameras, binoculars, cash, just that sort of thing, really. We sat there for about half an hour maybe. They arrived at about 6:30, so then at 7 P.M. or so, when John Childs came, they asked the men, Paul and Keith, to put warm clothes on because they said they would have to go to Aru, where someone could read their passports. They were worried in case the men were Israeli spies, and they had to be sure, so they said. It was their setup, I think, to take them away.

"So they took us from behind the hut, and we sat down on the porch of the other hut where the schoolboys were being kept, and then our guys put on the warm clothes, and then, well, the terrorists marched them down the river. They took off down the river, the ten armed men, the three guys, and John Childs's pony guide. They said he was coming along so that once they visited their commander in Aru to check out the passports, they could send him back with the others because the pony guide would know which way to go. But that wasn't the way it happened.

"I just sat there as Keith walked away. I sat there for a while mulling over what went on in that half hour. This has really happened, I kept saying to myself.

"And Cath turned round to me and said, 'I don't think they are coming back.' I said, 'Don't you worry about that; they are coming back.' I was trying to raise our hopes a bit, but in the back of my mind I didn't feel they were. I don't know why I said it, but I wanted to make her feel better. And I wanted to believe they would come back, and so by saying it, maybe it would happen. They will bring them back; of course they will bring them back, and in the back of your mind you're thinking, I bet they don't.''

At about 8 P.M., Jane and Don, still seated at the front of their tent, watched as an entourage of rebels and tourists marched into their camp—including the two Brits, the Japanese man and woman, the Swiss women, and John Childs. The American woman's tent was far enough away that to round her up would have strained the guarding capacity of the small band of terrorists. It was then, as the terrorists returned with the other trekkers, that Jane felt the first pang of fear—a frightful feeling that her well-ordered world was beginning to collapse.

Jane and Don immediately recognized Keith, the friendly Brit they had met in the mountains the day before. But it was the man next to him, John Childs, who stole their attention. He looked nervous and distraught, his eyes staring downward, as if he were too anxious to make eye contact. Jane was immediately concerned. She was even more concerned as she saw the terrorists talking to Jane and Don's guide. The guide then rushed to the tent to tell Don he must dress warmly for a trip to Aru, a town three hours away by foot. There Don, the two Brits, and the other American would spend the night, the guide said, and John Childs's ponyman would bring them back early the next morning. In the tent, Don slid his relatively new Gore-Tex pants over his shorts, then heavy wool socks, a shirt made of polypropylene, a fleece jacket, then a Gore-Tex jacket, and a balaclava, a hat that rolls up or folds down like a ski mask—all top-of-the-line gear.

When he emerged from the tent, he handed a pile of clothes to Jane and said, "These are yours; take them." It seemed a peculiar move at first—until she clutched the bundle. She knew then what he was doing. In the pile, he had concealed their money belt, which contained several hundred dollars in travelers' checks. In the same moment, his eyes darted to a pair of shoes at the front of the tent. They belonged to the Japanese woman, who with the other tourists had been motioned into Jane and Don's tent. Jane would soon learn that Don had stuffed their ready cash into the toe of one of the woman's hiking boots. This was classic Hutchings, so typical of him to be thinking ahead. He's looking out for me, she thought, and he knows they're going to pillage the campsite and he must be worried that he won't be returning soon. She looked up at him and nodded, forcing back a wave of fear and the beginnings of a tear. She was starting to understand what terror meant.

The militants told Jane she must leave now, walk back to the other camp, and stay there until 10 P.M. They told her that her husband would be back early the next morning. Then Jane, her guide, and the guide from the other camp left. There were no good-byes. In the approaching darkness, she stumbled up the road to the camp, as she was told, never looking back. At 10 P.M., Jane returned to the camp, finding the tents nearly empty. The militants had ransacked every bag, every pocket, taking items they apparently deemed useful to their cause such as batteries, shoes, and cameras. All she wanted back was her husband.

If it was a three-hour hike to Aru, Jane reasoned, and they left at first light, at 4 A.M., they should return by 7. She slept no more than an hour that night and stayed in her sleeping bag through first light until 6:30. Any minute, she thought, she would look through the opened tent flap and see that familiar smile and the bright hazel eyes that always illumined his face when he came home from work in Spokane or when they had met that day in Manali on the post office steps. But that didn't happen. And so she moved to the riverbank where she and Don had waited for dinner so calmly only twelve hours before. Waiting was not so easy now. Seven A.M. came and went, and then 8 A.M. Shortly after 9, the group from Julie's camp appeared, including John Childs's guide. He had returned from Aru alone— without the men the militants had promised to send back with him. He handed Jane a note from the rebels. "For the American government only," it said. She tucked it in her back pocket and joined the procession to Pahalgam, nearly six hours away.

"Walking out was a terribly difficult thing to do, terribly difficult," Jane would say later. "It was hard to leave the site. It was hard to see Bart, the young Japanese fellow, the American woman, and to know that they were coming out and Don wasn't. It wasn't anger but maybe envy—that they were lucky and we weren't. Why us? I kept thinking. Why Don? What had we done? It wasn't that I wanted anyone else to be taken. It was just hard to imagine why this was happening, that we were the ones with the bad luck that day."

Midafternoon, about 3 P.M., nearly fifty people—some, like Bart, on horseback—and dozens of gear-toting ponies paraded into the resort town of Pahalgam, like a band of displaced gypsies. Along the way, Jane and Julie and Cath had warned other trekkers of the lurking dangers, and they had packed up their ponies, following the cavalcade out of the mountains. In Pahalgam the crowd of anxious foreigners congregated at the local police station, some needing to report thefts of their cameras and equipment, while Jane, Julie, and Cath reported the kidnappings of the four men.

When Jane told an officer that she possessed a note from the militants—to be given to a U.S. official as soon as possible—she and her guide were pulled into a private room. At first she was hesitant to surrender the note. This man was obviously not an American, and she feared disobeying the rebels' request. But her guide encouraged her, nodding his head as she looked his way. The handwritten note, in Urdu, demanded the release of twenty-one jailed Kashmiri rebels, including Pakistani mercenaries, by July 15. "Accept our demands or face dire consequences. We are fighting against anti-Islamic forces. . . . Western countries are anti-Islam, and America is the biggest enemy of Islam."

It was July 5. Jane and the others traveled to Srinagar later that day, reporting the incident to the United Nations Military Observer Group for India and Pakistan (UNMOGIP), a small UN group based in both countries since 1949. UNMOGIP then contacted the U.S. embassy in New Delhi. The tourists stayed at the UN facility for two nights only, and then, because UNMOGIP was a neutral group that wanted to distance itself from the incident, the women moved to the Indian government compound, which consisted of several houses with grassy yards and tennis courts behind a high wall in the middle of Srinagar. A few days later they flew to New Delhi, where they would stay for most of the ordeal in the modern high-rise of the British High Commission. For days they would tell their story to diplomats, police, and military officials while the hostages would be forced deeper into the Himalayas, tracing paths no tourist could ever know, learning just how high the mountains can be and how long it is between dusk and dawn.

8

In the middle of a moonless night, silent but for the purring wind, at a time when even the native shepherds fear what they cannot see, the slender figure of a man crept soundlessly out of a stone hut, past a sleeping sentry, and into a forest of pine and birch.

Kneeling before a stream, the man quickly slathered handfuls of mud onto his fair-skinned face. Then, with his boots slung over one shoulder and never looking back, he darted, like a frightened cat, into the darkness. Though ill with dysentery and nearly lame from a blistered foot, he ran and ran, crisscrossing unfamiliar terrain of steep slopes and gorges that dropped almost vertically to rivers below. His eyes, like those of an animal of the night, adjusted to the keenest darkness he had ever known. Despite the throbbing pain in his foot, his taut, muscular legs carried him higher and higher into the Himalayas. And his will pushed him farther and farther beyond the vision of his own capabilities.

The man was John Childs, and, against all odds, he was doing what few hostages have ever done: escaping. Childs was a chemical engineer and manager at Ensign-Bickford Industries, a designer of explosives, based in Simsbury, Connecticut. A fitness devotee, he typically ran three to five miles a day. He also kayaked, skiied, biked, and hiked. It wasn't surprising, then, that the Himalayas were on Childs's mind in early June when his company informed him that he would soon be going to India to tour its facility in Calcutta and to explore possibilities for expansion in the vast Indian marketplace. He and the two other managers arrived in India on June 23.

For trekkers, the Himalayan range is a paradise, with its embracing vistas of dense forests, torrential rivers, and layers of soaring mountain walls. Because Katmandu, Nepal's capital, was only an hour from Calcutta, Childs, already imagining the clean scent of pine needles and mountain snow, decided that this trip was his chance to trek through paradise. But when he researched Nepal at his local library, he learned that early July was monsoon season and the western Himalayas in northern India would be the only dry place to hike. The best midsummer treks, the guidebooks informed him, were in Kashmir. None of the books he read mentioned the political instability of Kashmir, a region with such physical beauty that it was frequently described as India's Camelot. And although he later read the State Department's report on the conflict in Camelot, his false sense of security prevailed—something he would quite openly admit later.

On June 24, Childs made arrangements for a place to stay on the first and last nights of a six-day excursion after his business trip. After traveling to and from New Delhi and Srinagar and the resort town of Pahalgam, he would have four days to explore the Kashmiri Himalayas.

While in Calcutta, Childs spoke eagerly about his plans. Several people warned him about the tensions in Kashmir. One man advised him to consider another side trip, perhaps to Nepal. But a Kashmiri man he met at his company's plant assured him that tourists would not be bothered. Separatists, he was told, were battling the Indian army, and though there had been numerous abductions, the rebels weren't interested in foreigners. The worst that might happen, he was told, was a delay from Indian troop movements on the road; but trekkers were still trekking, and the terrain was truly spectacular in June and July.

On July 1, carrying a sleeping bag, tent, and backpack, Childs fled the heat and humidity of the Indian plains to temperate Srinagar, the "city of beauty," as it was called in the Kashmiri language, and once one of the greatest cultural centers of Asia. There he hired a taxi to take him to Pahalgam, a hilly resort town nestled in the mountains at the junction of two rivers. The sixty-mile route—winding in and out of shepherds' flocks, tunneling through mountains, and rising to an elevation of 7,000 feet—took nearly three hours. At Pahalgam, Childs commissioned a trail guide named Dasheer, a pony, and a pony handler, Rashide. The next day, the Connecticut trekker and his entourage hiked fifteen miles through forests and along rugged rivers to the alpine meadows of the Lidder Valley. Erecting a tent and a campsite, Childs planned to stay two days, taking day trips, first, on July 3, to Kolahoi Glacier, an eight-mile trek to 10,000 feet, and the next day to Tarsar Lake at an elevation of 13,000 feet.

On the afternoon of July 4, the forty-one-year-old engineer returned to his tent to recover from nearly seven hours of high-altitude hiking, a bout of altitude sickness, and a case of one very blistered foot. Nauseated and short of breath, he drifted off to sleep, comforted by the thought that in two days he would be on a plane home.

A few hours later, sometime between 6:30 and 7 P.M., Dasheer rushed to Childs's tent, awakening him and asking for his passport. The guide said there was trouble with some militants. Childs's first thought was that the Indian security forces were checking documents in search of Muslim separatists. But Dasheer, typically very calm, was extremely upset. When Childs emerged from his tent, he understood why.

Twenty yards away, a craggy-faced man cradling an AK-47 assault rifle was motioning Childs and his guides to move down the hill to the other campsite. There Childs was instructed to join the Brits sitting behind the stone hut. And soon, at gunpoint, Childs, one of his guides, and the two Brits, Keith and Paul, were forced to leave the camp. They were going to the town of Aru, they were told, where their leader would read their passports. This was six or seven miles to the south. Along the way they would stop at another campsite, where Donald Hutchings joined the caravan of captives. They were told they would be released the next morning.

During the three-hour hike to Aru, Childs convinced himself that this was nothing more than an inconvenient delay. He even began to fret over his plane reservation. Could he get the same flight a day or two later?

At Aru, the militants released one of the hostages, Childs's guide. Before leaving, Dasheer tried to assure Childs that there was nothing to worry about, but his face and his words delivered vastly disparate messages. It was Dasheer's expression, the strained moments of forced assurances, and their minute-long exchange that sent a first ripple of anxiety through Childs's body. That and the lie about Aru. There was no commander waiting to check passports. It was all a ruse, perhaps to ensure that the hostages would walk quietly away from the campsites and from their loved ones, moving deeper into the mountains. Dasheer watched as the rebels herded the hostages out of Aru. As Childs looked back and saw Dasheer standing there, a pained expression on his face, Childs sensed the full extent of his troubles for the first time. This, in combination with the lie about Aru, had raised his level of fear to one of terror.

Early on the morning of July 5—after walking much of the night—the four hostages, with at least a dozen armed escorts, began another journey, this one longer and more rugged than the well-worn path to Aru. They marched along a steep Alpine canyon through sun-flecked forests and across log bridges that spanned wide chasms over rivers roaring far below.

With a ratio of three militants to every hostage, it was impossible for Childs, Wells, Mangan, and Hutchings to move more than two steps from the barrel of a gun. Neither handcuffed nor chained, they were not restrained in any way. But, forced to walk from dawn to dusk, always on the move to dodge the detection of government troops, they became prisoners of their own exhaustion and fear. Each time they stopped, at the crest of a canyon or along the banks of rushing waters, Childs listened for the clicking of a rifle's chamber, certain that he was about to be shot and killed.

As the starkness of his situation pressed upon him, Childs grew increasingly anxious. On the second day of captivity, he began feeling angry at himself for getting into such a fix, and he grew frustrated at the helplessness of his plight. But halfway through the July 6 march, Childs's impatience overwhelmed him. As if tired of watching the reel of his own drama, Childs forced himself to stop thinking in the morbid, frightened terms of the defeated. Indeed, in an effort to ward off depression and despair, he began plotting and replotting his escape. He focused his attention on learning the habits and routines of his captors and on the characteristics of the terrain. He also hoarded food whenever possible.

Childs remembered what the Kashmiri factory worker had told him in Calcutta—that no foreign hostage had ever died at the hands of a Kashmiri separatist. The guide, Dasheer, had said the Kashmiris were not violent people. They were provoked to violence only in self-defense, in response to atrocities reportedly inflicted upon them by the Indian army. He trusted Dasheer as well as his own instincts regarding the Kashmiris he had met. These were reasons not to attempt an escape; any such attempt might compel his captors to defend their property, which now included him. But to Childs, to be sure, it was becoming increasingly clear that these were not necessarily Kashmiris. Some were clearly not locals, he thought, as he watched them. They stopped frequently along the trails to ask shepherds for directions. The way they walked and the choices they made indicated they knew mountain terrain, but they were not necessarily familiar with these mountains. Some of his captors, Childs began to believe, were Afghan or Pakistani mercenaries.

Childs also couldn't shake the memory of his encounter with the group's commander. On the first day of captivity, Childs had begged the leader to release him because of his two little girls back in Connecticut. He had opened his wallet and shown the leader the pictures: Mary, five, and Cathy, four. But the leader did not respond, and the look in his eye, as he motioned Childs away, was unapologetic, cold, and empty—as if he had never felt the touch of a child's hand or the warmth of a loved one's embrace. This was not the look of a man who had spent most of his life herding sheep nor one who, because of an impassioned desire for Kashmir's independence, was fighting the good fight.

To Childs, the leader had the look of a killer. At one point, he found himself sitting on a log next to the leader. On the leader's other side his AK-47 rifle was leaning against the log. Childs sneaked a few looks at the gun, thinking that, yes, he could grab it. He was indeed taller and perhaps more muscular than the man to his side. But as he was considering such a plot, the eyes of the militant caught his. And in that interlocking moment, Childs knew that the man knew exactly what Childs was thinking. The militant shifted his body in a very subtle way, as if to prepare for a confrontation and to send a signal that he was ready for conflict if Childs so chose. Had Childs missed his opportunity to escape during the split second before the look? Later, Childs learned that the leader, and the rest of the rebels, concealed in his clothing a knife, an extra gun, and at least one grenade. Beginning in midafternoon of the second day, Childs could think of nothing but his escape.

By the third day, Childs was having trouble walking largely because of blisters. This worried him because he feared that the weakest hostage, the one perceived to be incapable of continuing the rugged daily marches, would be the one the captors would choose to kill first, if that indeed was their plan. Still, he sensed that the militants were weary too. Out of desperation now, Childs, like a caged fox, began picking up the scent of opportunity for escape. While his captors concentrated on the path to the next campsite, he regularly tested their vigilance. He slowed his pace along the trail and then speeded up, all the while watching their response. The men ahead of him assumed he was trailing behind with the men at the back of the line. The ones behind clearly believed he was guarded by the men up front. This told him that his captors were not as organized and vigilant as they appeared to be. On the third day, too, Childs, who was suffering from dysentery, began to exaggerate his condition, giving him an excuse to be in the woods more often than usual.

Nights were spent in the huts of herders. The twelve militants, the four hostages, the herder's family, and their cows shared the same space. By the third night, Childs was practiced in the nocturnal routines and roles of his captors and hosts. The women hovered around the fire, boiling tea and cooking for hours each night. The rebels, who were devout Muslims, prayed five times a day: at dawn, noon, midafternoon, sunset, and at night between sunset and dawn. There was a possibility of escaping during the time when the men's praying coincided with the women's preparing of meals.

On the fourth day, the group, which had thus far been navigating unfamiliar terrain, traversed the valley that the Hindu pilgrims take to Amarnath Cave each summer—a path familiar at least to Hutchings, Mangan, and Childs. If they took a path down the valley, they would eventually arrive at the town of Pahalgam; if they went up, they would find themselves at the famed cave. This was the break Childs had been waiting for. In that vast and alien wilderness, he had a benchmark—a mental map on which he could chart his escape. The familiarity boosted his confidence. He knew where he was, and he knew he had to move soon. His feet aching, having more and more difficulty keeping up, he knew that he could not continue much farther without drawing attention to his current frailties. Fearing that he was becoming too much of a burden to the rebels, he could not stop the recurring image of himself as the first casualty, the terrorists' way to show the world how tough they could be. He could not forget the cold look in the leader's eyes when they were sitting on the log inches apart and yet worlds away.

When the parade of tired trekkers arrived at their destination on that fourth fateful night, thick clouds hovered above them, blocking the lights of the moon and stars and promising an evening of rain. Childs awaited nightfall with intense anticipation and with the hope of stealing away over terrain that his captors knew no better than he. Childs wasn't certain how long the sentries watched him when he left the group to relieve himself. And so late that night, he wandered out of the hut, past the sentries, and into the brush. He was tempted to bolt right then but decided instead on a trial run. While he stayed longer than usual, no one came looking for him. This established two things: a record of acceptably long trips away from the hut for Childs and a knowledge that the militants were unalarmed by a longer-than-usual trip.

He returned to the hut and pretended to sleep. Around 2 A.M. on July 8, Childs lumped his sleeping gear into the shape of a human body so that no one who awakened for the 4 A.M. prayer would notice a gap across the row of sleeping bodies in the hut. Then, in his stocking feet, with morsels of bread stuffed in his clothes and his shoes slung across his shoulders, he slipped past the sentries, wrapped himself in a cape of darkness, and fled.

For hours and hours, he ran nonstop, up and up, forging farther into the mountains—in the dark and the rain, without a path to follow—until the terrain grew so precipitous that he had to stop and lace on his boots. He had no choice but to climb and keep climbing, for he knew that down the mountain from the captors' encampment, there were shepherds with dogs which would surely bark on hearing the sound of his escape. And he knew, too, that the rebels would be awakening soon for morning prayers. He had no idea of the direction he was heading; all of his resources were focused on keeping his legs moving, testing the endurance he had built up from so many years of jogging and skiing and kayaking in what now seemed like someone else's life. Onward and upward he ran. For three hours, pushing through brush and scrambling over rocks, he ascended the Himalayan hills.

At first light, fearing he would be caught by the rebels or seen by nomads sympathetic to them, he found a place to hide and sat waiting in the cool shadows of a large rock. Still, as the day grew brighter, his hiding place seemed less secluded. So he continued his flight upward, gasping for air as he climbed toward 10,000 feet and more. Feeling hunted and paranoid, he kept looking for a place to hide. Eventually, he came upon a patch of hillside moss on which to rest; he had reached an elevation of nearly 14,000 feet, safe enough, he decided, to elude his captors—if they had, as he had hoped, searched for him down the mountain. That day, July 8, as dusk drew near, anticipating the cover of darkness, Childs began to wend his way down the mountain, with the hope of finding a stream or river that would lead him into the heart of a village.

It must have been close to 5 P.M., nearly fifteen hours after his escape, when Childs began to hear a sound that startled him. As he was moving slowly across a narrow ridge, he heard the faint whine of a motor, then a furious whirring sound, and then he felt the frantic gusts of wind. Suddenly a helicopter swooped into his vision. His first thought was that there had been a rescue operation and the captives had been released, and that it was just his dumb luck to have risked his life to escape when all the while a rescue team had been on their trail. Then he thought the men in the helicopter might belong to a Pakistani group operating in collusion with his abductors or be members of the same gang hunting him down. The pilot saw him and circled, cruising toward him. A soldier was pointing a gun at him. Childs said a prayer and kept on his path. When the helicopter came as close as fifty feet or so, he saw that the man in the passenger seat was using sign language to tell Childs to climb toward an area where the helicopter could land. Childs was hesitant. The helicopter moved dangerously close.

"What are you doing up here?" the man yelled.

"I was abducted," Childs said, trying to identify the man's uniform.

"You're German?" the man asked.

"No, American. I am American."

"Oh, my God, this is a miracle, this is a miracle of God," the man said.

He was right, Childs thought at the time, it was a miracle, nothing less. These men were not Pakistanis; nor were they terrorists from the group he so feared. Somehow he was still alive, and he was being rescued. His rescuers, General D. D. Saklani, the security adviser to the governor of Kashmir, and another police official, were inspecting the mountains in search of tourists. Earlier that day, the Al-Faran, as if exacting revenge for the successful escape, had abducted two more tourists: Dirk Hasert, a twenty-five-year-old student from the University of Erfurt in Germany, and Hans Christian Ostro, a twenty-seven-year-old actor and writer from Oslo, Norway. There were at least thirty-five trekkers in the Kashmir hills that day, and the Kashmiri government was trying to find them, warn them, and help them to a place of safety.

Childs stood for long seconds staring at the helicopter, feeling for the first time the extent of his fatigue, the pain in his legs, the cuts on his feet. From the helicopter he tried to see the path of his escape, but the vast terrain, with its endless layers of mountains and gorges, now covered his tracks, camouflaging his race to freedom. He scanned the landscape in the direction he had come, hoping to spot the rebel camp and somehow assist in the release of his fellow captives. The guilt of surviving was quickly diminishing the thrill of his escape. He could almost feel the pain of the captives as they continued the march, mile after mile, along uneven, rock-strewn trails. And now, because of Childs's escape, they would be watched more carefully, guarded more heavily.

In the days ahead, amid the grueling and tedious debriefings by the State Department and the FBI, Childs met with the families of the remaining hostages. He was more than pleased to share with them as much information as he could in the hope of allaying some of their fears. He told them that the rebels, whom he believed to be mostly Afghans and Pakistanis in their early to middle twenties, had not mistreated the hostages. The rebels were providing adequate food, typically rice, mutton, and chipatis, though the shelters, often stone huts with dirt floors, were uncomfortable and cold. Keith was very optimistic, Childs told Julie, though he was suffering from altitude sickness. And Don, who had been in the mountains for ten days and had already trekked along 13,000-foot passes, was helping Keith to overcome his illness. Long accustomed to mountain life, the rebels had little understanding of altitude sickness, but Don had explained to them how really ill Keith was and how the illness would soon pass if they just allowed him time to recover.

Both Don and Keith were schmoozing regularly with the rebels, who seemed curious to learn what the Westerners were all about. The rebels had nicknamed Don "ChaCha," John told Jane, which meant uncle. This was probably because, at forty-two years of age, Don was the oldest of the hostages and likely older than most of the rebels. Paul was the youngest at twenty-four, and Keith was thirty-three. Don was also friendly and generally good with the rebels, John said. This was a tremendous relief to Jane—although she had assumed, knowing Don, that he would naturally play the part of the elder statesman. Childs also told Jane that the rebels were fascinated with

Don's watch, a mountaineer's special with an altimeter and a stop-watch built in.

Later that year in a lecture at the University of Hartford's World Affairs Council, Childs elicited more: "We weren't physically tortured, but there was a form of psychological torture. For example, they slaughtered a sheep in front of us, cutting its throat and beheading it in much the same manner they later killed Hans Christian Ostro."

On July 15—the rebels' deadline—Childs flew home. At Bradley International Airport, in Hartford, Connecticut, his children rushed into his arms while his mother and father watched in disbelief, hoping that the sight of their son was in fact real and not a dream. And nothing that would ever happen again—certainly not the rebels' dubious claim later that they had allowed him to escape—could diminish the joy of the release and Childs's resolute conviction that he had indeed outsmarted the terrorists.

In the days that followed, Childs granted several interviews, but he declined offers for television appearances. He didn't care to spin his tale into a TV movie. He was more concerned that too much media coverage might somehow threaten the release and safety of the remaining hostages. Mostly he wanted his life back, his work, his children, his daily five-mile runs at the local high school track.

Weeks later, when the news broke about the murder of Hans Christian Ostro, Childs talked to the *Boston Globe* about his abduction. "I was very naive before this experience," the soft-spoken engineer said. "I always thought what happened like this happened to someone else."

9

Unshielded by bodyguards or armored cars, unprotected by alarm systems and double bolts, distracted by the pursuit of adventure, and often too trusting for their own good, tourists are the kidnappers' quintessential "soft target"—easy to spot, easy to lure, and easy to snatch. And there are plenty to choose from in this age of "innocents abroad."

As the world's biggest industry, tourism employs at least 10 percent of the global workforce, producing 10 percent of the world's gross national product and growing 20 percent faster than the global economy. The fall of communism and the end of ideological struggles—along with enhanced globalization and the coming of peace to countries long at war—opened the world's gates to travelers everywhere. A blend of capitalism and curiosity entices the masses, with their money and their unbounded enthusiasm, to circle the globe. At the same time, technology, particularly the Internet, has been shrinking that globe to the size of a computer screen, making even the most remote destinations seem easily accessible and even the most inhospitable lands seem friendly. Moreover, "adventure-travel" is in vogue, as if the breathless pace of technology and the materialism of Western culture—with the uniformity of shopping malls and fast-food franchises—has compelled people to seek out simpler, less-developed worlds. Whether it is the steppes of Mongolia or the jungles of Indonesia, what appeals to this army of explorers are the remoter reaches of the planet—as unusual, as virginal, and as distinctly un-Western as possible.

In past eras, terrorists avoided tourists, fearing they would alienate certain countries, including the United States, which would cost them sympathy as well as financial support for their various causes. But the 1970s wave of airline hijackings revealed the attention-grabbing value of snatching tourists, especially those from nations that were aiding Israel, the avowed enemy of Islamic terrorists. While hijacking eventually fell out of vogue—it was too costly and yielded too few benefits—the appeal of kidnapping tourists never faded.

The Shining Path, a Maoist guerrilla group in Peru, was one of the first in recent times to recognize the value of the individual tourist as hostage. Its crusade was to ruin Peru's tourist trade in the 1980s and hence help to derail the ruling regime. By the 1990s, as it became clear that tourism was playing a vital role in the economy of many developing nations, abductions of tourists grew enormously in appeal. Indeed, in the dawning age of CNN and the Internet, the act of abducting Western tourists held the potential for instantaneous worldwide publicity—TV cameras beaming the cause of the captors from mountain or jungle hideaways to the dinner tables of Middle America. For bandits and ransom seekers, too, abducting an entire tour group—thus exposing the "safety-in-numbers" myth—made it possible, as various incidents had demonstrated, to demand ransoms from more than one country, corporation, or family. As one government official put it, tourists as targets are "slow-moving, big, pink, and obvious."

In a July 1995 article about ways to avoid becoming "a bargaining chip in someone else's war," the travel editor of the *Independent*, a London newspaper, wrote: "Nothing in the guerrilla's repertoire compares with a Western hostage. Revolutionary movements can engage in bitter struggles for years without the world taking much notice. Capture a tourist, though, and suddenly the conflict will be plastered all over the Western media. The more important tourism is to the national economy, the greater the bargaining power."

"What is so sinister about today's terrorists," a June 1996 article in the *Times* (of London) read, "is that most of them believe that tourists in themselves embody the system and values the militants are trying to overthrow."

Caught up in the tourism wave, most travel sections of newspapers and magazines, however, are not so wise. Regaling readers with the glories of exploring exotic, once-forbidden lands, such as Cambodia, they rarely, if ever, mention the threat of abductions or the other violent crimes perpetrated against tourists. Yet during the six years from 1991 to 1997, tourists were abducted in India, Kashmir, Yemen, the Philippines, Turkey, Costa Rica, Ecuador, Venezuela, Greece, China, Panama, Indonesia, New Guinea, Bolivia, Peru, Egypt, Cambodia, Colombia, Pakistan, Guatemala, Honduras, Russia, Mexico, Tanzania (in a game park), Baja California, and the United States.

In the Philippines, where Islamic extremists, political rebels, former rebels, and criminal gangs all utilize the age-old crime, even the chairman of the nation's biggest travel and tour agency was abducted in 1995. He was released after his wife paid a ransom of five million pesos ($192,000).

In Ecuador, politically motivated kidnappings of tourists typically protest the ecological damage allegedly caused by oil exploration in the Amazonian jungles. One advisor to indigenous groups staging such protests commented that "lawsuits and negotiations confronting oil companies have gone on for many years and the people now seek to negotiate directly by whatever means possible, including abductions." In September of 1995, residents of the legendary Galápagos Islands threatened to kidnap tourists as a way of forcing the Ecuadoran government to send more money to the islands and to build a university there. But it was the northern region of Ecuador, along the Colombian border, that was perhaps the most worrisome. The area has been vulnerable to kidnappings perpetrated by Colombian guerrillas in collusion with local bandits venturing over the border for new prey. In the summer of 1996, a New Jersey computer scientist and his eighteen-year-old daughter were kidnapped while bird-watching near the precipitous northern edge.

Kurdish separatists snatched a young British couple as they were cycling through eastern Turkey on their way to Australia in 1993. Over the next two years, tourists from several nations were abducted in both India and Kashmir. In Mexico, the devaluation of the peso in December 1994 lured droves of tourists to its abundant, and suddenly inexpensive, resorts because vacationing was cheaper now in Mexico than in neighboring Costa Rica and other Latin American vacation spots. But the nation's growing economic troubles were also bolstering the kidnap trade, as rebels and street criminals alike engaged in the ancient crime for the love of lucre. In Yemen, armed tribesmen abducted seventeen French vacationers in 1996 while they were sightseeing. In late 1995, kidnappers seized four Americans and fifteen Filipinos vacationing at a Lake Sebu resort in the southern Philippines and demanded that the government stop oppressing the poor. Then, on January 1, 1996, in Costa Rica, nine masked men and a woman snatched two tourists, one from Germany and the other, a Swiss-born tour guide, from the dining room of a resort lodge surrounded by lush rain forests in an area loved by ecotourists. The kidnappers, former contra rebels from nearby Nicaragua, demanded a $1 million ransom in addition to job guarantees for workers, a cut in food prices, a rise in the Costa Rican minimum wage, and the release of fellow rebels from prison.

One of the most bone-chilling cases occurred in Cambodia in 1994, a boom year for tourism there, when three backpackers—from France, England, and Australia—were abducted from a train. The backpackers had heard the siren song of tourism promoting the white-sand beauty of Kampot, a port town dubbed by Cambodian government boosters as the country's greatest new resort. It was the latest in a series of Western hostage–takings in a country that had a new, independent government, and which, after twenty-five years of war, was hailed by travel magazines as being "at peace." The problem was that Cambodia, though not at war, was still an unsafe place, particularly for foreigners. There were, after all, 8.5 million land mines in the country.

The journey from Phnom Penh to the beaches of Kampot was hardly the road from London to the cliffs of Dover.

Despite the alluring coverage that Cambodia had recently received in magazines and newspapers worldwide—and despite its 1992 debut in the celebrated *Lonely Planet* guidebook series—the manifold dangers in its immediate past still lingered in the shadows of its supposedly vibrant present. The Khmer Rouge, Cambodia's vicious gang of guerrilla thugs that had murdered 2 million people between 1975 and 1979, was still trying in the mid-1990s to bring down the government and was marauding at will throughout various regions, including the Elephant Mountains around Kampot. Worse still, kidnapping was the Khmer Rouge way of making money, and while Cambodian villagers were the usual prey—for ransoms of rice and other supplies—word was out in 1994 that the guerrillas were targeting Westerners. After all, there were many more foreigners, including Western travelers, roaming Cambodia than at any time in recent history. And so it happened that in late July, on the train ride to romantic Kampot, the brutal Khmer Rouge snatched the backpackers at gunpoint. Forty or more fighters stormed the train, guns ablaze, taking at least twenty passengers hostage, including the three backpackers.

Commander Ramm and his team of negotiators were assigned to the case. The first ransom demands ranged from $50,000 to $150,000. But no sooner had the first demands been made than the three governments announced that they had strict policies forbidding the payment of ransoms to kidnappers. The rebels then took another tack. Knowing that the hostages came from three of the countries that were major financial supporters of the Cambodian government—the enemy of the Khmer Rouge—they proposed a release in exchange for the end of such support. Soon thereafter, the Royal Cambodian Armed Forces began an all-out attack of the rebel hideout where the hostages were being held. That was mid-August. Toward the end of the month, authorities received a videotape showing the thin young hostages. One pleaded, "If the governments won't pay for our release, please do the moral thing and give our families the opportunity to arrange our release."

On October 30, the bodies of the three young men were found in a shallow grave near a Khmer Rouge hideout surrounded by minefields. They were killed sometime during September, the coroner said. The Khmer Rouge took credit, claiming the hostages were war criminals.

A few months later, a college professor from Texas and her guide were shot and killed while touring the ancient temples and towers of Angkor Wat, Cambodia's most often touted tourist attraction. The Khmer Rouge took credit once again, and at the same time announced that hunting down, abducting, and killing Westerners was their new official strategy for derailing the Cambodian government.

Roughly a year later, the *New York Times* ran a bullish story in its travel section about tourist attractions in the "new" Cambodia. "Angkor emerges from the jungle," the headline read. "After years of neglect, the Cambodian temple complex is being restored and tourists are flocking back."

The article began: "True to the beliefs in reincarnation of the Hindu and Buddhist kings who built them, the temples of Angkor are being reborn in a new Cambodia. . . . Tourists, most of them Japanese and European, are returning by the thousands to what may soon become the leading attraction of Southeast Asia."

The article was right on target in terms of trends. By 1996, in addition to Angkor Wat, the Cambodian Ministry of Tourism was promoting nature-based tourism; the hip word was *ecotourism*. At tourism conferences throughout Europe that spring, the agency distributed its glossy brochure, the one with the headline "Cambodia: Journey of a Lifetime."

Later the same year, the *New York Times*—unlike many other publications—demonstrated that it had learned the importance of warning its readers about the perils of travel across the exciting, though sometimes dangerous, international frontier. In December, the *Times* ran a travel piece about Myanmar, "a country of old manners and a deep humanity that neither time nor a military dictatorship has been able to erase." Between 1991 and 1995, the number of tourists to Myanmar, which changed its name from Burma in 1989, had soared from about 8,000 to 100,000. Tourism dollars had jumped from $9 million in 1991 to $32 million by 1995. And in 1996, the Myanmar tourism agency's latest campaign, "Visit Myanmar Year 1996," had reached the vast readership of the *New York Times* in the form of a smooth-flowing and engaging article.

"Yangon is a slow and gracious capital, with a lingering European feel to its buildings and tree-lined avenues. . . . Visit Myanmar Year was advertised everywhere in our travels. The government is building new hotels, widening and even tarring the ubiquitous dirt roads, applying fresh gold leaf to pagodas," the article informed. And, alluding to a political controversy within the country over the issue of tourism, the article went on to say, "Many Burmese, including the leader of the National League for Democracy, feel that foreign dollars only benefit the existing Government, thereby strengthening an oppressive military dictatorship. They ask that tourists bypass Myanmar, especially during this year. On the other hand, we found the Burmese people so eager to talk—in angry whispers—about the curtailing of their freedom, and so wanting us to carry their message out, we felt satisfied that our own kind of tourism had helped, not hurt, their country's struggle for democracy. At the end of a walking day in Mandalay, food was on our minds."

On the same page of the Sunday travel section, showing social responsibility, the *Times* ran a story by Seth Mydans, the chief of its Bangkok (Thailand) bureau, who informed the reader that Myanmar, though one of Asia's loveliest nations, was "in the grip of a military junta that has drawn condemnation from around the world for its suppression of democracy and its abuses of human rights." And in the second paragraph of the story, which discussed in detail the political aspects of the "Visit Myanmar Year" campaign, Mydans quoted from the U.S. State Department's most recent announcement—only six days old—that "U.S. citizens exercise all due caution in traveling to Burma and should for the time being curtail travel to Burma (Myanmar) absent a compelling reason."

Clearly, an astute editor at the *Times* had checked with the bureau chief in nearby Thailand to get the latest news before publishing the travel piece. It was a move that many readers and law enforcement officers hoped would one day be standard journalistic practice in travel sections of newspapers and magazines.

Around the same time, in another *Times* travel piece, the writer posted a warning within the article itself. "We knew Yemen would be exotic," it began. Then, in the third paragraph: "We fared much better than the group of French tourists who were kidnapped near the same place, taken to a mountain stronghold for several days and released unharmed. Tribesmen in Yemen have a long tradition of hostage-taking."

The strange and scary juxtaposition of travel hype with travel danger seemed to be escalating every year. After Guatemala's civil war formally ended in late 1996, the government immediately threw open its doors to tourism, beckoning travelers to come to the now-peaceful nation. And although Guatemala was the cover story on travel magazines by spring and summer of 1997, it was not yet all that safe. By the end of January, there were reports of a new kidnapping wave in Guatemala, where abductions had already been a problem for several years, and analysts were looking at the demobilized soldiers and guerrillas as reasons. "Generations of men had been fighting and now suddenly what were they to do? An entire society didn't suddenly change because of a piece of paper," one kidnap consultant commented. By summer, six or so months after the peace treaty was signed, the government was downplaying the problem, saying there had been only 9 cases so far that year. Human rights groups put the tally at 900 for the half year. The truth was somewhere in the murky middle.

Kidnap negotiators, in both the private and public sectors, were often stunned by the presence of tourists in the very nations where they were deployed to gain the release of hostages. They liked to say that the more a travel brochure stressed the word *remote,* the greater the potential for danger and the greater the need for caution. Negotiators found themselves navigating through a strange new world, one in which most people had little understanding of what was going on. They were aghast at the trend toward "tribal tourism" in some countries, including Papua New Guinea, where travel agencies were sending tourists on field trips to gawk at the bow-and-arrow cultures of primitive tribes, some of which were at war.

One negotiator recalled working a case in the Philippines in 1993, in which the New People's Army had abducted a businessman. One morning, as the negotiator was leaving his hotel to go to Mindanao, he noticed a camera crew loading up to leave. They were also going to Mindanao, they told him, to work on a tourist film for trekkers. Alas, he was heading for the island to connect with a rebel intermediary to begin negotiations for the release of a hostage.

Negotiator Mike Ackerman remembered a similar scene in El Salvador a few years back when he was leaving his hotel to work on establishing contact with some kidnappers. "I was thinking how I couldn't wait to get out of there, and then suddenly I saw a busload of elderly tourists pull up and I thought, What the hell are they doing here in the middle of a civil war?"

Just as the tourism boom and the globalization of the economy in general have indirectly boosted the kidnap industry by providing new supplies of soft targets, the surge in both industries—tourism and kidnapping—has helped to spawn another boom: in the travel advisory business. The Ackerman Group, Pinkerton's, Control Risks Group (CRG), Kroll Associates, and other private companies with crisis management services have been issuing risk assessments of individual countries for their clients for at least the past decade. But now, with client lists burgeoning, their daily risk analyses have far surpassed the State Department advisories in detail, frequency, and—sometimes—objectivity. CRG has twenty-five analysts compiling information for its richly detailed daily assessments. At Pinkerton's, the analysts cull from daily press reports out of Reuters, the *Wall Street Journal,* and other papers as well as from Internet Web sites in the individual countries. The analysts also tap into field sources including Mormon missionaries and representatives of the Catholic Church.

The private companies have far more resources to allocate to their daily advisories than the State Department. This was especially true during the mid-1990s; ironically, State's budget was shrinking at the very time when the need for its protective services was dramatically expanding. By 1997, there were 3.27 million Americans living abroad, not including U.S. government employees and their dependents. And each year the number of Americans traveling abroad was increasing by 10 percent—from 46.45 million in 1994 to 50.76 million in 1995.

With the private groups, there is far less red tape. No hidden political agendas, no layers of red-pencil bureaucrats lined up between the reporting of facts and the publication of advisories, no need to be diplomatic nor to fear offending a trading partner. In consequence, the daily risk assessments spewing regularly and rapidly out of the private sector are simply more helpful than anything the government is able to provide.

"The government's biggest problem in this is that they do not want to say bad things about a country with whom the U.S. has a good relationship, for example, these days, Russia or Mexico," said Mike Ackerman, who in 1978 was the first to offer clients risk assessment reports, country by country. "A negative advisory does incite some anger. We've been threatened by countries and by airlines. They want to sue us because of giving them bad publicity when we're just trying to protect our clients."

The State Department, despite the input of astute crime and terrorism analysts, has an advisory system that is hampered by its sometimes conflicting missions of protecting American citizens abroad *and* exercising the nation's foreign policy through embassies and consulates. During an era when U.S. business interests are at the front lines of U.S. foreign policy, the two basic mandates have a greater-than-ever potential for clashing agendas.

To be sure, the government has long recognized the need for stepped-up vigilance abroad, at least regarding the security of the business community. In 1985, it paid special attention to corporate America in the creation of its Overseas Security Advisory Council (OSAC). Promoting cooperation between the public and private sectors on security issues abroad, OSAC provides information, guidance, and briefings to American firms operating overseas. But there is no equivalent for the ordinary citizen. The dilemma for the State Department is that some countries in which the United States wants to expand its markets are plagued with crimes, including kidnapping. These are societies in transition, experiencing fast growth and jolting exposure to the West. And for some, tourism is crucial to their financial development. Thus, a negative travel advisory from the United States is tantamount to an economic boycott.

Even if an advisory contains only one contrary phrase, it can incite rage from the targeted nation, enough to sometimes cause the United States to back down. On March 15, 1993, three days after a wave of bombings in Bombay, the State Department placed India on its dreaded travel warning list. The response was the political equivalent of a bomb, inspiring a series of indignant editorials, and provoking certain high-level Indian officials to vent their concerns to the American embassy and to business executives from the United States. Two weeks later, the State Department canceled its warning, saying, "While it is possible that terrorist events may occur for which the Department has no forewarning, the Department no longer believes it is necessary to defer travel to New Delhi."

In this era of expanding world markets, when the United States' economic future depends on its ability to compete successfully in a highly competitive international economy, the travel advisory has more political power—both positive and negative—than at any other time.

The government's system of advisories has been a target for critics of all sorts since advisories were first issued in the late 1970s. Until recently, they were issued sporadically and without uniformity. Embassies received little guidance about what conditions warranted advisories and what facts should be noted. By 1990, increasing concerns over safety abroad, the rapidly changing global scene, and the outbreak of numerous new conflicts had escalated concerns over the accuracy and immediacy of travel information released by the government. A 1991 study initiated by a congressional subcommittee revealed there were reasons for concern. It appeared that the government was publishing advisories for some countries in which violent crimes were occurring but not for others. Sometimes the delay between the beginning of a crime wave and the time it was announced to the American people was as long as three years. And there were instances when foreign policy appeared to be a factor in the decision-making process. The study cited numerous examples.

In Mexico, for instance, between June of 1989 and February of 1991, the government reported that 139 Americans were the victims of violent crimes in that nation: thirty-nine murders or attempted murders, twenty-nine rapes or attempted rapes, three kidnappings, and sixty-eight assaults and armed robberies. Yet the same agency that had accumulated those statistics did not issue an advisory or travel notice to warn Americans about the incidents. The State Department's explanation was that the ratio of Americans who were victims of crime to the millions of Americans visiting Mexico each year was quite low. Further, it believed that Mexican authorities were demonstrating a commitment to combating crime. During the same period, the government issued an advisory for Kenya because of a few violent incidents, including the murder of one American tourist at a game park. The State Department had been inconsistent in the way that it had dealt with the two countries.

It is no small wonder that private sector advisories have become as much of a daily habit for the business executives and the well-informed travelers of the 1990s as a cup of coffee and the morning paper—that is, for those who can afford them. Corporations, entrepreneurs, and wealthy individuals who engage private firms to advise them on the risks of traveling abroad and how to deal with problems such as kidnappings are well aware of the mercurial nature of global crime and the hazards of a borderless world. They well know that globalization is as much about the expansion of crime as it is about the expansion of markets. But the typical traveler without access to such services is often not aware enough of potential perils to even check a government advisory or to inquire beyond guidebooks, brochures, and travel agents.

And so, in the 1990s, droves of eager travelers—their curiosity stirred by scintillating brochures and enticing photo-rich articles—have operated under the illusion that their government still has the resources to protect them abroad if there is indeed a problem. The odds, of course, are in their favor. Kidnapping and violence against foreigners, though clearly on the rise, are still relatively uncommon. But they *do* happen and usually to those who are unaware of or misinformed about the unpredictable landscapes of the new age. In a borderless world, there are few official restrictions to traveling—a situation that requires more in-depth research before a trip.

Kashmir, though occasionally mentioned in travel magazines and tour books as a paradise on earth, was by 1995 no longer touted in major publications as a tourism Mecca. During the 1980s, an average of 80,000 foreigners visited Kashmir annually. By 1994, after Kashmir's war for independence escalated, barely 10,000 visitors watched the sun rise above the mountainous horizon of the vale of Kashmir.

The plummet caused a near-panic among owners of hotels and the various tourist attractions, including the luxurious houseboats on the still-shimmering Dal Lake in Srinagar. Hundreds of hotels had been boarded up, while the boat owners, who once earned 600 rupees a day, were now doing manual labor for barely 50.

The panic invited a battalion of Kashmiri con artists to devise all sorts of clever ways to prop up the tourism business in their war-struck land. Nattily dressed con men, experienced in spotting naive, first-time visitors, greeted new arrivals at the international airport in New Delhi and told them apocryphal stories about hotels being totally booked in the city, about riots that made it unsafe in the city at that time, or about record heat killing dozens of people daily in New Delhi. The tourists were then offered travel packages to cool and spectacular Kashmir at grossly inflated prices. Some were even led to what they were told, deceptively, were official branches of the government tourism office; there they handed over passports and traveler's checks to supposed staff members, who offered to help them cash their checks and redo their itineraries to include Kashmir. The lodgings were sometimes on a houseboat owned by a relative of the so-called tourism official in New Delhi. The offices also booked tours through the celebrated Himalayas—under the direction of a guide who, of course, was also a relative. A British official based in India told the *Daily Telegraph,* a British newspaper, in May 1996 that India's capital was "full of government tourist offices most of which were unofficial [and] that the Indian authorities did nothing to discourage the touts or deter people from visiting Kashmir."

Paul Wells, the Nottingham photographer and student taken hostage that summer in Kashmir, had experienced a version of this con. When he and Cath Moseley first arrived in New Delhi, they hired a cab at the airport to take them to the hotel they had booked in advance. The cabby told them there were riots near that hotel, and that it was dangerous for them to stay in that part of the city. But he did know of a hotel that was safe, the cabby said, and he took them to it. At the hotel, they were advised that it was cooler and safer to go north to Kashmir, and—presto—there appeared someone who would arrange for the accommodations and the tour. Thus the young couple ended up in Kashmir on a houseboat on Dal Lake. It was there that the houseboat owner encouraged them, as well as the Mangans, to trek in the vicinity of Pahalgam.

Still worried about safety, the two couples then went to the state tourism offices to inquire. It would haunt Julie Mangan for a very long time that the advice she and her husband received was so positive, especially after she learned that the militants had been controlling sectors of the Kashmir Valley for several months at least. Still, in asking about safety, both couples were told that hikers had been following the trails up and down the hills near Pahalgam all summer long, and that there had not been a hint of trouble from the rebels.

When Jane and Don checked local tourism offices in New Delhi and Srinagar, no one warned them of the hidden perils in the hill country of India's war-torn "Camelot." What they did not know, as they chose their passages through northern India, was that tourists had been kidnapped in the same region the year before, in the vicinity of Pahalgam as well as in Srinagar and New Delhi.

In Srinagar, a militant had killed an American tourist from Ogden, Utah, who was staying on one of the houseboats on Dal Lake. The thirty-two-year-old man had been shot in the back and chest while taking pictures with an impressive, attention-getting video camera. Militants thought he was a spy, according to some reports. Others said his killers simply wanted his fancy camera.

The incident in New Delhi involved three Brits and an American who were lured into captivity by a young man who offered his services as a tour guide through the villages outside of Delhi. The so-called guide showed them his passport and, in a thick British accent, explained that he had studied math at the London School of Economics. But on the way out of town, the man pulled a pistol on the young tourists and took them to a farmhouse somewhere on the outskirts of Delhi, where they were chained to the floor. The American hostage was later taken to a separate house, apparently back in town.

The man with the pistol and his fellow kidnappers called themselves Al-Hadid, which translates to "Blade," and while basically unknown, the group would later be revealed as a front or an extension of the Harkat-ul-Ansar (HUA), an Islamic band in Pakistan. In a very well planned kidnapping, which included rented houses, fake IDs, several cars and drivers, and a carefully executed entrapment, the Al-Hadid sent photos of the four captives at gunpoint to the BBC. "Our hostages are as yet unhurt. Unless our brothers are released, our Western hostages, the guests of the Indian government, will be beheaded one at a time," they wrote in a message sent with the photos. The "brothers" were jailed militants, including the lead kidnapper in an incident involving two Brits earlier the same year, whose name would also appear on the Al-Faran's list of demands in exchange for Hutchings, Wells, Mangan, and Hasert.

The four captives were rescued quite by accident by Indian police, who in the process of chasing down a burglar scared the Al-Hadid lookout on the roof of the house where the American was being held. Curious about why the man ran, they chased and apprehended him and freed the American. Eventually, the other captives were rescued, unharmed, in a police raid.

In all fairness to the tourism offices, Jane and Don were warned about the potential dangers of spending time in Srinagar. Urban centers were increasingly dangerous, they were told, while the outlying areas were well traveled and not problematic—not for the past twelve months, that is. On June 9, 1994, in the very same area where Don and Jane were hiking, Kashmiri separatists had kidnapped two Brits—an incident no tourism official cared to share with the couple from Spokane. One of the hostages, Kim Housego, was the sixteen-year-old son of Jenny and David Housego. Housego was a New Delhi businessman who was the former South Asia correspondent for the *Financial Times* who had taken his family on a trekking holiday to Kashmir on the occasion of his wife's 50th birthday. And the other, who was abducted from his hotel room in Aru, was thirty-six-year-old David Mackie, a video director from London. He was on an eighteen-month world tour with his wife, Cathy. The kidnappers were mostly Pathans, Housego would say later, mountain people from Afghanistan and northwestern Pakistan who had joined the fight to end Indian rule in Kashmir. At first they asked for the release of jailed militants. They then called for an end to the human rights abuses of Indian soldiers against Kashmiris. They promised they would not harm the hostages unless the Indian army launched a rescue.

Because of his work in India, David Housego had many contacts in the Pakistani government, in the press, and among the Kashmiri separatists. The press coverage of the crisis was unrelenting—one of the reasons, Housego would always believe, for his son's and Mackie's release—and so was Housego. Neither the Indian government nor the British Foreign Office could persuade him to sit back and wait. He was even interviewed while walking into the mountains to find the rebels and speak to them himself. A combination of his bravery, his contacts, and a groundswell of public sentiment among Pakistanis, Kashmiris, and militants—who unilaterally decried the hostage-taking—effectively shamed the kidnappers into freeing Mackie and Housego after seventeen days in captivity. Housego's connections must have been powerful because in less than a day after his initial contact with Pakistani leaders, the government issued a statement condemning the kidnapping of Housego and Mackie as acts of terrorism. The denunciation was "tremendous in shaping attitudes in the Valley and in isolating the group that had taken them," he later told a BBC reporter. Sadly, the man who had acted as the secret intermediary between Housego and the militant leaders was murdered three days after the hostages' release.

The Housego/Mackie ordeal occurred in June. A few weeks later, the Utah man was murdered on the streets of Srinagar, and then four months later, the four tourists were abducted in New Delhi. If Jane and Don had consulted the latest State Department information sheet on India, which was issued on November 25, 1994, they would have read that "during September/October 1994, in what appears to have been an isolated incident, one American and three British tourists in New Delhi were lured by friendly-seeming members of a hitherto-unknown Kashmiri terrorist group and taken hostage. After weeks in captivity, the four were released, unharmed, following a police action."

About Kashmir, the circular read, "In July 1994, an American tourist was fatally shot in Srinagar, and in June 1994 militants held two British hikers hostage for 18 [sic] days before releasing them. These recent events demonstrate that the Kashmir Valley in the State of Jammu and Kashmir remains a dangerous place where terrorist activities and violent civil disturbances continue."

But the American couple had gone to the Indian tourism offices believing this was the way to get the most up-to-date information. (As experienced travelers, they knew that things change quickly in areas like Kashmir.) They also found out what trekkers who had just returned from the trip had to say about the area. No one told them about the events of the year before. Everyone said the area near Pahalgam would be suitable for trekking.

And even in the summer of 1995, despite Jane's and Don's ordeals, the flow of tourists to Kashmir continued, much to the shock of everyone involved in resolving the incident. Leon Schenck, one of the FBI's hostage negotiators, would never forget the two trekkers sitting next to him on one of his plane rides to Srinagar. Schenck was thinking about Srinagar and the fact that it was really a town under military occupation, as in a war. Yes, this was a war, he was thinking as the trekkers, both English-speaking, sat down. "I was shocked to see that in August [1995], after so many problems, people were still traveling there. I asked them if they knew what was happening in Kashmir, and they looked at me, I swear almost with an air of excitement. 'Yes, we know, but we aren't worried. The trekking areas are fine; we'll be fine.' I couldn't respond."

In September of 1995, the *Guardian,* an English newspaper, published an article about a "miniboom" in tourism that year in Kashmir. The tourists were coming back, making 1995 the most successful season in six years. While Indian tourists were still staying away, according to the article, foreign tourists seemed undaunted. Between twenty and forty tourists were flying into Srinagar each day, despite severe flooding in August and the abductions of tourists in midsummer, the article said.

Around the same time, a British official, obviously concerned about the potential for more kidnappings, commented on the hidden dangers for tourists in both Kashmir and New Delhi. The Indian authorities, he maintained, were doing nothing to warn tourists. "There are still hundreds of people going to Kashmir, despite what's happened," he said. "We cannot dissuade them. They think, It can't happen to me."

10

⬦⬦⬦

At the State Department press briefing on the morning of July 17, Nicholas Burns expressed the U.S. position that the responsibility for resolving the kidnapping of the tourists in Kashmir belonged solely to the Indian government. The U.S. involvement consisted of one embassy officer in Srinagar. There was obvious concern, but there was also considerable confidence that this would not be a prolonged, complicated standoff. The last abduction of Westerners in Kashmir, the previous summer, had lasted only seventeen days. What seemed to slip through the cracks of memory, though, was the fact that the 1994 incident was resolved solely by the concerted efforts of family members—not the Indian government—and in several other recent kidnappings in India, the government had made concessions to the rebels.

> *Q:* Nick, can you bring us up to date on—if there's any news on—the hostage situation in Kashmir and the American being held? The deadline has passed, and I just wondered what the situation was.

> *Burns:* The United States remains very deeply concerned about the situation in Kashmir where five hostages are being held by the Al-Faran

group. We have an officer in New Delhi who is in Srinagar. He works continuously with the Indian authorities in their efforts to secure release of the hostages. We continue to hope for a peaceful outcome out of concern for the safety of the American involved and the others. . . . We are monitoring it very closely with the one person that we have there, and through the efforts of our embassy in New Delhi, we're hopeful for a peaceful outcome to this. We call upon, of course, the Al-Faran group to exercise reason and a humanitarian commitment to resolve this problem peacefully and to release all of the captives unharmed.

Q: Do you think there are any direct talks between your person on the scene and this group? Has there been any direct contact at all?

Burns: I can't say. I think I want to say as little as possible, so that I don't in any way affect negatively the efforts by the Indian government to bring this crisis to a successful and peaceful conclusion.

Q: Are you suggesting, though, it is in the hands of the Indian government right now, not—

Burns: It's certainly in the hands of the Indian government, yes. It most definitely is, and we are working with them. We have a direct interest, obviously, because an American citizen is being held, and for that reason we have an embassy officer in Srinagar.

The terrorists' July 15 deadline had come and gone, and, after ardent appeals from the families and from Amnesty International, the hostages were still alive, though they were forced to endure yet another day under the sword. A two-day extension of the previous threat gave the Indian government until midnight of July 17 to deliver the jailed militants and to save the lives of the hostages.

At precisely one hour before the new deadline, the Srinagar offices of the Associated Press received an audiocassette of messages from the captives.

"I am Don Hutchings of the United States of America," the neuropsychologist from Spokane began. "I am OK. We have walked many days and nights over the mountains, and I am tired. The mujahideen have been OK with me. Jane, I want to let you know I am OK. I do not know [if] today I will die or tomorrow I will die. I do not know what will happen. I appeal to the American government and the Indian government for help."

In the same packet, Al-Faran enclosed a written statement: "We made contact with the [Indian] government three days ago but the government does not seem to be prepared for any purposeful talks. They [the hostages] can be killed at any time after the expiry of the deadline. We will not extend the deadline again."

The Indian government refused once again to release the jailed rebels. After the clock struck twelve on the morning of July 18, the hostages could be executed at any moment. This marked the beginning of what some officials referred to as the "war of nerves."

At the State Department briefing that morning, a reporter asked Burns about the American in Kashmir. "We are continuing to work with the Indian authorities," he said, in a brief statement. "We remain hopeful there will be a peaceful outcome to this very great problem. We still have an embassy officer in Srinagar. We certainly would join the families in appealing to the people who are holding Mr. Hutchings captive and the others captive to release them unharmed. These people have done nothing wrong. These people are innocent, and they ought to be released unharmed and released immediately."

On the seventeenth day of captivity, July 20, the British families and authorities were filled with optimism because David Mackie and Kim Housego had been released the previous summer after seventeen days. Maybe history would repeat itself. But July 20 came and went without news of any release. Then, early the next morning, as the families and authorities tried to move past the disappointments of the previous day, the manipulations of the Al-Faran threw them off balance once again. That was the day the rebels announced that two hostages had been seriously wounded during a skirmish with Indian security forces in the hills near Pahalgam. It was the worst scare yet for the families—one that Jane Schelly would recall in the sitting room at the German embassy on the day of Ostro's death.

The Indian government fired back a denial that such a battle had ever occurred. "Although I still wanted proof that they were safe . . . it was reassuring," Jane wrote in her journal that night.

But reassurances were short-lived as the Al-Faran continued to play with the minds and hearts of its victims and their families, keeping them on the edge, off balance, uncertain—and, of course, in a perpetual state of terror. High drama, obfuscation, and misinformation were among the most powerful weapons in a kidnapper's arsenal, and the Al-Faran knew how to employ them all. Despite the disappointments, the continued captivity of the hostages, and the maneuverings of the Al-Faran, diplomats were somewhat optimistic by the end of July—an attitude that buoyed the families and worried the trained negotiators in New Delhi who had been excluded from the front line negotiations. The experts from Scotland Yard as well as the FBI wanted direct contact with the man who was speaking almost daily to the rebels. In this way, they could evaluate the content of the exchanges and help devise a negotiating strategy. But the diplomats, obviously pleased with how things were going, did not see the need for such assistance and did not extend an invitation to the outsiders.

To be sure, death threats and deadlines had come and gone, and the hostages were indeed alive. And now there were religious dates to look forward to, windows of time that might be convenient and useful for the rebels in drawing public sympathy and international attention to themselves and their cause in exchange for the release of their hostage-pawns. Most everyone was confident that the end of Yatra, a religious holiday that began in mid- to late July and ended after the full moon in August, would be such a time.

Each year, during Yatra, at least 20,000 Hindus walked to the Amarnath Cave, where a Hindu god, Lord Shiva, supposedly once lived, to renew spiritual life and convictions. To protect the pilgrims from Muslim rebels, the hills were swarming with thousands of Indian troops who normally spent their time patrolling the 730-mile border—called the Line of Control—between the Indian and Pakistani parts of Kashmir. With more troops roaming about, releasing the hostages during Yatra would heighten the risk for the Al-Faran to be caught and for the hostages to be killed or wounded in a skirmish with the government soldiers. And so, by the end of July, there was much speculation that the hostages could indeed be released on the occasion of Yatra, but not until the end of Yatra when the countryside would be safer. By then, after five weeks of holding the men, the rebels might be relieved to be rid of the burden of feeding and housing five extra people. They might also be persuaded that holding the hostages was a futile method for getting what they wanted.

During the last week of July, as negotiations languished, Jane was grappling with the question of whether to go home. Her return ticket to the States would expire on July 31, and she was tempted to use it. Back home, she thought, she could lobby for Don's release through political channels, possibly pressing for a diplomatic move that could help to resolve the crisis. But Julie and Cath were staying. The family of Hans Christian Ostro had recently arrived. And there was a strong scent of optimism in the air.

Jane later recalled: "By Monday, July 24, which was Day 21 of Don's captivity, I awakened, as always it seemed, at 4 A.M., the time of morning [Muslim] prayers, which were broadcast on loudspeakers near the Srinagar compound where we were staying. I was able to go back to sleep, but at 6:30 A.M. I was back up and my mind was busy turning things over and over. I was giving serious thought to going back home to try to find out what I could in the States. On the plus side, I couldn't do much more in Srinagar, and I think the embassies preferred us to be in New Delhi or the United States simply because we wouldn't be as at risk as we were in Srinagar. The ticket wouldn't need to be changed, and it wouldn't require extra money. Don would respect my judgment if I chose to go home; I never doubted that. I could be comforted by family and friends. I could attend to some of Don's business appointments, and he may need quiet time after all the questioning, once he is released, I thought. On the negative side, I thought Don would be disappointed if I were not there, or feel that I had bailed out and possibly feel deserted. I might feel guilty about leaving. Other people might think that I was bailing out, and it would have the appearance of not sticking with it. If Don were injured, I would want to be there quickly, and from Spokane it's nearly a thirty-five-hour trip. I would want to be there if Don is actually set free."

Partly because of the heightened anticipation of their release and because she simply did not want to leave India without her husband,

Jane decided to stay. Then, on August 4, only six days before the end of Yatra, came the next big scare. The Al-Faran sent color photos of Donald Hutchings and Keith Mangan to the local press offices as apparent proof that the two hostages had been wounded during crossfire between the rebels and the Indian security forces.

Lying on a mat on the floor of what appeared to be a wooden hut, Hutchings, in one of the photos, wore a bandage wrapped around his abdomen and waist. Along his right side there appeared to be blood seeping through the gauze. In another picture was the thirty-three-year-old Brit, Keith Mangan, his chest swathed in a bloodstained bandage. A second photo of Mangan showed him with a wounded and bandaged left leg and what was supposed to be an intravenous needle stuck in his right arm.

"I do not have the strength to speak much, but I think Keith is critically ill with many wounds in his broken leg. We have no medicines," Hutchings said in a tape that accompanied the photos.

The militants, in their own message, reported that in addition to Hutchings and Mangan, the German hostage, Dirk Hasert, was ill. "For the last three days they have stopped eating. Unless immediate treatment is given, they may die, and for that the Indian government will be responsible," the rebels said.

The rebels did not issue a threat this time, but they did stress a new angle: an appeal to foreign governments to put pressure on India to meet the terrorists' demands. They also lowered their demand for the release of jailed rebels, from twenty-one down to fifteen.

The Indian government continued to deny that the hostages had been wounded in any clash at any time with their troops. One official said that if the men were wounded, which could be true, then they likely were shot during an attempt to escape.

At the State Department on August 4, the official briefer, David Johnson, told reporters: "Our primary concern in this case continues to be the safety of American citizen John Hutchings [sic] and the other Western hostages being held in Srinagar. This is especially true given the reported illness of one [sic] of the hostages and makes it even more important that the kidnappers release the hostages immediately. I'd note the responsibility for the hostages' safety rests entirely with their captors. The United States, as well as interested groups in Kashmir and throughout the region, have condemned the kidnapping and have appealed for the release of the hostages immediately on humanitarian grounds. Out of concern for the safety of the hostages, we have in the past and will continue to decline to discuss specifics of our efforts and the efforts of others to gain their release."

In Middlesbrough, England, later that day, Mavis Mangan, Keith's fifty-eight-year-old mother, picked up the ringing telephone, anxiously hoping for news of Keith. Neither she nor her husband Charles, a sixty-year-old retired steelworker with a round, ruddy face and a cheery disposition, would leave the house together now; one had to stay behind to answer the phone in case of any news involving Keith. As she lifted the receiver, Mavis, a short-haired bespectacled woman whose bubbly spirit belied a matronly appearance, reflected on the fact that the day before had been Keith and Julie's tenth wedding anniversary and that they had planned to spend it at the Taj Mahal. Perhaps there would be good news now. But the caller was a local radio reporter informing the Mangans about the photos. Mavis and Charlie would later recall the episode:

> *Mavis:* "Would you like to see the photos?" the reporter asked us. And I said, "Yes, of course, I want to see my son." And so they, the people from the radio station, came out to our house. I have no idea how they got the pictures; we didn't know about them. "Is this your son Keith?" they wanted to know. And I said, "Yes, this definitely is Keith." And it looked so authentic, in the black-and-white version that they had.

> *Charlie:* Well, we obviously believed it.

> *M:* We had a few days of hell because of that photo, waiting to see if it was true because the Foreign Office said they didn't know yet.

> *C:* "We'll let you know," they said, and for a couple of days we were worried sick.

M: Then we got the call from the Foreign Office telling us the photos were definitely a fraud.

C: When you saw the color photo, you could tell that the blood looked like Tabasco sauce and the needle in his arm was not stuck in.

M: You see, it was on his arm, not in it.

C: Yes, on it. That was a relief, wasn't it, Mavis?

M: Yes, but oh, it was a few days of absolute terror for us. Oh, and the questions. Terrible. What do you think about this and that, your son, the wounds? What the hell do you think we feel about this? That's our son who is supposedly shot. Oh it was horrendous, awful. Wasn't it? If those men holding our son wanted us to feel the terror, they did with that, they certainly did. This was real terror.

C (with a sigh): Oh my, yes.

The Sunday paper on August 6 in Spokane bore the headline "Hostage Shot, Critically Ill, Rebels Report." The phone tree, a network of twenty or so of Don and Jane's friends set up during the first week of the incident, was buzzing from the early morning hours. The consensus among Don's friends in the medical community was that the photo must be a fake. The bandages were clean except for one almost perfectly round spot of blood. This was not the way people bleed, they reasoned. Everyone commented on the unnatural position of his right hand. His left hand lay out of sight, presumably along the left side of his body. But his right hand, lying along the side of the mat, was not in a relaxed position. The fingers were bent in such a way as to create various lengths, as if the arrangement had been carefully staged.

One of his friends, who was certain Don knew some of the basics of sign language, sent a copy of the photo to a signage expert in town, who said that the fingers were close to the positions that would send the message "I'm OK." Whether he had meant to do that or not, no one knew. But those who believed it did so because they felt Don would not miss such an opportunity to communicate. "When we were told this, that it might mean something like 'I'm OK,' then we thought, Well, that's how smart he is, and this is in a picture that went all over the world basically. That's Don. Always thinking," Jacki McManus said later.

The full moon occurred at 2:16 P.M. on August 10, the birthday of the prophet Muhammad. Yatra ended the next day. But there was no sign of an impending release—no cassettes, no statements, no photos. The silence, especially in the wake of high expectations, was almost as painful and haunting as a death threat.

On Saturday afternoon of August 12, one of the outside experts made a secret plan that he would speak to the G4 on Monday about the negotiations. He was worried that they may have been too confident about the possibility of a release following Yatra. He had seen far too many cases in which the curtain came crashing down just at the moment when the drama seemed to be moving toward a peaceful finale. He didn't trust what was happening now, despite the local diplomats' apparent optimism. He was concerned that there didn't appear to be a backup plan, in case something went horribly wrong. He told a colleague that he was worried about stirring things up but he felt he needed to remind people that this case might not be like any other. "What will you do when you get the first finger or ear or someone dies? What is your plan?" he would ask.

That same afternoon, Jane Schelly, Julie Mangan, Cath Moseley, Hans Christian's sister, Anette, and Dirk Hasert's girlfriend, Anna-Katrin Hennig, sent their third appeal in five weeks to the Al-Faran, this time in the form of an advertisement to be published in local newspapers on Sunday, August 13. The statement, written in Urdu, begged the hostage-takers:

> In the name of Allah the most merciful, the most gracious, in whom we and you too trust, we make a compassionate appeal to you for the unconditional release of these five innocent and faultless men. It would be showing great regard for the great values of the faith and you would also be telling the world that humanity is still alive. We are very anxious over the reports that Don and Keith have been seriously injured. You will not gain anything by these tourists being in trouble

or by our being in distress. We had come to Kashmir only as tourists and we all are now to a great extent aware of the problems and troubles with which the people of Kashmir are faced. But we are not in a position to help to resolve the extraordinary problems existing here. We are ordinary human beings. We can only show our sympathies for the Kashmiris who are caught amid great difficulties and troubles. We can only pray before the Almighty to shower mercy on them. In the name of Allah, the most beneficent, the most gracious, we appeal to you to take pity on us and release our dear ones without further delay.

11

⬦⬥⬦

Hans Gustav Ostro could not sleep the nights of August 11 and 12, not even for an hour. He felt he could not let himself slip into the comfort of sleep until he saw his son again. And until then, he was tormented by the frustration of not knowing what to do. At first, after he had received the call about his son's abduction, he had decided to stay at home in Norway. The government had advised the family against going to India partly because there was much optimism that the incident would be quickly resolved. But after a week, it was simply too painful for him to be so far away. He wanted to be there when Hans Christian was released, to help with the trip home, or if his son were hurt, to be with him and comfort him. Moreover, the media pressure in Norway was relentless. It was uncommon for a Norwegian to be taken hostage in a foreign country and nearly every second of the day, it seemed, Hans Gustav, his daughter, and his ex-wife were beseiged by ringing phones and clicking cameras—until they fled to a secret residence in Oslo known only to the closest of friends. So intense was the coverage that the information from India had to be sent to Norway in code. The lead time between the messages going out from India and those coming in was often too much for even the most patient man to endure, and no one is patient in a kidnapping ordeal. And so, with the help of an understanding foreign office, during the few dark hours of a Norwegian summer night, Hans Gustav and his daughter Anette were covertly flown out of Oslo to New Delhi.

That had been nearly three weeks ago and now the feeling of help-lessness was returning. In those lonely hours in New Delhi, Hans Gustav wanted to write to his son, to tell him all of the things he might have forgotten to say in times past. He was unable to turn off the reel of Hans Christian's life that ran through his mind. As images flashed before him, he smiled, momentarily forgetting the harsh real-ity of the present. During these sleepless nights, the present and past seemed to converge. As if he were half awake and half dreaming, he saw Hans Christian as a boy playing in the yard at their cabin in Tons-berg, as an adult strumming his guitar at his favorite Indian restau-rant in Oslo. These images seemed so real that Hans Gustav believed his son would step out of the scene any minute and appear by his side, and all that had happened since July 8 would be nothing more than a wicked dream.

He also thought about writing to the diplomats of the four coun-tries and asking them to consider some sort of concessions to the rebels. Wasn't there any negotiation tactic that would straddle the line between outright concessions to terrorists—that is, giving in to their demands for releasing prisoners or paying ransoms—and giving them something that would be valuable enough for them to release his son and the others? Was India's hard line approach absolutely necessary? Hadn't India offered concessions in the past—for example, to gain the release of Rubiya Sayeed, the twenty-three-year-old daughter of a top Indian official, in 1989?

In the early hours of August 13, as Hans Gustav waited for dawn, he decided to ask the Norwegian ambassador at breakfast to meet with him after lunch. At the meeting, he would explain that he wanted to do something more than what was already being done. He would ask for a press conference, during which he would place the blame on the Indian government and urge that it meet at least some of the demands of the Al-Faran. And then, perhaps, the terrorists would release his son.

Having decided this, he leaned back against the headboard of his bed in his suite at the Norwegian embassy and began to think about his son and the irony of the situation. Hans Christian, an inveterate champion of the underdog, could not tolerate injustices. He simply could not stand to see anyone hurt. A few months before Hans Christian left for India, he was in Oslo one night and saw two boys beating up an immigrant black man. People were watching, Hans Christian later told his father, and doing nothing. And so Hans Christian stepped in and tried to stop the attack. One of the boys had a knife and slashed Hans Christian's right arm during the attempted rescue. Hans Gustav cringed at the memory of the anger he felt toward his son after the incident. Did he tell Hans Christian that he was furious because he had done something wrong or because he didn't like to see him get hurt? He couldn't remember now. He did remember Hans Christian's remark: "I couldn't think of myself; I had to stop it."

Though strong in spirit and able-bodied, Hans Christian had always been a sensitive boy, which had sometimes worried Hans Gustav. One summer Hans Gustav found his son crying on the porch of the cabin at Tonsberg. No more than ten years old at the time, he was reading a book about the American West, and the pictures showed Indians falling off their horses as they were shot in battle. He even held a lecture for the family on the topic of how the Indians had been wronged. Hans Gustav smiled as he remembered the day Hans Christian bought a first-class ticket on the train to Tonsberg. The family was surprised at such an extravagance because they knew that Hans Christian, a struggling actor and street musician at the time, could not afford the luxury. But he had a cat that he wanted to bring along on the trip and felt that the animal would have more freedom to roam around in first class. As Hans Gustav would say, tapping his fist on the left side of his chest, "Hans Christian has a good heart."

Hans Gustav, a tall, lean man with thick white hair and a friendly, open demeanor, was the general manager at one of Norway's largest savings banks. He was the type of person who, if told by a restaurant maitre d' that the wait for a table was an hour, would smile and say, "It is no wonder there is a wait for such a fine eatery." He would schmooze some more until the maitre d' would ask him to wait at the bar, and then, ten minutes later, the maitre d' would be showing him to his table. His son was just as friendly.

Hans Gustav's father was a shopkeeper; his grandfather, a construction worker. Hans Gustav's only son was an artist. And now he was thinking, in the early hours of August 13, that perhaps he hadn't understood his son as well as he could have. He enjoyed him and loved him, and he was certain that Hans Christian knew that. But had he really understood what his son was trying to do creatively? Perhaps every father of an unconventional, artistic son has trouble with this.

As a boy, Hans Christian had shown keen acumen in most academic subjects. In watching his inordinately bright child grow into a spirited, strong-minded young man, Hans Gustav came to believe his son would study business or law. He had a sense for many years that Hans Christian would become a well-known figure in Norway, though fame was nothing that he particularly wished for his son.

Hans Christian was not the sort to follow an orderly career path in the cultural establishment. He was an artist in the purest sense; that is, he sought to develop his chosen arts, dance and theater, beyond their current levels in his culture. What he sought to do in India—and the reason he was there in the first place—was to bring the Indian culture to Norway through a kind of artistic symbiosis. He believed that the two cultures were linked, from the earliest evidence of each, and that a union on a cultural level would spawn a hybrid—a rich, colorful expression in both music and dance.

In the autumn of 1994, Hans Christian received an artist's scholarship to support his studies. With it, he began his own theater company in Oslo, called Katarsis, and traveled to India to learn certain traditional Indian dances for the choreography of a play he planned to produce in Oslo. He was also working on organizing a troupe of Indian performers to take back home to Norway.

He arrived in India on February 3, 1995, and spent four months living with an Indian family in Seekrishnapuram, a village in the state of Kerala in southern India. His days began with meditation, then hours of practicing what was called Kathakali dance with his Indian teacher, and in the evenings he would play his guitar and sing with his Indian hosts. Like a traveling minstrel, Ostro could entice the most reticent of any group to join him in song. His passion and talent were utterly engaging. He could play the piano and the guitar. He wrote, directed, and acted in plays. He had a beautiful voice.

Looking once again at the communications from Hans Christian since his captivity began, his father—and others—believed the written messages were coded. These messages, which Hans Christian had somehow managed to send through villagers, were written on the backs of four photos. Three of the photos showed Hans Christian in elaborate traditional Kathakali costume on the night of the performance of an Indian play he produced in Kerala. The fourth showed him meditating with his teacher. The seemingly innocuous messages, all in English, stuck with the topic of the photos. But surely, thought Hans Gustav, they were communicating more.

The first message: This from the Kathakali training. I hope to start a Theatre school with Kathakali as an important ingredient. It takes totally five hours to put on all the makeup and costumes in Kathakali.

The second: This is from my first play in Ishavaran Ganesh Temple, Sreelerishnapuram, Kerala. I am playing Phima, the half-god who is son of the wind and has 100 [in numbers larger than the letters] elephants' strength. The play's name is *Shouria Gunam* (Divine Anger), and I am the one being angry. I am the first foreigner ever to study this play which is very difficult.

The third: I have bought a full costume and recorded the music in studios. I am planning to perform in Norway and Europe next year. There are so many Indians [lines drawn through *Indians* but not enough to make it illegible] people living on our continent that come from the Sub-Indian continent [sic]. It's time we get to know some[thing] about their culture. Our roots are related and deep. This play will be especially suitable for schools and the growing generations.

The fourth: "It's hard for a king to live in exile in a forest wearing leather clothes." The special importance in Kathakali are the hands and the eyes. It's a silent play, to drums, cymbals and camatic [sic] vocal. Thank you, embassy.

After receiving the messages, Hans Gustav and embassy officials sought help in interpreting exactly what his son might be trying to communicate through references to Indian literature. Someone in the political section of the U.S. embassy called people at the International Kathakali Center in New Delhi, including Usha Balakrishnan, who then found Shanta Verma, a professor of political science at New Delhi University. Verma had studied and performed Kathakali for more than twenty years, and her father was a Kathakali dancer. She examined the photographs, trying to explain the language of the eyes and hands in Kathakali and to identify the play from which Hans Christian quoted.

This Kathakali play is based on an epic drama of Indian lore, she determined. At the point in the story where the quote appears, the five Pandava brothers are dwelling in exile in the forest after their stepbrother has usurped the throne that rightfully belongs to the eldest brother, Yudhisthra. Arjun, one of the brothers, has gone to a shrine to the Lord Shiva to seek divine weapons, while Bhim, another brother, remains in the forest with Yudhisthra, and the two younger brothers are living as religious ascetics.

Bhim says to Yudhisthra, "Oh, king, do not forget to see our plight. Wearing skins and with forest tribes, we are wandering in the forest because you, being the virtuous one, have relinquished the duty of king. For this reason, we find ourselves in these circumstances, while he who is most cruel and dishonest rules in Hasinapur [the Pandavas' capital city]. We are in a helpless situation, just like a person who has no eyes, helpless though he has other things. I can defeat these people myself alone if you permit me."

The scholars speculated about Hans Christian's reasons for choosing a quote from this story out of all the Indian literature that was familiar to him. The story was consistent with the hostages' situation in several ways, the scholars noted. The five "brothers" in exile might have been a way to communicate that there were five hostages, a fact that the hostages might have thought the authorities did not or could not know. That Arjun visits a shrine of the Lord Shiva could indicate that they were being held somewhere in the vicinity of the Amarnath Cave, one of India's main shrines to Shiva. The reference to the forest could also have been a clue to their location. Not all of the Kashmiri hills are forested. The vicinity around Pahalgam is heavily forested, but areas a little higher are barren and rocky. Hans Christian substituted *leather clothes* for *skins* in the original play, which may have been done for the purpose of telling his readers that he was near the Lidder River, which is basically the path from the Amarnath Cave to Pahalgam. The scholars concluded that the use of the quote, leading them to a body of work as it did, was a "fine tribute to Hans Christian's artistic intellect."

The words in the messages could be seen in more than one way, and there was endless speculation about their true meaning. A few examples: The "100 elephants" meant that the Al-Faran was 100 strong. In message number three, Hans Christian was saying that the kidnappers were in fact controlled beneath the surface by a covert Indian group; that it was important for the world to know this; and that it was a movement that was growing. By alluding to a play, he was trying to say that the kidnapping was itself a play, meaning that the rebels were merely acting like Kashmiri freedom fighters when, in fact, they were actually Indians trying to discredit the rebel movement, or perhaps even a splinter group operating independently from the rebel stronghold in Pakistan. All this speculation made Hans Gustav even more anxious.

The father fretted a good deal about the danger his son was in. He knew from information gleaned from villagers that Hans Christian had put up a fight when the five rebels had invaded his campsite on July 8. Alone without a guide, Hans Christian was only a few days from his destination, the Amarnath Cave. He wanted to make the journey before the Yatra holiday lured hordes of pilgrims to the cave. But he also wanted to see what they would see during the full moon of August, so he had planned to be there for the full moon of July, which fell that year on the twelfth. The Amarnath is a vast cave, nearly 500 feet high and wide, swirling with sacred stories. Legend has it that on the night of a full moon many centuries ago, Lord Shiva told his disciple about his belief in reincarnation. The cave, at the head of a large tributary of the Indus River, is considered ideal for meditation. And because of the way water trickles through its limestone roof in summer, a lingam—the symbol of Shiva—forms in the cave, reaching its maximum size around the time of the full moon. Hans Christian believed in reincarnation and was thrilled to be traveling to the cave before returning to Oslo on July 31. He had checked with the Indian tourism office and one Kashmiri tourism agency to be certain that his pilgrimage would be safe and then, just as Jane and Julie and their entourage were heading into Pahalgam, had headed out from Srinagar on an alternate path, toward the cave.

In his last message home, he sent a postcard of Srinagar and its scenic Dal Lake and wrote (in Norwegian): "The Himalaya is fantastic and I want to hire a pony and travel to a Buddhist cloister. I am looking forward to the mystery and silence of the mountains. I am worn out from the Kathakali dance and my trips to New Delhi, Calcutta and Bombay, all exhausting cities. It's good to be with mountain people here in Kashmir. I will be home on July 31st, on SK501 from London in at 8 P.M. Much love, [his signature]"

It was ironic, Hans Gustav thought, that his son was at that spot along the trail to the cave that particular day. His tent was very near the path. Pitched on a flat stretch of ground, it was quite visible. Hans Christian never made it a habit to be early to anything, and yet on July 8 he was probably only two days from the cave, and the full moon would not occur for yet another two days. He was early, and the reward was to be abducted, his father thought cynically.

Hans Christian was the only one who put up a fight when his captors came for him. In fact he was fighting so intensely that the two men who were sent to capture him couldn't manage alone and had to beckon another militant for help, according to the villagers who apparently witnessed the ambush. It was possible that Hans Christian pulled a knife on one and might have wounded him, but this was never confirmed. He was physically very strong and in excellent shape because of the exercises and dance he had been doing for the past several months and because he had been trained for one year in Norway's compulsory military. He was rebellious by nature, though, and it was in his character to resist any sort of captivity. So his son may have caused a stir that day, Hans Gustav thought. Such details, however, did not give him peace of mind. He also knew that the rebels had brought in a teacher to give lessons to the hostages about the Koran, a book that Hans Christian had studied very thoroughly. And he knew that his son would not accept the Islamic fundamentalists' interpretation of this holy book. The teachings, he was told later, had lasted only about three days. He would also learn that his son had meditated regularly and was heard singing loudly at times. Some villagers spoke of "the singing hostage." And though it may have been a delight to hear the Norwegian's melodic voice ringing through the hills, it could not have pleased the militants to hear a man singing loud enough to alert the Indian troops of their position. In addition, he would learn that his son had tried to escape at least once and had probably tried to flag a helicopter, running into an open area when he heard the chopper approaching.

Hans Gustav looked around the room at the furniture and finery of the embassy and thought of how gracious and generous the ambassador and his staff had been. He had a private chauffeur to go anywhere he wanted to go, and the embassy staff planned all sorts of activities, tours mostly, to distract Hans Gustav, Anette, and Hans Christian's mother, who had arrived from England in early August. But Hans Gustav wanted to spend his time at the embassy so he wouldn't miss hearing any news about his son. And besides, he couldn't relax and enjoy himself as long as his son was in captivity. It was hard to do anything without thinking of what the hostages were doing, difficult even to take a shower without remembering that the hostages were enduring without life's simplest amenities.

That morning at breakfast, Hans Gustav told the Norwegian ambassador that he wanted to meet with him after lunch, which was to be held that day at the German embassy. He would then explain his concerns regarding the Al-Faran and his belief that India must give in to some demand, must give them something, and must allow him to hold a press conference. But at lunch Hans Gustav saw what Jane Schelly saw: a foreboding restlessness and nervous eyes darting quickly away from contact with the hostage families. When, in the middle of the luncheon, the German ambassador left the table for a phone call or a meeting, Hans Gustav felt "that sinking feeling."

Once the ambassador returned to his seat, between Jane and Hans Christian's mother, it was hard not to notice the solemn aspect of his countenance and demeanor. He was clearly trying to pretend that nothing had happened. And after the German ambassador announced that one of the hostages had been killed, Hans Gustav was frightened for the first time in many years—truly frightened. It was as if the walls and floors were disappearing around and beneath him and he was floating through an unknown space that was dark and cold and terrifying.

The chauffeur took the Ostro family back to the Norwegian embassy, where they were asked if Hans Christian had any distinguishing birthmarks or scars, such as the recent one left over from his attempted rescue of the black man in Oslo. Hans Gustav sat in the living room of the embassy, his hands clasped as if in prayer and his head shaking. No, no, it cannot be Hans Christian. He is too strong, too full of life, too passionate. No one could kill such a boy.

12

AUGUST 24, 1995
TONSBERG, NORWAY

Hans Christian Ostro was the first Norwegian hostage to be killed since World War II. In Norway and elsewhere, commentators spoke of war and its many faces. They called for an end to the decades-long conflict in Kashmir—the "war at the top of the world," they called it—and stressed that the tragedy of Ostro's death should be a catalyst for peace. In the *Times* of London, an editorial said the incident had "shocked many observers into taking notice for the first time of the gravity of Kashmir's troubles. At a time when politically-motivated kidnapping is far from uncommon worldwide . . . capitulation to [rebel] demands will only lead to a growth in this unsavoury industry."

Some observers used the occasion to declare that the world was at war again, but in a different, far less predictable, and clearly less obvious way. The international frontier was ablaze with conflicts, as the post–Cold War world redefined its cultural, political, economic, religious, and moral boundaries. And Ostro, in his efforts to blend two cultures, represented the hope of a potentially dark age: that globalization and borderless trade could do more than make some people rich and keep others poor. They could help to spread the richness of cultures, to blend the beauty and spirit of diverse lands, to build a stronger, more peaceful planet.

Though firmly embedded in the political rhetoric of the developed nations, such idealistic notions, in 1995, came about as close to reality as a walk in Jurassic Park. And Ostro's fate, in its grisly way, had helped to expose the sham. His passionate quest had collided with the equally ardent agenda of a Muslim insurgency. The impact was the very definition of tragedy, for his family and his country.

For the rest of the world, Ostro's death symbolized the chaos and disorder of the century's last decade and the speed with which things could change in any region. Given the new availability of rebel manpower and weapons, a new border dispute could erupt at any time, or a long-simmering, decades-old conflict could intensify. And governments, it was clear, could neither control the outbursts within their borders nor assure protection for citizens beyond them.

The death of Hans Christian Ostro sounded an alarm—as did many other such incidents during the 1990s—warning the world that things were different now, that old ways of thinking and coping had to change, and that the efficacy of governments in the midst of such crises could not be assumed, much less guaranteed. Governments are designed to deal with other governments, using time-honored protocols and following well-established rules and laws. Ostro's death demonstrated that citizens abroad—regardless of the imprint on the passport they carried—were less the representatives of a foreign land moving under the protection of their native flags than they were free agents, traveling at increasing risk in a disordered world. It appeared that a new global individualism was required to survive on the new global frontier.

Ostro was not a political person, not well versed in the politics, economics, and conflicts of the world. He had lived in India for five months and so it was only natural that he would ask the locals about the wisdom of his trip to India's legendary Kashmir, a place he had described to his family as a Garden of Eden. What he did not know was that the world had become like an M. C. Escher drawing, in which things could appear one way or the other depending on how you looked at them or what you chose to see.

It took about thirty hours to move Ostro's body and head from the village of Prazmulla to the All India Institute of Medical Sciences in New Delhi. First, the body and the head were sent to Anantnag where they were stitched together. Then the corpse was flown in a helicopter to an army hospital in Srinagar, then on to New Delhi the next day in a special aircraft of the Indian air force. The postmortem revealed that he had been dead for approximately thirty-six hours, which meant he had been murdered early on the morning of August 13. Medical experts surmised that Ostro was alive when the terrorists slit his throat. Since there was little evidence of a struggle, however, everyone hoped that he was asleep when it happened. And because there was no sign of bleeding from the chest, pathologists believed that he was certainly dead when the rebels carved *Al-Faran* onto his body.

The autopsy disproved the hideous news reports that his body had been badly bruised. Such accounts suggested that the rebels had beaten him—a fact that terrified the families of the remaining hostages and deepened the pain for Ostro's family.

"I remember hearing the messages, one message and then the other, that he was beaten and he was starved, that he had been sick, and even one saying that every bone in his body was broken," said Tora Mellbye, a friend of the family, in an interview in Norway. "It was absolutely terrible—terrible and untrue. And therefore after a few days, we just didn't read the newspapers and the family didn't see them, thankfully. But so many of his friends and everyone in Norway was reading them and"—she stopped to hold back tears.

In fact, the autopsy showed that Ostro was in excellent physical condition. But because of the terrible anguish caused by the rumors and speculations, the Norwegian ambassador asked the family for permission, which it granted, to release the autopsy report to the press.

Numb and exhausted, Ostro's father, sister, and mother left India on August 17. They brought with them the young man's body and a multitude of unanswered questions. It would take them years to piece together what had happened, and still they could never be certain about which stories and details to believe. What was puzzling about the murder was that there were no rebel threats immediately preceding it, nor had the government recently refused to meet their demands. Some intelligence sources said that Abdul Hamid Turki, the Muslim leader of the Al-Faran, had performed a special prayer the night before, asking for guidance. After falling asleep, he supposedly dreamed that Allah had come to him saying that one of the hostages must die. It was only then, probably because Ostro was the most strident and rebellious of the hostages, that they chose the Norwegian for their sacrifice. Another source claimed that, during an attempt to escape, Ostro had broken the nose of a rebel, who, from then on, targeted him for revenge.

There was also the theory that the rebels had planned to release Ostro, whom they had separated from the other hostages a week or so before his death. Perhaps the sounds of Indian troops, which were scouring the hills around the shepherd's hut where they were hiding with their hostage, had awakened them in the middle of the night. Some sources also speculated that Ostro, unable to sleep, had been singing again—no doubt too loudly for the rebels, who were trying to evade detection. And so, that theory goes, they killed him suddenly that morning when they heard troops approaching and when Ostro refused to be silent. This theory, as well as one that he was trying to escape, would strengthen with time, especially after the Indian government finally released all of the papers found on the young man's body.

Much to the shock and puzzlement of the families, for nearly eight months the Indian government held certain letters and poems found on Ostro's body. One such item was a note from fellow hostage Paul Wells to his girlfriend, Cath Moseley. This was a mysterious piece of paper so tightly rolled that Ostro was able to conceal it in the seam of his shirt. The fact that Ostro was carrying such a missive gave some credence to the possibility that the rebels had planned to release him that morning and that something had gone wrong, such as the unexpected arrival of the Indian troops.

Far more convincing, however, was the theory that Wells had given Ostro the note because the Norwegian was determined to escape and Wells wanted to send a message out with him. He may have been separated from the others because he was too rebellious and because he had tried to escape at least once, leading the rebels to suspect he would try again. One of the notes found on Ostro's body and addressed to the other hostages read: "Escape Plan, Part Two. 6 August. I'm doing it now. Good luck."

Bits and pieces. That's what the family had brought back with them from India, and that's what they would continue to have for a long time. Hans Gustav would always believe that the Indian officials were holding back far more than the rolled-up note. They knew something that they were not revealing, he would later say, and he and his family, with the help of the Norwegian government, would continue to probe until they found the truth. They did know, beyond doubt, that Ostro had a strong personality and was not, by nature, a submissive man. "He was very secure within himself," his father said. "A very intense kind of person, whom, I have been told through the years, is quite memorable. He's the kind of person who looks you in the eye when he talks to you, and he doesn't babble. Every word is important and thought out. He asks 'why' a lot. He always did that. He demanded explanations. Why do you do that? Why do you study that? Why do you think that?"

Friends described him as charismatic. He "was so strong," said Tora, "that he would attract people to him, pull them into him, partly because he was such an intense listener."

But the combination of such admirable traits could have been deadly for a hostage. While Ostro's strength—both physical and mental—helped him to endure captivity, his refusal to submit no doubt agitated his captors, especially the leaders.

Still, Hans Gustav believed that his son had listened to and even befriended some members of the rebel gang. "He liked to explore people and find out what made them behave as they do, to plow ever deeper into their minds and souls," Tora recalled. Though sympathetic to the rebel cause, he revealed in his letters that he disapproved of their tactics. And so the father surmised that his son might have tried to persuade the rank-and-file rebels to disobey their leader and to abandon the kidnapping. This behavior and the escape attempts would have been enough to anger the rebels. There was also the rumor that he had punched a rebel in the nose during one such attempt.

And so it was altogether possible that the Norwegian, with his singing and his strength, had been too difficult for his rebel keepers to control. Hans Gustav believed that "because he could get messages out of the camp, through rebels and villagers or whomever, on his own, his captors perceived him and his spirit as dangerous. That is what I believed happened. He was a threat to them."

An Indian newspaper ran an editorial around the time of Ostro's funeral offering another theory: "Ostro was not chosen by accident. Nor was he chosen because he came from the smallest of the countries whose nationals had been kidnapped. He was beheaded because in their weeks together the kidnappers found out that unlike the others who were simply tourists, Ostro genuinely loved India and its culture, had studied Kathakali and intended to give performances on his return to Europe. Killing him was, therefore, a way of simultaneously giving vent to their insensate hatred of India and its Hindu culture."

The father's only peace came with the recollection that his son was a devout believer in reincarnation and did not appear to fear death. "He was afraid of nothing, never had been," his father would say later. "He was not afraid of death; I am certain of that."

On August 24, in the seaside town of Tonsberg, about two hours south of Oslo on the Oslo Fjord, more than 300 people gathered to pay tribute to the dead Norwegian hostage. Tonsberg, Norway's oldest settlement (A.D. 871), was the place where Ostro's family had spent summers when he was a boy, and now, in a wooden cathedral perched on a cliff above the sea, it was where family and friends would say good-bye to him. The mourners included well-known Norwegian artists and statesmen. The Swedish actress Liv Ullmann was among the crowd. She and other Scandinavian artists were in the process of launching the Hans Christian Ostro Memorial Fund, which would reward promising artists trying through their art to build bridges between cultures and peace among countries.

With the grace and wisdom of a woman far beyond her twenty-five years, Anette, the sister of Hans Christian, stood at the pulpit of the crowded church and delivered a eulogy (translated from Norwegian):

> Dear brother, we've waited for you. We've waited for you every day and every night since you were taken in Kashmir.

Some of us have felt the thoughts you were sending us. Some of us have felt your strength.

We felt how your hands were tied; we felt how you were suffering. But we were waiting for you to be free from captivity. The hope was extinguished Sunday the thirteenth of August.

Now our prayers and our faith are tied to the four other innocent hostages still being held captive. You were brutally murdered by homicidal primitives, the greatest contrast to your lively openness.

You lived and you died because you had a faith and trust in life, in art, in people, and in passions.

Your death is as meaningless as it is possible to be. There's no meaning in what you went through; there is no meaning in your death.

But perhaps there is a meaning by this bringing forth some good in us, the humans here on this earth. That we through your person, your power, your soul, and your goodness can be better people ourselves.

Hans Christian, I believe and I feel that. In our thoughts and our hearts, you will never be gone. You will live and breathe together with us each day, each month, and each year. You will never be forgotten.

You represented a peaceful, artistic, and global spirit of our age, which will also live on. You honestly cared for all the small and weak. You didn't once even kill a fly. You would release them outdoors. That was one part of your healthy philosophy of life, your appreciation of people and of all living things on this earth.

When your cat had difficulty giving birth, three times you gave life to her kittens, with your warm hands and your love. You even gave her the name Liv [Norwegian for "life"].

The cats send their best greetings, as does Trim, the dog you loved so much and at whose death you wept. Maybe you are together with him now. Also the most loving of greetings to you from Mama and Papa. They miss you so terribly, and they hurt so much in the midst of all the good you have given and are giving to them.

I promise you, Hans Christian, that I will do all in my power to comfort and support them in the future. I know that they will do the same for me.

Warmest of greetings as well from your grandparents on your father's side and your grandmother on your mother's side, John, Erik, the rest of the family, and all your friends and those who love you. They were all so enormously fond of you.

But for me, you were my big brother. I have endless memories of being with you, from childhood, from adolescence, and from our short life together as adults.

We were so different in many ways; but also we were so much alike. We were also bound together in such a way that I cannot manage to put into words. It is beyond the indescribable.

We held together and supported each other, and there were all those fine times with you. All the times you came to me, the little bashful one, and tried to ask me questions about love, infatuation, about people, and about yourself. All the times I came to you, and you gave me hope, believed in me with good humor; you put your protective arms around me and gave me a sense of worth.

You said I had to take care of the nobility in myself, and I promise you, Hans Christian, that I will do that.

I will continue to be your cheerful half. I will continue to believe in myself. I will keep the faith with you.

How many times you played the prettiest songs on your guitar and sang for me, for our family, and for our friends with your voice of emotion, your radiating magic! How many times you entertained us with your humor, your zest for life, and your love!

You were so good, Hans Christian.

You were my protective big brother, but you were also my best friend. For me, you will never be some kind of saint or martyr; you will be my handsome brother. And I miss you so much.

Forgive me for all the times I didn't understand you. Forgive me for all I did or should have done.

Thank you for giving me the power to love music. Thank you for giving me the power to love the written word. Thank you for giving me insight into drama by your expressions about nature, about mankind's suffering, joy, and elemental strength. Thank you for giving me the power to rejoice in life and beauty. Thank you for giving me a glow in my soul. Thank you for giving me the power to love. Thank you for permitting me to love you. Thank you for all the strength you will give me the rest of my life. Thank you that we heard your last song.

My friend, I know you're in good shape now. We'll meet again in another world, in a fantasy, in a paradise. Peace be with you.

In the months ahead, the family would receive thousands of letters from people all over the world who had also lost a child or sibling, and who had read about the tragedy and wanted to send condolences. Many of the writers were Indians expressing their shame about what had happened. The Indian community in Oslo was especially attentive. Hans Gustav felt a certain comfort in visiting the Village Tandoori, an Indian restaurant where he had dined with Hans Christian shortly before the young man's trip to India, early in 1995. He spent many hours there now, sometimes taking with him the messages that Ostro had sent out of the mountains. These he would read over and over, searching for clues, for answers, for reasons, and for a way to simply reconnect with his son's vibrant spirit.

"My dear family: I am fine. I keep on believing in the good in people. My biggest concern is what you think and feel. Please be strong because I am. Love you, Hans."

13

Midnight, August 15, was the new execution deadline—the end of the forty-eight-hour ultimatum delivered in the note pinned to Ostro's shirt. The government again refused to give in to any of the rebel demands, and the fate of the hostages remained unknown. By midmorning on the sixteenth, there were no reports of bodies found along rivers or roads. Nor were there any grisly announcements from rebel intermediaries. "One has to be optimistic," a Kashmiri official told a gathering of reporters in Srinagar. "In the absence of any adverse report, we must assume they are safe."

Everyone was told to trust the silence. But in a deadly, psychological game like this one, silence functioned more as a weapon of intimidation, a void designed to provoke fear, than as a thing to trust. As long as there was contact between the Al-Faran and the government, hope existed. And when there was no contact, the silence extinguished the hope as the moon sometimes blocks the sun.

Later that morning, merchants in Srinagar shuttered their storefronts and bazaar stalls as part of a statewide strike to protest the killing of Ostro. Kashmir's pro-rebel political and religious groups—

at least thirty in all—had organized the protest to broadcast their condemnation of the Al-Faran's tactics. Even the Pakistan-based HUA,
which was considered the most rapacious of the terrorists operating in
the Kashmir Valley, denounced the Al-Faran. The day of the strike, the
HUA, whose members had reportedly also participated in insurgent
and terrorist operations in Myanmar (Burma), Tajikistan, and Bosnia,
released a statement to the press denying it had anything to do with
the Al-Faran, the latest kidnappings, or the death of Ostro.

The Al-Faran, in turn, protested the protest. In Anantnag, a town
adjacent to the hamlet of Prazmulla where Ostro's body was found, a
lone insurgent tacked a small, printed leaflet to a telephone pole a few
feet from a local mosque and told the passersby to spread its message
to their friends in other towns. In the flyer, the Al-Faran warned that
any Kashmiri observing the strike would be dealt with as "an infidel."
The Muslim "mountain warriors" scorned the Kashmiris for protesting the death of one Christian tourist when they had been silent after
Christians had slain hundreds of Muslims in both Bosnia-Herzegovina
and Chechnya.

The strike inspired both hope and fear regarding the welfare of the
hostages. In response, the Al-Faran, stung and humiliated by the lack
of support among other rebels, could end the ordeal and begin negotiating their own safe passage to Pakistan in exchange for the tourists'
freedom. At the same time, the terrorists could react to the protest by
harming another captive. There was always the prospect that one
angry zealot yielding to the high emotions of the moment might lose
control and take matters into his own deadly hands.

It was in the midst of these fretful uncertainties, early on the morning of the sixteenth, that Roy Ramm arrived in New Delhi. As he had
anticipated, British diplomats met him at the gate, briskly shaking his
hand, yanking his canvas bag off the luggage wagon, and stealing him
away in the British High Commission's white Range Rover. On the
road leading out of the airport, as he prepared for a long day of meetings, the commander gazed out the window at the traffic drilling past,
noticing, as visitors often do, the shiny presence of the old British
standard—the Morris Oxford, a made-in-India classic marketed now
as the Hindustan Ambassador. The highway, he thought, was much

like India itself. An occasional Fiat or Opel cruised by, followed by a fleet of Marutis, a Peugeot 309, a Mercedes 220, even a Ford Escort, all parading as if to show off the new India and its emergence from economic exile as a Third World state.

As he listened that day to the observations and concerns of diplomats and other officials, the commander felt for the first time the tension surrounding the death of Hans Christian Ostro. The day the body was found, diplomats from the four affected countries had gone to Anantnag to identify, beyond all doubt, which of the hostages had been killed. They now could not hide the horror of what they had seen in that village two days before. Indeed, the commander wished the diplomats had been spared the sight of the mutilated body. Police were accustomed to such scenes; diplomats were not. Someone should have stopped them from going. Of course, such an amateurish gaffe seemed an inherent part of the very problem he was facing, with everyone trying to do the right thing but no one, no single authority, experienced enough with the murder of a tourist or the abductions of foreigners to know exactly what to do. If only one of his men had attended the body and had seen it just after it was discovered, thought Ramm, there might have been revealing clues as to what precisely had transpired in the hours before the killing. But to question what had happened after the discovery of the body was to question India itself, imposing Western attitudes of superiority and aggravating Ramm's already sensitive position as an outside adviser.

The main worry now was whether Ostro's murder would be the first in a series of executions. And what could they do to stop it? What intelligence could Ramm or any of the outside negotiators bring to the dilemma? Would the Indians continue to pridefully resist the help of outside experts, such as those from the FBI and Scotland Yard? The commander's presence at the meeting that morning assured him that things would be different now. But the delay in bringing professional negotiators to the front lines was still troubling.

Ramm knew that what transpires during the first few days—sometimes hours, depending on when the kidnappers first begin to communicate—sets the tone for the entire ordeal. If, for example, promises are made to the rebels during the first panicky hours after the abduction, and the promises cannot be kept, the damage to negotiations is almost irreversible. What Ramm did not know at that time was that during the first several days after the abductions, on or around July 10, the government had asked for the names of the militants that the Al-Faran wanted released from Indian jails.

"You either hit the ground running or you don't," he would say later. "And when you don't, it is hard to make up ground and to break patterns—sometimes damaging patterns—in the communications with the rebels and in the strategy or lack of strategy. From the start, you are sending signals to the other side about how their concerns and demands will be interpreted and understood by the Western governments."

The negotiators were eager to set up a system—their "cell"—for recording, organizing, and analyzing all communications with the rebels. The "cell" would provide a network of professionals to back the government's communicator, Kashmir's Inspector General Rajinder Tikoo (pronounced TEE-koo), so that he did not have to handle such sensitive contacts alone. Until then, Tikoo had waited alone in a house in Srinagar for the rebel intermediary to call, with little or no relief. Tikoo needed feedback after each call in order to interpret exactly what the rebels were saying and to devise the most useful response. Words were the bridges connecting the hostages to safety, and each word from Tikoo to the rebels, like a carefully placed beam, required attention and planning.

The moves and strategies of negotiation were all the more crucial because of India's continuing hard line against the militants. The government was unwilling to bend, to yield even slightly in its dealings with them. This was partly because the government firmly believed that the Al-Faran was an extension of a Pakistani group and not a local Kashmiri band. There was also the fact that four Western governments—all with overt policies of no concessions to terrorists—were watching and advising. But the biggest reason was likely the national election coming up in several months.

The tourist abductions had become a politically sensitive issue, one that Indian officials clearly could not ignore. Along with the Communists, the main opposition party—the right-wing Hindu Bharatiya

Janata Party—was warning India's Prime Minister P. V. Narasimha Rao that he would face severe criticism if he traded Kashmiri prisoners for Westerners. In the past, Rao had been accused of being too soft on the Muslim separatists in Kashmir. Now, his party was taking the stand of preserving northern India and protecting it from balkanization. And Rao was seizing the spotlight on the Kashmir crisis for his own political security.

Rao's intransigent posturing was putting the hostages at risk, for the terrorists had grown accustomed to a far more flexible and yielding India, as recently as that first week of the tourists' abductions when the government had asked the kidnappers for the names of the jailed militants. This sent a subtle yet powerful message to the terrorists that indeed they might get what they had demanded. And it was a move that only reinforced the pattern of India's behavior in past cases. Indeed, the likelihood of concessions may have lured the kidnappers to Hutchings and the tourists in the first place, though so far it had led the rebels down a trail of expectations unfulfilled.

Like bears returning to a campsite, the rebels had begun the ordeal with expectations of rewards. Since 1989, when separatists abducted the twenty-three-year-old daughter of the Indian home minister, India had periodically swapped jailed insurgents for hostages. After five days of captivity, Rubiya Sayeed regained her freedom in exchange for the release of five militants from India's prisons. In the coming years, a Kashmiri politician's daughter was freed after ten days, in exchange for one jailed guerrilla—down from the original demand of five rebels. An oil-company executive was released after fifty-three days for six freed rebels. A bank officer was swapped for one guerrilla; an Indian minister's brother-in-law, after four months in captivity, walked to his freedom after India freed three jailed insurgents. A kidnapped scientist and two others were freed in exchange for seven guerrillas.

In other cases, there had been raids—some more successful than others. And several hundred civilians had been kidnapped to extort money from their families. In 1994, approximately 315 people were kidnapped in Kashmir; about 70 of them were killed, according to the Indian High Commission in London. In 1995, there would be 430 kidnappings, in which nearly half of the hostages would be killed. In total, the Indian High Commission reported that over the period from 1990 to 1995, about 2,000 people had been kidnapped in Kashmir: 50 percent were known to be dead, 25 percent returned to their families in various conditions, and 25 percent were still missing. Most of the hostages were Kashmiris or Indians; very few were foreigners. And, to be fair, it was not always clear who was conducting the kidnappings. Some of the Kashmiris returning home with bruise-covered bodies and broken or missing limbs were victims of the Indian security forces. It was, after all, a war.

Under such circumstances, the pressure on negotiators could not have been greater, though most admitted that negotiations could only accomplish so much. It was not their country, after all. And even after they were brought to the front lines, they were still just advisers to the Indian government, though the authorities were clearly more open to advice in the aftermath of Ostro's death. The negotiators, through Tikoo, might be able to convince the rebels that the kidnappings had damaged their cause and that releasing the hostages would redeem their image. Tikoo could offer international publicity in the event of a release. Most important, Tikoo, following the scripts and advice of the various negotiators, could keep the hostages alive while trying to wear down the rebels, who might just release the hostages and move on, especially with winter fast approaching.

For now, the immediate job was to determine the opposition's agenda, to devise a strategy to disrupt it, and to herd the rebels toward a resolution. If there was, in fact, a plan for more executions, then the government must intercede and Tikoo must persuade the rebels that such a plan was futile and again remind them of how their behavior was undermining their cause.

During the meetings that morning, Ramm was struck by the complexity of the situation. "When you are listening to four ambassadors in session, each with their own domestic post and agenda, trying very hard to work together, pooling their knowledge about the very complicated domestic Indian politics, you'd have to have the wisdom of Solomon and a computer between your ears to retain the massive amount of data you are hearing and to process it," the commander said. "I knew then, that day, that this would be a long process because the sheer mechanics of it were so evidently complex. In a typical hostage situation (in London, say)—and by this I mean a kidnapping that is contained—you know where everyone is and you pick up the telephone and you know where to ring. But in a kidnapping like this, you normally don't know where they are. In a developing nation, even when you do know where they are, when you finally find them and you then have a containment situation, you often cannot telephone them. You are relying on emissaries and on translators. Your primary function as a negotiator is to establish a conduit of communications with the kidnappers, and that is logistically quite difficult in remote places, such as the Himalayas.

"I don't mean to overdramatize, but with these cases you've got people's lives in your hands. That's the feeling you've got. And the people around you are making or have made crucial decisions, and they are asking your advice. And you look out your window every day and think, not how beautiful or exotic the lands before you are, but that somewhere out there is the hostage or hostages. If you are in London, and you have a kidnapping, you are so proximate to it and the policeman says, 'OK, let's cordon off the area and kick in doors until we find this guy.' That's the basic reaction. But in these cases, in Kashmir or wherever, you know that's not achievable; you know it's not going to work. It's just not the way to resolve these things. You must talk to them; you must negotiate, from the very start of the thing, if you want the hostages to live. What was going through my head that morning was just what a challenge we had ahead of us. My heart ached for the hostage families that day."

Finally, on the night of the sixteenth, the rebels sent a message to the government, via an intermediary, announcing they had "not yet killed" the hostages. The government responded by asking for tapes and photos to confirm that the hostages were alive. Two days later, the rebels gathered the hostages together to pose for photos and interviews. In a black-and-white group portrait, the four men posed, sitting in a row in a stone hut, left to right, Keith, Don, Dirk, and Paul. A thin-looking Don, with his balaclava wrapped around his head, held an Urdu-language newspaper that prominently displayed the date, August 18. Then in four individual shots, each of the men held a sheet of paper on which the same date was written. Each man spoke individually in messages that were as similar as they were controlled.

"My name is Donald Hutchings. This interview is taking place on August 18, 1995. I am fit, well, and have no problems. Jane, I love you."

Each hostage ended his message by telling his partner "I love you."

It would be days before the hostages' loved ones would hear the tapes and see the pictures. As the cameras were clicking in the rebel hideaway and the captives were possibly feeling a touch of optimism, the local press was running off the latest scoop: a leak about American, British, and German experts flying to Srinagar with Black Cat commandos, including the chief commando, Lieutenant General Ashok Tandon. Newspapers reported that Tandon was meeting with the governor of Kashmir, other senior officials, and nine Western antiterror experts. There was much speculation that a new strategy would soon be announced: perhaps, the long-awaited raid. Though for weeks now Indian officials had resisted pressure, especially from Indian security forces, to storm the hideout, Tandon's arrival certainly presented the altogether logical, though unsettling, possibility that Ostro's death had moved some minds in the direction of a raid.

That very night, after the proof-of-life photos were taken, the Al-Faran issued a statement, delivered to news offices in Srinagar, threatening to kill the hostages if India went ahead with a raid. "Upon learning of an army operation, we will immediately kill the hostages," the note stated, in Urdu. "By adopting a rigid attitude, one tourist already has been killed. The government wants the rest of them killed so that this [Kashmir] issue is propagated at the international level in a negative sense. . . . We fully know that the hands of Big Boss [the West] are long. But Allah is greater and more gracious than it."

The Al-Faran intermediary rang up Tikoo to announce that it was time to say "farewell" because the hostages would now indeed be killed. The Al-Faran leaders, he said, would let the captors know when it was time to execute the hostages by sending a press statement to the BBC that contained the code words *within twelve hours*. Because the rebels' wireless was not always working—between the leaders and the captors in the mountain hideaway—the group often used the press to send coded messages to each other.

On the nineteenth, the rebels dispatched a statement containing the doomsday phrase. But Tikoo urged the rebel intermediary to withdraw it in exchange for assurances from the government that no raids or commando operations would occur. Behind the scenes, Ramm and others, including security officers from Britain, Germany, and the United States, had been trying to persuade the Indian military and the government that any attempt to capture or to kill the kidnappers at this point would undoubtedly endanger the hostages, who could be killed in the inevitable gun battle. Or, the rebels would kill them at the mere sight of approaching troops to punish the government for launching a raid, whether or not the government had deployed the troops to that location or the troops accidentally discovered the rebel campsite. Only a few weeks before the Kashmir ordeal began, two American missionaries had been killed by their captors in Colombia after nearly eighteen months of captivity when a government security patrol had stumbled upon their location. The Indian government must order its battalions to avoid the rebel hideouts at all costs, the advisers stressed. At the same time, all governments must pull back their commando forces.

The terrain was such that it would be nearly impossible to pull off a successful raid. Rebel guards and lookouts could be hiding in the forests above a hideout that could be surrounded by flat, rock-strewn lands, rice fields, or perhaps a grove of willow trees whose chopped branches and stubby profiles could not even shield the sun. Troops could be easily spotted. A helicopter could be easily heard. And the rebels, upon hearing or seeing the signs of a raid, would inevitably kill the hostages in the seconds before the commandos arrived.

And so the government, after very lengthy discourse, concluded that although it did know the approximate area where the hostages were located, a raid would serve only as the last resort—initiated only if more hostages were killed. The problem in Kashmir must be resolved, it had been decided, through diplomatic channels. Staving off yet another potential crisis, an Indian official went on TV that night to announce that there were no plans for a raid.

The proof-of-life tapes and photos reached the authorities finally on August 22, bringing tender moments of relief and temporary joy to the families and officials. For Jane and Don to connect on that day was especially meaningful because it was the eve of their wedding anniversary. Others, too, were moved by the occasion, including the officials overseeing the case. Ramm took his copy of the group photo and silently tucked it into a compartment of his wallet next to the letter from his son that he always carried with him—one of the first letters James, now nineteen, had ever written to him. The photo of the hostages would remain in his wallet for a very long time. "I carried it," he would say later, "as a kind of reminder that amid the stifling bureaucracy of the G4 and the complications of negotiating, there were lives at risk."

But the relief, as always, was short-lived. The information—dating from August 18—was already too old to be trusted. With the latest death threat issued the night after the photos were taken, the government, once again, asked for proof that the hostages were alive. This time they demanded to speak with one of the hostages. And so the government, following the suggestion of the kidnap experts, offered to supply the kidnappers two-way radios that would be powerful enough for communications out of the layered hills of the Himalayas.

So far, communications had been conducted by telephone through intermediaries in Srinagar. The problem was that no one on the government end could initiate contact. And the telephones were frequently out of order. For the longest time, the outside consultants had been urging the government to send better radio equipment into the rebel camp. But the Indians were reluctant to give the rebels anything of value, especially expensive radio equipment.

The kidnappers were likely hiding very high in the alpine hills, probably at about 12,000 feet, an elevation that would soon be lost to the snows and winds of winter. Their exact location was difficult to surmise, though it had periodically been known through intelligence reports. U.S. spy satellites, like the ones used in the movie *Patriot Games,* had not been especially helpful. Reacting to the intensity of heat waves rising from the earth, these highly sensitive devices could detect the presence and movements of people on the ground. But because of the combination of the mountainous terrain, the deep valleys, and the barren expanses, the devices could not safely get close enough to identify individuals. Radio waves, though a far less sophisticated technique, might help to keep closer track of the hostages.

Finally, it was agreed that the two-way radio sets would be given to an intermediary, who would hand them over to a messenger from the Al-Faran, who would then deliver them to the rebel group. After much trial and error—the radios sat for days at a secret location—the rebels toted the radios to their waiting comrades high in the hills. And after some discussions, they agreed to put Donald Hutchings on the radio, at a mutually agreed-upon frequency, established by using codes, on August 28. It was the first direct contact with a hostage.

"We are safe," Hutchings said.

Tikoo told Hutchings that the families wanted the hostages to know they were all right and to be as strong as possible. Then Tikoo asked him the kind of questions that are typically used in proof-of-life exchanges—details from the lives of the hostages, carefully chosen by the families, that only they could know.

> *Tikoo:* What are the names of your dogs?
>
> *Hutchings:* Homer and Bodhi.
>
> *T:* What happened to your twin brother?
>
> *H:* He died when he was three days old.

Then Tikoo gave Hutchings questions for the other hostages and told him he would call again in two days for the answers.

On August 30, the rebel intermediary rang up Tikoo and put Hutchings on the line again. The doctor from Spokane then proceeded to give the answers that the hostages had delivered the day before—tiny morsels of information that would give the families something comforting to cling to longer than they could ever have imagined at the time.

For Dirk Hasert: Where did you first meet Anna Katrin [his girlfriend]? *At the Anger Kino* [a theater]. What is your father's date of birth? *August 22, 1932.* What is the name of your cat? *Mayer.*

For Paul Wells: Where and when did you first meet Catherine Moseley? *On October 1, 1992, at Rocky City in Nottingham.*

For Keith Mangan: What is the name of the school that you and your wife Julie went to? *Bertrem Ramsey school.* Who was "Septimus"? *Keith's grandfather.*

And so on this day, August 30, it was confirmed, beyond a doubt, that the four remaining hostages were indeed alive. What no one knew at the time, including the hostages, was that during those late days of summer one of them, Donald Hutchings, came close to being released.

In the U.S. Department of State press briefing the next day, Nicholas Burns, the official briefer, talked of India.

Burns: Since you've raised [the subject of India], let me just say, we're very pleased with the state of our relationship with India. One of our most senior diplomats, Frank Wisner, is our ambassador, and I think it's our very firm view that our relationship with India has improved quite dramatically over the last year or so due to the efforts of both governments to recognize that India and the United States have a lot in common; that we have a lot of issues that we can work on cooperatively and with great benefit to both countries. So I'm glad you raised India. It gave me the chance to comment on our relationship.

Q: Anything on the hostages?

Burns: I don't have a lot that takes us beyond yesterday, but I can say that we have been briefed by the Indian government on their telephone conversation with our American citizen, Donald Hutchings. They were able to be in touch with him yesterday. And we believe as of yesterday that all four of the Western hostages were alive and well, based on their responses to personal questions put to them by the Indian government on the telephone—questions that only they could answer.

We are encouraged by this news, but we continue to urge the Al-Faran organization to release the hostages immediately, and we continue to emphasize that the responsibility for the safety of Mr. Hutchings and the other Western hostages rests entirely with the Al-Faran organization.

During that last week of August, several dramas—one, quite significant—were unraveling behind the scenes. For one, the U.S. Delta Force had tried to launch what everyone was waiting for: a rescue. But the commandos ran into more than a slight obstacle when Indian customs officials impounded their weapons. The U.S. State Department intervened, and twenty-four hours later the equipment was released. Trying to proceed, the commandos then asked Indian authorities for detailed maps of certain parts of Kashmir. They were told no such maps existed because the area had simply never been adequately mapped. One of the Americans then produced aerial photographs taken two years before by the Indian air force. What the Americans needed, they explained again, were maps with greater detail. Still, they were told, this was an area that had never been properly surveyed. There were no detailed maps. The special troops were eventually confined to a military air base in Kashmir while the Indians initiated an inquiry into actions tantamount to what they viewed as a breach in national security. The incident came very close to erupting into a diplomatic crisis, but, by most accounts, the U.S. ambassador astutely brought it to a peaceful conclusion.

Then there was the episode of the near release. In hindsight, the story would differ with the person telling it, perhaps because some felt guilt and others, anger. Some said it was a crucial moment, while others called it "not such a big deal, not a close call, not a serious offer from the rebels." But to some, negotiators in particular, it was a painful ordeal. In the late days of summer, the rebels appeared to be ready to discuss a partial release, and the chosen one was the American, Donald Hutchings. There were various theories about why they would be ready for such a move. One was that the rebels, in the aftermath of Ostro's death, had been the recipients of a public battering from everyone on both sides of the battle—from their own comrades in Islamic extremism to the Kashmiris, whose cause they supposedly represented, to the government spokesman Tikoo, who was constantly reminding them that killing Ostro was a very bad move and that releasing a hostage would counteract the damage to their international image. There was also the possibility that the rebels had been led to believe, from the early stages of the ordeal, that a release of at least one of their jailed militants would actually occur. The rebels were apparently aware that the government was checking the incarceration records of each name on their list in case a release of one so-named militant was already scheduled under the Indian laws. Whatever the reason and whatever the confidence in the rebels' intent, it is clear that a partial release was in the works. What nixed it, by every account, was the G4 and its resolution to stick together.

At the very beginning of the incident, the four governments comprising the G4 had established "an all for one and one for all" pact. One country would not act independently of another. They were in it together. If any one of them had wanted to covertly make a move toward any sort of concession, it would have been difficult to do so without the others knowing. And a covert move, without the knowledge of the others, would have been frowned upon—an overt betrayal. If, for example, the incident had involved only German hostages, it was altogether possible that Germany would have pressured India toward a concession or dispatched its own rescue mission into the vale of Kashmir. In one case when a German operative was arrested in Colombia for associating with guerrillas to free a German hostage held for ransom, a high-level government official told reporters, "We will have more cases where German citizens are taken hostage. We are obliged in those emergency circumstances to help. Unconventional procedures for the solution of humanitarian problems are justified."

But in working with each other, no Western government wanted to be seen as giving in to terrorists, and likewise none would accept a deal in which one country benefited and the others didn't. And so it was that when the American hostage was offered in a partial release that summer, the offer was declined.

For the negotiators, it was a wrenching moment, but it was a decision that none of them could override. They simply did not have the authority. The G4 did. Said one negotiator, lamenting that day, "In negotiation we think that every person we can get out unharmed . . . well, that's one less person in captivity. This is our goal."

By the end of August, press commentaries were beginning to describe India as a government "at its wits end," and the rebels were beginning to issue death threats once again, now with a name attached. The man they threatened to kill first was Donald Hutchings.

14

As in the first wakeful moments after a pleasant dream, the hours that followed the contact with Hutchings were nearly sublime for the hostage families. But too soon the clouds of concern would return, and a routine of terror would resume.

On the night of August 30, Jane Schelly wrote in her diary: "They [the experts] are going through every possible strategy, trying to decide what changes should be made, what's the best way to handle each situation. We have been warned today that we could have a very, very difficult period coming up and that they were all ready, as ready as they can be, to react quickly. I think what they mean is that the appropriate people are on alert in the UK and the USA to make important decisions. We have been told that things could get tough and that there is only a 50-50 chance of them getting out alive."

Jane, Julie Mangan, and the girlfriends of Dirk Hasert and Paul Wells—respectively, Anna-Katrin Hennig and Cath Moseley—shared a spacious two-story suite on a high floor of the British High Commission in New Delhi. They had moved down from the military compound in Srinagar toward the end of July. It was safer in Delhi, officials thought, and slightly less intense. The embassies attended to their every need, including psychological counseling under the tender care of a German psychologist who was an employee of the State Department in Germany. They spent their very long days in briefings, on sightseeing tours, or sometimes catching up on lost sleep. The nights were often rugged. Everyone suffered from some sort of sleep disturbance, whether it was bad dreams or insomnia or chronically fitful sleep. If they weren't up with their own bad dreams, they were helping someone else cope with theirs. Jane, being the oldest, assumed the role of leader. To lead was her natural disposition. She spent many nights consoling the others, especially Julie, whose nightmares were torturous and unrelenting.

For Jane, early mornings were the hardest time. To ward off the anxiety, she had a rule that she followed throughout the ordeal. She never allowed herself to think more than once about a regret, a particular scene from the abduction, or a frustration. Whatever it was that occurred to her, she would think it through carefully and thoroughly, sometimes expressing it on the pages of her journal, and then she would drop it. In this way, she didn't dwell on anything negative. First thing in the morning, she would stretch, watch the news on television, and then go for a run. She wrote in her journal regularly and took as many tours as possible. She simply did not allow herself to stew over that which she had no control. But occasionally a bad dream would emerge from her unconscious, seeping through the cracks of her carefully designed system of control.

In one dream, she later recalled: "We're in a building in a hallway with these metal steps, ones that you can see through. The terrorists are in there, and so is Don, somewhere. What I remember so clearly was that one of the terrorists was sitting on a step above me, and I was down one or two steps, and he had his arm around my neck and was holding a knife to my throat. If I moved at all, the knife started to cut in, and in the dream, the blood was starting to drip down my neck onto my clothes. And the terrorists were yelling and threatening to kill. Julie was down a little farther on the steps, just kind of frozen. Then suddenly I was facing a guy who had just appeared, dressed completely in black; he was a commando, a rescue guy. Just as quickly, there was a shot, and the guy's head went flying into the air. I kept watching it, as the knife dug deeper into my throat and as I looked all around hoping to see Don. Then, thankfully, I awakened."

Only forty-eight hours after Hutchings's voice had connected two worlds, the Al-Faran, with the swiftness of a guillotine, severed them once again. "We won't hesitate to kill the foreigners if our demands aren't met," the militants warned in a radio message. Two of the hostages, they added, were ill now, though they would not name the two. The message prompted an emergency meeting of diplomats, kidnap experts, and government officials. The government warned the families to brace themselves for a tough period, presumably in part because the rebels had provided proof-of-life and offered to consider a partial release but had received nothing in return.

On September 1, the exchange between Tikoo and the rebel intermediary seemed like two boxers sizing each other up:

Tikoo: How are you, my friend? I hope the tourists are all right and you are looking after them.

Al-Faran: What have you done about our demands?

T: It was proceeding really fast but what to do? Beant Singh [chief minister of India's Punjab state assassinated by terrorists seeking independence] was killed yesterday.

AF: What are we supposed to do about that?

T: Listen to me, friend. You have no idea of how governments function. Why don't you speak to me tomorrow evening and by then—

AF: It can't be done. I've told you, we know how to kill. Last time you found the body. This time we'll throw the bodies at such a place you won't even be able to find them.

T: Don't do that. Look up. Allah is also listening to you.

AF: Are you giving me a date or not?

T: I am telling you, we are working out something. . . . Why don't you understand that such things take time? Unfortunately, Beant Singh was killed.

AF: Today you are saying Beant Singh is killed, tomorrow you'll say some other Singh has been killed. Are you giving a date or not?

  T: Why don't you call me on the telephone tomorrow? By then, I may have some news.

AF: This will not happen at any cost. I am telling you, the decision has been taken. We are going to kill them.

  T: For God's sake, don't do this. Call me tomorrow, and I may have some news for you. You and I will both regret the fact that you were not patient. What will you gain by killing innocent, unarmed tourists? *Bahut badnami hogi.* [You will get a bad name.]

AF: *Hamari kya badnami hogi, hamne kaunsi hukumat karni hai.* [What bad name will we get? We are not planning to form a government.]

  T: Then why do it? You kidnapped them for a specific purpose. Aren't you worried about the safety of your accomplices?

AF: I've told you, we know how to kill, and as for them, these people don't really matter to us.

  T: So, then, why are you demanding their release?

AF: Are you giving me a date or not?

  T: Please wait. And speak to me on the telephone tomorrow at nine in the morning.

AF: Let me make myself clear. If by nine you don't talk in specifics, by 9:30 all four of them will be dead and you won't know where to find them.

Then, a day later, on September 2:

Tikoo: I need some more time. We have moved ahead, so you should also be patient.

Al-Faran: It is impossible for us to wait.

  T: Why don't you speak to me on the telephone? I may have something to tell you.

AF: What are you going to tell us now that you haven't already said in the past two months? You are just wasting time.

T: Why don't you understand? The decision has to be taken 600 miles away from here [in New Delhi]. Please call me in the evening.

AF: We told you yesterday too that we can't give you an extra second. If you give us a date, we can wait even for a year, but first give us a firm date.

T: So many people are involved in such a decision, why don't you understand? And I've assured you that the government is not planning any [rescue] operation, so why can't you wait?

AF: We are not scared of an operation. We are prepared to die. . . . *Hum marna jaante hein.* [We know how to meet death.] What's it to us? Those four will also die in the process.

T: Can I make a request? Please call me in the evening.

AF: What is the use? You have been saying the same thing for the past two months. We decided yesterday to kill them, and let me tell you, there is no difference in what we say and what we do.

Finally, the intermediary agreed to call Tikoo that evening. The government's advisers, meanwhile, decided that a new voice might give the rebels a feeling that something was being done about their demands. It was a delay tactic to keep the negotiations—and the hostages—alive.

With the new person, Kashmir's director-general of police, M. N. Sabharwal, at his side, Tikoo began the exchange at about 5 P.M.

Tikoo: How are you? What about the guests? I hope they are OK too. Mr. Sabharwal, my boss, went to New Delhi by special plane. We are all at it. Why don't you talk to him?

Sabharwal: Solutions take time. If you had not killed Ostro, we would have been closer to the destination. After all, you also know that the tourists are innocent, not involved in your fight. Why don't you leave them first, and then we can carry on with our discussions? I will convey your demands to the government, but you also consider our appeal—what is the point of working by deadlines? That's not how governments work. One or two people don't take decisions—[the line was suddenly cut].

Soon the phone rang again, and Tikoo once again urged the militants to be patient.

Tikoo: I don't want to give you a date because if we can't stick to it, you'll curse me. Tell me, how can I help you? Do you need any rations or blankets? Some wheat or rice?

Al-Faran: We are not arranging a wedding here.

Sabharwal: It will take time. In the end there will be a solution. Why don't you speak to your commanders and appeal for time?

AF: It can't be done.

S: Speak to Tikoo at five tomorrow.

AF: This can't be done.

T: Wait for some more time. Call me tomorrow and I'll tell you where we have reached.

AF: Give me a date.

T: Please be patient.

AF: Impossible.

T: Think it over. It will only go against you. No one will gain. You are a good Muslim. Does Allah give you the permission to kill?

AF: At best, I can give you another two hours.

T: My dear friend, what can I do in two hours?

AF: This is our last conversation.

T: Don't act in haste. It is a question of human lives.

The rebel intermediary then said he would not wait beyond seven o'clock that night for a date, and he cut the line. The back and forth was agonizing, with Tikoo trying to buy time and the rebels repeating their threat to kill, as if chanting an evil mantra. An Indian official told reporters the Al-Faran group was "extremely unreasonable," while the rebels repeatedly complained that India was stalling.

On September 3, the Al-Faran called back.

> *Tikoo:* The director-general went to New Delhi and returned by special plane, but what to do? Things are getting a bit delayed. Appeal to your commander and please be patient.

> *Al-Faran:* *Sabar ki had ho gayi.* [There is a limit to waiting.] Give me a date, even if it is a year from now.

> *T:* Why are you talking of a year? It will take much less. What are you going to achieve by taking a hasty step?

> *AF:* Don't waste time unnecessarily. You asked for proof of their safety, and we have given you that.

> *T:* Give me a few days. How, where, and when they are to be released. So many things have to be decided.

> *AF:* If you say two years, we'll wait two years. Give me a date.

> *T:* It will take much less than a year. Only if you were a government official, you would have known.

> *AF:* Don't teach me things. The government released militants in exchange for Rubiya Sayeed [the former Indian home minister's daughter] and K. Doraiswamy [executive of the state-run Indian Oil Company], and it took less than two months.

> *T:* But they were locals. This time, four governments are involved.

> *AF:* Yes, we have realized that it is better to deal with you through locals only.

> *T:* Is there any possibility of any other kind of deal?

> *AF:* There is not.

> *T:* Call me tomorrow.

> *AF:* It is futile, unless you can specify a date.

> *T:* I can't because I don't want to give you a wrong date.

AF: Remember the date, the fifteenth [of September]. We'll bring the government down on its knees. We can get them [our comrades] released ourselves, and I'll even get one of them to speak to you on the phone.

T: You are a very brave man.

AF: I have told you, this time you won't even find their dead bodies.

T: Call me at ten. The news will not be bad, that much I can tell you.

AF: Buri hi hogi. [It can only be bad.]

T: Why do you want to harm them? Why kill poor, unarmed guests?

AF: Ab hum zid per utar gaye hain. [Now we have decided to be stubborn.] We will show you. I can give it to you in blood. I have told my accomplices.

T: Please don't. They are innocent people, guests from other countries. What will you gain from being stubborn? Everything will work out fine.

AF: You will know by the fifteenth.

T: I swear to God, we are doing something. Call me in the morning. That way I'll get the whole night to do something. We may even have to send a special plane.

AF: Remember the date, the fifteenth.

T: Take care of the hostages.

AF: Yeh khayal nahi ho sakta. [This can't be done.]

The Al-Faran intermediary then hung up.

The next day, September 4, was a trying one. The intermediary rang up Tikoo at 10 A.M., but the government negotiator wasn't home; then, silence from the rebel camp.

"We're at a delicate stage," an Indian police official told a reporter that day. "It could go either way. They could free the hostages or, just as easily, carry out their threats to kill them."

That evening the intermediary called again—to reiterate a threat to kill.

> *Tikoo:* How are you? What is happening?
>
> *Al-Faran:* *Aap ne rishta hi taud diya.* [You have broken the relationship.] . . .
>
> > *T:* *Yeh rishta toot sakta hai kya?* [Can this relationship be broken?]
>
> *AF:* *Toot chuka hai.* [It has been broken.]
>
> > *T:* I am talking to very senior people, don't worry.
>
> *AF:* There is no need for you to explain things anymore.
>
> > *T:* Tell me, the papers are saying our contact has snapped, and here we are talking to each other.
>
> *AF:* *Lambi baaten karne ki zarurat nahi hai.* [Forget all this long talk.] I am going.
>
> > *T:* Tell me what I can do for you . . .
>
> *AF:* I asked you for one thing, and you have not done that.
>
> > *T:* I am a government official, why don't you try and understand? You are upset because you want a date. I understand that you are having problems in the mountains. It is getting cold. Tell me what you need—food or grains—and I'll have it sent in tons.
>
> *AF:* There is no need. We know how to get what we want. You will not even find their ashes.
>
> > *T:* Listen to me, you are in this for your friends. Then wait, they'll be out in a day or two.
>
> *AF:* We don't see that happening.

The rebel spokesman hung up, once again, and for four days there was no contact at all.

Behind the scenes, during this period of silence, an inmate at New Delhi's maximum security Tihar Prison was making his move. Sajjad Afgani, one of the jailed Kashmiri separatists whose release the Al-

Faran was demanding, handed a note to a messenger on September 5 and ordered him to deliver it to the kidnappers. The note commanded his followers, the kidnappers, to kill the hostages unless he and his fellow inmates and associates were freed. One of the Brits must be killed first, the note reportedly instructed. Then, if the Indian government still did nothing, the rest of the hostages would have to be killed.

Those days of early September were torturous for the families, who were beginning to believe that contact might be lost indefinitely. Government officials insisted that contact would resume any day, though they would not reveal how they had come to know this.

Meanwhile, news accounts were less sunny. "The grim turn to the hostage negotiations," wrote one British journalist (in the *Independent*), "seems to have arisen because neither the Indians nor Al-Faran have budged in nearly two months. Al-Faran insists that in exchange for the hostages' lives, India must free at least four jailed Kashmir insurgent commanders. After initial signs that it might do that, Narasimha Rao's government has toughened its stand against the rebel kidnappers. The main opposition party, the right-wing Hindu Bharatiya Janata Party, along with the Communists, warned Mr. Rao that he would face a roasting if he traded Kashmiri prisoners for the Westerners. . . . Prospects of a rescue raid on the kidnappers' hideout, thought to be somewhere in the mountains of southern Kashmir near Anantnag, have also dimmed. Not only would such an assault endanger the hostages' lives, but the Indian army is reported to be angered by the presence of more than 60 foreign 'anti-terrorist experts' in Kashmir. This force, said to include men from the SAS as well as German commandos, is now at a secluded army base near Srinagar. The Indian press reported that the highest ranking Indian officer in Kashmir, Lt.-Gen. Surinder Singh, handed in his resignation to the Prime Minister in protest over the blow to the army's 'prestige' in letting in foreign commandos. Mr. Rao refused the general's resignation, but the hostage negotiations have taken on a political slant inside India which he cannot ignore."

In their now-frequent meetings, kidnap experts, on Ramm's team as well as in the FBI, suggested dropping all lines in Tikoo's script that referred to any potential release of the jailed rebels. Promising such a concession could only frustrate the captors, they argued, since the release of the jailed militants was, in fact, not imminent. One of the most widely acknowledged verities in the business of hostage negotiations is that no promises should be made that cannot be kept; promises serve only to heighten expectations and any failure to fulfill them can lead to deadly consequences. The message that had to be stressed to the Al-Faran was simply that the kidnappings of tourists and the killing of Ostro did nothing for their cause and that if the rebels released the hostages, the freed men could act as their ambassadors, communicating to the West the Kashmiris' desire to be free from India. Among other things, the experts advised the government to tell the kidnappers to leave the hostages in a village and disappear into the mountains.

On September 6, the second day of silence, a report was leaked from the military compound at Srinagar—where negotiators and others on the case were staying—that an Indian army patrol had been spotted about two kilometers (1.2 miles) from where the rebels were supposedly keeping the hostages. The obvious fear was that the hostages might be wounded in a skirmish. This led to another sleepless night for the families, and still there was no word from the rebels. Yet no news reports of any so-called bloody battle surfaced at the time.

Finally, on September 8, the rebels broke the silence with a press release in which they threatened to kill the hostages, yet again, in twenty-four hours—on Saturday night, the ninth—if their demands were not met. The rebels stressed that if they were forced to carry out this threat, India's unyielding attitude would be held to blame. The dilemma was, as always, whether the statement was authentic, whether the threat was serious, and whether the hostages were alive when the statement was made.

In the statement, the group called the Indian government "very irresponsible," adding that "the government should announce the release of our jailed militants without mentioning a number. The exchange of hostages could be discussed later. We will wait until tomorrow evening. We will take the extreme step after the expiration of the deadline and the authorities will be responsible for it."

Late in the night of September 8, several hours after the guerrillas had sent out their latest warning, the intermediary rang up a weary Tikoo. The conversation lasted an hour and ended with the rebels agreeing to call again on the evening of September 9.

And then the government heard more disheartening news. The next day, September 9, brought word of yet another incident of kidnapped tourists in the region. As many as twenty European and Australian hikers had been snatched from a hotel in the area of Ladakh. Using words such as *detained*, state officials were careful to avoid the word *kidnapping*. The "detainers" this time were Buddhists from the Zanskar Valley, where 18,000 people, mostly Buddhists with Tibetan origins, live and where snow closes the valley for most of the year. A Kashmir government spokesman told reporters that the Buddhist "detainers" were demanding more federal funds for "developmental works." And "they are angry." Seeking their autonomy, the Buddhists accused the Indian government of ignoring them because they are so geographically isolated.

Meanwhile, that night, the Al-Faran extended its deadline, again. And Tikoo urged the rebels to release the hostages because they could and would act as the rebels' "ambassadors." In response, the intermediary, as always, wanted a date for the release of the militants.

Parts of the conversation that evening went like this:

> *Tikoo:* Hello, how are you? . . . Why can't you do one thing? Release one or two as a goodwill gesture and let them act as your ambassadors.

> *Al-Faran:* It is out of the question. . . .

> *T:* Okay, tell me, is your commander from here or from across the border?

> *AF:* He is from here only.

> *T:* Aren't you worried about harming your cause, the movement?

> *AF:* The movement can go to hell.

> *T:* Can you do one thing? Why don't you leave at least one of them?

AF: It is all in my hands—to kill them or leave them. But there is no need to waste my time and yours.

T: So many governments are involved, why don't you try and understand?

AF: They obviously want them killed, that's why we are ready to kill.

T: Even their wives have appealed.

AF: I am not willing to listen to any appeals. I'll write to the families myself and tell them that we had to kill the hostages because of the government's adamant stand.

T: You can't do this. . . . I've told you I can't give you a date. . . . The entire Islamic world is appealing to you . . . even Mecca has appealed.

AF: I don't know who all are appealing. Don't think that we can't kill them; we can kill them anytime. . . . We can't be patient anymore.

T: Call me tomorrow. Don't break communication . . . and look after the tourists. I'll wait for your call tomorrow.

A trace of hope, like the first rays of sunlight following a storm, came on September 10 when the rebels lifted the deadline—set to expire at midnight on the tenth—without any changes in the government's position. Perhaps the government would win the waiting game. The next day Reuters ran a story with the headline "Hopes Grow in Kashmir." And the wives and girlfriends of the hostages sent a message to the kidnappers: "We welcome your decision to extend the deadline as a first step toward their release. We appeal directly to Al-Faran to release safely the ones we hold so dear."

There were other scraps of good news the next day. The Buddhists released the twenty or so tourists after four days' captivity, leaving them in a guest house in the Zanskar Valley; no one had been harmed. And newspapers were reporting that the September 5 note from the rebel in Tihar Prison to the kidnappers had been intercepted by Indian intelligence agents. The rebels never received the orders to kill, which were intended to override any exchanges between the kidnappers and Tikoo.

But hope was never lasting. And behind the scenes the terrorists had managed to weave yet another web of horror. On September 11, the families of the hostages gathered at their apartment in the British High Commission at about 11:30 A.M. for a briefing. The news was not good. The rebels had contacted the government at 7 P.M. on the tenth—only half a day after lifting the most recent deadline—to issue yet another, diabolical threat: Donald Hutchings would be killed at 8 P.M. on the night of the eleventh.

Jane Schelly remembers the moment vividly: "I was busy writing, taking notes as always, and as I was writing I heard them say that Don had been singled out. The way I was sitting, I had my legs crossed. And as they told us this recent development, I could tell that all eyes were on me, but I couldn't look up. And then I realized that my leg, the one that was hanging over the other, had begun to shake uncontrollably, a violent shaking that made it nearly impossible for me to write. I had had this experience before, in rock climbing. They call it 'sewing machine leg.' It's when you have too much tension, are too tired, and the stress causes this uncontrollable shake. And the way you can stop it is to weight it, pushing against the floor in this case. And so I uncrossed my leg and put my foot on the floor because I didn't want it to shake so violently. All the while I was looking at my notepad, clenching my pen so very tightly, as if stunned, unable to look up. I'm sure everyone thought I was crazy, but I just couldn't look up and make eye contact with anybody. They must have thought I wasn't reacting. I just kept writing."

Leaving the hostage families with a renewed sense of vertigo, the rebels, the next night, canceled the threat against Don.

By then, the rebels were reportedly holding the hostages in an area far beyond radio range, high in the mountains, over 14,000 feet above the Wadwan Valley. Troublesome, too, was a series of leaks in the press throughout September, all of which whittled away at what little trust the rebels had in Tikoo and the governmental authorities.

Uncontrolled leaks to the press are almost always harmful to the process of negotiation, especially in nations where rebel kidnappers assume that the press is government controlled. Negotiators spend weeks, even months, slowly building bridges of trust to kidnappers;

leaks are the bombs dropped on the bridges. Every kidnap expert has stories about talks breaking down or negotiations being stalled for weeks, thus endangering the lives of the hostages, because of leaks.

In Sierra Leone, for example, earlier that year, talks were cut off the night before rebel kidnappers were scheduled to discuss plans to free two British engineers. Negotiators had carefully worked out a strategy slowly leading to a threat to end talks altogether if the rebels refused to drop their ransom demand. One night the rebels announced that they were willing to talk about ways to release their hostages. They did not even raise the issue of ransom money. Up to that point, the rebels had said they would not discuss anything until an exact amount of money was agreed on, but now they were talking about releasing the hostages without the entanglement of ransom. This was stunning progress—just the kind of breakthrough event for which negotiators are always aiming. Alas, among those present when this event occurred was one diplomat who either was dumber than a stone or saw personal gain in the breakthrough. That night, on national television, he announced that the rebels had capitulated, that they would release the hostages in exchange for nothing, and that the whole affair had simply shown how weak the rebels were. He also took credit for the capitulation. As a result, the rebels did not call the next day. Nor the next. Nor the next. For several nerve-racking weeks, no one knew whether the hostages were alive or dead or whether the rebels would ever call again. Finally, after nearly a month of silence, talks resumed, resulting in the eventual release of the captives—without the payment of a ransom. The diplomat was dismissed because of the leak, which could easily have cost the lives of the engineers.

Who was leaking the information in Kashmir was unclear; the source would never be revealed. Most observers were certain it was some government official, but what that meant was not exactly clear. "Government" could mean New Delhi or Kashmir or Srinagar. And within each of those, it could be the military or the police or politicians. Several people were certain it was a local politician who reputedly was sleeping with a member of the press, but this rumor was never substantiated. Others claimed there was a conspiracy designed to sabotage the negotiations and thus damage the standing of Prime Minister Rao, but this notion was as leaky as the government itself. Besides, there were so many competing interests in the case that it would be almost impossible for enough people to agree long enough to conspire on anything.

Commander Ramm dismissed the idea of a conspiracy. He was a stout believer in the "chaos theory of leaks," which holds that the leaker is usually some low-level functionary who obtains a juicy piece of information and then uses it to advance his or her career or sells it to the highest media bidder. "He thinks, Bloody hell, I've never had one of these before; with whom shall I share this?" said the commander. "I honestly don't think that when people do this, they understand fully how much they are endangering the lives of hostages."

On September 18, a highly sensitive detail found its way into the news: that the Indian government was considering the payment of a "ransom" for the release of the hostages. What had happened was this: Earlier in the month, perhaps a week or more before the leak, the rebels had proposed a deal in which they would be granted safe passage, out of range of the marauding Indian security troops, in exchange for the hostages. As a "guarantee" for this, the Indian government must agree to put $1.2 million into an escrow account payable to the rebels when the hostages were returned. For one of the few times since they had been kidnapped the beleaguered hostages appeared to have a chance to be out of the woods. The greatest hope in recent days seemed to be that the government was indeed willing to consider safe passage in exchange for the hostages. Now the rebels' new proposal, though far from perfect, was a variation on that theme. After more than two months of the same back-and-forth negotiations, stuck impossibly on the demands for released prisoners, people believed this proposal was a step toward a resolution.

Around this time, there were reports that India was expecting a "happy ending" because the terrorists had actually achieved some of their goals and therefore might be willing to take the offer of safe passage and flee, leaving the hostages behind, of course. Although their jailed comrades had not been released, the kidnappers had gained international attention to their cause, and they had certainly discouraged tourism in Kashmir, which meant that their enemy, the Indian government, would lose tourism dollars.

But soon the sunny picture was dim once again—very dim, in fact. On Monday morning, the eighteenth, an Indian news report exposed the ongoing negotiations regarding the "guarantee." But the word used was *ransom*. There could be a release as soon as Sunday night (September 24) or during the following week, the article said, because of this so-called ransom deal. Other news services picked up the story. One wire service reported that the government of India was offering $1.2 million for the release of the hostages. There had been rumors about possible ransom demands in early weeks of the kidnappings, but none had been confirmed and none was taken very seriously. Like a lighted match thrown into a dry field, the news of this so-called ransom deal spread quickly across the globe. Though the story came in different versions with varying sums of money, ranging from $750,000 to $50 million, all stories used the word *ransom*.

The leak immediately caused a snag in any potential consummation of such an arrangement. The Al-Faran was apparently fuming. The militants accused the Indians and the negotiators of betraying them and claimed that the news had been purposely leaked by the Indian government to give the militants an image of "cheap mercenaries" and to prolong the negotiations. The delay, said the militants, was pleasing to the Indians because it gave them more time to use the incident to discredit the Kashmiri separatists and their cause—a convenient strategy especially during a year when an election was likely to be held in Kashmir.

"The problem was clearly that the news leaked as a 'ransom,' giving the Al-Faran an image it did not want," Jane said later. "An obnoxious image. This was repulsive to them. So it just didn't go anywhere. It all happened very, very quickly, I recall, from the time the thing was proposed, to the time it was leaked, to the time when it was just out of the question. We all wondered, Was this a serious opportunity, one that we would regret missing?"

The afternoon following the leak, an Al-Faran representative phoned the Associated Press in Srinagar to report a skirmish between Indian army commandos and rebels. The commandos, they claimed, had attacked one of their hideouts near the town of Pahalgam, causing several casualties. They would not disclose whether the hostages were among them.

"There are casualties, but we don't have the details," the rebel told the press. "We have no information about the whereabouts of the hostages and whether they are alive or were killed."

The group also announced, in a written statement, that the Al-Faran leadership had lost contact with their colleagues who were holding the hostages. They accused the Indian government, once again, of prolonging the crisis. The government, meanwhile, claimed there had been no such battle and that the rebels' message was a "pressure tactic." Relations between the government and the rebels were deteriorating—no doubt in response to the ransom leak.

Also on the eighteenth, the rebels secretly escorted a doctor from the Marwah village in nearby Jammu to their campsite—perhaps half a day away—to treat one of the hostages for an eye infection. An official would later say that Donald Hutchings might be suffering from conjunctivitis. There would be more nettlesome rumors surrounding the doctor's journey—that the other hostages, for example, were suffering from snow blindness. Though none of this was ever confirmed, there was a strong likelihood that Hutchings did in fact have eye problems.

And on the same day, HUA released a statement to the press outlining in detail its theory that India was carrying out these kidnappings and had killed the other hostage, Ostro, to vilify Kashmir's independence struggle. "There is every likelihood that India may kill the four remaining hostages and ascribe it to the Mujahedeen of Kashmir," the statement said. An Indian official had only one comment, "Ridiculous."

As if the ups and downs that month were not dizzying enough, another nasty rumor echoed through the timeless hills: that the hostages were dead. There was so much concern about this, and so many locals claiming that it was absolutely true, that the Indian government called a news conference on September 19 to announce that an intermediary had confirmed again the well-being of the captives. "We don't have other evidence, but we believe that the information provided by the intermediator is correct," said an official, in Srinagar.

The next roller-coaster ride began only two days later when the news was out that a respected and widely read newsmagazine would soon publish parts of conversations between Tikoo and the rebel intermediary. The week before, an article in the same publication, *India Today,* had quoted an official as saying it would be "nothing short of a miracle if the hostages were released unharmed." The story, in an attempt to analyze the current crisis, concluded that the kidnappers were ruthless and that the negotiators had had little space in which to maneuver.

The new article, the one with the partial transcripts of the negotiations, said that the government's strategy was twofold: "Waiting for tomorrow" and "Hoping that the Al-Faran doesn't stop talking." The article described the progress as abysmal, saying that the government "limps along from day to day as if in a collective daze, even as the Al-Faran issues threats that are as ominous as they are sinister," and that the only thing the government was banking on was "hope and time— keeping its fingers crossed and wishing that the captors might finally relent and free the hostages."

More than any of the other leaks thus far, authorities worried about the exposed transcripts of the process of negotiation. (Later, however, it would be the leaked ransom story and another leak in mid-October that stood out most.) Such a betrayal of confidentiality between rebels and authorities could damage—even sever—the delicate strands connecting the two sides. A negotiation is all about compromise, and it requires giving and taking, explaining and reexplaining, a constant shuffling and reshuffling of wishes, expectations, and demands. If these delicate balancing acts are suddenly exposed in the publication of transcripts describing them, the effect is to undermine the whole process. To place the transcripts in the lap of the public, which included the rebel leadership, was to open the process to disruptive commentary and criticism. In such a context, suspicion and doubt would appear where hope was tentatively renting space.

Though it was clear to everyone involved that the rivalry among the three Indian sectors—the military, the intelligence, and the police— could easily have provoked such a leak, the source of the tapes would remain a mystery. It was virtually agreed, however, that extremely sensitive information had once again seeped out of the government. There were rumors that the source was Tikoo, though negotiators who knew him well denounced such talk as folly. He was the one, after all, who had to deal with the unpleasant repercussions—a negotiating atmosphere suffused with uncertainty and renewed hostility.

Whatever the source, reports of the leaked transcripts, soon to be in the hands of the public, certainly had the predicted result: silence from the rebel camp. It was a grueling silence, more painful perhaps because just before the cutoff there had appeared to be some progress toward a release. On September 28, the government announced, "We have reasons to believe that the hostages are safe and no harm has come to them."

As the hostages entered their third month of captivity, the routine of contact between the government and the Al-Faran had broken down. The bridge so carefully built since the days after Ostro's death was blocked. It was no small success that the negotiator, Tikoo, a gifted conversationalist, and his advisers had kept the dialogue alive as long as they did. But there had been no progress toward a compromise. India, despite a hint of flexibility in the earliest days of the ordeal, was unwilling to bend. A rescue, which some observers believed should have occurred back in August, was considered far too dangerous and now, with winter approaching, almost impossible.

Perhaps the only reason the hostages were alive at this point was that Tikoo's scripted messages, despite the apparent droning repetition, reminded the rebels over and over how futile it would be for them to kill the hostages and how damaging the death of Ostro had been to their image and to their cause. The thinking, of course, was that the rebels would eventually tire of feeding and guarding the hostages and realize the kidnapping was not reaping the desired rewards. Unless a behind-the-scenes diplomatic move by the United States or one of the other countries could end the standoff, time and the ability of the negotiators to persuade the rebels to keep the hostages alive was the only hope.

But soon a new enemy would appear, one that would make the waiting game even more dangerous: winter in Kashmir.

PART III

A Day in October

⟨⇥⟩

Negotiation is an art and the art lies in looking through the eyes of the adversary.

—Richard Clutterbuck, author and
terrorism expert, October 1995

15

OCTOBER 11, 1995
KASHMIR

For three months, the hostages and their Muslim guards had marched deeper into the layers of overlapping mountains, traversing vistas that had dazzled travelers for centuries. At dawn they awoke to the brooding grandeur of the Himalayas, watching for the sun to appear above the peaks, like a loyal friend dispatched to lead them home. But as winter drew near and first light awakened the hues of dying leaves, a merciless chill had begun to set in.

October 11 was the 100th day of captivity for the prisoners of Al-Faran. In Srinagar, temperatures were averaging sixty to sixty-five degrees Fahrenheit during the day, dropping to the forties at night. It was roughly ten degrees cooler in the surrounding hills. By then the hostages were often held in Anantnag, near the village where the body of Ostro was found, or sometimes in the adjacent hills, where the first snows typically fell by early November. And by then temperatures could plummet to as low as minus-ten degrees Fahrenheit. Even in late October, there would be rumors that Donald Hutchings already was suffering from frostbite.

But winter was worrisome for more than what the cold and the snow could do to the health of the hostages. There was also some concern about how the kidnappers could meet the increasing needs of their prisoners. In winter, not only would the hostages require more food to survive the elements, but their medical needs would likely grow more acute. And surely the weather would slow them all down as they moved from hideout to hideout, forcing them to lower altitudes, to where the forests met the roads and where the risk of running into Indian troops was higher. While the "mountain warriors" were used to the rigors of the Himalayas, the hostages, despite their trekking experience and physical prowess, were not. If the four men became too burdensome, as John Childs had feared, winter could compel the rebels to choose between two extreme options: to kill or to release. And such a decision would depend partly on whether the kidnappers still perceived the hostages as valuable bait to trade.

Although the fragile bridge between the rebels and the Indian government had not yet collapsed and there were periodic hints of progress, a compromise appeared less and less likely. For whatever reasons, a nation that had granted concessions in several past cases, including the release of political prisoners, had grown intransigent on accommodations to win the freedom of Hutchings and his fellow captives. The Indian government, steering confidently as though it knew the bends in the road, held ever proudly to its course. The rebels, too, were stuck on the same dialogue of demands, though, early on, they had reduced their initial demand for the release of twenty-one jailed militants to fifteen and there would eventually be an offer of a one-for-one swap.

Although everyone who had a stake in the negotiations kept a wary eye on the calendar, winter was but one of many daunting challenges in Kashmir. For one thing, India's so-called Camelot was less a paradise than a bleeding wound. "Asia's Bosnia," some experts called it. Despite the continuing flow of tourists to Srinagar's Dal Lake and to picturesque Pahalgam, the region was effectively a war zone, with sandbagged bunkers on the streets of Srinagar, troops occupying lakeside hotels, and roving military cars with automatic rifles perched in readiness on hoods and roofs.

The Indian and Pakistani struggle over Kashmir was the longest-running border dispute in the history of the United Nations, beginning shortly after India achieved independence from Britain in 1947. In partitioning its Indian empire, Britain created two independent nations: Pakistan as the homeland for the Muslims, and India, a secular state where Muslims, Christians, and the dominant Hindus coexisted. Both vied for control of the 86,000 square miles of the state of Jammu and Kashmir. While the majority of Kashmiris were Muslim, the region's royal leader at the time of the partition was Hindu, and at the sign of the first Pakistani invasion in 1948, the Hindu maharaja called in the Indian troops. In the cease-fire agreement following a bloody conflict, India retained over two-thirds of Kashmir while Pakistan claimed the rest, an area it calls "Free Kashmir." India refers to the same area as "Pakistan-occupied Kashmir."

Since 1947, India and Pakistan have fought three wars, two of them over Kashmir. Seeking to add Kashmir to the Islamic empire, Pakistan, in recent years, has allegedly trained fighters, supplied weapons, and provided safe havens to Muslim extremists crusading to sever Kashmir's ties to India. Islamabad consistently has denied such charges. India, in turn, has escalated the numbers of Indian security troops in the once-idyllic Kashmir Valley. As for the Kashmiris, many dream of independence, while others seek to join Pakistan, and still others want to remain part of India, though with more local autonomy.

In January 1990, the long-simmering discontent in Kashmir ignited into a popular uprising in which, according to Muslims, the Indian army, without provocation, massacred hundreds of innocent Kashmiri civilians. The Indian government accused Muslim demonstrators of attacking the Hindus first. Since then, the hills of Kashmir and especially the areas bordering Pakistan have been overrun with hundreds of thousands of Indian troops—reports range from 300,000 to 600,000—as well as hordes of militants that include new Islamic mercenaries from Pakistan, Afghanistan, and the Sudan. The 1990 massacre swelled the ranks of militant groups with young recruits, and because of the atrocities of the Indian troops, many more joined the fight for independence. By most accounts, in the mid-1990s the militants overtook strategic centers within the vale of Kashmir, including the town of Anantnag and its environs. As in most such conflicts, both sides have disputed the death toll, with Indians claiming 14,000 Kashmiris have died and human rights groups setting the toll at nearly 40,000 Kashmiris killed, sometimes after being tortured.

Whatever the political pronouncements might be, the hard, irreducible fact was that masses of people were at war in northern India and many were dying. With scores of troops, foreign mercenaries, and local militants scattered throughout Kashmir, the task of negotiating a kidnapping was impossibly difficult. Normally, kidnap negotiators venture into the countryside to cultivate reliable sources of information regarding the rebels and their movements. But such a routine task was life-threatening in Kashmir. For negotiators to find even a trustworthy intermediary—always a challenge in kidnappings—was doubly difficult in a land intractably locked in internecine conflict.

The war and all that went with it also blocked at least one opportunity for a rescue. At one point, the hostages were known to be at a hideout in the town of Anantnag. Such a situation often facilitates a rescue, but in this case the ubiquity of Muslim militants made a raid in Anantnag nearly impossible. Indeed, at the very least, the militants would certainly know of the attempt to rescue the hostages before the commandos arrived. And they would likely kill the hostages to give the appearance of a botched military rescue, thus shifting the blame of the deaths onto the Indian government. It was too much to risk.

Equally formidable, and a hindrance to rescues, was the terrain. The kidnappers and their captives could slip into the mountains and disappear as easily as water into sand. The hills provided innumerable lookout posts allowing militants to detect troops or helicopters for miles across the valley's open expanses, making a surprise rescue unfeasible.

At the same time, one of the more mysterious and seemingly insurmountable problems was the true identity of the enemy. The conundrum of the Al-Faran complicated India's and the G4's roles in resolving the crisis, especially in its early days. With whom was India supposed to negotiate and against what nation or group should the G4 apply diplomatic pressure? The variety of militant groups in Kashmir had recently spawned new gangs that were using the cover of patriotism and freedom-fighting to pillage, kidnap, and extort. At first, it seemed Al-Faran could be one of these, operating like a gang of bandits, independently and ruthlessly, for their own profit. The original intent of the kidnappings, however, appeared to be to force the international spotlight on the desperate nature of the Kashmiri cause for independence. This led to the notion that the Al-Faran must be a new offshoot of one of the many Kashmiri militant groups—a notion that was a dangerous one in the early days of the incident because it allowed the governments involved to believe that pressuring Pakistan would be useless. It was a theory that should have been dropped like hot coals after John Childs came out of the mountains and informed his debriefers that most, if not all, of his captors were Pakistanis or Afghanis.

David Mackie and Kim Housego believed "Al-Faran" was part of the same group that had kidnapped them the previous summer, the Harkat-ul-Ansar, or HUA, the Islamic extremists based in Pakistan, possibly within the sphere of influence of the Pakistan government. Both groups had included a Kashmiri area commander whose familiarity with the valley and its inhabitants helped the band to move swiftly and secretly through the mountains, as well as a cadre of Afghani and Pakistani warriors. Al-Faran's leader, Abdul Hamid al-Turki, was a former field commander for the HUA. The list of jailed militants whose release the Al-Faran sought was strikingly similar to the list submitted the previous summer for the release of Housego and Mackie. And intelligence agencies informed Kim Housego, who returned the next year to lend his support to the families of the 1995 victims, that the 1995 hostages had initially followed the same route that Housego and Mackie and their captors had taken. Further, they were held for two months in the same house on the edge of a village called Sukhoi where Housego and Mackie were held for three days. And there was some evidence that one of the Al-Faran militants had been involved in the 1994 incident. The only differences were that Housego and Mackie had been released very quickly. They had even been given souvenirs, including a wall clock with the inscription: "Teacher-Hitler/Pupils-Indian Occupational Forces/With Best Wishes to Kim Housego from Harkat-ul-Ansar International."

The Pakistani government and the HUA repeatedly denied affiliation with the Al-Faran.

There was also that persistent theory, originating in Pakistan, that the so-called rebels were, in fact, part of the Indian security forces, perhaps a renegade group. Even the *New York Times* gave the theory a modicum of credence. In one article John Burns wrote, "Nobody can even be sure whether the kidnappers, who call themselves Al-Faran, are real insurgents or, as many better known Kashmiri guerrillas assert, are Indian-backed renegades trying to discredit the entire movement."

If so, the abduction was perfectly timed, for it occurred during the months preceding the Kashmiri election that was supposed to be held that fall. While such a scheme may have seemed preposterous, it had happened before in India. In 1971, for example, the Indian secret service had set up a bogus group called Al-Fatah to discredit Islamic separatists. Al-Fatah hijacked an Indian airliner and blew it up on the runway at the Lahore airport. And so it was that Pakistan, denying it had anything to do with Ostro's death, pointed its finger south.

"It is clear that the inhumane kidnapping and the ghastly murder are the acts of forces that are seeking to discredit the legitimate struggle of the Kashmiri people and to damage their cause," the Pakistan Foreign Ministry said in a statement to Reuters after the death of Ostro. Pakistan's then Prime Minister Benazir Bhutto called Ostro's murder "an act of terrorism committed by enemies of Kashmir's fight for freedom."

But just as vexing as the terrain, the weather, the war, and the warriors were the intertwining, endlessly complicated political relationships of the major players—a potpourri of potentially conflicting egos, agendas, bureaucracies, policies, and theories that made for a troubling, sometimes rudderless force, amounting to an unseen power potentially as damaging to the hostages as a winter storm.

An unwieldy mix, it included: the central government in New Delhi, the government in Kashmir, the Indian security forces, the Kashmiri police, the ambassadors of four countries, the Pakistani government, the Pakistani intelligence agency ISI, the HUA leaders, the Islamic religious leaders (also in Pakistan), the negotiators from Scotland Yard and the U.S. Federal Bureau of Investigation, the British

Foreign Office, the U.S. State Department, the U.S. Central Intelligence Agency, the U.S. National Security Council, the German counterterrorist squad GSG9, the local Kashmiri militants, the local Al-Faran leaders, the rebels holding the hostages, the government intermediary, India's ruling political party and the opposition party, the families of the hostages, independent mercenaries, and the local, national, and international media.

India, the country running the case, and Pakistan, the country that was likely home to the kidnappers' leaders, were wrangling over Kashmir, a potential flashpoint for a nuclear clash; India owned a cache of nuclear weapons, and intelligence suggested that Pakistan had them too. That alone was enough to complicate the resolution of a hostage-taking in Kashmir. But there were other frictions as well: between the central Indian government in New Delhi and the Kashmiri state authorities in Srinagar, between the military troops and the police, between the police who handled investigations and the police who handled everyday affairs, between the U.S. State Department and the FBI, and even between agents of the FBI, the ones investigating the case and the ones negotiating the hostages' release.

And then there were the four Western nations—the G4—striving for consensus, each with a separate foreign policy and mind-set regarding both India and Pakistan, each with a different history in dealing with hostage incidents, and each with a unique internal bureaucracy. Because of this, the demands and replies shuttled back and forth between the rebels and the government passed through many channels, sometimes moving as slowly as a glacier. Although Tikoo spoke with the rebels daily, three or four days could elapse before he could deliver the official response to a particular demand. It was like a game of "telephone" in which a message follows a long path from start to finish with the risk of it being altered or misinterpreted along the way. Picking up critiques at every stop, the message would follow this path: from rebel intermediary, to Tikoo, to the head of the Indian military, to the negotiators, to the diplomats, to the heads of state and others in authority in each of the affected countries. After analyzing the demand and all the critiques and suggestions sent with it, the central governments would issue orders and comments to their ambassadors, who would then send the rebels' demand with the official response back along the same serpentine route.

At the same time that the G4 presented a sometimes unwieldy bureaucracy, there was also the issue of occasional rigidity and, of course, the ever-present pact that no nation was to act alone in resolving the case. Thus, when the rebels offered a partial release, the G4 had turned it down. "They wanted all or nothing, they said. It was tough. A partial release could have been the beginning of a total release," said one close observer.

India, as a former colony, was burdened with a complex of attitudes and concerns regarding its relationships with the G4—especially, of course, with its nineteenth-century noblesse oblige colonizer Great Britain. India's sovereignty was an issue from the start of the case; the Indians were not at all comfortable in taking advice from the Brits or from anyone else, for that matter, though Roy Ramm and the British negotiators who rotated in and out of the case likely felt the chill the most.

"Before the death of Ostro," says an individual familiar with the case, "there was a sort of standoff—rooted in the colonial past, a combination of India's paranoia and pride and, to be fair, the arrogance of the West. A lot of political garbage got in the way. India seemed to be reacting to what could be called collective arrogance on the part of the participating nations. You had the Western powers trying to use *their* assets and intelligence instead of India's. And India: whether they were being offered the help or they were accepting help, it made them feel incompetent or rather feel that they might look incompetent. But the expertise being offered was quite good, and, especially in the beginning stages, they should have been less proud and more focused on the potential for a tragedy in the making."

Another close observer said: "Just imagine British soldiers and experts coming to America in the 1820s. India's independence is fairly new, and this was an incident that touched every sensitive nerve. Of course, there was the intriguing possibility that India was putting on an act. What for? Well, to stall a resolution, to make themselves look good and the militants look worse. India isn't easy, you know; it's simply not easy. You remember what Rudyard Kipling said, don't you? 'A fool lies here who tried to hustle the East.' "

Pride was a prickly issue, as well, in the relationship between the State Department and the FBI. Diplomats, responsible for maintaining sound, amiable ties with their host countries, are sometimes skeptical of other agencies engaging in international crises; especially suspect would be a bureau of the U.S. Justice Department whose sphere of influence has been confined traditionally to domestic shores. While attitudes change from embassy to embassy, the consensus is that foreign lands are not the natural habitat of the FBI. The diplomats' point of view is this: After FBI agents have swooped into a country, done their work, and gone home, it is the diplomats who are left to face the music—to answer for any political or cultural gaffs that their itinerant colleagues may have committed. On the other hand, in the event of a kidnapping, the FBI has the near equivalent of a special forces unit, a specially trained crisis team operating internationally as well as domestically. And although hostage cases abroad are often different from most kidnappings in the United States, the agency's negotiators at least have experience with the crime and strong instincts about what works and what doesn't. By the summer of 1995, the FBI had advised foreign governments on nearly fifty kidnappings abroad. "They made some mistakes in the beginning, in their earlier international cases," said a former FBI agent, "and their reputations as 'Rambo'-like intruders followed them abroad, but they learned fast. The agents in Kashmir were quite good."

Even after officials invited the FBI to the front lines of the Kashmir incident in Srinagar—more than a month after the abductions—the agencies danced an uneasy two-step. Although individuals working the case were clearly devoted to gaining the release of the four hostages, there were lingering resentments on both sides. The FBI was dismayed at its belated entry into the case, and the State Department, still skeptical of the FBI's expanding international role, could not be persuaded that the FBI presence was a boon.

Like a giant chessboard, the political terrain of the Kashmir case with its multitude of players and agendas was filled with opportunities

for good moves and bad moves, though everyone seemed to be waiting for a move by the superpowerful United States. An *India Today*
article in late September 1995 had ended with the comment that all
that was left to hope for was a diplomatic breakthrough "perhaps initiated by the U.S." But considering the strategic position of the
United States in South Asia that summer, the American giant resembled an emperor without clothes more than an omnipotent superhero.

Nothing about diplomacy is ever simple, particularly under crisis
pressure, and the changeable bonds between the United States and
both Pakistan and India more than proved the point. Since the partitioning of British India, the United States had faced a daunting challenge in trying to balance its relationships with these two inimical
nations. Getting too close to one could damage the alliance with the
other. And always in the middle, there was the wild card of Kashmir—
a card that any of the nations could play in trying to manipulate one
another. U.S. sympathy, for instance, to the Indian or Pakistani cause
in Kashmir could win points in the respective nations.

Every U.S. president since Harry Truman had had to face the
conundrum of how to deal with India and Pakistan, whether it was
the threat of India strengthening ties to the Soviets or the importance
of India as an effective brake against Chinese aggression. During the
Kennedy years, when the president's close friend John Kenneth Gal-
braith was the ambassador to India, the United States tried to bolster
its ties with India without alienating Pakistan, a very valuable strategic
ally. But for much of the Cold War era, India's links to the Soviet
Union, as well as its nuclear capability, provoked enough suspicion in
the United States to inspire a policy favorable to Pakistan. Efforts to
help effect a truce in Kashmir obviously failed. When Kennedy tried
to interest India's President Jawaharlal Nehru in a Kashmir settlement, Nehru stressed that India could not accept the Pakistani argument of Kashmir's adhering to the Islamic nation because of its
Muslim majority.

Until the summer of 1995, no U.S. president had faced a hostage
crisis in Kashmir, the beating heart of the animosity between India and
Pakistan. And to do so was to face an unusually complicated and delicate situation. The central question was where the United States, in

the multitude of diplomatic concerns it had in that region, would place Donald Hutchings. How important was the life of one American in a region where the United States was deeply concerned over the growth of U.S. markets, the proliferation of nuclear weapons, and the threat of Chinese expansion?

Pakistan was the obvious target for a diplomatic move. But U.S. pressure on Pakistan would be effective only if Islamic extremists were, in fact, sponsoring the Al-Faran, and if the Pakistan government actually did have influence over the extremists. The quicksands of Pakistani politics made it unclear where the ever-changing lines of power were drawn. That summer, Prime Minister Bhutto needed to win the support of the extremist groups in her power struggle against Nawaz Sharif, the opposition leader, which meant that she was more interested in wooing them than in bringing them to heel at the bargaining table. She also feared the fundamentalists, who had reportedly been behind an attempt to assassinate her the previous year.

Another problem was that the fundamentalist leadership recently had accused Bhutto of pandering to U.S. interests. And they were right. Bhutto had long cultivated a good relationship with the United States, a superpower that could supply her country with military and scientific expertise and state-of-the-art technologies. Now, however, she was compelled to put a chill on that relationship. Clearly trapped between conflicting domestic and international pressures, Bhutto was in a political vise and might very well have had little, if any, real power over the Islamic fundamentalists. In light of all this, for the United States or any other country to strong-arm Pakistan regarding the hostages and risk losing ground on other issues, such as nuclear nonproliferation, appeared to be a futile and counterproductive strategy.

There were political analysts, however, who believed that the Pakistan government was faking its inability to control the extremists and that the United States simply wanted to accept such a view. One editorial writer in an Indian daily commented in late August: "If Al-Faran is only another name for Harkat-ul-Ansar and is controlled by the ISI [Pakistani intelligence bureau], then the U.S. refusal to even take cognizance of this possibility and let it be reflected in its dealings with Pakistan is directly increasing the risk to the hostages' lives."

For the United States, there were numerous mitigating circumstances, such as an ongoing drama about some F-16 fighter planes—
known as the Fighting Falcons—that Pakistan had purchased from the
United States and had never received. While Pakistani officials had paid
about $370 million for the aircraft, missile launchers, and other equip-
ment, the United States had reneged on the deal because Pakistan had
failed to meet the requirements of the 1990 Pressler Amendment,
which mandates that any nation receiving U.S. economic or military
aid be nuclear-free. This barred Pakistan from receiving U.S. arms until
the U.S. president had satisfied Congress that Pakistan did not have a
nuclear arms program. By the summer of 1995, not only was Pakistan
shopping at the military stores of other countries, but it was frustrated
and agitated with the United States over the F-16 fiasco.

There was also the possibility that the U.S. quest for Pakistani
cooperation in apprehending Mir Aimal Kansi, the alleged killer of
two CIA officials in January 1993, required just about as much pressure as the United States could exert on Pakistan at that moment in
time. It was in fact during June of 1995, a few weeks before Hutchings and the others were taken, that a special order was issued in the
United States: the Presidential Decision Directive, which calls for eliciting cooperation from foreign nations where terrorists and other suspected criminals reside. The directive was applied to Pakistan that
June to gain cooperation in finding Kansi. To press that country
again, at a time when the U.S. relationship with Pakistan was not as
stable as it once was—and would be again—might have been difficult.

"Face it," said one source close to the case. "Two murdered CIA
officials held a higher priority than one tourist in captivity whom
everyone believed would be set free by August, like the others had
been the summer before. At the time, there would have been no comparison between the seriousness of the cases, and if pressure was
brought to bear on Pakistan, it would be in the matter regarding the
CIA. . . . Later, the [U.S.] government did pressure Pakistan, but not
in the beginning part of the crisis. Of course some would tell you
that's when the pressure counted most."

As for pressing India, that was never easy. Since the United States
mouthed the policy of never dealing with terrorists, any U.S. attempt

to pressure India into making concessions, as previous Indian administrations had done, would have to be covert—certainly without the knowledge of the other G4 members.

At the same time, this was, after all, an age of intense globalization, and for most Western nations, economic interest in the vast Indian marketplace gave India a political advantage. In the United States, economics dictated the major foreign policy moves of the first year of the Clinton administration, such as the North American Free Trade Agreement and the rewriting of the General Agreement on Tariffs and Trade. There were those who liked to say—especially during Clinton's reelection campaign when the president was comparing himself to Teddy Roosevelt—that the new U.S. motto should be: Speak Softly and Carry a Business Card. Indeed, it was a time when the U.S. secretary of state, Warren Christopher, the chief U.S. negotiator in the talks that ended the Iranian hostage crisis in 1981, was openly talking about the role of business in U.S. foreign policy. In a July 1996 speech in Indonesia, Christopher said, "We are trying to put the bottom lines of American business on the front lines of American diplomacy. And I do believe that it is working."

India, with its 920 million people, has the largest middle class in the world, with 200 million potential consumers—an irresistible market, especially for utilities, transportation companies, and financial service institutions. As of 1995, there were only .8 telephones per 100 Indians—a vast, untapped market for telecommunications companies. By then, the United States was already India's number one foreign investor, and corporations such as AT&T, Ford, Coca-Cola, IBM, and General Electric had staked a claim. With the World Bank predicting that India would be the world's fourth largest economy by the year 2020, U.S. businesses saw cooperation between the two nations as a political imperative—crucial to the United States' financial well-being in the twenty-first century.

And, to be sure, by the summer of 1995, the animus that had characterized the interaction between New Delhi and Washington for years, like ice weighing down the branches of diplomacy, was vanishing. In its place, a bond, though a fragile one, had formed. In trying to hold hands with India, the United States faced a double challenge: moving beyond a tenuous, difficult Cold War relationship and overcoming what could be seen as blunders or mishaps in the early Clinton years.

The Cold War's end and Prime Minister Rao's stunning free-market, open-door policies, beginning in 1991, had forced the United States into a radical reassessment of its South Asia policy, moving it to focus on ways to ingratiate itself with India. But no sooner had the frosty diplomacy of the past begun to melt away than the Clinton administration came to power, sending a sudden chill over India once again. One of Clinton's first acts as president was to move Ambassador Thomas R. Pickering, one of the most highly respected of American career diplomats, from New Delhi, where he had served only a few months, to Moscow. And then Clinton allowed the post of U.S. ambassador to India to remain vacant for sixteen months—a blatant insult to the host nation. Meanwhile, an assistant secretary of state, Robin Raphael, caused an uproar in New Delhi by referring to Kashmir as a "disputed" territory—New Delhi believes Kashmir to be part of India—and by acknowledging the need to protect the human rights of civilian Kashmiris against the documented violence of Indian security forces. Such comments suggested to the Indians that the new administration in the United States was more sympathetic to the Kashmiri cause of self-determination than to India's claims to the region.

Indeed, that had been the U.S. stand throughout much of the fifty-year dispute. In the 1950s, Adlai Stevenson and other politicians had pushed for Kashmiri independence. At that time, Kashmir was a political pawn between the United States and the Soviet Union regarding their respective relationships with India and Pakistan. The Soviets backed India's claims to Kashmir, whereas the United States questioned them. In the 1960s, in response to Chinese aggression into South Asia, the United States pushed for a new round of talks over Kashmir. Again the United States did not accept India's vision of an automatic right to Kashmir. Then, in the early Clinton years, the president's emphasis on human rights and his criticism of abuses in Kashmir deeply offended New Delhi.

To take the chill out of the air, in the spring of 1994, newly appointed Deputy Secretary Strobe Talbott, on his inaugural trip, stopped first in India "to mend fences." Talbott spread the word that the U.S. position was to do everything in its power to effect a resolution between India and Pakistan over Kashmir. The United States, much like Prime Minister Rao himself, was running as fast as possible away from the politically damaging image of softness toward Kashmiri separatists. When it came to Kashmir, the United States was neutral at the very least and perhaps even leaning ever so slightly toward India.

But in late spring of 1995, the protean nature of the bond between the United States and India became suddenly apparent. The $2.8 billion Dabhol power project, headed by a U.S. consortium called Enron Corporation and known as the biggest U.S. investment in India, fell from grace in the eyes of Indian politicians. In the state where the project was located, a newly elected regime had scorned Enron, alleging corruption in the negotiation of the deal.

Throughout the months ahead, certain officials within the U.S. government would closely monitor the Enron problem. Even the U.S. president would get involved, as a *Time* magazine article would reveal two years later. In November 1995, President Clinton reportedly sent a note to his then chief of staff, Mack McLarty, with a newspaper clip about Enron and its difficulties. Interestingly, the Democratic National Committee received a $100,000 donation from Enron, which later denied the money was a repayment for any high-level favors or special pressure on the Indian government in its behalf. The project was reinstated in June 1996. And shortly after Ambassador Frank Wisner resigned from his post in New Delhi, in 1997, he was appointed to the Enron board.

In late June 1995, at a meeting in Santa Clara, California, the United States and India formed the U.S.-Indo Commercial Alliance. Ambassador Wisner told reporters that the alliance "is as clear a signal as the U.S. government has to say we think this is a good time to do business in India."

Then, a week or so before that fateful July 4 in Kashmir, the bond grew even stronger when Ambassador Wisner made his first trip to Kashmir. For most of his short visit, he attended meetings with political leaders, government officials, teachers and students, human rights activists, local merchants, and leaders of the All Parties Hurriyat Conference, the umbrella organization for the many groups of militants. He also made time to go shopping in Srinagar with his daughter, tour parts of the great Dal Lake, visit shrines, and spend time at a camp of Kashmiri migrants who had fled their homes because of violence. It was truly a mission of goodwill. In his talks with leaders, he lamented the suffering of the Kashmiri people and called for a peaceful resolution of the Kashmir dispute. He said that the friendship between India and the United States was growing fast and that "we will extend all possible help for a peaceful and political understanding of the situation [in Kashmir]." But in discussing the path toward such a resolution, Wisner appeared to be expressing a subtle tactical shift—one that was perhaps unintended, but which unfortunately incensed the insurgents.

He said repeatedly that the United States, though committed to peace in Kashmir, did not have a formula to attain it. The United States did, however, strongly support the Indian point of view on holding elections in Kashmir as set forth in the Indian Constitution. The problem with Wisner's comments stemmed from the fact that the Hurriyat leaders and the Kashmir separatists, as well as the Kashmir Chamber of Commerce and Trade, wanted the solution to evolve out of tripartite talks involving India, Pakistan, and the people of the state. These groups stressed that the people of Kashmir no longer had faith in elections alone to resolve the problem.

In 1994, the militants, protesting the election process, had stolen Srinagar's electoral rolls out of a government office and burned them. And in late spring 1995, the Hurriyat leaders had announced that their people would not participate in any election. One leader vowed to immolate himself in protest, saying: "If the world conscience will come forward, they can stop the Indian government in this so-called election process."

But Wisner told them that the elections must be the focus for now. At the same time, the Kashmiri governor, General K. V. Krishna Rao, reportedly told Wisner that the Kashmiri people were tired of the militancy and were longing for the return of normalcy.

In the days ahead, the U.S. ambassador's support of an election, as called for under the Indian Constitution, was viewed by Kashmiri sep-

aratists as well as Indian politicians as a step away from the earlier policy as expressed by Robin Raphael and others before her. The Indian
politicians hailed it as a victory, while the Kashmiri separatists railed
against it. One Kashmiri newspaper editorial read, "The fact that Mr.
Wisner has tried to canvass for the election process implies that the
U.S. now acknowledges however belatedly the finality of Kashmir's
accession to India. . . . Quite a long way the U.S. Administration has
had to travel to reach the point where Ambassador Wisner has advised
the Kashmiri leaders to participate in the election under the Indian
Constitution. Incidentally, the large-scale supply of arms which has for
the last four years helped the militants to augment their firepower
came via Pakistan from the stocks sent by the U.S., originally meant
for the Afghan Mujahideens to fight the Soviet forces, but quite a lot
of it later found its way to a whole host of desperadoes for the entire
area from Karachi to Kashmir. It is therefore refreshing to find the
U.S. ambassador advising the Kashmiri militants to participate in the
election after all the havoc that the American supply of deadly arms
has been playing in the region."

The shift was perceived by the separatists as a slap in the face. Some
observers even claimed that this was what provoked the riverbank kidnappings on July 4. On July 6 one British journalist wrote: "What
seems to have goaded the militants into grabbing a few hostages was a
well-publicised [sic] visit to Kashmir the week before by America's
outspoken ambassador in Delhi, Frank Wisner. Not only did Mr. Wisner go fly-fishing in a river tauntingly close to the militants, but his
statements after the trip angered many Kashmiris who were hoping,
irrationally, that the U.S. would arm-twist India into granting them
autonomy. Instead, Mr. Wisner claimed that Kashmiris were tired of
the militancy and that the Indian prime minister, Narasimha Rao,
should be encouraged in his plans to hold state elections."

At the same time, some newspaper commentaries blamed the
United States' erstwhile sympathy for the Kashmiri cause as the insti-
gation for the kidnappings. The United States had been "mollycod-
dling the separatist sentiment," wrote the *Hindu,* a weekly. The logic
was that the shift in policy would not have seemed so drastic to the
insurgents if the sympathy preceding it had not been so dramatic.

Whatever the reasoning, there were a multitude of rumors and opinions backing up the concept that the United States had somehow precipitated the incident and therefore should resolve it.

Behind the scenes and beyond the view of newspaper commentators, intelligence agents were culling evidence that pointed to the possibility that the abductions had been fortuitous. The militants, whose leaders were likely in the HUA, had been walking along the Lidder River, following it as they often did as a pathway through the valley, and they happened upon the flocks of tourists. A captured militant, in a confession in 1996, substantiated the theory, though he would later recant the confession. The militants, he said, had disobeyed their leader's instructions to kidnap foreign engineers in another region.

On the day of the abduction, July 4, the U.S. ambassador told the press, "I can think of no better way to celebrate our own independence day than to reaffirm the commitment of the U.S. to a long-term relationship with India that will serve our common interests and protect our common ideals."

The next day, Jane would deliver to the police in Pahalgam the note from the militants in the sealed envelope labeled: "For the American Government only. Accept our demands or face dire consequences. We are fighting against anti-Islamic forces. . . . Western countries are anti-Islam, and America is the biggest enemy of Islam."

By October, it was clear that if the standoff in northern India ended in tragedy, it would be difficult to focus the blame on any one agency, government, or individual. Such was the incredible complexity of the crisis. And as seasoned negotiators knew best, the outcomes in all such cases could not be predicted or controlled. The lives of captives blew with the moods, whims, desires, and even dreams of their captors as well as the policies of nations and the strategies of negotiators.

There is a general belief among law enforcement officers that in an investigation, most of the mistakes that come back to haunt them are made in the first few hours. It was an axiom that also applied to hostage crises, though "hours" would mean "days." The truth of the tenet was never more vividly revealed than it was in this case—when, in that single fateful moment on July 10, the Indian government made a blunder from which the negotiations might never recover. It asked the kidnappers to supply the names of all the militants whose release from prison they were demanding. It was a message of hope, like an arrow sent into the rebel camp. From that point on, the expectations of the rebels, already raised by India's recent history of occasional prisoner swaps for hostages, would be impossible to satisfy unless, of course, the Indians were prepared to trade jailed militants for hostages. For the kidnappers, now, nothing less would do. And their increased expectations intensified every challenge of the case, requiring a greater effort on everyone's part. Negotiators had to devise all sorts of strategies to try to offset the damage. And diplomatic moves were more critical than ever.

In the early stages, too, there was a problem, by some accounts, of the diplomats depending too much on Indian authorities to deal with the kidnappers. A few journalists commented that some of the diplomats were too new to their posts to have good, reliable contacts among the militant and religious groups in Kashmir and Pakistan, groups that could have helped in those immediate days after the abduction. It was such contacts that former journalist David Housego set into gear after the kidnapping of his son and David Mackie in Kashmir the previous summer.

By October, around the time of the 100th day of Hutchings's captivity, there were news stories about weary rebels on the verge of capitulation. Negotiators like to use national holidays, holy days, or significant passages, such as the 100th day—basically any day that can be defined as an occasion—to persuade kidnappers to end a standoff. The occasion gives the kidnappers a way out, an opportunity to end it, save face, and get publicity for it. Toward this end, on this particular occasion, officials were telling the press, and negotiators were trying to persuade the rebels, that the Al-Faran had already gotten plenty out of the ordeal. Once again, they stressed that the international press was shining a spotlight on the struggle in Kashmir and that the kidnappings had cut a considerable chunk of profits out of the 1995 tourism season in northern India—a tough blow to the militants' enemy, India. This was progress, one official told the press, adding, "There is much speculation now about an imminent release. They [the rebels] should be satisfied that they have accomplished something."

But they were not—especially when they heard the latest press leak. Around the time of Day 100, newspapers ran a story that the Indian government had agreed to free two of the fifteen detained militants who were on the Al-Faran list and who were supposedly scheduled to be released soon under Indian law. One article revealed that the designated two had been shifted from their prison cells to detention centers in the Kashmir Valley while the details of an imminent swap were being discussed.

But such a swap would never happen. Because of the ruling regime in India and its political concerns about appearing to be too soft on militants, most officials in New Delhi were hesitant to release any men named on the insurgents' list, much less ones who were high on the list. And these men, the ones rumored to be released soon, were apparently among the top three. Throughout the ordeal, there was some debate within the government on what to do. Officials were also discussing the possible leverage to be gained from changing the accommodations—"the place and manner of the incarceration," so said one source—of certain jailed militants. Hence they had moved two men out of their jail cells to detention centers.

When the talks hit the media in a distorted form, however, the Indian government panicked, according to a source close to the case. Whatever possible progress might have been made in further discussions regarding such a swap was now lost. "To release men so high on the list would have been too embarrassing for the government; they worried that it would give the masses the wrong impression," said the source. "And they literally raced away from it after it was exposed, never to return to the notion, though you must understand that the [Indian] government, the ones in the government who did not favor any level of concession, may have used the occasion of the leak to force everyone away from the idea of such a swap, ever."

And so it was that the 100th day of captivity for the prisoners of the Al-Faran had begun, like all the other ninety-nine days, with the hope that this would be *the* day. And, for everyone involved, it would end with the stinging realization that the earth had turned on its axis one full revolution once again without the news of imminent release.

16

There has never been a good time or place to be a hostage; but for Hutchings, Mangan, Wells, and Hasert, being kidnapped in 1995 in Kashmir was bad timing indeed. The political landscape was as precarious and unpredictable as the jagged, irregular topography. And prospects for a resolution seemed bleak. It was a time when the Indian government was dodging an image of being too soft on militants, a time when the ruling regime in Pakistan was trying to mollycoddle the extremists who might be supporting the Al-Faran, and a time when neither India nor Pakistan was kissing the feet of Americans. And, after much deliberation and expensive deployment of military troops out of the G4 nations, a rescue had been ruled out. Concessions, scorned as a problem, not a solution, were political venom for the Indian government and the G4. There wasn't even publicity for the cause—that is, the cause of the hostages. No one was drumming up a public crusade that might then put extra pressure on the governments. No yellow ribbons from sea to shining sea for Donald Hutchings.

In the United States, the 1990s appeared to be the decade of the forgotten hostage. There were at least nine other Americans in captivity during the autumn of 1995, and the snatching of foreigners and nationals was occurring ever more frequently worldwide as the ranks of kidnappers increased and as kidnap gangs slowly expanded beyond the prey of diplomats and wealthy, top-level executives. It was as if hostages had been swept into a dark corner of foreign policy, hidden in the shadows of the economic goals of an era.

The hostage families were advised to keep a low profile, to protect the delicate nature of the negotiations. And, of course, having had no experience with kidnappings, they did what they believed would protect their loved ones. What they didn't know and couldn't know was that the issue of publicity versus silence in kidnapping cases had been debated since the media became a force.

Undoubtedly, silence in the early stages of a kidnap crisis is often important. Publicity raises the perceived value of the hostages, and this inevitably has the effect of raising the kidnappers' demands and prolonging the hostages' captivity. In the abduction of an American in Ecuador in early 1997, the captor's demand of $1 million advanced to $2 million the day after the first blitz of international coverage. Without publicity, the rebels might begin to believe that the kidnapping is a futile endeavor and then end the ordeal. Keeping a case out of the press can also help negotiators, who might want to use the promise of publicity in exchange for the hostages if international attention is one of the kidnappers' goals. And leaks to the press, especially in the first hours, days, and weeks, can disrupt critical communications, as many cases have demonstrated. Leaks can even endanger the lives of the hostages, particularly if the leak agitates a violent or deranged captor. In the Kashmir incident, there had already been several damaging leaks. There was the one regarding the so-called ransom, back in September, sending the rebels into high-gear rage over the image of being money-hungry mercenaries, rather than rebels hungering only for the freedom of Kashmir, and then the one on the 100th day of captivity.

But while leaks can kill, there are also dangers in news embargoes and low-profile strategies, particularly in a prolonged ordeal involving ordinary citizens without political clout. Silence can lead to government passivity and can protect political leaders from the damaging fall-out that often occurs in hostage crises. When hostages are unknown individuals, as in Kashmir, there is little publicity following news of the abduction, unless, of course, a victim's family initiates it. In a case in 1996 in which seven French monks were kidnapped and killed, silence was one of the culprits, subsequent studies revealed. "The first lesson to be drawn was that since the kidnapping of anonymous monks stirred only moderate media interest, the government was slow to really take up the case, losing precious time," read one intelligence report. The other big problem in the case was the size of the team of people trying to resolve it, the report said. With twenty to thirty people involved, it was hard to make decisions and there were rivalries and personal grudges.

In the 1994 abduction of Kim Housego and David Mackie in Kashmir, the quick release, after seventeen days, was attributed in large part to the unrelenting press coverage. Kim's father, David, a former journalist, kept the story alive in the press through his many newspaper contacts while he utilized his political contacts among insurgents and Kashmiris to find the rebels and negotiate the freedom of the hostages. Housego firmly believed that he got his son out because of the media coverage. In a televised BBC interview in 1996, Housego said, "It seemed to me the only thing to do was to create maximum publicity about it.

"It's only the relatives who fundamentally care about the hostages. Clearly, governments are committed to it as well, but they have all sorts of other objectives. And I think it's only the relatives who systematically, persistently keep up the pressure."

In the same BBC show, *The Big Story: Search for the Forgotten Hostages,* a reporter pressed a British Foreign Office official, Dr. Liam Fox, on the issue of media coverage in the Kashmir case. The interview took place on the 500th day of captivity for the Kashmir hostages, and the show had just revealed that the British Foreign Office had asked the families of the British hostages to say little, if anything, to the press. The conversation went like this:

BBC: In light of the fact that the hostages have now been 500 days in captivity, do you regret that decision?

Foreign Office: I don't think that the fate of the hostages is dependent, frankly, on what happens in the media. I think it's naive to think that in a country like the United Kingdom where the media is quite powerful, to assume that that is equally true—well, you've been to Kashmir. You know what it's like. It's not the same world. We're dealing with somewhere very different.

BBC: But there was another case: David Housego and his son. He definitely went for the publicity option and had his son released in 17 days.

FO: Obviously, I am not able to go into the details about why we see that as a very different case. Except to say that we believe it was not an intentional kidnapping.

BBC: But the fact remains that Housego succeeded in 17 days and in 500 days you have failed.

FO: Whether the tactics applied in the media [in the Housego case] were the defining difference, I don't think anyone can say.

Sometime during the Kashmir ordeal, the *Los Angeles Times* ran an article about the hostages of the 1990s, calling them "America's forgotten people." "Their plight is in contrast to the seizure of the U.S. embassy in Tehran in 1979," the article said, "when the detention of 52 Americans held this country hostage for 444 days and elevated the yellow ribbon to the status of a national symbol."

Implying that the government was less than vigilant about Americans abroad, the article quoted families and friends of hostages who had tried to enlist the government's help without much result. "The public may believe that if an American is kidnapped you can go to the embassy and get help. That may be true of State Department and military folks," said Scott Ross, an attorney for New Tribes Mission, a Protestant evangelical group whose three missionaries Mark Rich, Rick Tenenoff, and Dave Mankins were abducted in Panama in 1993. "But for private individuals it's up to that person, his family or his employer to work through the situation."

The article suggested also that kidnapping and terrorism were so common now as to effectively lose their marquee value. Snatching for money or for the release of jailed comrades no longer captivated politicians or the public. It was simply part of the international terrain; in some parts of the world, such as Russia, it was even a routine part of doing business.

The State Department, in defense of its policy, fired off a letter in response to the *Times* article: " 'Hostages Languish as Public Interest Wanes' misses the mark in depicting the U.S. government as unresponsive to the families of kidnap victims. The safety of Americans abroad is the Department of State's paramount concern, and while current kidnapping cases may receive less media coverage than in the past, we have never stopped doing everything possible to resolve them. But we must deal with the realities of international law and rely on local law enforcement officials, who also face constraints on their action."

The letter went on to say that the State Department warns Americans of potential dangers through travel advisories and when an American is kidnapped, the agency gives such cases a top priority, serving as a liaison with foreign law enforcement and foreign diplomats. The letter stressed that the U.S. government "does not pay ransom because that encourages further hostage-taking. The nature of hostage-taking has changed dramatically. Rarely are kidnappings undertaken now with the goal of influencing U.S. government policy. The great majority of hostage incidents today involve demands for monetary ransom. This may explain the change in the public attention given these deplorable incidents."

Indeed, what the State Department was saying was true. Kidnappings were no longer about military-political alignments for or against the Soviet Union, and kidnappers were rarely, if ever, within the control of governments. But perhaps the State Department letter didn't go far enough. Not only had the nature of hostage-taking changed dramatically, but also the nature of governments. In every non-Communist nation, governments were adjusting to a world without a single enemy. It was a new, complex, chaotic world, and in response, government agencies were redefining themselves. Perhaps what was really happening

was that governments simply didn't have the power to resolve kidnappings in the new era, that they were applying old patterns of behavior
to new circumstances. In the end, what the captivity of Donald Hutchings and his fellow hostages revealed, perhaps more than anything, was
just how independent and self-protective citizens abroad in the new age
had to be.

17

As winter was approaching, there were painful questions to consider. Just how long, for example, should the families remain in India? It was clear that the ordeal was a marathon, not a sprint. Endurance was the word of the day—for the families as well as the captives.

It was common now, more than ever perhaps, to be thinking about past cases. How had other hostages won their freedom? After how many months, or years? What had the families done to hasten the process? Had they helped the government? Had they always followed orders? Had they privately hired mercenaries or orchestrated their own rescues? Had they commandeered the media to pressure their governments? For over 200 years, the families of American hostages taken abroad had considered such questions.

Few Americans kidnapped overseas—except in the course of war—had ever been killed. In recent times, three Americans were killed in Lebanon: William Buckley in 1985, Peter Kilburn in 1986, and William Higgins in 1989. Usually, however, there was a way out. The journey toward resolution was often long and arduous, and the path was littered with sacrifices, compromises, and occasional acts of chicanery. But there had been successful military and police rescues, covert bargains, hard-fisted diplomacy, and ransoms paid by families, by friends, by corporations, and even, secretly, at least once by Congress. These were the ways that had freed hostages of the past. But none of this was happening in Kashmir.

That the United States held firm to a no-concessions policy was the honorable route. No one could criticize such a stand. After all, such a critic could be viewed as adhering to policies promoting terrorism. Nonetheless, it was a policy that had proven impractical in past cases. And it was a departure from U.S. actions throughout the twentieth century, for this had been a time of conciliation and concession. Despite the fiery retaliatory rhetoric of presidents such as Ronald Reagan, Harry Truman, and Teddy Roosevelt, the truth was that almost every twentieth-century U.S. president had had to bargain with kidnappers in some way for the release of an American hostage.

The U.S. experience with kidnappings abroad was a hodgepodge of policies and strategies, whether the snatchers were freelance terrorists and criminals or political groups sanctioned by foreign governments. To be sure, the United States, in coping with such crises, stumbled long before it learned to walk. Its first hostage crisis, which could have been scripted as a comic farce, was a lesson in how not to negotiate a kidnapping.

The drama began in July of 1785 when Barbary pirates from the coast of North Africa captured two U.S. merchant vessels and took twenty-one men into captivity, to be released only after the payment of a ransom. Thomas Jefferson and John Adams, the two U.S. officials in charge of securing the release, hired a Connecticut sea captain named John Lamb to travel to Algiers. Congress authorized Lamb—the nation's first hostage negotiator—to pay $4,700 for the return of the hostages, who were kept like animals, barely fed, and regularly beaten. It took Lamb more than six months to get from the United States to Algiers, largely because he stopped in Spain on the way for what appeared to be a vacation. Upon his arrival in Africa, he offered the dey of Algiers $10,000 for the release of the Americans. The dey then demanded $50,000; Lamb countered with $30,000, which was

$25,300 above Congress's limit. Lamb, whose negotiation skills left much to be desired, could not persuade the dey to budge from the $50,000 figure. And fearing the wrath of Congress, Lamb fled Algiers for Spain, leaving the hostages on a veritable death row, the case unresolved, and Congress uninformed about the so-called negotiated ransom.

Jefferson turned next to a French religious group called the Order of the Holy Trinity and Redemption of Captives. This group was in many ways a precursor of the private sector kidnap negotiators of the 1980s and 1990s, who hire themselves out to corporations, wealthy individuals, and even governments needing professional negotiators to secure the release of hostages. For a fee, this holy order had for years been involved in negotiating the return of hostages of all nationalities from the many prisons along the Barbary Coast. But in this particular case, they ultimately failed. And so by 1793, ten of the original twenty-one hostages had died of bubonic plague and other ravages of a long captivity. At that time, too, more than 100 additional seamen were kidnapped; three years later, most were released, in addition to the eleven men who had been held for more than a decade.

The ransom, eventually negotiated by a U.S. envoy, had by then reached $585,000 plus various naval supplies and presents—for a total value of more than $1 million. With an incentive like that, the pirating did not end in 1797 when most of the hostages arrived home. By 1815, Barbary pirates had kidnapped at least 700 American seamen. Private groups and the U.S. government had managed to secure the release of most of the men, though at least twenty-eight died in captivity.

In the early part of the nineteenth century, a very young United States, fueled by a heightened sense of power and a surge of nationalism in the aftermath of the War of 1812, began to rely on force and military prowess in dealing with kidnappers abroad. The government's response throughout the nineteenth century was militarily aggressive and retaliatory until, ironically, the administration of Theodore Roosevelt. Roosevelt, the bellicose wielder of the big stick whose every instinct pushed him toward the use of force in facing foes of the United States, established a new precedent in the handling of kidnappings: conciliation.

Whatever the State Department and President Clinton were analyzing in relation to the Kashmir incident, they would have done well to revisit the actions of Roosevelt—the man in whose image Bill Clinton claimed to be modeling himself—in the case of Ellen Stone, which effectively set the standard in the twentieth century for every president who faced a hostage crisis. The ordeal began on September 3, 1901, when a gang of Macedonian rebels, seeking U.S. money and support in Macedonia's struggle for independence from Turkey, disguised themselves as the Turkish enemy and kidnapped an American missionary from Massachusetts working in Turkey and nine others. They quickly released seven, keeping the missionary, who was fifty-five-year-old Ellen Stone, and Katarina Tsilka, a trained nurse from Bulgaria who happened to be five months pregnant. By posing as Turks, the rebels hoped to turn U.S. sentiment against Turkey and thus elicit support in the United States for their independence movement.

For six months, the Macedonian rebels dragged Stone and Tsilka across jagged, mountainous terrain, as Kashmiri rebels had done to Hutchings and his fellow captives. Often Stone and her captors were barely one jump ahead of Turkish troops crawling along the craggy slopes in search of them, in the way that the Kashmiri kidnappers found themselves dodging the Indian soldiers.

Needing money to fund their movement, the Macedonian kidnappers demanded a ransom payment for Stone. Almost immediately the Missions Board in Boston, fearing that the Massachusetts native could not withstand the rigors of captivity, agreed to consider it.

Roosevelt was facing the quandary that would plague his fellow presidents throughout the century: how to devise a policy that would at once save the hostage's life, prevent future abductions, and present a strong international image for his country. What was different in the twentieth century—setting Roosevelt apart from his predecessors—and what would add another nettlesome problem to the already vexing ordeal of kidnapping was the change in the coverage and dissemination of news. Altering the speed and manner in which public opinion was molded in the United States, it was this change that would affect how every president, from Roosevelt on, reacted to every hostage crisis—and all crises for that matter. This technological revolution launched by the Linotype machine, which made rapid typesetting and mass circulation dailies possible, was propelled through the twentieth century by the advent of radio and the explosive growth of television. And the new informed citizenry, taking the side of humanity in the cause to free the hostages, would usher in an era of policies of negotiation and bargains, replacing the tough approach of the nineteenth century.

Among the thorns of Roosevelt's dilemma was the fact that Stone was a woman and that, according to the accepted social canons of the day, she required special consideration. In general, Roosevelt believed that there were certain risks inherent in being a missionary in the wild hinterlands of the world, and that because the missions were not sanctioned by the American public, the government had no obligation to bail the missionaries out of their difficulties.

"If a man goes out as a missionary," Roosevelt once wrote, "he has no kind of business to venture to wild lands with the expectation that somehow the government will protect him as well as if he had stayed at home. If he is fit for his work, he has no more right to complain of what may befall him than a soldier has in getting shot. But it is impossible to adopt this standard about women."

What the president ultimately did in helping to settle the dispute was hardly in keeping with his sabor-rattling style. To avoid the appearance of groveling and caving in to the kidnappers, he encouraged the missionaries to raise the ransom privately, with the promise that Congress would reimburse them later. But no sooner had the government and the missionaries reached an agreement on a plan to free Stone than the U.S. general consul in Constantinople, Charles Dickinson, following an old custom in which U.S. representatives abroad dictated their own policies, decided that if the kidnapping was indeed successful and the ransom sums were paid, the precedent would make life intolerably dangerous for any Westerner abroad.

Dickinson declined even to entertain the idea of paying a ransom, regardless of his president's commitment to such a payment. One of Dickinson's notions was to intervene with Bulgarian troops, using them to set a trap for the kidnappers. But knowing that such a plan could endanger the life of Stone, the U.S. government quickly blocked that scheme, as it did Dickinson's second idea, which was to bribe the rebels guarding Stone.

Finally, the government appointed emissaries to negotiate a ransom-for-hostages swap with the kidnappers. In the end, with hundreds of Turkish troops lurking in the hills around them, the emissaries found the brigands and handed over $66,000 in gold—$34,000 less than the kidnappers' demand. A few weeks later, the now-three captives—the baby was born three months into the captivity—were released.

"The only real alternative available to Roosevelt was to ignore the kidnapping, thereby making it a non-event requiring no American response," wrote historian Russell D. Buhite in his 1995 book *Lives at Risk: Hostages and Victims in American Foreign Policy.* "In a sense, this crisis foreshadowed the difficulties the United States would experience with terrorist groups in the latter half of the twentieth century. World power makes a nation susceptible to terrorist acts when indigenous groups assume that a particular country can make a difference in local or regional disputes. In 1901, the United States was a world-class power economically, although not militarily, but the [Macedonian rebels] thought (correctly as it turned out) that the American response would influence events in Macedonia. As in later cases, it would be difficult to determine responsibility and more difficult still to act once blame had been assigned. To use force—the instinctive response for Roosevelt and many of his successors—would result in the killing of the hostages. To do nothing, as the Stone kidnapping proved and as later episodes would further demonstrate, would be impossible given the public pressure."

When faced with their own hostage crises, U.S. presidents after Roosevelt, in most cases, sought solutions through bargaining. Presidents Wilson and Harding provided food and medical relief to the Kremlin to gain the release of Americans held in the Soviet Union. President Truman was known for his use of force from Hiroshima to South Korea. But in a year-long hostage crisis, in which Consul General Angus Ward, his wife, and staff were detained by Chinese Communists at the U.S. consulate in Manchuria, he found himself helpless to do anything but negotiate to obtain their release. And when the North Koreans seized the crew of the USS *Pueblo,* the American spy ship working the Korean coast, President Lyndon Johnson mulled over every conceivable military option until finally, in order to ensure the crew's safe return, he agreed to sign a phony apology and an even more counterfeit admission of guilt.

If Roosevelt had a twentieth-century presidential rival on the Richter scale of bellicosity, at least after the days of Truman, surely it was Ronald Reagan, whose rise to power ushered in a no-negotiation "swift and effective retribution" policy toward terrorists. And, to be sure, his chest-thumping rhetoric got a big boost early in his presidential career with the release of U.S. Brigadier General James Dozier in 1982. The irony was that Reagan and his policy had little, if anything, to do with Dozier's rescue.

On December 17, 1981, two members of the then-notorious Red Brigades, disguised as plumbers, gained entry to Dozier's flat in Verona, Italy. They were followed by six others, who kidnapped Dozier and took him to another flat, where he was forced into a pup tent wearing chains, a hood, and earphones blaring out loud rock music. Reagan dispatched a cadre of advisers to work with the Italian police. Ross Perot, at the behest of Oliver North and the National Security Council, put up $500,000 as a reward for information. And among other strategies, the CIA sent in a psychic to locate Dozier and his captors. In the end, U.S. intelligence did help, but it was the Italian police—with capabilities considerably enhanced in response to the 1977 kidnapping and murder of statesman Aldo Moro—who ended Dozier's captivity, after forty-two days, by pulling off a brilliant rescue. The key to the resolution was the arrest of several members of the Brigades, including one who was apparently the driver of the car for the Dozier kidnapping and who assisted in locating the hideout.

In the Middle East, Reagan wasn't so lucky. In 1985, the year terrorists snatched seven Americans in Lebanon and hijacked a TWA jet, he learned about the implacable difficulties inherent in trying to pursue a no-negotiation policy in a kidnapping, that most vexing of terrorist acts. In June that year, the hijackers of TWA Flight 847 asked Israel to release jailed Shiites in return for the hostages, including dozens of Americans. At that time, Reagan told reporters, "America will never make concessions to terrorists. To do so would only invite more terrorism. Nor will we ask nor pressure any other government to do so. Once we head down that path, there will be no end to it—no end to the suffering of innocent people, no end to the ransom all civilized nations must pay."

He also said that the United States would not "interfere" with Israel's decision on whether to release the prisoners. With this comment, Reagan placed the public spotlight on Israel. If prisoners were released, it would be Israel who had conceded to terrorist demands, not the United States. And Israel had done this before; in 1983, for example, it reportedly swapped 4,500 guerrillas and 100 jailed Palestine Liberation Organization members for six Israelis. Meanwhile, behind the scenes, maneuvers were in the works to pressure Israel into such a move. Then Prime Minister Menachem Begin made a brilliant political move. He announced that Israel would release the prisoners only if *the United States* requested such a move. This stymied the under-the-table moves the Americans were planning. Now, if the prisoners were released, it would always be assumed that it was U.S. pressure on Israel that precipitated it. The key to the dilemma lay partly in the fact that Israel had been releasing Lebanese prisoners before the hijacking. In the end, to avoid giving the impression that a link existed between the release of American hostages and the freeing of Lebanese prisoners, Israel said it would not discharge any more prisoners until the American hostages were freed.

"This indirect negotiation," wrote the scholar Buhite, "allowed the administration to maintain an appearance of non-negotiation but did not fool anybody, least of all Middle Eastern terrorists. American involvement in the bargaining, although behind the scenes, proved critical in the successful conclusion of the deal."

Throughout the TWA crisis, the Reagan administration hoped to gain the freedom of the Beirut hostages and the TWA hostages using the same maneuverings. But that didn't happen, and eventually Reagan was forced into the star-crossed arms-for-hostage deals to free the Americans in Lebanon. "President Reagan, like his predecessors," wrote Buhite, "had come to understand, despite his rhetoric to the contrary, that deals with terrorists were often necessary."

Just as Roosevelt, in the case of Ellen Stone, had set the standard for the twentieth century, what was happening in the 1990s could be setting the tone for the new era. Perhaps the Kashmir crisis would be the witching hour for the hostages of the twenty-first century, leaving behind the retaliatory ways of the nineteenth century and the conciliatory ways of the twentieth century and ushering in a new era—in which governments held back, citizens abroad had to be more cautious than ever, and negotiators (in both the public and private sectors) assumed more responsibility for the release of hostages.

18

October 11, the 100th day of captivity for Donald Hutchings and his fellow captives was the 559th day for Minnesotan Raymond Rising somewhere in the jungles of Colombia. It was the 299th day for the Emberlys, the couple from Peterborough, Canada, also in Colombia. And for the bird-watcher, British Sargeant Timothy Cowley, whose search for the Andean duck was interrupted by kidnappers in August, it was the 59th day of captivity in the Andes Mountains.

On that same day, lawyers for Thomas Hargrove, the science writer from Texas, were signing off on a $100 million lawsuit against a kidnap negotiation firm, an insurance company, and Hargrove's employer for allegedly neglecting their responsibilities to gain his swift release from Colombian guerrillas. Seven weeks earlier, on the morning of August 22, after 334 days in captivity, Hargrove had walked out of the mountains in exchange for two ransoms totaling at least $250,000.

Meanwhile, at FBI headquarters in Washington, D.C., an unprecedented meeting was taking place throughout the day. The topic: the astounding surge of kidnappings in Colombia. As of October, there were an estimated eighty-five foreigners held in captivity there, as well as hundreds of Colombian ranchers, lawyers, and businessmen. Eight were Americans. And the incidence of kidnappings in countries bordering Colombia was on the rise.

A thunder of panic was rolling through the Colombian government. For the first time ever, it had asked the FBI to advise and assist in trying to end the devastating wave of kidnappings that had gripped the nation for more than five years and that seemed to be escalating almost daily. Moreover, in September, the government had created a new post, the national antikidnap coordinator. Its first appointee, Dr. Alberto Villamizar, whose mother and daughter were abducted by drug traffickers in 1990, had flown to Washington for the conference that October day. During the discussions, he would stun his fellow conferees as he explained how Colombia's crackdown on cocaine cartels and cultivators was spawning a class of unemployed drug operatives who were now perpetrating other crimes, including kidnapping, to make a living.

The meeting began at exactly 9 A.M. in a large, nondescript room with a small table for coffee and croissants at one end, a row of vinyl-covered chairs standing guard at the other, and a common conference table with chairs in the middle. The gathering, however, was far from ordinary. In attendance were FBI agents from the Critical Incident Negotiation Team, known as CINT, and from the bureau's counterterrorism unit, including one hostage negotiator who was between stints in Kashmir. There were also State Department analysts and counterterrorism experts. And there were representatives from the burgeoning industry of private kidnap consultants, including the London-based Control Risks Group; Corporate Risk International, based in Fairfax, Virginia; Kroll Associates, out of New York; former CIA agent Mike Ackerman's firm from Miami; and Crisis Consultant International, a California-based group that had helped to free missionaries from captivity.

It was a room filled with inherent conflicts. The private groups were competing fiercely in a market on the brink of a boom. Control Risks Group (CRG), the most established, had sued one of the industry's newcomers, Corporate Risk International (CRI), for trademark infringement. The similar acronyms were intended to confuse clients, the older firm argued; a jury ruled in favor of CRI. Kroll, meanwhile, was trying to snatch a king's ransom's worth of the market for kidnap cases from the others, mainly CRG, its leading competitor. There was the pervasive friction between public and private sector policies governing the resolution of kidnapping cases. And there was interagency friction, to say the least, between the State Department and the FBI regarding attitudes and procedures for getting Americans out of trouble abroad.

The government preached no ransoms, no bargains, and no concessions, while the private negotiators effectively made their living from bargaining for the release of hostages through concessions— often by facilitating the payment of ransoms for their clients. The business of private negotiation was thriving by filling the gaps, often dangerous ones, created by governments' inabilities to protect the ever-growing numbers of citizens abroad. The private companies issued daily risk reports on the countries where their clients lived and worked, and in the event of a crisis—such as a kidnapping—they dispatched kidnap consultants who were on call twenty-four hours a day. During this period, the State Department's budget was diminishing annually, with embassy staffs shrinking in some parts of the world and consulate posts disappearing in others. The agency's ability to protect Americans abroad, despite all its rhetoric about having a mandate to do so, had become increasingly starved by federal bean counters. To be sure, State sensed that this time-honored mandate was slipping from its once-gargantuan grasp, thus introducing that other conflict in evidence that autumn day: FBI versus State Department.

Indeed, State was beginning to squirm as the FBI, in its ever-expanding international role, encroached on the traditional domain of diplomats. It was a conflict that would heat up during the next few years as both agencies became involved in more international kidnapping cases. Far deeper than the issue of one agency invading the turf of another, the problem was becoming one of policy. When these cases arose, the State Department typically followed the strict U.S. policy prohibiting concessions of any kind to kidnappers, whether they were terrorists or criminals—groups that were sometimes indistinguishable.

U.S. embassies often apprised families of hostages that this was U.S. policy. Negotiating with terrorists encouraged the spread of terrorism. But, from the point of view of negotiators, such strict adherence to the policy in each and every case limited the possibilities for devising creative strategies for the release of hostages. The heart of the problem, according to one government source, was that kidnapping was already a huge problem. "The fox is already in the henhouse," he said. And a rigid refusal to bargain with kidnappers—a position that could lead to the death of the hostage—would not stop a problem that in some regions was out of control. Better law enforcement, less poverty, more attention to demobilized soldiers. These might be the ways to stop the spread of kidnappings. The sacrifice of one or two American lives was not going to stop the crime.

"The irony here is that negotiation can lead to the ultimate deterrence of the crime, which is apprehension and arrest," said the government source. "What the State Department wants isn't practical. They worry only about how our government appears to the world. It's political. But the reality is that only through negotiation do we stand a chance of identifying the kidnappers. The dialogue provides an interaction that we hope to exploit. Being engaged in such a way does not equate to capitulation."

The debate, which seemed academic at first, had become more serious as more incidents occurred. For an embassy to tell families of kidnap victims that it was the policy of the U.S. government not to negotiate with terrorists and then to hold their hands while putting the fate of the hostage's life into the hands of the host government was not fair, some agents asserted. For one thing, U.S. policy did not prohibit the families of hostages from doing everything in their power to free their loved ones from the grip of kidnappers. The no-concessions policy applied only to U.S. personnel—staffers who knew when they took their jobs that there was potential danger in working overseas for the U.S. government. Citizens who had enough money to hire private kidnap consultants or who had jobs with companies that retained such expertise knew about this fine line.

But between these worlds of the business executive and the U.S. government employee, there were plenty of tourists, employees of small companies, and self-employed workers such as freelance geologists, who relied totally on their government to help them get out of trouble abroad. These were the people that the FBI was trying to help, the people who were neither wealthy enough to hire private negotiators nor protected by the war chest of a large firm. The people who fell through the cracks.

For years, business executives, with the help of companies such as CRG, had been handling kidnappings on their own, and the State Department had given them wide latitude to do so. When ransoms were paid, for example, companies sometimes issued statements attributing the hostages' freedom to all sorts of other reasons. The kidnappers, a statement might say, had grown tired of the care and feeding of captives and so released the hostages to end the ordeal. When it came to the kidnapping of ordinary citizens, negotiators felt that the government must do all it can to get them out of trouble. If the families of hostages wanted to negotiate with the kidnappers, and even to pay a ransom, then the FBI felt legally and morally obligated to offer its expertise about the best way of doing this. After all, U.S. citizens had the right to pay ransoms within U.S. borders. And kidnappers were often caught while collecting ransoms. Ransoms were even tax-deductible in the United States, as "theft" losses.

The simple truth was that the agents working the cases abroad were beginning to see that current policy was based more on the chest-thumping, get-tough rhetoric of politicians than on the evolving exigencies of the international frontier in the post–Cold War era. The policy that embassies applied to kidnappings was the U.S. terrorist policy, and clearly part of the problem was that kidnappers of the new era were not always terrorists. The State Department seemed to be talking about terrorists, and the FBI was talking about kidnappers—all kidnappers. No one in either agency wanted the United States or any other government to open the floodgates to terrorists or criminals by swapping weapons for hostages or by changing foreign policy in response to kidnappers' demands. But there had to be a middle ground between such extreme concessions—what law enforcement called "substantive concessions"—and no concessions at all. It was along this middle ground, where creative resolutions could be sought, that the FBI stood—and more firmly each day.

For the first time since the United States had adopted a policy of not paying ransoms in cases of political kidnappings, FBI agents were bravely questioning it. In the age of globalization, when unprecedented numbers of Americans were traveling, working, and living abroad, was it still practical? And could the wording simply be changed from *no concessions* to *no substantive concessions*? Just that simple change would legitimize negotiating and bargaining and give agents more latitude in dealing with kidnappers.

"The reality is that we long ago lost the ability to play tough with the bad guys. Kidnappings are out of control. Why should an American lose his or her life because of an outdated policy?" said an individual within the FBI who requested anonymity.

And another said, "It's like the movie *Jaws*, when the politicians wouldn't close the beaches despite the sharks feeding on the local citizens. And the cops shouting the reality of it. Here, too, the politicians call the shots. They don't want to see things as they really are because that requires change and possibly the loss of votes. Meanwhile it's up to law enforcement to protect people in any way possible until the politicians see the light. The problem is that it usually takes a terrible tragedy for that to happen."

But for one intriguing day in that room on Pennsylvania Avenue, differences gave way to the singular challenge at hand: the kidnapping plague and how to stop it. The morning began with a presentation on the history of the FBI's "extraterritorial investigations," followed by an FBI negotiator speaking on the agency's response to overseas kidnappings. After a brief break, the private consultants spoke about their responsibilities in kidnap cases and their strategies. In the afternoon, State Department representatives talked of the "Embassy Response to Kidnap Matters" and "Consular Functions and Responsibilities." For the rest of the day, the focus was on Colombia.

Despite the uneasy peace among various participants, the meeting, by its very existence, broke new ground. There was, of course, fresh information exchanged. But more profound by far was the fact that the FBI had invited private sector experts in for consultation. As one attending observer put it: "The fact that State was there at the FBI that day spoke volumes about the seriousness of the problem at hand, that is, kidnappings, and about the apparent new flexibility and openness at the FBI. Also the ability of both agencies, when called upon, to work together. But the fact that the FBI was bringing in private experts signaled a near revolution. The FBI wanted to hear from the people who had been where they were heading. They wanted to get it right, and so they were amassing as much information, outside and in, before developing a strategy. It was different, to say the least."

For an agency with a dogmatic culture whose style was to cling to the past like a pit bull clutching a T-bone, change was atypical. But there were changes aplenty—and big ones. According to one agent, the FBI was trying to shift its attitude from "reactive" to "proactive"; from simply reacting to crises to anticipating and preparing for them. The meeting that day was a good example.

Another sign of change was the long-deserved recognition of the bureau's hostage negotiation unit. Rambo had apparently moved to the back of the class and the Roy Ramms of the world were now teaching. One of the new mottoes around the halls of the FBI was: Restraint Does Not Equate to Weakness.

Only a disaster could compel an agency so stuck in its ways even to consider changing. And in this case the disaster had happened two years earlier in Waco, Texas, when at least seventy-eight members of the Branch Davidian cult were killed in a fire after a fifty-one-day standoff. How the Waco incident was handled, or rather mishandled, had been the subject of a congressional hearing that autumn. The tragedy was blamed largely on poor communications between the FBI's Hostage Rescue Team (HRT) and the CINT negotiators—in particular, the failure of the FBI command, headed by HRT agents, to listen to the suggestions of the negotiators. Several months after the bloody finale, in 1993, Alan A. Stone, a professor of psychiatry and law at Harvard, who studied the incident, wrote to then Deputy Attorney General Philip Heymann: "I have concluded that the FBI command failed to give adequate consideration to their own behavioral science and negotiation experts. They also failed to make use of the Agency's own prior successful experience in similar circumstances. They embarked on a misguided and punishing law enforcement strategy that contributed to the tragic ending at Waco."

Among those testifying before the Senate Judiciary Committee investigating the Waco case was Clint Van Zandt, an FBI hostage negotiator for almost twenty of his twenty-five years at the bureau. He offered a blistering assessment of his five weeks on the case: "Our written assignments warning of the dangers associated with too much tactical pressure went unheeded. The negotiation team leaders were refused access to the HRT to discuss the role of negotiations in attempting to resolve the incident. Instead of cooperation, we had discord. When we attempted to force the cooperation issue with the tactical commander, we were told that anything the tactical teams needed to hear about negotiations, they'd hear from him. He also indicated that were it not for the negotiators and their gentle handling of the Davidians, the tactical teams would have routed the Davidians from their compound in the first week. For almost every positive concession the negotiators were able to obtain from the Davidians, the tactical team was ordered to counter with a negative response. We did not trust David Koresh [the cult leader], and the Davidians learned not to trust us. These are but a few examples to say that 'We [the FBI teams] were not on the same sheet of music.' "

Until Waco, HRT, which began in 1983 as a domestic version of the military's Delta Force, had an elite "golden boy" image. These were the guys who stormed, raided, and rescued to get hostages out. On the other end of the spectrum there were the crisis negotiators in CINT, which was created in 1985 partly in response to a rising number of long-term hostage situations in the United States. Their training included a two-week negotiation course at New Scotland Yard, taught in recent years by Roy Ramm. For their international cases, they were taught strategies for responding to ransom demands and for tactfully coordinating the agendas of the host country police, the U.S. embassy staff, the intelligence agencies, the employers, if involved, and the families of the hostages. As was evident in Kashmir, on international cases they also had to juggle the demands of the FBI investigative agents to apprehend the culprits with their own desires to negotiate the captive's release.

Well schooled in psychology, CINT team members conveyed a hint of "new age" culture, speaking, for instance, of "holistic" approaches to resolving crises. This meant having the ability and willingness to study the lessons of past incidents and to consult many experts before taking action—in short, to have an open mind and embrace many possibilities in search of the best resolution. It meant attending meetings like the one on kidnapping that day in October. These were the guys who considered the ability to listen far more critical to resolving a case than firepower and bravado. They formed the chorus of restraint that by the autumn of 1995 had a receptive audience.

Whether hostages were held behind barricades in Texas or in Andes mountain hideouts or in "hostage hotels" in Rio, the meticulously plotted strategies of negotiators allowed everyone—from investigators to rescuers to diplomats—the much-needed time to plan and pull off the best possible resolution. Negotiation was also a way to ensure that the hostages were still alive and to glean all sorts of intelligence about the conditions of their captivity, including the daily habits of their captors—details helpful in achieving a successful rescue if negotiations broke down. Such extended maneuverings also gave the hostages more time to bond with their captors, often making it more difficult for the kidnappers to kill them.

Indeed, a key concept in modern negotiation was recognizing the positive benefits of the passage of time. In fact, one of the mottoes of the guru of modern negotiation, Dr. Harvey Schlossberg, was the simple declarative: Throw Away the Clock. A psychologist with the New York Police Department, Schlossberg, along with NYPD Detective Lieutenant Frank Bolz, set up the first hostage crisis unit in the world. At the Waco hearings, Bolz commented on time as a weapon. "Time permits the police and other law enforcement people to gather intelligence, to gather manpower, to gather equipment. Time permits perpetrators to get tired, to make mistakes. And if negotiating fails, you can always escalate up, but if you engage in a violent course of action first, you cannot step back and say, 'Hey, now I want to talk to you.' "

Modern negotiation, in both the public and private sectors, origi-nated in the early 1970s as a weapon to counter emerging variations of the crime of kidnapping. While the taking of hostages was hardly original, the advent of airplane hijackings as well as the September 1972 tragedy at the Olympic games in Munich—in which eleven Israeli athletes/hostages were killed—demanded new responses from those charged with trying to free hostages. In Munich, the eight Palestinian terrorists holding the young athletes demanded the release of hundreds of prisoners held in Israel and West Germany; they also demanded an airplane to fly them from Munich to Cairo. West Ger-many was willing to meet their demands, but Israel would not negoti-ate. The German police and army, both ill prepared for such an ordeal, conducted an abortive sniper attack and a direct assault that provoked the terrorists to blow up the helicopters where the hostages were held. The disaster spawned new counterterrorist groups in the militaries of numerous countries: Germany's GSG9, France's GIGN, the Counter-Revolutionary Warfare branch of Britain's SAS, and in the Nether-lands, the Special Air Unit.

In New York City, however, the reaction took a more unusual form. In late September of 1972, Schlossberg and Bolz and other NYPD administrators, anticipating and fearing this new terrorism would spread to their city, formed a committee of officers from every division of the force to create guidelines for a new age. It was a move that would one day be viewed as revolutionary. Above all else, the new mantra went: human life must be the most important consideration. Not the gathering of evidence. Not the recovery of property. Not even the apprehension of culprits, though this was clearly high on the list of priorities. Bolz and Schlossberg were charged with devising negotiation procedures and training the first negotiation team. The New York City guidelines, comprising the seminal theory of hostage negotiation, influenced the philosophical core of negotiation teams in Israel, Great Britain, back home at the FBI, and throughout the West-ern world, though with time and new experiences, the strategies would change considerably.

Law enforcement strategies evolve as the face of crime changes. And Waco, much like the incident at Munich, was another variation of a crime that ended in tragedy, thus prompting immense and irreversible change. In 1994, the FBI launched a new crisis management group, the Critical Incident Response Group, or CIRG, to better coordinate the agency's response to crises by uniting the agency's crisis units under the same authority—thus placing the crisis negotiators in CINT and the HRT rescuers on that "same sheet of music." When the CINT negotiators had something to say, HRT had no choice now but to listen. For negotiators, there was no Hollywood equivalent to Rambo—yet—but the spotlight was now on them. A renaissance of negotiation had clearly arrived at the FBI, both domestically and internationally. "What was really happening was that the agency was going back to the ideals of the 1970s," said one agent. "Somehow in the 1980s the tactical, the rescue end of things, got all the power. Waco returned us to a normal balance where negotiators' assessments and advice are given equal priority ranking. The use of a tactical resolution is now the last resort. We use force not because we can, but only when we have to."

While the FBI, since the mid-1980s, had had the legal right to venture beyond U.S. borders, what stepped up its presence abroad was the end of the Cold War and the concomitant increase of global crime and terrorist threats. With the USSR no longer serving as archenemy, government agencies mirrored the confusing changes of the post–Cold War era. Some officials and agencies were rigidly clinging to the past. Others, such as the FBI's ambitious new director, Louis B. Freeh, were trying to adjust their agency's roles to the new world—sometimes with prescience and wisdom and sometimes with sheer ambition. For his agency, Freeh saw opportunity in the chaos. He looked at the changing landscape of global crime, the increasing presence of Americans abroad, and the inevitability of crimes in foreign lands spreading to the United States, and he envisioned a new global FBI, an expanded bureau with a new mandate as cops of the world.

In a speech in Washington, D.C., that October of 1995, Freeh said, "The world has become a much smaller and much more dangerous place. We are confronting dangers today—here in the United States and abroad—that even a short time ago were incomprehensible. And the FBI is responding accordingly."

It was the 1984 Act for the Prevention and Punishment of the Crime of Hostage Taking that, for the first time, gave the FBI the legal right to deploy agents abroad to investigate kidnappings and, among other things, to help gain the release of hostages. By the fall of 1995, CINT negotiators had assisted in getting Americans out of captivity in Ecuador, Chile, El Salvador, Bolivia, Colombia, Panama, Costa Rica, Guatemala, Cambodia, the Philippines, Mexico, and Zaire. And now they were in Kashmir.

At the October 1995 meeting, though, it was clear that not everyone in the room was persuaded that the FBI had mastered the international kidnap scene. Kroll, for one, had attacked the FBI in a recent promotional flyer, sent to insurance brokers and others, saying, "Corporate Risk International trumpets their 'FBI' connection and expertise. They imply that the FBI kidnap experience and reputation in the U.S. carries over to foreign incidents, giving CRI an advantage. But there is no relationship between dealing with a U.S. kidnap and a foreign kidnap."

What Kroll was criticizing was that the experience of most agents was on the domestic front, where kidnappings are often contained, and not on the international stage, where they so often are not. The goal in the international "hidden-hostage" cases is to use the information and the time provided through negotiations to locate the hostage hideout and effectively to create a contained situation—the type for which most government negotiators are trained. But containment is a rare achievement in the remote jungles and mountain ranges of India or Colombia, Cambodia or Indonesia. Without containment, a raid, which is always an option in domestic cases if negotiations break down, is so often not feasible. And even when there is containment, a raid may still be inadvisable. For example, in Kashmir when the hostages were kept in Anantnag, the ongoing war and the militants' occupation of the town made it too risky to launch a raid. In such circumstances, all the more pressure is placed on negotiators. The hostages' lives may depend entirely on the ability of the negotiators to understand the temperaments, motives, and intentions of kidnappers from a foreign culture who are often communicating on inferior radio equipment or telephones in countries where power outages are common. Sometimes communications depend on emissaries running in and out of the mountains carrying messages of questionable authenticity.

But it was more than the lack of containment that at first hindered the agents abroad. It was the isolation. They were accustomed to working with a network of people, domestic swat teams and databases, not to mention local police forces trained in hostage negotiation. In international cases, the agents had nothing comparable to that. They were working with foreign governments and with local cops who might be inept, corrupt, or hostile—at times all three at once. The transition from domestic to international cases was sometimes as rough as the terrain itself. In one case, in Asia, the American agents could not adjust to the indigenous food and had to have canned spreadables and other items shipped to their remote station. On the lighter side, in one case in Zaire, an agent pulled out a Diner's Club card to pay a hotel bill, much to the surprise of the hotel clerk and the other American negotiators standing by.

The learning curve, at first, was steep. In one early case in Mexico, the FBI came to the aid of an employee of a multinational company who had been abducted. During the incident, the bureau took pictures of the kidnappers' intermediary and sent them back to the United States, where an arrest warrant was issued. Five years later, the intermediary took his family to Disney World for a vacation and was arrested. The FBI never told the company about the pending arrest warrant, according to an individual knowledgeable about the case, nor did the FBI warn the company that the arrest had taken place, effectively putting the company's 400 workers in Mexico at risk. When the company did find out, its executives were horrified. Fortunately, there were no repercussions.

"The first time I ever saw them in action was in 1991 and they were very Rambo-like; now they've made a 180-degree turn," said David Lattin, CRG's operations director in the American division. "They don't want Rambo. They want peace. They want to keep the dialogue with the kidnappers to get more information, to keep the hostages alive. The tactical guys think like North Americans, a linear, cause-effect way of thinking; do it fast. The negotiators must and do

think more like the cultures they are dealing with; they will take whatever time is needed. They know very well how to use time just as the
kidnappers use it: as a weapon."

It was difficult to determine who was best at this waiting game. If
the hostages did not survive, it was often because of a botched escape,
a gory rescue, or a kidnapper either taking revenge or losing control.
To identify one moment or one strategy as the reason for failure was
problematic, though sometimes the negotiators were the scapegoats
when diplomacy or other government efforts had failed. And if the
hostages were freed, the behind-the-scenes maneuverings were typically never revealed.

It was all so very secretive. Governments were inclined to take
credit for victorious cases, while the private consultants typically did
not, though some of the industry newcomers had taken to bragging
publicly to attract new business. To boast of participation in a specific
case lacked dignity, most of the consultants agreed, and it betrayed
clients who often did not want the world to know what measures they
had taken to obtain the release of their employees.

Despite the meeting that day, there was normally little praise flowing between the public and private sectors of negotiation. The private
companies quietly glowered at one another and at the FBI officials,
whose agents, they claimed, were too inexperienced in foreign cultures. Members of secret military rescue teams—such as the Special
Air Services in Britain or the Delta Force in the United States—
derided the private groups, calling them "intrusive," "foolish," and
"mercenary." Cops in the United States and Britain openly disapproved of their counterparts in the private sector because of the
volatile issue of concessions and ransoms. Government officials typically frowned upon private negotiators, also because of the ransom
issue, though some governments had secretly allowed ransoms to be
paid and had sought the advice of private consultants, such as CRG's
experts, on a number of occasions. As in the case of that October
meeting at the FBI, some government agencies culled valuable information from the veteran negotiators in the private sector. And then
there was that quiet revolution occurring within the FBI in which
negotiators were trying to do for the ordinary citizen what the private

negotiators had been doing for corporations for years: give them the assurance that if they got into trouble on the international frontier, there would be someone they could turn to.

In planning the meeting, what the FBI clearly recognized—and what everyone there understood—was that experience was the key factor in countering kidnappers. There was only so much that Roy Ramm or anyone else could teach about achieving the release of hostages.

To be sure, there were many basic lessons of psychology and semantics: No promises. No lies. No threats. Never say yes. Never say no. Never condescend. And never, never engage in the language of hostage-taking. The word *hostage* acknowledges that there are, indeed, hostages, and this triggers a set of responses in the kidnappers' minds. *Hostage* leads to the word *demands,* which sets off the idea of *deadlines,* which raises the prospect of unmet demands, and then, inevitably, the dreaded fear of *retaliation.*

But what couldn't be taught was a long-practiced ability to listen— a heightened sensitivity to the nuance of voices, like the skill of the blind listening in the absence of sight. And what mattered most was as primal as the crime itself: instinct based on years of probing the twisted, unpredictable psyches of kidnappers. To negotiate a kidnapping was to tread across a frozen lake, listening for the cracks that signaled danger, avoiding the thinly crusted areas, and ultimately finding the tortuous way to the other side.

19

Down the street and across a small London park from the offices of Roy Ramm and the suntan squad, under the crown of a white wooden cornice etched with the date 1885, is a narrow, red-hued brick building wedged inconspicuously between Lord's Food & Wine and a modest Italian eatery called the Queen Anne Restaurant. In its lobby, to the left of the elevator, is a white-and-yellow sign that reads:

> BOMBS.
> BE ALERT.
> IF YOU SEE ANYTHING SUSPICIOUS:
> • KEEP CALM.
> • KEEP CLEAR.
> • DON'T TOUCH.
> PHONE POLICE.
> DIAL 999.

The first stop off the elevator is the Westminster City Council; then the elevator rises to the second floor and opens onto a small reception room flanked by two conspicuous metal doors. The doors are bullet-proof and gray, with tiny little windows, like the doors of a Brink's truck, keeping out intruders—and sealing in secrets.

This is 83 Victoria Street, headquarters of Control Risks Group, Ltd. Variously described as a "paramilitary," "counterterrorist," "counterinsurgent," "supersecretive" firm, CRG, as it is typically called, advises companies, governments, and wealthy individuals on how to minimize risks from kidnappers and terrorists and, in the event of a kidnapping crisis, how to bargain for the life of the hostage. Holding the hands of investors and corporations as they venture into the wilds of the international frontier to the unsettled and sometimes angry reaches of undeveloped nations, CRG does what governments don't have the resources to do. And CRG, like other private groups, can consider a variety of concessions that most government policies prohibit, such as the option of advising clients to pay ransoms. Like the government agencies charged with protecting citizens, gathering intelligence, and securing the nation, much of what CRG has done through the years is wrapped tightly in a cocoon of secrecy.

It's a world rarely chronicled. British mystery writer Dick Francis offered a glimpse of it through his fictional kidnap consultancy Liberty Market Ltd. and his character, kidnap negotiator Andrew Douglas, in the book *The Danger.* "Kidnapping, you see, is my business," Douglas says. "My job, that is to say, as a partner in the firm of Liberty Market Ltd., is both to advise people at risk how best not to be kidnapped and also to help negotiate with the kidnappers once a grab has taken place: to get the victim back alive for the least possible cost. Every form of crime generates an opposing force, and to fraud, drugs, and murder, one could add the Kidnap Squad, except that the Kidnap Squad is unofficial and highly discreet . . . and is often *us.*"

In his dedication Francis writes: "Liberty Market Ltd. is fictional, though similar organizations exist. No one who has helped me with the background of this book wants to be mentioned, but my thanks to them just the same." Just as no one from CRG wanted to be acknowledged by Francis, no one wanted credit for advising Frederick Forsyth in shaping the main character of his book *The Negotiator.* In that book, the eccentric, engaging American named Quinn, an ex-military man turned negotiator, spends ten years working for "a firm of Lloyd's underwriters in London, a firm specializing in personal security and hostage negotiation."

Terrorism expert Richard Clutterbuck hinted at the intriguing world behind the bulletproof doors when he dedicated one of his books, *Kidnap, Hijack, and Extortion,* to CRG: "To my friends in Control Risks who don't know what it means to have a quiet life; who are prepared without notice to take the next flight to places facing the highest risks in the world, and to work there under intense pressure until the job is done; who have thereby saved many lives and helped the police catch dangerous criminals and terrorists who, but for that, would have deprived more people of their right to life and liberty."

CRG's strike force of ten full-time antikidnap operatives is on call twenty-four hours a day to fly to any part of the world to work a case, like the kidnap specialists at Scotland Yard and the FBI, but with some critical differences. For one, CRG is a private, for-profit organization, majority-owned by its employees, who are typically ex-soldiers, ex-spies, ex–Scotland Yard, ex-FBI, and even ex-diplomats, and who hail from both sides of the Atlantic. Independent of any government, CRG works above the shifting sands of political agendas and foreign policies. As an organization—with the exception of the International Committee of the Red Cross, the Catholic Church, and the Anglican Church of England—it has more collective experience than any single group in handling kidnap incidents. At least twenty-eight staffers have what is called "response" capabilities, meaning experience and training in responding to kidnap crises. Its kidnap services are automatically tied to the Kidnap and Ransom (K&R) insurance coverage underwritten out of Lloyd's of London. CRG, as part of the insurance package, will automatically respond to anyone with the specific consortium (Cassidy-Davis, Hiscox) of Lloyd's underwriters. It will also work, on a fee-paying basis, for the uninsured and does the occasional pro bono work for families and individuals in trouble. As part of the

K&R agreement, the company or individual with the policy cannot reveal to anyone that it has such coverage. Exposure will result in automatic cancellation of the policy.

The K&R policies are kept in a locked safe at Lloyd's. The clients' folders are filed under coded names. And the case files are kept in a vault in a rather secretive room at CRG's London headquarters. Even if a reporter confirms the presence of a CRG negotiator at the scene of a high-profile kidnapping, neither CRG nor the policyholder will confirm the firm's involvement.

The other big difference is ransoms. If a ransom is the only viable option, CRG will help its clients devise a strategy to pay. Because of this, the thick metal doors have not yet been able to hold back an occasional flood of controversy.

As Victoria Street comes alive each morning, the world behind those doors is already bustling, and a dozen or so people are beginning their days with the intensity of journalists on deadline. They ring up their on-the-ground sources from Rio to Cairo to Moscow. Between calls, they scan newspapers and wire services to dig up the latest details of crises round the world. A coup in Sierra Leone, a rash of kidnappings in Lima, an abducted American in Venezuela, a murdered tourist in Guatemala, a Hong Kong executive missing in Manila. The analysts cover a total of fifty countries. Each specializes in a region of the world and scrutinizes the dangers and risks of traveling to, remaining in, or doing business with the particular countries of that region. There are two analysts to an office; their desks are cluttered with reports and books and file folders set in piles surrounding a computer terminal, a Rolodex, and perhaps a mug half filled with tea left over from the long day before. In the corridor outside the offices is a wall of white wooden cubbyholes with large mail slots marked "The Americas," "Africa (south of the Sahara)," "Middle East," "North Africa," "Asia," and "Europe." Down the hall is a conference room, its walls covered with framed regional world maps. There, every day at 9:15 A.M., the analysts meet, much like a morning gathering of newspaper reporters and editors, to discuss the information they have culled from their morning calls and readings and to assess the global hot spots of the moment. At 9:30 A.M., they adjourn to write their first reports of the day, which must be on-line to their clients by 10:30 A.M. Like news stories, these reports highlight the most important events on their "beats." At 11:30 A.M. and again at 12:30 P.M., they must file two more reports. By lunchtime they will have written and sent out their on-line assessments and advisories to thousands of clients, including corporations, governments, venture capitalists, and wealthy travelers. During the rest of their day, they are updating advisories as events happen in the countries they cover, as well as attending meetings and writing up special threat-assessment reports for the myriad projects the firm manages—for example, working in a kidnap-plagued nation to set up a special antikidnap unit within a government police force.

On Thursdays, their work may require attending the weekly, high-level parley in which ongoing kidnappings are reviewed. There, in a deceptively quaint room with blue-print wallpaper and antiquarian maps of South America, a review committee scrutinizes the progress, or lack of it, in every case. A case manager brings reports from the kidnap consultant who is on the scene. Another consultant-negotiator, who has already rotated off the case after the usual three-week stint, offers critical details. Other kidnap specialists, with experience in guerrilla activity in the affected country or in kidnap cases resembling the one in progress, advise the committee. One analyst brings a printout of similar cases from the CRG data, which document kidnappings worldwide since the early 1970s. A government relations adviser could be present and, if in town, one of CRG's most seasoned kidnap consultants will attend. At least one had been at the game for twenty years, going back to the beginning of CRG—back to the far-off days of Julian Radcliffe and his fledgling invention.

⸺⸺

If Julian Radcliffe had lived centuries ago, he would have been an explorer ready to set sail at any moment in pursuit of a new, unknown land, driven by the passionate belief that he would discover something far better than what he saw before him now. But instead of claiming new territories for the British Empire, the restless, inventive Radcliffe concocted one commercial enterprise after the other, launching small businesses in the time it takes others to climb a single rung of the corporate ladder. His most recent invention: the Art Loss Registry, a massive computer system that matches police lists of artworks confiscated in drug busts and other crimes worldwide, with clients' descriptions of the paintings, sculptures, rings, and brooches of their stolen collections.

Thin and wiry, Radcliffe, with his finely tailored suits, his exquisite command of the English language, and his brisk, proud walk, has the almost clichéd air of a British statesman—a modern-day Neville Chamberlain. In a style that perhaps only a Brit could possess, he seems to stand at the juncture of two distinct classes, with the ambition of the middle and the bracing coolness of the upper. There is a scent of ambivalence about him, as if he wants the world to know of his achievements and innovations and yet hesitates to mention them, because seeking fame, or even enjoying it, lacks a certain dignity. That he is an insurance director at Lloyd's—for the Bain Hogg Group, a political risk broker for Lloyd's—seems suitably traditional and staid. Yet the puckish glint in Radcliffe's eye and his irresistible desire to tell a good, sometimes rakish story belie any hint of stodginess. This is a man who radiates creativity and seizes opportunities long before others see them. He has launched enough enterprises that he says his worst fear is that "I will awaken one morning to discover that I am competing with myself; I have created a company in competition with one I had created years before; and I will never be able to do anything but work for the rest of my life."

At the age of twenty-six, Radcliffe, fresh out of Oxford University with a degree in philosophy, came up with the idea for Control Risks, the first ever kidnap consultancy. It would be offered as a service as part of the Lloyd's K&R package. It was 1975. Airplane hijackings had only recently debuted on the stage of world terrorism. And since the late 1960s, it had become increasingly clear, particularly to oil and mining companies exploring and sometimes exploiting the Third World, that governments were not equipped to protect them. The opportunity was there amid the chaos of the changing currents of the early 1970s. And Radcliffe saw it. He envisioned a private agency that would fill the gap between citizens, mostly businessmen, venturing into potentially dangerous territories, and governments struggling to fulfill their mandates to protect.

The Control Risks consultants would advise policyholders on how to prevent kidnappings and on what to do when such a crisis occurs. In the event of a kidnapping, the policy, which already covered the expense of a ransom payment, would include the cost of consultants sent to the scene to advise companies and families on the negotiations with the kidnappers. Lloyd's would pay the cost of the consultants out of the premium, which would be reduced if the client implemented the firm's suggestions for crisis-management plans and engaged in its prevention training.

Part of Radcliffe's idea was to recruit from the rosters of former members of the British army's SAS unit—considered the best-trained counterterrorists in England. The SAS men were perfectly suited for CRG because of their international experience. And so Radcliffe enlisted the services first of David Walker, a former SAS major, and then three more former officers, Arish Turle, Mark Winthrop, and Simon Adamsdale. With a tiny staff in place, CRG came into being— for a while on very wobbly legs.

One of the firm's first big cases nearly toppled it: the 1976 abduction of Gustavo Curtis in Colombia. During the summer of 1976, Curtis, a fifty-one-year-old New Yorker who was then the manager of Beatrice Foods' Colombia affiliate, was called to the U.S. embassy in Bogotá. There an official showed him a surveillance photo that the embassy believed to be Curtis. The photo had been taken at a party by an underworld criminal. The embassy advised him that the photo could mean he was a kidnap target. But the man in the photo, Curtis told them, was wearing a ring and a necktie that he did not own. Though unpersuaded that he was the man in the photo, he talked about it with another executive, who advised him, "To hell with everything; get on a plane and get out."

Curtis then began a two-and-a-half-month campaign to get transferred out of Colombia to a new post—to any comparable position— in another subsidiary of the Chicago-based multinational. During that time Curtis, a tall, prosperous-looking man who was married to a local TV personality, spoke with a local security firm about buying a gun and a two-way radio unit for his car. He also inquired about bodyguards and ways to bolster the security of his plant.

In hindsight, his company would be critical of the fact that he did not contact the Colombian police authorities to request physical protection; nor did he contact Control Risks, which, among other things, would have reminded him to alternate his routes to and from work and the times he left for the office and for home each day. Curtis had attended a meeting of all Beatrice international managers, in Monaco, at which Control Risks conducted a security briefing offering such advice. The services of the then-tiny consultancy came with the company's purchase of kidnap insurance, including $2 million in coverage with Lloyd's and $1 million with Hartford. In the first half of the 1970s, Beatrice had experienced numerous threats, including a bomb threat at its Chicago headquarters and a threat to the life of its CEO.

Curtis's number-one priority was to flee the country. And so, toward this end, he continued to urge his company to transfer him out of the heart of danger. But, he was told, there were simply no suitable openings. Besides, kidnapping was "part of what it means to be an executive," a company official told Curtis, according to court records filed in U.S. District Court in New York.

And so what he feared most happened. On September 28, at 7:30 P.M., Curtis was abducted on his way home from work—he left at the usual time—when a car driven by the kidnappers entered the narrow side road along which Curtis's white Dodge was traveling. The car blocked Curtis's passage, and when his driver tried to back into a broader, more heavily trafficked street, another bandit-filled car zoomed in, spitting dust and screeching brakes, behind the Dodge. When Curtis got out of the car to sort out the confusion, he suddenly felt a gun at his temple and was shoved into one of the other cars. He was bound and gagged, taken to an unknown location, and lowered into a long shaft leading to a damp, dingy, four-by-eight-foot cell some sixty feet underground. The kidnappers wanted $5 million for his release—the same amount as the ransom wanted the year before in Colombia for a Sears executive who was released after eighty-nine days in captivity and after payment of a $1.2 million ransom.

Within a few hours, Beatrice was informed of the abduction, but no one at the subsidiary or the parent company, not even the director overseeing security, had any experience with kidnappings. The director, a former FBI agent, immediately phoned Control Risks in London, and Radcliffe dispatched a team of two men to Bogotá.

CRG recommended, and Beatrice agreed, that no counteroffer should exceed $100,000, according to the New York court records. So the negotiations began with Beatrice offering 750,000 Colombian pesos, then equal to about $22,500. The offer, always in pesos, inched up to the equivalent of about $100,000. Sometimes weeks would go by without hearing from the kidnappers; for example, from November 18 until December 2, there were no calls. Finally, on February 15, the kidnappers, for the first time, reduced their demand, to $3 million in response to a 5.5 million peso offer; and again on March 18 to $2 million, after the company had upped the offer to 6.5 million pesos, or nearly $200,000, according to the court records. (The rate of exchange at the time was about three cents to one Colombian peso.) On March 22, the kidnappers came down to $1 million, and thirteen days later, on April 4, the company—on the advice of CRG, of course—upped its ante to 7.5 million pesos, or about $225,000. On April 27, the kidnappers switched to pesos, lowering their demand to 16 million, or nearly $480,000, in response to the other side coming up to 12.5 million pesos. And at last on April 29, 1977, the company offered 15.5 million Colombian pesos, which was about $465,000. The kidnappers agreed.

After a reduction in ransom from $5 million to approximately $465,000, and eight months of captivity, Curtis, emaciated from the loss of forty-five pounds, was set free. CRG had fulfilled its duty to its client, and the ordeal was over for Curtis. But there was one remaining problem: the local law banning the payment of ransoms. The Colombian authorities had been especially unhappy the year before when the $1.2 million was paid for the Sears executive. This, they claimed, was the starting gun for a race to kidnap foreign executives in their country. And so as soon as Curtis was free, they took action.

Radcliffe will always remember the before-dawn call he received from Colombia telling him that his two former British Army majors, Turle and Adamsdale, were in trouble. It was two days before their return home, and, feeling a sense of satisfaction in securing Curtis's safe release, they were enjoying a leisurely dinner when suddenly two immigration police officers interrupted them. There was a problem with their passports, they were told as they were led away. And, as Radcliffe learned, they were later arrested and held against the charge that they were members of the gang that had kidnapped Curtis.

The problem, it appeared, was a classic one: the right hand of government had no knowledge of what the left hand knew. From the start, CRG and its negotiators had permission from the Colombian police to negotiate Curtis's release under certain conditions. The negotiators had to share with the police any information about whom they were talking to as they developed their conduit to the kidnappers. The ransom must come under the current market value, which was then at $2 million, preferably below $1 million. And they wanted the ransom paid in pesos, not U.S. dollars. In return, the police said they would share information to help the negotiators and they would not make any moves that could be harmful to the negotiations. Everyone had abided by the agreement. When they reached the ransom level of $465,000, the negotiators obtained the approval of the police, who asked them if they would serialize the bank notes. They did, and in the hope that the police would apprehend the kidnappers, they turned over all their information. Even the kidnappers had behaved well. Until dinner the night of the arrests, it had been a textbook-smooth case. The police had even commented on the excellent cooperation.

The problem was that during the negotiations a state of emergency had been declared in Colombia, which gave the military jurisdiction over certain crimes, including kidnappings. A military judge initiated the move to arrest Turle and Adamsdale—a move that later resulted in his dismissal for abusing his powers. Meanwhile, the two young former SAS majors were stuck in a Colombian jail. "At that point, everyone told me we were finished. I should wind it up, I was told," Radcliffe recalled later. "My negotiators were in jail, the business was finished, and I had to concentrate my efforts on getting them out. Then we called on the pope, the British ambassador, the archbishop of Canterbury to assist us."

Unmarried at the time, Radcliffe visited the wives of the jailed CRG negotiators to inform them of his plan to offer himself to the Colombian authorities in exchange for Turle and Adamsdale. "That didn't work. It was, to say the very least, a real trial period for CRG, considering that two-fifths of its staff was in captivity."

With much negotiation and coercion, an agreement was finally struck, but only after the negotiators had spent ten weeks in a wretched Colombian jail.

The following year, Curtis filed a $185 million lawsuit against his employer's parent company, claiming it had "performed ransom negotiations inadequately." Among other things, he complained that Beatrice had been well aware of the terrorist threat to his life prior to the abduction and had done nothing to prevent it—mainly, finding a job for him away from Colombia. Eventually the case was decided in favor of Beatrice. When asked in court why he didn't leave, after he had been warned by the embassy of the danger, Curtis told the court, "I am not a quitter."

In the midst of legal claims flying back and forth, CRG was gaining a stellar reputation among potential clients for the handling of the Colombian ordeal. While Radcliffe had feared the incident might dash his plans for a bustling business, quite the opposite occurred. The story spread like prairie fire through the corporate community, heightening the awareness of the need to retain consultants like CRG. In the end, the incident smoothed CRG's path into the U.S. marketplace.

By 1978, CRG had handled more than fifty kidnappings and had offices in Washington, D.C., and Paris as well as London. Early that year, Radcliffe gave a speech in D.C. at an elite gathering of chairmen of major U.S. corporations. Looking out over an audience that included then-President Jimmy Carter, Radcliffe confronted some of the troubling issues of his business—including the vexing, centuries-old conundrums at the heart of the crime of kidnapping. How can you justify facilitating the payment of ransoms when the ransoms help to fund terrorists and criminals and to encourage more kidnappings, thus endangering the lives of people in the countries where the ransoms are paid? Is the payment of ransoms fueling the crime of kidnapping? And how do you respond to the critics who attack K&R insurance, which Lloyd's had been offering since the 1932 Lindbergh kidnapping, as an irresponsible enterprise making profits by brokering fear while fanning the flames of terrorism?

"Societies faced by the threat of assassination, kidnappings, or other misfortunes, whether politically or criminally inspired, look to governments for protection," he began. "Then, realizing that total security is not possible and is very expensive, they seek to shift the losses of the few to the shoulders of many by means of insurance. . . . Dutch shipowners of the eighteenth century formed mutual insurance companies to collect ransoms from their members to release crews held hostage by pirates in the East Indies."

There were no studies, he went on to say, showing that the presence of K&R insurance had increased either ransom demands or the number of kidnap incidents. No matter what could be said about insurance companies making money from fear—whether it was fear of fires or burglaries or kidnappings—there was no way to deny that insurance increased the awareness of a problem. Fire drills and all the other prerequisites of insurance coverage required informing people of the problem and teaching them how to prevent it. Radcliffe stressed that governments simply didn't have the resources to do this for the fast-growing multitudes of people beginning to explore the sometimes dangerous outer reaches of the globe. The private sector was stepping in.

In a kidnapping, the immediate reaction of families and corporations is to get the victim back alive as soon as possible. And in a panic, their first impulse is to pay the full amount of the ransom demand. It is the payment of a top price, Radcliffe said, that makes the crime look profitable and alluring. Negotiators, with their experience and aplomb, tame the hysteria of the victims' loved ones and employers and get the price down. If the ransom is so low that it cannot cover the cost of the kidnapping, which in some cases can be costly, then the negotiation has helped to discourage the crime.

"Some governments have considered outlawing the payment of ransom or even negotiations themselves. It may be tempting to do so," Radcliffe continued, "since the initial reaction of many responsible citizens when they are faced with the demand for ransom and negotiation under duress is to stand firm in the belief that sacrifices must be made to prevent terrorism or similar criminal activity from spreading. The U.S. State Department has publicly endorsed this policy with respect to its own employees; it has also encouraged the same policy for U.S. corporations. The State Department adopted a no-pay policy early on in the attacks on U.S. diplomats in Latin America. It is probably the correct policy for a government to take, but it is worth considering whether corporations or families could adopt the same policy."

For a no-pay policy to be effective, Radcliffe said, hundreds of thousands of families and corporations, including their overseas subsidiaries, would have to agree to hold the same tough line. If one gave in, the deterrent would not be effective. Considering the pain and impatience of families during kidnappings, it was impossible that such a policy could ever be enacted, he contended. And if families and corporations did pay, they should have access to the very best advice from consultants who were experienced in negotiation. "Considering how some governments, such as Japan and Austria, have continued to give in to terrorists' demands, it is denying the natural dictates of human nature to expect families not to do so. Efforts have been made to make negotiations illegal, and police have tried to seize ransoms when they were due to be paid. The effect of these measures has been to make certain that families conducted secret negotiations without informing the police, and this is obviously the worst of all possible worlds.

"It is probably just as unrealistic to try to make the payment of ransom illegal as it would be to forbid a person to hand over his or her wallet if he or she was mugged on the street. It would therefore appear to be difficult to maintain either voluntarily or legally a policy of no payment or no concessions. . . . In theory, it is simple to favor a no-pay policy, particularly for an unknown individual. In practice, few would deny that they would be prepared to pay a ransom for their own eight-year-old daughter."

By the early 1980s, business was brisk at CRG, but controversies and conflicts periodically surfaced, like the sometimes violent tremors from an otherwise dormant underground fault. In 1982, Arish Turle led a management buyout of CRG, which until then had been a wholly owned subsidiary of the broker Hogg Robinson. Radcliffe was forced to choose between CRG and Hogg Robinson. He chose to leave CRG—just in time to miss the first big round of controversy.

In the highly secretive K&R business, public scrutiny ebbs and flows with the incidence of high-profile cases, such as the 1986 abduction of Jennifer Guinness that brought torrents of attention—of the unpleasant kind—to CRG. Guinness, the forty-eight-year-old wife of John Guinness, a member of the famed Guinness brewing family and the chairman of Dublin's Guinness and Mahon Merchant Bank, was snatched by three masked men from her secluded mansion on Dublin Bay. It was April 8, her husband's birthday. The kidnappers, who were suspected to have ties to the Irish Republican Army, demanded $2.6 million for her return.

This was a time when the Provisional IRA was strapped for cash to run its military and political campaigns, estimated to cost a total of at least $5 million. To raise money for its war chest, it had resorted to kidnapping. And, much to the dismay of the Irish government and the Garda (police), some ransoms apparently had been paid. There was, for example, the nearly $1 million paid to free Ben Dunne, an executive of one of the nation's biggest chain stores, following his abduction in 1981. Against this backdrop, CRG's involvement somehow leaked to the press, sending up red flares seen by government officials in both Ireland and England. As always, CRG's only comment to the press was, "We will not officially confirm or deny that we are involved. It would not be company policy to do so."

In the Guinness case, after several days without contact with the kidnappers—a harrowing time for the families of hostages—the family retained the London firm. As one newspaper had said, CRG "has a team of very experienced ex–Scotland Yard experts, many of them long-standing senior officers on the Anti-Terrorist Branch as well as one former head of the Yard Bomb Squad, a West End detective, and former members of the British Army's best, the SAS."

Throughout the ordeal, Mrs. Guinness, who had heroically volunteered herself as a hostage to protect her daughter from abduction, talked to her captors about her husband being a mere banker who had worked hard for a living and who, though bearing the Guinness name, was only from a modestly endowed branch of the beer-brewing dynasty. "You have the wrong Guinness," she reportedly insisted. On the eighth day of the ordeal, April 16, the Dublin police raided the house on Waterloo Road where she was held. And during the five-hour siege, she was rescued, unharmed. The very next day, political sparks were flying.

Dale Campbell-Savours, a member of Parliament in the Labour Party, called for the prosecution of CRG and its K&R underwriter for allegedly breaching prevention of terrorism laws. In a page-one story on April 17, the *Times* of London announced that Home Secretary Douglas Hurd would review K&R insurance in response to the call for prosecution. A top police official told the press, "Private security firms such as the one called in on the Guinness kidnapping are operating 'at the very frontiers' of official tolerance."

In response, the then Attorney General Sir Michael Havers said that he saw no evidence of either CRG or the underwriter breaching such laws. Still, for several months kidnap insurance and kidnap nego-tiators became pariahs, with Margaret Thatcher leading the parade of critics and naysayers. Thatcher was persuaded that what CRG did was directly in opposition to what governments were trying to do to counter terrorism. And by May, following her lead, politicians from two more parties, Tory and Alliance, joined with Labour in expressing their concern over K&R as an encouragement to kidnapping—which, they stressed, was a source of funding for paramilitary groups and for terrorism in general.

The Commons passed a motion to put the issue before the world leaders at the Tokyo summit that May (1986) and asked them to take action. The Hague, meanwhile, was already studying possible mea-sures against the payment of ransoms. And soon the Irish govern-ment, charging that the availability of such insurance was an incentive to kidnappers, would lobby the European Economic Community for a Europe-wide ban on K&R insurance. "I will consider bringing in legislation to make it illegal here and take it up with other countries to prevent policies being issued, and paid out abroad," said Irish Justice Minister Alan Dukes.

Columns and editorials, as well as news stories and letters-to-the-editor pages, brimmed with commentary attacking K&R for promot-ing the crime of kidnapping and, among other things, for violating nearly every government's party line—the unequivocal, hard-line policy propounded by most Western governments toward any form of concession to terrorist or criminal organizations.

Around the same time, a respected British journalist, James Adams, came out with a new book in which he made the case that ransom kidnappings were funding terrorist activities far more than anyone realized. "For every penny that a terrorist group gathers in from kidnaps," he wrote, "a substantial proportion goes toward the funding of future operations and the maintenance of the terrorist organization." And he pointed to the rise of kidnap insurance as a damaging trend. Wrote Adams: "In an unintentional conspiracy, the terrorist, the victim, and the insurance companies have found a level at which they are all prepared to work. The kidnappers get their cash, the victims have insurance, and the insurance companies get their premiums."

When the issue was debated before the EEC, some delegates pointed out that a K&R policy had very little bearing on whether a businessman or diplomat was targeted by kidnappers. What was more relevant, they argued, was the appearance of the wealth of the targets. They said, too, that a standard condition of K&R insurance was that full cooperation be given to law enforcement agencies in the country where the incident occurred—thus striking out another argument. And then, one or two delegates pointed out that the Americans, described as vociferous anticoncessionists, had been recently exposed as "anything but that," as one man put it, in the recent arms-for-hostages incident. The problem of kidnapping should be discussed by governments, law enforcement agencies, the insurance industry, and all interested parties, wrote one delegate in the aftermath of the meeting, "because of the needs of private individuals and corporate bodies in an increasingly violent world." Cooperation among all concerned groups, he went on to say, was the way to fight terrorism—not a witch-hunt against one sector of the community.

Toward the end of May that year, the *Post,* an insurance trade magazine, tried to restore the diminished status of the industry by saying that the "irrational" targeting of the insurance industry, following the abduction of Jennifer Guinness, was provoked by a "disgust and fear of terrorism." No one wanted to come out on the side of the insurance industry—an industry perceived to be making money off of human fear while filling the coffers of terrorists. And politicians— some quite sincerely—wanted to find a way as soon as possible to curtail kidnappings and other terrorist acts. "The main claim put forward by the would-be banners is that insurance encourages kidnappers and terrorists," the article read. "The facts do not support this argument. . . . Only 2% of all victims are likely to be insured. The insurance has to be kept secret. Otherwise it is void; so it is difficult to see where the encouragement to the terrorist comes from. The existence of an insurance policy ensures that the authorities are informed as soon as the kidnap takes place and that expert negotiators are called in, thus eliminating the possibility of a family parting with money before the police are even aware that a kidnap has taken place. Kidnap insurance is thus more likely to result in less money getting into the hands of terrorist organizations, surely something that the likes of Labour MP Dale Campbell-Savours and Irish Justice Minister Alan Dukes would welcome. Why, then, are they arguing for such insurance to be outlawed?"

The *Post* also pointed out that Lloyd's of London could lose 22 million pounds a year if a ban were introduced. Eventually, after it was confirmed that CRG had broken no laws and could not be prosecuted, the furor faded from the front pages. But the issue did not. As long as there were politicians and kidnappings and K&R, the issue would be debated. In some camps, K&R would always be the culprit in the rising numbers of kidnappings in certain regions such as Latin America. And Campbell-Savours and others would continue to push for the prevention of ransom payments as part of the campaign to curtail terrorist fund-raising.

Despite the rumpus, the business of CRG continued to grow. Between 1987 and 1990, the firm logged 1,370 kidnap cases, plus 90 kidnap attempts. In some cases, cash ransoms were paid. In others, negotiations resulted in giving the kidnappers something other than money in return for hostages—such as international publicity, shiploads of food, or money-backed guarantees for new schools, roads, or hospitals.

Ransom, in the jargon of negotiation, means anything demanded in exchange for a hostage. In one case, a company gave money to several international newspapers for ad space to publicize the kidnappers' manifesto of rights and their campaign for independence. To resolve an incident in Brazil, a company distributed $3 million to a school district. In a case in Asia involving two American executives, Islamic insurgents at first asked for a seven-figure ransom, but a few days into the negotiations, the kidnap experts discerned that money wasn't really the issue. Negotiators, through the daily exchanges, learned that the local provincial government wanted new schools and new roofs for several buildings. They also wanted recognition and respect from the company that was making big bucks from their resources. And so, without paying a cash ransom, the company obtained the release of the two men by promising a new school, new roofs, and a new full-time salaried position: community relations director. If they did not follow through, they were threatened with more kidnappings; so far, the compromise has worked.

Rice, jeeps, medical supplies, radios, even basketballs have all been used in negotiations to gain the release of hostages. In one quite memorable case, in which Asian insurgents had kidnapped an American manager, CRG's kidnap specialists learned that the kidnappers loved to play basketball, and so the deal was struck that the manager would get his freedom in exchange for basketball uniforms for two teams as well as two basketballs.

In 1990, Control Risks released a study of the outcomes of kidnappings worldwide over the previous three years: 40 percent of the victims were set free after a ransom was paid; 35 percent were rescued; 11 percent were released without payment; 9 percent died in captivity or were killed; and 5 percent escaped. Ninety percent of kidnappings were in twelve countries: Brazil, Colombia, India, Italy, Lebanon, Mexico, Pakistan, Peru, the Philippines, Spain, the United States, and Venezuela.

By the mid-1990s, it was abundantly clear that Radcliffe, in his invention of CRG, had dropped a spark into a dry field. The idea of private industry kidnap negotiators and crisis management consultants had spread across the globe, and new companies, on the model of CRG, were changing the face of a once elite and low-profile business—forcing even CRG to utter an occasional boast for the sake of competition and to open its bulletproof doors wide enough for a few outsiders to enter, or at least to look in. Suddenly, the highly secretive professionals who had spent most of their careers concealing what they did from the outside world were forced to market their skills.

20

The chaos and opportunity flowing out of the Cold War thaw, along with the anxiety over national security that the Gulf War had precipitated, was causing a minor industry to emerge from the shadows and, in the fervent light of a new era, begin to flourish. The potential market for Kidnap and Ransom insurance (K&R) and kidnap consultants was far greater in the 1990s than it had been during the days when Radcliffe was struggling for his firm's credibility. In a world of shifting governmental alliances and unlimited economic opportunities, the need for protection beyond what governments could deliver—and the equally pressing demand for resolutions to crises beyond what governments could feasibly allow—was perhaps never greater than at the end of the twentieth century. Private security consultants were advising people on where the risks were, how to prevent a crisis, such as a kidnapping, and how to negotiate the release of a hostage. They were telling people what the travel industry was reluctant to reveal and what governments admitted when politically useful: that the borderless world was a dangerous place.

Large multinational companies, especially in the extracting industries of oil and mining, had been quietly training employees in kidnap
prevention practices and buying K&R coverage for years. Now there
were planeloads of new players traveling across the wild and woolly
international landscape. It appeared that small and medium-sized
companies were the fastest-growing markets, and in companies of all
sizes, top executives were no longer the only ones covered. Employees
at all levels were insured because kidnappers were no longer distinguishing rank and title, as they once did during the era when diplomats and celebrities were the frequent prey. While eagerly buying
K&R coverage, wealthy families and well-to-do travelers were also
subscribing to daily travel advisories and risk reports offered by CRG
and similar companies.

It was a rare occasion when private consultants were not somehow
involved in a kidnapping or extortion case abroad. In the 1995 Kashmir
incident, for example, John Childs, the American businessman who
escaped, had access to an on-call outside negotiator, Sean McWeeney at
Corporate Risk International, through Childs's company. And because
of the challenging nature of the Kashmir case, government advisers discreetly sought the advice of firms in the private sector.

In the new order of unlimited opportunities and untold dangers,
private security firms, along with insurance companies, were reaping
profits at a level that even Radcliffe could not have predicted—
$2,000 a day for some kidnap negotiators, plus expenses, and $750
to $1,500 in annual premiums per $1 million of K&R coverage.
K&R underwriting at Lloyd's had jumped 50 percent each year from
1990 onward.

Even those who had protested the concept, in the 1970s and
1980s, were getting in on the act. In Ireland, for example, where there
were a half dozen high-profile kidnappings in the years following the
Guinness abduction, crisis management firms, some with kidnap consultant services, were doing a steady business. This was also where
politicians and the police had joined the 1980s outcry to outlaw CRG.
Sitting on the board of directors of one Dublin company were a former
Irish military police captain, a former assistant commissioner of the
Garda, and a former Garda superintendent. And in England, where

CRG was not at all popular among the military ranks of the SAS—despite the fact that its early recruits came from the SAS—a new company was formed by one of the SAS founders.

In the United States, the first in the private sector to offer kidnap negotiation services was Emanuel C. "Mike" Ackerman, an ex-CIA agent, who in 1977 at the age of thirty-six started Ackerman & Palumbo with another former agent, Lou Palumbo. By 1978, Chubb Insurance had chosen the new firm as the "response" professionals automatically called in the event of a kidnapping or other terrorist incident involving its clients covered under its new K&R insurance package. In 1989, Ackerman bought out Palumbo and renamed the firm the Ackerman Group.

Ackerman, a Phi Beta Kappa with a degree from Dartmouth, never boasted any prescience in getting into the kidnap business. In 1975, when congressional hearings were exposing a multitude of CIA secrets, he knew it was time to leave what he had intended to be his life work. With eleven years of experience and a reputation for being an aggressive agent, he was outspoken against government meddling. He knew it would change the CIA forever, and he firmly believed the agency's best years were suddenly behind it. And so, young enough to change careers, he did, but only after he denounced Congress in a book called *Street Man* and ran for a congressional seat in Florida and lost. His next move was clearly a winner.

Ackerman was perfect for the job of kidnap negotiator. He was fluent in Spanish and Russian. He had spent years in both Latin America and Europe, mostly recruiting informants. He had tracked international terrorists, and he was adept at posing as someone he wasn't—for example, the employee of a company or a member of a Latin American family. Whatever he had to do to get the hostage out alive, he would do. The difference between CRG and Ackerman was that Ackerman himself actually paid the ransoms. Like the CRG experts, he would act as a consultant when necessary, advising families and companies every step of the way on what they should or should not do. But for the most part, he was the one doing the negotiating—the guy on the front lines. It was Ackerman, not an intermediary, who was sitting in the helicopter dropping a bag filled with $500,000 into a

Guatemalan jungle to gain the freedom of an American executive. He conducted negotiations, paid ransoms, and helped local law enforcement to track down the culprits. He was hands-on all the way, for $2,000 a day plus expenses. And he typically handled four cases a year.

It was Ackerman, too, who was the first, even before CRG or Pinkerton's, to offer clients a country-specific risk analysis report. In early 1978 he was meeting with an executive in Dallas, who told him that what he needed most was for someone to pinpoint exactly where on the globe the dangers existed. Ackerman thought at the time that it was impossible to do this. By the fall, the firm had launched a service that eventually covered eighty countries. Clients began to realize that Ackerman knew what he was doing when the shah of Iran was ousted. Several months before, in September of 1978, Ackerman had advised his clients to prepare to evacuate. In November, nearly two months before the coup, he told them to leave.

The enterprising ex-spook had plenty of company in the North American marketplace of the 1990s when a surge of opportunism had brought one new crisis management firm after the other onto the business terrain, all pledging to protect, to prevent, to resolve. Although the "it-can't-happen-to-me" and "it-certainly-can't-happen-here" syndromes were still common throughout the United States, there was a slow-moving awareness of a potential threat, reflected in part by the burgeoning client lists of private firms such as Ackerman's and the numbers of new start-up firms.

And while the U.S. miniboom for kidnap experts owed a lot to the Cold War's end and to the Gulf crisis, there was one other factor: several high-profile incidents at home. Except for the well-informed traveler and employees of international firms, kidnap prevention was the last thing on anyone's mind in the United States—until, that is, a specific case made the headlines. And in the 1990s, there seemed to be more than the usual number of these.

To be mentioned on the annual *Forbes* list of wealthiest Americans, replete with an estimate of your millions or billions in assets, was once the height of status—for some, the culmination of the American dream. Now it was tantamount to donning a bull's eye for a mask and sending up a red flare for all criminal opportunists to see.

In the plot to kidnap Texas billionaire Robert M. Bass—for a $5 million ransom—the kidnapper, as he later told prosecutors, selected his target after reading business magazines in which Bass, along with speculations about his wealth, was frequently mentioned during the go-go 1980s. California executive Charles Geschke, whose abductors were well aware of his assets, was targeted in 1992 after the publication of a news article about his $50,000 donation to his college alma mater. A Seattle man, in an elaborate kidnapping scheme devised in 1989, had researched various publications and annual reports to determine the assets of prominent Idaho businessmen for his ambitious hit list. Targets included the CEO of Boise Cascade, the CEO of Morrison-Knudsen, both based in Boise, as well as potato baron J. R. Simplot and his son-in-law, who was Idaho's lieutenant governor. The kidnapper was caught after the abduction and subsequent murder of his first victim. In his car, investigators found the complete roster of names, addresses, home numbers, and occupations of his intended victims. And it included other useful intelligence, such as their daily routines and their hobbies.

Among the cases in 1990, there was the New Jersey abduction of the sixteen-year-old son of Richard Traa, who owned numerous McDonald's franchises throughout the state. First Bank System chairman John Grundhofer was snatched at 8 A.M. a few months later from his reserved parking space in the garage of his Minneapolis company. And there was the December kidnapping of the thirty-year-old daughter of multimillionaire Jim Pattison, just over the Canadian border in Vancouver. The victims in all three cases survived.

In 1992, Sidney Reso, the immensely powerful president of Exxon International—sometimes called "Mr. Exxon"—was abducted from the driveway of his $680,000 home in an affluent New Jersey suburb, 250 feet from his front door, between 7:30 and 8:00 A.M. It was recycling day, and Reso, a private man who, despite money and power, chose to live an unpretentious life, always took out his own garbage. He also declined the executive privilege, which Exxon would have provided, of a driver trained as a bodyguard and armed for crises such as kidnappings. His hands cuffed, his legs bound with hemp, his eyes and mouth trapped beneath layers of tightly wrapped duct tape, the fifty-seven-year-old executive spent his captivity in a six-by-four-foot wooden crate. His captors were a former New Jersey police officer, who had also worked for both Exxon Security and a private security consulting firm, and the man's wife. Pretending to be part of a radical environmental group, they asked for $18.5 million from Exxon for Reso's return. That was on April 29.

A few weeks later—while Reso was still missing—the president of Adobe Systems, Charles Geschke, was easing his Mercedes sports coupe into a parking space in Mountain View, California, south of San Francisco, when a man approached him holding a map. The unsuspecting Geschke was about to offer his help with directions when suddenly the man moved the map aside to reveal a very large gun—pointed at Geschke's chest. This was the man who, during the next four days, would repeatedly explain to the fifty-two-year-old Geschke, as he lay helplessly bound and gagged in a closet, that he had wired the bedrooms of Geschke's three children with nitroglycerin and would explode at least one by remote control if Geschke failed to cooperate in any way. He would also warn Geschke that he planned to make him "shark bait" in his native country of Jordan, if his ransom demand of $650,000 was not met.

Rescued after four days in captivity, Geschke lived. But Reso did not. His abductor, the former Exxon security officer, shot Reso during the first minutes of the abduction, and, although negotiations lasted for fifty-nine days, Reso died on the fourth day of his captivity as a result of the wound.

In 1993, a tuxedo executive from New York, Harvey Weinstein, endured a captivity that was the epitome of claustrophobic terror. The sixty-eight-year-old owner of Lord West Formalwear, one of the nation's largest tuxedo manufacturers, was abducted at knifepoint outside the Queens diner where every day, for many years, he had eaten his breakfast of raisin bran, cranberry juice, black coffee, and toast. For twelve days, while his abductors tried to extort a $3 million ransom, Weinstein, known as an affable, generous man with no enemies, was buried in a four-by-eight-foot pit beneath an abandoned rail yard near the Hudson River in upper Manhattan. To endure, he carried himself mentally back to foxholes in the tropical darkness of the South Pacific during his days as a marine in World War II. He tried to remember lessons on solitary confinement from Arthur Koestler's book *Darkness at Noon*. And he wrote his verbal autobiography. All he could hear were trains in the distance and an occasional helicopter overhead. "I knew the biggest challenge would be to keep my sanity," he said at the 1995 trial of his abductors. Weinstein was rescued after one of his captors was arrested and revealed the vicinity of his captivity.

The week before the August abduction of Weinstein, casino magnate Steve Wynn picked up the ringing phone at his Las Vegas Mirage Hotel and Casino and heard: "Mr. Wynn, we have your daughter." Kevin Wynn, his twenty-six-year-old daughter, had been abducted from her luxury townhouse, despite an elaborate system of gates and alarms surrounding it. The men on the phone said they wanted $2.5 million and warned him not to go to the police. He didn't. And he paid about $1.45 million. His daughter was quickly released. The kidnappers were eventually apprehended and convicted. But only part of the ransom was recovered. While the details of the incident were kept out of the press, sources close to the case have said that Kevin Wynn had taken her car to a garage for repairs. In the glove compartment was the remote control for the gates to her luxury complex and her garage. Through a twisted trail of connections, her abductors reportedly obtained a copy of the remote control, which facilitated their scheme.

In January 1994, Jay Bhagat, the executive vice president of Mobile Telecommunications Technologies, opened the front door of his home in Jackson, Mississippi, at about 10:40 P.M. to the sight of his wife with her hands tied and her mouth taped shut. Seated nearby in the living room was his daughter, bound to a chair and blindfolded. The abductor, who had carefully researched Bhagat's company's financial reports to select a target, told Bhagat that he had considered other executives. But, said Bhagat later, "He said I was an easier target. He said the other fellow had more security at his home." The kidnapper was later killed by FBI agents at a shopping mall, after releasing Bhagat and picking up the $750,000 ransom.

By 1995, there was a minisurge in what some private investigators called "doorbell abductions." "There's a knock at the door, the doorbell rings," said former FBI agent Paul Chamberlain, in Los Angeles. "Then a guy takes the wife and child of a bank officer hostage while another guy takes the banker to the bank to get money."

In Silicon Valley, the fast-turnaround style of kidnapping—some called it "fast-food kidnapping"—showed a new twist. In several incidents, executives of high-tech firms were ambushed while driving home from work by a carload of gun-toting kidnappers. Blocking the executive's car with their own, the kidnappers then forced the executive, at gunpoint, to return to his office and hand over, not money, but valuable computer components. In a globalized, high-tech marketplace, chips, the tiny, semiprecious items in huge demand throughout the world, could be as hot as drugs and as pricey as gold. And so it was only logical that criminals would depend on the usual methods to gain access to the booty—burglary, robbery, and kidnapping. A Fremont, California, detective issued warnings to owners and managers of computer companies with inventories of memory chips and computer processing units: "Be aware of the vehicles around you when traveling to and from work, and be wary of cars parked near your houses and your businesses."

Indeed, by the mid-1990s, robbing high-tech firms and warehouses was clearly passé. The state-of-the-art way of obtaining chips was to abduct executives or the spouses and children of executives, which was happening rather frequently to Asian owners of facilities storing the chips. Art Fonda, chief executive officer of Piiceon, a San José memory-module maker, spoke for many in the Bay Area when he told a reporter that he feared this new use of kidnapping. "We have lines of prevention [security] that I don't even know about because I don't want to be able to say anything if I'm a hostage."

But the concern over kidnappings in the United States—still fortunately low-key—centered more on the importation of the crime through various groups, such as the Russian mafia, for whom kidnapping and extortion are part of the culture of doing business, as well as the potential for the kidnapping wave in Mexico spilling over the border. By 1996, there were kidnappings in parts of the nearby Baja region, and there was the high-profile abduction of the Sanyo executive who was snatched in Mexico, a heartbeat away from his home south of San Diego. After the $2 million ransom was paid and the man was set free, a surge of anxiety pumped through the veins of businessmen working in Mexico. Kidnap experts, too, worried about the ramifications, though some were too busy counting new clients.

In the United States, the crisis management biz, replete with an antikidnap advisory service, was indeed booming, which signaled a consumer-beware atmosphere, especially regarding kidnap negotiation. To be good required experience. Some firms had it and others didn't, but it was difficult to tell from brochures alone. In tallying the number of kidnap incidents it had handled, a given company might count a single phone call as an incident, even though it had merely discussed a case or offered armchair advice, and had not actually deployed staff for the weeks and possibly months it took to resolve the case. Some clients were aware of the need to ask questions about level of experience and training among negotiators, while most were not. But like so much of crime and crime fighting in the 1990s, this was a new frontier.

In addition to Ackerman and the U.S. branch of CRG, competitors included former FBI agent Paul Chamberlain, renowned for his extensive work on the Patty Hearst kidnapping. A short, tightly wound man with a fast-paced, animated style and a boisterous bent for storytelling—his anecdotes are enriched with characters and dialogue—Chamberlain is married to a former FBI agent. He launched his firm in Los Angeles in 1981 with a $500,000 gift from the family of a kidnapping victim whose life he had saved thirteen years before. He had worked with several insurance companies, including Firemen's Fund, which launched its K&R coverage in 1994. Its brochure that year described a "crisis response service—a kind of SWAT team composed of former FBI and law enforcement officers at Paul Chamberlain International." By 1995, Chamberlain's firm had handled at least 300 kidnapping and extortion cases—half international and half in the United States. In one case, he bargained the kidnappers down from a $1 million ransom demand to $125,000.

Sean McWeeney, another former FBI agent, worked for a number of years at Chamberlain's firm, heading up the East Coast operations. In 1991, McWeeney left Chamberlain to start his own company, Corporate Risk International, in Fairfax, Virginia, just down the road and over the freeways from Control Risks Group's U.S. headquarters, in McLean. By October 1995, CRI was telling clients that it had handled seventy-eight kidnapping and extortion incidents—thirty-six in the United States and the rest abroad.

The dangers and risks of the new era seemed to be pumping new life into Pinkerton's, the country's oldest "private eye" operation. "While you seek the opportunities of a global economy, we stand beside you," a Pinkerton's brochure read. Though most of the firm's revenue came from its bodyguard services, its image was changing. In 1990, the firm bought Business Risks International, a Nashville operation run by former FBI agent Don Walker. BRI had been handling kidnap cases for decades. With its risk assessment reports and travel advisories, both online and hardbound; its "Danger Spots of the World" column in the London *Times;* and K&R coverage through CIGNA International, Pinkerton's was alive and well. Its Internet Web site read, "Pinkerton Risk Assessment services is like having your own counterintelligence agency at your fingertips." The firm boasted a database chronicling more than 56,000 terrorist incidents worldwide from 1970 to the present. And it had its own "response" crew, including Lou Palumbo, Ackerman's former partner, and Daniel F. Donahue, a former Kroll kidnap and crisis "response" person who was the managing partner of Incident Management Group, another crisis management company.

The big kid on the block, however—and sometimes the bully—was Kroll Associates, Wall Street's high-rolling star investigation firm, whose story was worthy of a book unto itself. Kroll was to white-collar crime what CRG was to kidnapping. Their vital statistics nearly mirrored each other's, though Kroll's staff was larger. Nearly two-thirds of Kroll's staff was devoted to an array of white-collar investigations; the rest worked on kidnappings. At CRG, it was just the opposite. And while Kroll was boosting its antikidnap business, CRG was channeling its investigative talents into more and more business intelligence and fraud work. Jules Kroll, a New York lawyer who had worked in Bobby Kennedy's Senate office during his law school days at Georgetown, started his firm in 1972 with a tiny staff doing small-time security consulting and minor probes. But during the heady 1980s when the feverish pace of mergers and acquisitions required companies to watch their backs and to know everything possible about their enemies, the firm became almost legendary. Kroll worked for Drexel Burnham Lambert to help dig up dirt on Ivan Boesky when Boesky began singing to the government in 1986. It helped to unearth the U.S. holdings of deposed Haitian dictator Jean-Claude "Baby Doc" Duvalier. Its staff had included a long line of ex-federal prosecutors, ex-FBI agents, and ex-spooks. In 1985, CRG's bold and bright Arish Turle, a former SAS captain, jumped to Kroll, as did a well-known counterterrorist specialist, once at the Rand Corporation, Brian Jenkins. Bill Ilsley, a shimmering star of Scotland Yard, took over the post of European director of crisis management at Kroll, in 1995, at the London branch. And former New York police commissioner Robert McGuire, also a former head of Pinkerton's, was at one point the company's president.

Along the perilous peaks of Wall Street in the 1980s, there was no doubt that Kroll was king of the sleuths—a renowned keeper of secrets. And by the 1990s, it was handling at least 2,500 investigations a year. But as it began its third decade, the firm, in the grip of nettlesome internal problems—such as high staff turnover and late payment of bills—was beginning to show some sizable cracks in its foundation. Still, the ever-confident, dauntless, imposing Jules Kroll, explaining away any problems as the price of such a fast-growing and highly sensitive business, continued to expand his firm. He opened new offices in Latin America, Australia, and Russia, and launched a campaign to escalate Kroll's counterkidnapping operations worldwide. And part of the push was to try to grab a significant market share from the top kidnap consultants at CRG.

Around the time of the October 1995 meeting at the FBI, Kroll came out with a marketing circular, *Kroll vs. The Competition,* distributed to insurance brokers, among others. It boasted that the firm had responded to 51 kidnap incidents since 1991 and its consultants had experience with over 120 kidnap incidents. In April of 1995 alone, it said, Kroll had deployed nine kidnap consultants—all fluent in the local languages—to handle nine kidnappings worldwide. "Do our competitors have this operational capability?" the brochure queried. "Do our competitors have this language capability? [Kroll] has experienced personnel assigned to offices around the world. This facilitates response speed and offers the benefits of local resources and knowledge."

Then, scorning its competitors, it went on to say that "CRG assigns most full-time response consultants to London. Most of their staff in overseas locations are marketing personnel. CRI has no additional offices. Chamberlain (a Los Angeles–based firm) has no additional offices. Ackerman Group has no additional offices."

CRG fired back with its own promotional flyer. Though known for a culture of secrecy and reluctant to advertise its counterkidnap capabilities, the current marketplace was forcing the firm to change. CRG had worked 253 kidnap cases since 1975—104 of them since 1991, the flyer noted. Each of its twenty-eight full-time crisis consultants spoke at least one foreign language, and as a group there was a facility in nineteen languages, it said. And countering the Kroll offensive, it stressed, "CRG has 14 full-service offices worldwide. These are not merely sales offices, but offices which employ full-time consultants." In the first ten months of 1995, they had worked twenty-eight kidnap cases in twenty-one countries.

21

OCTOBER 11, 1995
EN ROUTE TO RIO

The man in the window seat of row seven, business class, stared into the darkness of a Caribbean night. It was about 1 A.M., on October 11, 1995, and he was removing his headphones, replacing a Beethoven sonata with the hum of the jet plane. He was an ordinary-looking middle-aged traveler in his white button-down shirt, his pressed blue jeans, his brown penny-loafers buffed to a soft shine, and his Timex watch with its plain black vinyl band. Slinging an equally common green canvas bag casually over his shoulder, as he typically did, this passenger could easily blend with the airport crowd in any major city of the world. And to blend was his intention.

At the airport in Rio, his destination, he hoped no one would notice that the label of his designer jeans had been carefully removed or that the tan mark on his left wrist did not match the shape of the Timex watch or that there were no address tags on his canvas bag. He would avoid talking to anyone in the terminal, and when he had to, he would speak to them in Portuguese, perfected with a touch of slang. If it were Bogotá, he would speak Spanish with the appropriate regional accent; and in Mexico City, the same. Dropping the broad *a*s of his own Boston accent, he would not use his own name when he checked into a Rio hotel. And no one would ever know about his expensive Rolex watch back home in Florida on top of his bureau next to his college ring with the ruby setting and the note from his secretary—the message he received only twelve hours earlier about a new case in Rio, a kidnapping of the twenty-three-year-old brother of a millionaire supermarket magnate.

That Bob Dwyer, a compact, bespectacled man who almost always has a classic novel or a philosophical work in his hand, is a kidnap negotiator never crossed the minds of his fellow passengers that night. Few people know such a job exists, and no one watching this unpretentious ex–Marine officer and former FBI agent would have even suspected that he was an American. Such is the level of his understanding of Latin American cultures and his ability to slip in and out of the countries of his specialty: Brazil, Mexico, and Colombia. To Dwyer, a deep knowledge of the culture in which the kidnapping has occurred is as important as experience with the crime itself. To be an excellent listener is imperative, but in each culture, as the nuances of language and custom change, so does the lexicon of cues to which a negotiator must listen. And so Dwyer, who lived in Puerto Rico for eleven of his twenty-one FBI years, is fluent in Spanish and has worked hard to master the dialects of specific regions in Mexico and Colombia, not to mention the long hours spent listening to Portuguese language tapes and taking private lessons. His learning has never stopped, which is why he often spends more time with the locals than with fellow Americans, to expand his education. Dwyer knew from years of working cases in Bogotá and Rio how to ease in and out of a country without being recognized as a negotiator or even as an American, and without ever being stopped.

Dwyer was always noticing little details about local customs that helped him to further conceal his identity and origins. He had observed, for example, that it's almost second nature for men in the United States to have one or both hands in their pockets when they are waiting for a train or cab or for their luggage at baggage claim areas. But Latin American men rarely do that. And so, among other gestures and habits, Dwyer adopted this local convention to mask his identity, which was essential not only for his own safety but also for the families who employed him. He remembered once being with a family during the celebration of the return of a kidnap victim in Mexico. While he was there, he heard one of the guests refer to him as "El recomendado," meaning "the recommended one." He then realized that the guest knew what his role had been in gaining the release of the victim, and he panicked, wondering who else in the Mexican town knew. He quickly left the party and within an hour, the town.

Dwyer's green canvas bag was like a pilot's emergency kit, ready for bailing out over a jungle. In it, he packed a Swiss army knife, the most expensive model; a microcassette player; notebooks and journals; extra batteries of various sizes; two flashlights; and a file containing his basic medical history. Power outages were common in some of the regions where he worked cases, and batteries were not always easy to find. Once, while working a case in Honduras, he needed batteries for his tape recorder and had to travel to another town an hour or so away to find a store that carried them, and then the store had only one.

In addition to his classical tapes, he had brought along on this trip his Berlitz "Advanced Portuguese" tapes. He would listen to them during the last few hours of the flight. But for now, as rain streamed silently across the cabin window next to him, he did what his counterpart in the public sector end of negotiation, Roy Ramm, typically did on long flights to new cases: he thought about earlier cases and about the chaos that likely awaited him this time.

Going into a case, Dwyer had little information: the name of the victim, the name of the family member to contact, how many communications there had been since the abduction, and a few details about when and where the abduction took place. If the kidnapping was in a rural area in a Latin American country, the perpetrators were likely a guerrilla gang; if in an urban area, they were often former guerrillas who had turned to kidnapping as a livelihood, or common criminals who had turned their wicked trade into an industry.

Dwyer likened his job to that of an oncologist. The family of the hostage, like the family of a patient, turns to him for strength. He must listen carefully to the unrelenting fears, the grief, the imagined horrors. He must reassure them that it will all be OK, and, at the same time, he must deal with the reality of the situation. His job was to balance hope with reality. He must project an image of self-confidence, no matter what concerns he might have. Above all, he must never allow them to know that he shares their worst fear: that the hostage will be killed.

It was part of Dwyer's job to mitigate the mayhem and panic that could cause the family to make impulsive, unreasonable decisions. He assured them that what might seem strange behavior on the part of the kidnappers was typical. After working these cases since 1988, he knew most of the emotional tactics that kidnappers are likely to use, and he knew how to minimize the impact of their psychological assaults by explaining to the family that it was all part of a game. Using time as a weapon, kidnappers might give a family twenty-four hours to respond to a specific demand and then not call them back for another week. During this time, the collective pulse rate of the family soars, and unless they are told that this is a strategy on the part of the enemy, the delay will succeed in controlling and weakening them, making them more susceptible to the kidnappers' demands. Whatever the kidnappers do or fail to do, it was Dwyer's job to protect the family from surprises. And again, like a good doctor, he explained to them what must be done and the reasons for every move.

One of his first moves was always to choose a communicator, often someone from the victim's family, or perhaps a family lawyer, or a friend of the victim. For the negotiator to speak directly with the kidnappers could jeopardize the well-being of the hostage, whose captors might believe that they were being tricked and that government or law enforcement officials had been called in, against their wishes. It was his job to analyze the motives and intentions of the kidnappers— people he would never meet face-to-face—listening carefully to the words and intonations on the taped conversations between the family's designated communicator and the kidnapper's intermediary to determine the next move. He must learn as much as possible about the strengths and weaknesses of the victim, the kidnappers, and the family. He must take into consideration the interests and needs of the family, the kidnappers, the company (if applicable), the communicator, local law enforcement, embassy officials, the kidnapper's intermediary, the evolving relationship between the victim and the kidnappers, the health, stamina, and personality of the victim, and, of course, the government of the host country.

The family naturally wanted the victim back as soon as possible, but if the payment was too quick or too high, the kidnappers would get the message that these were easy targets and they'd hit again, soon, taking a sister or brother or son or daughter of the current victim and asking for even more in return for a safe release. A fast delivery could also cause a "double-dip" or "double-tap" case, in which the kidnappers ask for a second ransom before releasing the victim. Exercising patience was the only way to win this waiting game. Time in a kidnapping case was like a life span, Dwyer liked to say: "You never know exactly when the case will end."

Strategies varied from case to case. If he was negotiating for the release of an executive of a U.S. company captured in Brazil, he might tell the kidnappers, in an effort to dissuade them and to discourage kidnapping in general, that American corporations are heartless and cold about kidnappings. And that from their point of view, kidnappings in Brazil are a Brazilian problem. These corporations don't even want to know about kidnappings, much less concede to the kidnappers' demands. He might also try to divert ransom demands from U.S. currency to the Brazilian currency, the real, which would require numerous hard-to-deliver duffle bags of cash rather than a ransom payment neatly stuffed in a slim, easy-to-transfer briefcase. The weight of the ransom was something kidnappers rarely thought about. Yet it was a strategy for apprehending them. In the case of Sidney Reso in 1992, for example, the FBI was quite aware that the $18.5 million ransom request translated to 600 pounds. It wasn't exactly easy to lug a 600-pound bag without being noticed or caught. There were psychological reasons, also, to use the local currency: negotiating down from "billions" instead of "millions" was more effective. This was one of the reasons the negotiators in the Beatrice case talked in terms of pesos and not dollars.

Unlike most FBI agents, Dwyer had spent his entire career out in the field actively investigating. For twenty-one years he worked criminal cases, interviewing hundreds upon hundreds of criminals, taking signed statements, urging confessions, gathering evidence, developing informants—all of which gave him an advanced degree in human nature. His instincts formed a sharply honed mechanism for detecting lies, deception, fear, and panic—indispensable to his current work.

What was so different now in his private sector career was that he operated, for the most part, alone. The long stretches of blank time between the communications with the kidnappers and the strategy sessions with the family and the communicator could be deadly. Kidnappers usually call at dusk or nighttime, which leaves a good portion of the negotiator's day open. On one case in Medellín, Dwyer started every day swimming fifty laps at the hotel pool before meeting with the family. He knew a guy who wrote a book during a year-long rotation on and off a case. Another negotiator made quilts. One guy he knew on a case in Cali had always wanted to learn to play tennis and so took lessons every day during his thirty-day rotations on the case. By the time the hostage was free, he was more than a decent player.

Dwyer typically worked cases for Kroll, though he had also been retained by Paul Chamberlain and Pinkerton's. And he had never lost a hostage, though he knew guys who had. What he liked best about his job was that incredible rush he got when the hostage was set free— that moment when he could turn to the family and instead of offering reassurance, announce the time and place for the release. What he hated most about it, though, was the ransom. It was his job to personally count the money, bill by bill, of a cash ransom before it was handed over to the kidnappers. And while he counted, a bad feeling usually rolled over him, like a wave of anxiety. He knew that in just a few hours, the kidnappers would be doing the same thing, touching the same bills, and then using them to fund more kidnappings: to pay the bills for more hostage hotels, more cars to block the way to work for more executives, more rope to bind the ankles of more terrified sons, daughters, brothers, and mothers.

He had no moral qualms about negotiating the payment of a ransom. It was human nature to pay, and, in his opinion, no law against paying ransoms would ever be successful. If a country passed a law freezing a family's assets the moment a loved one was abducted, the family would conduct all negotiations in seclusion and perhaps not even bring in a professional negotiator. Or they would sequester assets in another country. And because he had endured so many hours with so many families during abductions, Dwyer knew that they would likely have no qualms about breaking the law. That minor act paled in comparison with living with the guilt of not doing everything possible to get the victim out alive.

Dwyer felt very strongly that as long as a government could not protect the vast number of its citizens living, working, and traveling abroad, it could not forbid its citizens—whether tourists or business executives—from doing everything possible to gain the release of hostages, including the payment of a ransom. He likened the situation to telling people who are threatened with a potentially fatal illness that they cannot use certain drugs or treatments that are not FDA-approved. "A person who is dying is not going to worry about the niceties of the law," Dwyer liked to say, "nor is a family who is worried about whether a loved one will be killed at any second of any day from the first moment of captivity."

In his view, the only solution was to improve the legal infrastructures of the countries where kidnapping was a problem. The cops needed training in sophisticated methods of investigation to increase the apprehension and conviction rate, which, in Dwyer's estimation, was really the best deterrent to the crime. And the cops needed to be better paid to eliminate the temptation to participate in kidnappings, which happened more frequently than anyone could ever know in most developing nations.

What agitated Dwyer, who was very proud of the work he did, was the public misconception about negotiators trying to get the ransom demand down to the lowest possible amount, whether it was money or prisoners or land grants. When insurance companies were involved, the inference was that the negotiators were working more for the companies than for the victim's life—a notion that incensed Dwyer.

"It's more like we make sure the highest possible ransom isn't paid," he said. "I worked a case where the family had an enormous amount of money, and we reached a point where the abductors were demanding $1 million. I knew if they were patient, the ransom could be considerably less. But the victim's mother was in her early seven-ties, and she was insistent that this amount should be paid. I spoke with the children and the in-laws, and I told them that I would not stand in their way if that is what they wanted to do. But I also said there were two very adverse consequences they should take into account. If they paid $1 million, another member of the family would likely be kidnapped within the next few months because of the image of being an easy-target family. And the second thing was that if a mil-lion was paid, this would become the new minimum standard for themselves and their relatives, their region, and their country. It was a difficult situation. They had trouble listening to their mother, who desperately wanted her son back. But they also respected her. In the end, they allowed me to bargain for a much less substantial sum, and the son was released, unharmed."

Dwyer stressed the importance of the negotiator's instinct, espe-cially when negotiations have reached a critical point: "[Instinct] is invaluable, cannot be taught, cannot be programmed on a computer. It's what makes this a very subjective job. The negotiator's wiliness, self-confidence, and experience must work like a sonata, a fine piece of classical music. It must be practiced over and over."

Dwyer had watched the crime of kidnapping transform the cultures of several countries over the past seven or so years. In Rio, the crime had been growing since about 1990 largely due to the growing gap between rich and poor, though the financial needs of drug traffickers were another cause. Dwyer knew families in Rio who had never even thought of a bodyguard six years ago and now had as many as fifteen. In some of the most beautiful towns in Mexico, he knew Americans who lived in houses surrounded by ten-foot walls topped with rows of electrical wiring and who drove only armored cars. He remembered looking out from a penthouse balcony in Bogotá across a neighbor-hood of one walled-in yard after the other, like forts, each with a guard sitting in a chair balancing an AK-47 or some other weapon on his knee. He knew well-to-do families—not all that rich—who were forced to save as much as possible to send their children to school in the United States because they feared being mistaken for a rich family with deep pockets. The rich feared abductions, and the poor feared being accused of abducting. The crime was transforming societies into regions ruled by fear.

But despite what was happening, there were still so many secretive, unreported cases and so many people who believed it would never happen to them—even in Latin America. It was a known fact that 98 percent of all kidnappings occurred while the person was driving to or from work. But the problem has always been that it takes an enormous amount of discipline to alter a route, day after day, to change work hours, to eliminate all routine, to constantly watch for something that might never happen. Dwyer understood this, but he was still unnerved when he debriefed victims upon their release and learned that the victim or his driver or someone close to him had "seen things" that might have been early warning signs. Even in the case of the Banamex chairman in Mexico, who was released in 1994 for more than $11 million, two or three of the bodyguards and chauffeurs of this very powerful billionaire told the debriefer that they had seen suspicious people watching the target, but that because they were neither instructed to report such activity nor asked about it, it somehow, in the course of daily life, seemed unimportant.

The lifestyle of a kidnap negotiator required the willingness and flexibility to drop everything for thirty days, within twenty-four hours of getting a call. It was like being in the military when you're told you have thirty minutes to evacuate. Among other preparations, Dwyer was in the habit of paying bills early. And vacations, as his wife of thirty years and four children well knew, were a chancy proposition. This October, Dwyer and his wife had planned to spend a week in Nantucket. The trip was to begin on the nineteenth. He would resolve this Rio case in five days, returning to Tampa on the sixteenth. But Nantucket would not be his next destination. Within twenty-four hours of returning to Tampa, he would get another call, to return to Rio to work a case involving yet another supermarket executive. This year it was supermarkets; last year it was bus companies—both businesses known to deal in large amounts of cash. "I just came home to do my laundry," he would tell his friends on the eve of yet another long, twelve-hour journey to Rio.

For now, as he checked his Timex to determine how much Berlitz time he could squeeze in before the end of the flight, Dwyer thought about his last trip to Rio, which had been in September. At that time, there were six ongoing cases that he knew of, and four of the five other negotiators were staying at his hotel. This was a new experience. He had bumped into negotiators he recognized at hotel bars in Bogotá once or twice, but five in one hotel—that was different. It was also fun and edifying. They would meet for breakfast each morning, and, without revealing names, they would compare notes, swap stories, and offer feedback. One of them had just finished a case in which the hostage was killed, and now he was determined to give the family closure by finding the body—not an easy task. He eventually had the Rio authorities, much to their dismay, exhume bodies until they found the victim; thirty bodies later, the victim was found.

Some negotiators lived with the families throughout the ordeal. Dwyer didn't. These were families that could be facing a death, and while he was sympathetic and wanted to understand the family and all of their needs throughout the ordeal, he could not get so close as to be distracted by their grief. He needed a daily dose of distance and solitude.

Raised an Irish Catholic in Boston, Dwyer was always grappling with basic philosophical and theological issues. He didn't understand why, for example, it was permissible to kill civilians during wars. It bothered him that issues regarding the widening gap between the rich and the poor couldn't be faced and discussed before violent eruptions of crime—including kidnapping waves—brought attention to the problem. In his line of work, he saw an endless stream of stolen lives, which caused him to question good and evil, especially the source of evil. On his last plane ride to Latin America, only a month before, he had read Hannah Arendt's *Eichmann in Jerusalem,* a historical commentary revealing the banality of evil. He had also recently reread *The Confessions of St. Augustine,* paying special attention to the passages on evil.

And now, as his plane cut across northern Brazil, with two hours left in the flight, he pulled a book out of the green canvas bag. *Wickedness: A Philosophical Essay,* by Mary Midgley. He turned to an underlined and familiar passage on page three: "To approach evil merely by noting its outside causes is to trivialize it. Unless we are willing to grasp imaginatively how it works in the human heart and particularly in our own hearts, we cannot understand it."

Although secrets hovered like wisps of smoke around his profession, Dwyer found his work far from mysterious. It was stressful, demanding, emotionally taxing. But the only mystery about it, in Dwyer's mind, was the fact that kidnappings happened so frequently. He well understood the economic and political factors provoking the crime and how it had changed since the end of the Cold War. He had actually studied the reasons for the apparent surge in ransom kidnaps in recent years. That wasn't the mystery. What was so utterly incomprehensible to Dwyer was how people could be so cruel as to trade in such human misery.

22

As the wheels of Dwyer's jet were touching down on the landing strip in Rio, a small cadre of Brazilian police was discussing strategies to fight the war on kidnapping. One new idea was to kidnap the spouses or parents of kidnappers and hold them until the kidnappers released their own hostages. It was an idea that would be tested in Rio and several other places, officially or unofficially, though, like all short-term remedies, it would fail. Around the same time, in Rio, the Jewish community was banding together to fight the war alone. They planned to supply negotiators from their own ranks and to bankroll their own ransoms. Their belief in how to proceed was bolstered by the centuries-old teachings of their religious book the Talmud, which read, "The duty of ransoming captives supersedes [the duty of] charity to the poor."

Meanwhile, in parts of China and the Philippines, vigilante groups were forming to fight kidnappers. In the Philippines, citizens were staging daylong strikes to protest the government's inability to stop the crime. In China the respected deterrent to kidnappers was the firing squad.

In Colombia, the government had new intelligence units devoted specifically to apprehending kidnappers. It was offering rewards for information about kidnappers, and it had slashed penalties for kidnappers who helped to free hostages. There were now 2,000 agents and twenty-four prosecutors fighting the kidnap war.

And in Mexico, while politicians grappled with the horrors of a culture transformed by fear, the nation's potential targets found their own quick-fix solutions: round-the-clock bodyguards, twelve-foot-walls, elaborate alarms, and kidnap-proof cars. Ford Broncos and Suburbans now made customized models with a James Bond twist that were selling well in Mexico. At the push of a dashboard button, tear gas could be dispersed from hidden ducts built into the exterior of the car. At the push of another, gun ports would open and the bulletproof windows would roll up. And, for the very well-heeled Mexican resident, Mercedes-Benz was making the Supercar, which offered the ducts and the ports as well as slash-proof tires and oil slick dispensers for those suspicious vehicles tailing too closely.

There was always some clever new idea to foil kidnappers, but, like cockroaches, they would adapt and survive. Some would even thrive. There were simply no surefire short-term deterrents to terrorist kidnappings or to the criminally motivated ones that were so common in Rio.

To be sure, some short-term tactics had worked. The day after the release of Michael Barnes, an executive vice president of a Philippine subsidiary of Unocal Corporation snatched in Manila's financial district and held for sixty-one days, newspapers ran front-page stories showing photos of the bodies of the fourteen kidnappers, who were killed during the rescue. "It took a while for anyone to even think of kidnapping an American after that," says one State Department analyst. "That's what you call a deterrent. Of course it would have been a different story if Barnes had been killed too."

And in Rio, the creation of a special tourist police force in 1992 was lessening the crimes on Rio's alluring beaches and, by most accounts, deterring the spread of kidnapping to tourists. Informing tourists of potential dangers helped, too. Awareness was, after all, the first step toward any solution.

The only real solutions were long-term—such as dramatically improved law enforcement to increase the arrest rates, elimination of police corruption to enhance the reporting of kidnappings, international cooperation in cracking down on kidnappers, and programs for reintegrating demobilized government and guerrilla forces in countries ending years of war. Economic changes to narrow the crime-fertile gap between rich and poor were critical to diminishing the crime. In places like Rio, social conditions had to be improved. In all parts of the world, the only way to eradicate kidnapping was to deal with its root causes. Governments had to listen to the protests of their disenfranchised populations and not be quick to ban or violently silence such groups, which could then resort to kidnapping and other crimes for their voices to be heard.

In confronting the rising problem in Ecuador, one government consultant pointed to the need for his nation's justice system to change. "We need to pay more attention to groups that have been marginalized up until now. If we don't, kidnapping will be seen as an exemplary method for securing quick solutions to long-standing conflicts. And I don't think that is the path we want to go down."

Even former hostages recognized and sometimes publicly condemned the conditions that had provoked their captors. In some cases, experts pointed to the Stockholm Syndrome, the psychological condition in which captives become sympathetic to the causes of their captors. But in others, the hostages were clearly in touch with reality. John Emberly, the Canadian held in Colombia for eleven months, saw his kidnappers as mere "pawns on a chessboard. They were a bunch of lads younger than my children—aged sixteen and twenty—who have been forced into a life like this because of the poverty of the country."

Long-term solutions, however, required governments to understand what it meant to be global in terms of human relations and social conditions as well as economics. Governments, such as the United States, needed to encourage human rights in tandem with economic development in their foreign policies. And companies expanding into lands where inhabitants resented the intrusion needed to contribute a portion of their profits to the communities they were entering.

The older multinationals understood the importance of this. It was the companies that had made hideous mistakes in their exploitation of workers and environments twenty years earlier that were among the more responsible explorers of the 1990s. They had learned the hard way that being insensitive to local cultures could precipitate a violent backlash.

One of Control Risks Group's tactics for countering insurgents was to deflate their cause—that is, to give the insurgents' communities what they were seeking before they were compelled to kidnap a company employee to demand the same thing. Projects to build schools and roads, to equip schools with computers, to operate roving medical clinics. Whatever was needed, the intruders should provide. CRG advised companies to include community relations programs in their budgets as a fixed item long before the first oil drill or bulldozer touched the ground.

But long-term cures required time and patience, which governments and politicians rarely possessed. Needing short-term elixirs, both frequently looked to new laws as solutions. In Guatemala, the ruling party's antidote in the mid-1990s was to promote the death penalty for kidnappers and accomplices who threatened to kill hostages. This was a country where in 1995 two people a week were being kidnapped and where kidnappers had hauled in more than $34 million in ransoms in 1994. Politicians were under extreme pressure to do something. New laws or revisions of existing laws were the preferred panaceas. The death penalty in Guatemala already applied to premeditated murder and multiple killings. And nearly 75 percent of the polled public approved of extending it to kidnappers. In Peru, President Alberto Fujimori passed a law toughening jail sentences for kidnappers, who could now face life in prison if they caused physical or psychological harm to their victims. And then there were the laws against ransoms.

The logic of the ransom laws was, of course, that the payment of ransoms encourages the kidnappers and hence the crime. Ransoms also help to fill the coffers of terrorists. Some experts contend that during the 1970s and 1980s, terrorist groups obtained more funding from kidnapping and drug trafficking than from government sponsors. And now, in the aftermath of the Cold War—partly because of those demobilized soldiers and displaced rebels, as well as ethnic and tribal uprisings—the kidnap activity had escalated in some parts of the world. To pay ransoms could therefore be tantamount to financing terrorism, though it was impossible to know how many ransom kidnaps were criminally motivated and how many benefited political groups and religious extremists. For politicians, these were catchy concepts, and it was easy to buy into the idea that stopping the payment of ransoms would indeed stop kidnappers in their tracks and even contribute to eliminating terrorism.

And no one could deny that paying ransoms was an incentive for more abductions. In the annals of reported kidnaps, the biggest ransoms ever were $60 million paid in Hong Kong in 1990 for the return of the fifty-seven-year-old billionaire property tycoon Teddy Wang Teh-huei and the $60 million paid in 1975 in Argentina for the release of Juan and Jorge Born after nine months in captivity. Wang, who was Hong Kong's fifteenth richest person, had also been kidnapped in 1983, when his wife had paid $11 million for his return. The second time, despite the ransom payment, Wang was never released; no body has ever been found. In Argentina, the Born brothers were the sons of the chairman and founder of Bunge Born, a grain-exporting firm that was the country's largest private company. The kidnappers' demands included the distribution of food and clothing worth about $1 million and the installation of busts of former President Juan Perón and Eva Perón in all branch offices of the Borns' empire. The ransom monies, according to an individual familiar with the case, were distributed under various names to bank accounts throughout Europe and used to finance more political terrorism on the part of the kidnappers, the Monteneros. They reaped at least $240 million in ransoms before they were stopped, following Argentina's military coup in 1976.

Among unreported kidnaps settled secretly through private negotiations, the largest ransom occurred in early 1977 when a supermarket chain in Germany paid $65 million to get back one of its top executives. Some intelligence analysts indicate that it was the success of this kidnapping that could have inspired others that year, including the tragic kidnapping and murder of Dr. Hanns-Martin Schleyer, the president of Mercedes-Benz. One of the largest ransoms ever paid by a U.S. corporation was Exxon's $14.2 million in exchange for a general manager abducted in Argentina in December 1973. More recently, in Mexico, the $20 million in ransoms paid within several weeks to kidnappers to get back the Banamex chairman and the supermarket chain tycoon helped to spread kidnapping throughout that nation.

But while it was true that hefty ransom payments encouraged more kidnappings, there was no way of forcing a halt to them—unless, that is, families were willing to sacrifice their loved ones, and companies, their employees. This was highly unlikely. There was also the logic imparted by the FBI negotiators: the problem was already widespread in some regions of the world and therefore to risk the lives of hostages by not bargaining was simply wrong.

By 1997, only four countries had laws addressing the issue. Spain required families of hostages to work with local law enforcement authorities. Germany outlawed the sale of kidnap insurance but did not ban the payment of ransoms. Italy and Colombia had laws prohibiting ransoms *and* negotiators, though neither country had proven conclusively that the laws had stymied kidnapping. In both Italy and Colombia, families and companies were still paying ransoms.

Italy's law, passed in March 1991, called for freezing the assets of the families of kidnap victims to prevent ransom payments, for banning the sale of kidnap insurance policies, and for the arrest of anyone assisting a family member in paying a ransom, which meant, of course, outside negotiators. In the years that followed, it was easy to assume that the law in Italy was the quintessential solution because the number of reported kidnaps was plummeting at a time when other countries were witnessing rises. But kidnappings were still occurring in Italy, mainly in the regions of Calabria and Sardinia, where kidnapping of locals was almost a pastime. The Italians had simply learned to circumvent the law. They were not reporting abductions and they made covert arrangements to pay ransoms. Former hostages were known to have sent property deeds to kidnappers via a neutral party months after their release. There were instances, too, in which land had been sold by a former captive, in the months following his abduction, at a price far below its assessed value to people who were fronts for their former abductors. In some instances, ransoms were delivered over the border in other countries, such as Switzerland. At the same time, there were allegations that Italian authorities, in some special cases, had paid portions of the kidnappers' monies.

What had changed in Italy was that there no longer were politically motivated, ideologically based incidents in which kidnappers targeted high-profile individuals such as Aldo Moro, who had been Italy's prime minister six times and was slated to be the nation's next president. Political kidnappings began to die out when the Red Brigades disbanded in the 1980s. The abduction of General Dozier in 1981 was probably their last big undertaking. The death of the high-flying Brigades diminished the visibility of kidnapping in Italy, though splinter groups and criminal gangs continued to exploit the crime. By the time the ransom law was passed, the targets had become local businessmen, merchants, chemists, farmers, and other middle-level professionals who were not as heavily guarded as multimillionaire industrialists and politicians. However, the occasional multimillionaire was hit. In one case in 1992, the parents of a seven-year-old hostage paid a $6.7 million ransom after receiving the child's chopped-off ear as an incentive to pay.

Undoubtedly the pace of kidnappings in Italy was slowing, especially in comparison to the 1970s and the days of the Red Brigades when Italy was considered the kidnapping capital of the world. But the change was less a result of the law and more the impact of two developments: the eclipse of ideologically based kidnappings and a shift in the economic priorities of the criminals. By the 1990s, in both Sardinia and Calabria the motivation behind kidnapping was money and the targets were low-profile locals. The gangs of Sardinia were bandits with no ties to organized crime. And in Calabria, it was all about organized crime. There, the presence of drug labs in the mountains had increased the numbers of government troops roaming the hills. It was not as easy as it once was to conceal hostages. In addition to the labs, the mountains also hid huge caches of weapons, which were being smuggled through the heel of Italy. The labs and the weapons reportedly brought in more money than the ransoms. And so it appeared that what was really curtailing kidnappings in Italy were other phenomena that just happened to coincide with the passage of the law.

In Colombia, in 1993, controversy raged around a new law to freeze the assets of captives' families and employers to prevent ransom payments. The law also made it illegal for families and companies to open secret negotiations with kidnappers, hence outlawing the work of private negotiators. It called for the termination of contracts with foreign companies that pay ransom. And it outlawed K&R insurance and all that went with it, including the kidnap consultants. But clearly kidnappings still flourish, and both families and companies have coped by setting up financial systems for ransom payments and elaborate instructions for families on what to do in the event of an abduction.

The same year the law was enacted, the Colombian Supreme Court ruled that to deny a family the right to try to save the life of a relative was unconstitutional. The judges wrote: "The payment of ransom is in itself a neutral act, neither good nor bad. It is the intention that determines the moral justification. Therefore, the payment of ransom to save a life or to obtain freedom has an altruistic motive universally recognized by the law. . . . Those operating through altruistic, noble and economically neutral motives and acting in the state of necessity according to the laws that penalize kidnapping have the sufficient force and virtue to strip away the illegality of the act of negotiating a kidnap."

Families in the midst of kidnappings want shorter than short-term solutions. They don't have time to wait for laws to be tested or police officers to be trained. They need results—fast. But because governments are often unable to help, and because experienced negotiators such as Dwyer or Ramm are either unavailable or summoned to the front too late, as in Kashmir, families, in desperation, have at times taken matters into their own hands.

The annals of global kidnapping are brimming with such tales. If it were not for the go-go spirit of David Housego, whose son was kidnapped in Kashmir in 1994, many believe that the case would have had a far different outcome. In the 1990s, there were several cases in which families wrested the reins of control: in Costa Rica, in Ecuador, in Colombia, in Mexico, in Hong Kong. There was the case of Thomas Hargrove, the Texan abducted in Cali, Colombia, in 1994 and released after eleven months in captivity. When his company announced that it would not negotiate a ransom, his wife, Susan, shifted into high gear, learning everything she could about how kidnappings were typically handled. Her brother, who lived in Kuwait, rang up oil executives knowledgeable about the steps hostage families should take. Kidnap negotiators from Kroll and Control Risks, in town on other cases, also offered advice. And much to her surprise, the American embassy and the FBI were very helpful. "Having lived abroad for years, I expected nothing from my government. What can the government really do, after all?" she said later.

Hargrove's company advised Susan not to negotiate for his release, but she felt that she had no alternative. After his family hired two professional negotiators and paid two ransoms, Hargrove was freed, in August 1995. "If you're in a country where ransom is an accepted thing, then you must pay it to get out," Susan Hargrove said two years after her husband's release. "You do it as legally as possible in the country where the kidnapping occurred. The choice of not paying is death."

Then there was the unforgettable story of Scott Heimdal, a 27-year-old engineer from Peoria, Illinois, whose ordeal seemed to be tailor-made for a Frank Capra movie of the 1990s.

Heimdal, who worked for a gold-mining company in Ecuador, was traveling by canoe down the Bermeja River about five miles from the Colombian border when a band of Colombian guerrillas, wearing green fatigues and wielding assault rifles, ambushed Heimdal and his companions in the boat. They killed the skipper and seized Heimdal and another man, whom they released several hours later with the message of a ransom demand for Heimdal's freedom. That was on April 28, 1990.

By June, Heimdal was still in captivity, still surviving on armadillo and monkey meat, still trudging daily through the jungles of Colombia somewhere on the east side of the Andes mountains. The Ecuadoran military's land and air searches had failed to find him. There were apparently no professional negotiators helping to devise a strategy. And back in the American heartland in Heimdal's blue-collar hometown of Peoria, folks were "mad as hell," as one editorial put it.

Peoria, a working-class community with strong allegiances and patriotic sentiments, took the family's plight to heart. The Heimdals quickly became Peoria's cause célèbre. Everyone, literally, got into the act of saving Scott Heimdal.

The ransom demand was originally $1.5 million, but was quickly and inexplicably lowered to $1.2 million. Then, after more than a month of Scott Heimdal's assuring the rebels that no one in his family had that kind of money, the demand had plummeted to $60,000, which was still far beyond the means of Heimdal's parents and two sisters. Scott's fifty-two-year-old father, Roy, sold kitchen cabinets, and his mother, Marge, was the activities director of a local nursing home. In recent years, they had been teetering near the edge of bankruptcy because of medical bills from an accident in which an uninsured drunk driver had hit and injured Marge.

Mayor Jim Maloof, a longtime friend of the family, told the citizens of Peoria that all it took was one dollar per household—there were about 60,000 households—to raise the funds. The activities director of another local nursing home—a friend of Marge's—contributed $1,200 from bake sales. Radio stations held call-in promotions to give away concert tickets, but only after each caller promised a five-dollar donation to the Heimdal cause. J. Michael Sullivan, the owner of Sullivan's Irish Pub and Rock Cafe, orchestrated a very profitable steak fry, raising $2,000 for the cause. Waitresses donated tips. Children collected money in jars. Ryan Hayden and Katie Bowles, two nine-year-olds, raised $275 at a picnic table at a neighbor's garage sale. PLEASE HELP FREE SCOTT HEIMDAL, the sign on the jar read. A neighbor boy who found a twenty-dollar bill in the street rode his bike to the Heimdal home to add it to the Peoria war chest. A four-year-old girl raised $61.17 at her lemonade stand. And at the end of four days, the town had anted up more than $100,000, which the family delivered to the local bank in coffee cans. Of that, the family sent $60,000 to Ecuador and eventually gave the rest to charity. Meanwhile, Peoria's *Journal Star* newspaper ran an editorial about the vexing issue of paying ransoms. "The Heimdal kidnapping affair demonstrates how easy it is to oppose paying ransom to terrorists in general and how hard it is when the matter becomes personal. . . . Is every American down there [Ecuador] looked upon as a $60,000 ticket? Maybe, but who among us could resist trying to help the Heimdal family in their hour of need? Obviously, not many. For most people, this was not the time for philosophical discussions; it was the time for compassion and help. Once Scott Heimdal gets home, we can return to philosophy."

In Ecuador, a go-between took the money, in U.S. dollars, to a jungle rendezvous near the Colombian border, only to find the kidnappers refusing to accept the U.S. currency. They demanded that the dollars be changed for Colombian pesos, roughly thirty million. The go-between then traveled twenty or so miles by canoe down a river to the nearest large town to exchange the funds. But there were not enough pesos in the entire town for the exchange, and so he traveled back to the kidnappers and gave them as much as he could in pesos, with a promise to deliver the rest later in the month. It was after this episode that the Heimdals were told that the kidnappers now were saying that the $60,000 was only a down payment to guarantee their son's life. The money required for his release, they were told, was far more: 350 million pesos, or about $600,000.

The snafu, by most accounts, was the result of a news broadcast the kidnappers had seen that had led them to believe that the Heimdals were far richer than Scott Heimdal had informed them. What angered them was apparently a Cable News Network broadcast about the fund-raising efforts in Peoria, from which the rebels got the impression that the Heimdals were a prominent family with money. There was also a slight misunderstanding. The kidnappers had said that the $60,000 was "to guarantee his life," while the Heimdals and others had believed that the payment would set him free.

When the Heimdals learned that the ransom and the efforts of the town had not resulted in the release of their son, the family went into seclusion. The town, meanwhile, erupted into a fury of indignation and rage. "We're taking it pretty hard," Michael Sullivan told the *Chicago Tribune*. "We thought that $60,000 would be pretty difficult to collect in a workingman's community, but we did it. And now we are beginning to wonder who we are really dealing with here. If this stuff is going to continue, everybody traveling outside the U.S. is going to be in jeopardy. A lot of people feel the government should do something."

On June 14, in a signed editorial on the front page of the afternoon edition of the *Journal Star,* Henry P. Slane, the newspaper board's chairman, lambasted the U.S. government for failing to take action against the Colombian rebels to bring Heimdal home. Slane called the government a "toothless tiger."

"Why doesn't the government act?" Slane wrote. "You want a suggestion? Here's one: Drop napalm in the jungle where these kidnappers hang out, as a warning to return Heimdal unharmed within 48 hours or else."

He went on to say that the kidnappers should be threatened with incineration, and if they aren't, then "every crackpot in the world is going to decide that any American citizen is a fair target if they want to fatten their purses."

A few days later, not only did Marge and Roy Heimdal emerge from seclusion, but they flew to Quito to retrieve their son themselves. "I am not coming back without my son," the forty-seven-year-old mother told reporters before boarding the plane in Chicago. In Ecuador, the U.S. embassy released a statement from the Heimdals saying they were taking "direct charge of all negotiations with the persons who have our son Scott. We have relieved all other persons that represent us in these negotiations. We're trying to establish direct contact with the persons that have Scott to try and obtain his freedom. We're confident and optimistic that they will hear our pleas and deal directly with us and understand the suffering we're going through."

Soon, the Ecuadoran press was calling the nursing home worker from Peoria "the lioness" because of her fearless, determined, unrelenting campaign to get back her son. She and Roy dealt directly with the rebel intermediary, explaining things like their financial difficulty in raising the hundreds of thousands of dollars the rebels were now demanding. The kidnappers could not get any more. On June 29, after sixty-one days in captivity, Scott Heimdal was released. A few days later, wearing an "I [heart] Peoria" T-shirt, Heimdal walked off a plane in the Peoria airport, amid a cheering crowd.

23

On Donald Hutchings's 100th day of captivity, the friends of Don and Jane gathered at the couple's Spokane home, as they had done nearly every Wednesday since July, to discuss the latest news from Jane, who was still in New Delhi, and to effectively "will" Don's safe return. The teachers, doctors, nurses, psychologists—all outdoors enthusiasts and mostly Mountaineers—left their jobs around dusk that October day and drove north along the leafy banks of the Spokane River, up a winding road to a hilly subdivision called Northwoods, and into the driveway of a cedar-sided house surrounded by fastidiously tended gardens. As the wind droned through the towering Ponderosa pines, bringing the scent of autumn and the promise of winter, the friends entered the house and greeted each other, walking across Tibetan and Persian rugs, past walls of Don's photos in Jane's frames and the colorful wooden masks collected on their many trips abroad, down the redwood outdoor stairs, and along a meandering brick path to the backyard garden. There, amid the white flowers aglow from the last brilliant rays of daylight, the friends joined hands and formed a circle.

Depending on their religious and spiritual beliefs, they meditated or prayed as they had done in this garden so many times by now.

Although Don's return was the ultimate hope, the very least that they wanted to do was to send both Don and Jane their strength by setting aside that one evening every week just for them. Some people were aware that it was the 100th day of Don's captivity; some also knew that Jane might be home within the next few weeks. And all were optimistic that the upcoming holidays would include more festivities than usual because Don, too, would be home at last. As friends go, these were top of the line. They had spared the time each week not only to practice this leap of faith, this serene meditation that could, if there was indeed some higher force, assist their friend, wherever he might be, but also to maintain as much order as possible in Jane and Don's household. A few Mountaineers routinely worked the garden, pruning and weeding, mulching and mowing, as Don and Jane would have done. One Mountaineer and dear friend, Emily Gordon, had volunteered during the first weeks of the ordeal to fly to India to help Jane, but Jane declined the help. Others took care of the dogs Bodhi and Homer. Still others handled very sensitive tasks such as relations with the press and the occasional calls from individuals who claimed they knew how to get Don out and wanted a chance to help.

There was the man who called St. Thomas More Church in August, after the death of Ostro, to offer his services in rescuing Don. The church had held a candlelight vigil for Don during July, which the man had seen on television. Now, he wanted to secretly travel to Kashmir and rescue the hostages himself. The secretary of the church was unnerved by the call and by others that followed and wanted to shift the responsibility of dealing with him to someone else. It was downright scary just talking about the abduction in India, much less hearing the offers of a mercenary, or whatever he was. The secretary finally called Don's office and someone there rang up Debbie Pierce, one of Jane and Don's friends, who, after a few days of thinking about it, mustered the nerve to call the man. His number was in Sandpoint, Idaho, the home, reportedly, of some of the nation's budding militia groups. And his phone calls had all the markings of quackery, Debbie thought. With visions of Aryan Nation and other white supremacy groups, she was immediately suspicious. But when she spoke with him, he assured her, in deep, confident tones, that his company routinely did this sort of thing. And he had nothing to do with the new militias. He knew negotiation skills and had a military background. He genuinely wanted to help, he said, though he cautioned that it would have to be very secretive, meaning no government involvement. His experience was mostly with companies who hired him to negotiate ransoms to gain the release of their employees.

"The question was whether he was capable," Debbie recalled later, "and whether it was appropriate for him to be doing this, in this particular case. Could he do more harm than good?" She worried too about whether his credentials were valid, whether he was who he said he was. Debbie spent several sleepless nights fretting over what to do. Meanwhile, the man from Idaho kept saying to her, "This is your friend; you must help your friend." But Debbie, a nurse anesthetist who had climbed six or seven summits with Don, was still skeptical. Knowing that she did not have the experience to judge his paramilitary abilities, she called on a friend who worked for the air force and had some experience counseling hostage survivors. He and a colleague agreed to meet with her and the gentleman from Idaho, which they did, secretly, one night at the church library.

At the meeting, the Idaho man presented credentials and spoke about his track record in negotiating ransoms. He said he had gained the release of hostages by negotiating things like the payment of college tuition for the children of the kidnappers or helping a child of a kidnapper to get cardiac surgery. He described all kinds of inventive concessions, all based on the information he was able to gain through his exchanges with the hostage-takers. He thought these things might work for Don, and he said he required only that his expenses be paid. When asked how he would get into the Kashmir Valley without being noticed by the Indian troops or the roving bands of militants, he said he had done it before. He seemed to have answers for everything. But there were problems: his credentials didn't all check out; he wanted a blanket tab for his expenses. And, even without those two negatives, the two military men concluded that he didn't have enough political experience. The Kashmiri incident was a delicate, complicated political tangle—perhaps too messy for a man with such skills to be successful.

It was Debbie, too, who handled what the Mountaineers affectionately referred to as "the posterman episode." The posterman was Roland Smith, a local man whose daughter had been treated years before by Don Hutchings. He claimed that without Don his daughter, a head injury victim, could never have lived a normal life; he wanted to do something to help the man he considered a hero. When the news of Ostro's death hit Spokane, Smith hit the streets. He decided he could no longer wait idly for the government to bring Don back. And so he clipped the photo of Don out of the local paper—the one depicting Don with a bloody bandage across his stomach—and designed a poster using the picture and the phrase "Free Dr. Hutchings." He hocked one of his favorite possessions, a fine set of tools, and used the money for the printing of hundreds and hundreds of posters. He then took the posters and tacked them onto telephone poles and light posts in what he considered the wealthiest parts of town. He covered the country clubs, golf courses, and ritzy suburban developments. "These are the people with the money and power who can help," he later told Debbie.

A local television reporter spotted the posterman as he was positioning a poster on the pole of a stop sign and wanted to do a story on it. Somehow Debbie found out about this and called the station to ask that it not air the story. Jane had briefed her friends on the importance of silence at this stage of the negotiations, explaining, as she had been informed, that publicity could influence the rebels' perception of the value of their hostages (the more valuable they perceived their catch, the more they would want in return and the tougher they would bargain). Publicity, in short, could prolong their captivity, she had stressed. Everyone respected Jane's wishes, though it was tough for many of her friends to hold back their inclinations to aggressively fight for the return of their beloved friend. The Mountaineers, for example, had wanted to picket the Spokane airport with signs protesting travel to India until the kidnappers in India released Don. And they wanted to launch a nationwide crusade in the press to draw attention to his plight. But they refrained.

When Debbie explained Jane's wishes regarding the publicity, the station understood and agreed to withdraw its story. Debbie then found out the posterman's name and called him. Explaining how publicity could hurt his hero, she asked Smith to end his campaign. He was hesitant at first and said he would think about it. After a second call, he still didn't consent to her request. Finally at about eight one evening, he called Debbie to announce that he planned to spend the evening tearing down posters. Several hours later, at about 1 A.M., Debbie was awakened by the ringing phone. It was the posterman. He had completed his poster removal. The Mountaineers club was so moved by his crusade and his cooperation in ending it that they offered to pay the $300 or so to get his tools out of hock. But he declined. He had done it for Don, he told Debbie, and he didn't regret it. He proudly assured her that he would eventually earn enough money to buy back his tools.

The Wednesday night meetings at the Hutchings house had a special meaning to most everyone gathered there. Although the group spanned the scope of most spiritual and religious beliefs—from agnostic to Catholic to Buddhist—and some participants had at first been embarrassed by the trancelike "willing" of Don's release, their shared experiences on those Wednesday nights had created bonds as strong as the ones they felt while scaling summits or climbing frozen waterfalls.

None would forget the second meeting in July when, gathering as usual in the garden, the phone in the kitchen rang. There was a silent, collective decision not to interrupt the messages they were trying to send to Don. It was probably the press, after all. But the phone continued to ring. It persistently rang off and on for nearly an hour until Jacki McManus couldn't stand it any longer and sprinted up the stairs to answer it. The evening had seemed more intense than usual, with everyone deeply concentrating. When Jacki answered, she felt dazed and shocked as she heard Jane's voice on the other end. No one had heard from Jane since the incident and Jane had not been told about their weekly ritual at her house. "Jane, we're here at your house," Jacki said, as the familiarity of Jane's voice jolted her out of her near trance. "Yes, I know, I somehow knew you were there. That's why I called." After that, the skeptics held their thoughts, some even believing that perhaps they could accomplish something in their weekly meetings beyond holding hands and communing with friends.

About two weeks after the October 11 meeting of her faithful Mountaineers, Jane left India for Spokane, first spending a week in Allentown, Pennsylvania, with her parents. At home, her mother had created a new version of the family prayer: "God is great. God is good. God we thank thee for our food. And please look after Don, Dirk, Keith, and Paul. May they have food to eat too." Jane, touched by her mother's words and well aware of Don's love of food, especially exotic food, added, "Good food."

In Spokane, the McManuses held a pot-luck dinner in honor of Jane's return, inviting about twenty people, many of whom had attended the Wednesday night meditations. And Jane held court, as she so often would do from then on, answering questions and explaining the details of the incident and the complexity of its resolution. She was hopeful, she told friends. Don might even be home by Christmas.

Jane and the other hostage families now faced the new challenge of appearing to move along the stream of a normal life while enduring the constant ups and downs of the rapidly unraveling events in Kashmir. Standing in a grocery store line, looking for a parking space, or forcing a smile as a colleague says good morning, all the while thinking about your loved one's ability to live through another day, was a new form of torment. Jane felt especially blessed for having such good friends, though it was impossible for her to communicate all that she knew and felt about the case, and so there were times when she felt very alone. Some things at first were difficult, such as walking past Don's study on the second floor of their home. It was hard to look at his neatly arranged works of Joseph Campbell, the canes that his father, once a cowboy, had whittled from various woods and that Don displayed in one corner, and the stunning crystal ball that Jane had bought for Don's birthday that year but that he had not yet seen. Most haunting perhaps was another present she had purchased for Don in India in late July: the latest addition to Don's collection of wooden masks from ancient and tribal cultures. While in New Delhi, Jane toured a museum of ancient Indian art and purchased a green mask with red and white accents rooted in the Kathakali tradition. What she did not know at the time, and would not know until many weeks later, was that Hans Christian Ostro had depicted this very same mask when he painted his face for his big theatrical production in India prior to his trip to Kashmir.

To calm herself, she exercised a good deal, as much as her schedule permitted. Balancing her work with her crusade to seek the truth in India kept her very busy. There were sweet memories, too, to keep her anchored. Sometimes, for example, when she was out in the yard with Bodhi and Homer, she would look up to the kitchen window and remember how Don loved to cook. While he prepared dinner she would work in the garden, occasionally glancing at that window in anticipation of a gesture motioning her back into the house for the meal. And whenever there was a full moon, Jane would sit on the back steps gazing up at it and thinking how Don, wherever he was, might be looking at the moon and thinking of her.

Within four days of her return home, there were news accounts saying that Don was suffering from gangrene. The Al-Faran had reportedly kidnapped a surgeon to treat him. But like so many other reports, it was never confirmed. In the ensuing weeks, Jane, though accustomed somewhat to the roller coaster of emotions, would feel the impact of this new report in the form of a dream. One morning in mid-November, she awakened with a start after dreaming that Don's frostbitten foot was sent to her by parcel post in Spokane.

Two weeks after her return, the rebels broke their two-month silence. Since September 18, after speaking with the Indian negotiator by short-wave radio or telephone nearly every day, they had cut off talks, saying that India was refusing even to consider their demands. While this was true, the real reason for the silence might have been the press leaks of mid-September. Whatever the reasons, it had been an unbearable time for the families and the three calls to Indian officials on November 9 brought back that feeling of hope they had had frequently during the early weeks of the ordeal. As always, though, the hope faded quickly as a new round of terror settled in. This time it began when the rebels imparted the news that Hutchings and one unidentified Brit were both critically ill. At the same time, they reiterated their demand for the release of fifteen jailed militants and their persistent threat to kill the hostages.

In Spokane, Jane responded to reporters' requests in her usual succinct, reserved manner. Still fearing that extensive media coverage could endanger the lives of the hostages and prolong their captivity, and honoring the advice of the State Department, she declined to take questions from reporters. But she did say: "They are innocent tourists who have never done any harm to the people of Kashmir. It would be honorable and humanitarian to release them unharmed so they can return to their families where they belong. I will return to India when events indicate my presence can contribute in any way to Don's safety or to his release. My greatest hope is that when I do return, it will be to rejoin him and to bring him back home. The governments of India, Germany, Great Britain, Norway, and the United States have worked tirelessly to win the release of the captives. I am most grateful for their efforts."

Soon, less than a week later, the militants scaled back their demands to the release of six of their jailed comrades. India rejected the offer and instead issued the demand for the release of Hutchings and the unnamed Brit whom the militants had repeatedly claimed were critically ill. In response to that, the Al-Faran, two days later—one week before Thanksgiving—sent statements to reporters stressing the dire nature of Hutchings's condition. "The foreigner is ill and could die at any time. All responsibility will be on the Indian government. The foreigners' relatives have been told to reach Srinagar as soon as possible so that we can hand over the body if he dies. The government has been told many times but is not agreeing to demands. The government of India is fooling the world by false media statements."

The day before Thanksgiving, the militants reduced their demand once again, this time to a one-for-one swap. And to India they sent the message that if this was not acceptable, "you will regret it." The Indian government refused the swap.

At the State Department, on the day before Thanksgiving, the briefing, given by Nicholas Burns, went like this:

Q: [We have been told] that Donald Hutchings [who is] being held there is now critically ill. Al-Faran is evidently anxious to turn him over, to swap him. The Indian government is refusing. Can you comment on the urgency now that he is apparently very ill, and India's decision not to negotiate or to deal, if you will, with the group?

Burns: Mr. Hutchings is an American citizen. He's been held captive for many, many months. It's unjustified. It's a terrible injustice that he's been taken captive. We do understand that one of the hostages is critically ill. At least, that's what the Al-Faran organization has said. I cannot confirm that is Mr. Hutchings because we simply have no independent basis to corroborate that. We continue to work very closely with the Indian government in the very strong hope that Mr. Hutchings and the other detainees will be released very soon. We have not forgotten about him—those of us here in the Department of State, my colleagues here in the South Asia Bureau, and the Consular Affairs Bureau who have a responsibility to communicate with his family, to follow the situation. We have an excellent ambassador in Delhi, Frank Wisner, one of our most senior Foreign Service officers, who is working on this. We have not forgotten about him. We're hoping and praying for his release.

Q: Does the U.S. agree with India's decision not to deal with this group and not to conduct, for example, a rescue raid, if you will?

Burns: We are working very closely with the Indian government. We support the Indian government. We share its views that this hostage-taking cannot be condoned, cannot be justified, and must be ended. We hope it ends soon.

Two days later, the demand reportedly plummeted to an all-time low: the release of one jailed militant. But it was not low enough for the Indian government, which said no. On November 26, the Al-Faran countered with a new threat: if their demand was not met, they would kill the hostages and never call back. On November 27, an eerie silence descended on the Srinagar compound where the calls were received. The designated phone never rang that day, nor did it ring the next day, nor the next, nor the next. Never again would the Al-Faran communicate directly with the government of India. Never again would it be possible to confirm any fact, theory, supposition, or hope regarding the four tourists in Kashmir. From then on, Indian authorities could only communicate with the Al-Faran through the media, in response to statements dropped off at the local press office by the group's intermediary. It would be harder than ever to authenticate the rebels' intentions, demands, and activities. Without codes and special communications to detect the real representatives of the kidnappers, no information could be totally trusted.

On the last day of the month, the All Parties Hurriyat Conference, an umbrella organization of nearly thirty pro-separatist groups, urged the Al-Faran to release the hostages "on humanitarian grounds." "We want to make it clear to Al-Faran that such acts [of kidnapping] will only bring shame to Islam and will not help our freedom struggle."

The Al-Faran responded by asking the Hurriyat to intervene and mediate with the Indian government to end the five-month crisis. "If the Hurriyat desires to save the lives of the four foreigners, it should come forward to mediate and get the government to concede to our demands, because we will under no circumstance free the hostages without achieving our aim."

But the group declined to mediate, saying the Indian government had never heeded its own demands "either to free or bring to trial tens of thousands of Kashmiris languishing in jails." Its leader told the press, "to negotiate with such a government is out of the question."

What happened next would result in controversy, confusion, and extreme concern for a long, long time. On December 4, several militants, including the commander in chief, Abdul Hamid al Turki, supposedly left the hostages under guard at an abandoned tourist lodge in Kokarnag and then ventured down the mountains on an expedition for supplies. Several kilometers later, on a ridge overlooking the town of Anantnag, a battalion of Indian troops ambushed them, killing Turki and three other militants. In the days following the skirmish, the rebels released a statement saying that three of the hostages had been "captured" by the Indian army. The fourth hostage had disappeared. The Indian government denied this, pointing out that the hostages were nowhere near the battle and that the Indian army had assured Western diplomats that it would avoid rescue operations that could endanger the captives' lives—a promise that was still in force.

"We have made our own investigation, and we have found that all four are with the abductors," said Ramamohan Rao, a Kashmiri government spokesman. "This is nothing but a pressure tactic by the abductors, who want to spread the lie that the hostages are with the army."

In the months ahead, an array of theories, some replete with witnesses, would emerge about the soon-to-be legendary battle in which the leader of the Al-Faran had perished. While the Indians would always claim that the encounter was purely one of chance, others saw it as a deliberate attack: the Indians knew the Al-Faran was moving the hostages along the outskirts of Anantnag that day, and they purposely met the entourage, killing the hostages to shuttle blame onto the militants. Others would say, with great resolve, that the militants recognized the danger of a chance encounter in the Anantnag vicinity and so had kept the hostages in a safe shelter that day.

While the Indian press was filled with stories about the government "being overcome by a sense of resignation" in the now four-month hostage crisis, the U.S. State Department had apparently not lost faith in India's ability to resolve the crisis. The State Department briefing by official Glyn Davies on December 6 went as follows:

> *Q:* Can you talk about South Asia for a second, Mr. Spokesman? Some political groups in India promote a view that the U.S. supports Pakistan in the issue of Kashmir with India. I would like to know if the U.S. consciously follows a policy of favoring Pakistan over India?

> *Davies:* No, we don't consciously follow such a policy. Our policy on Kashmir hasn't changed. We encourage an immediate end to the violence. Our long-standing position is that it should be resolved through negotiations between the two countries—India and Pakistan. We're more than willing to help in the process, to assist in it, but only if desired by both sides. That hasn't changed.

> *Q:* In the same region, about a week—maybe it was two weeks—ago, there were reports that the American that's being held by Kashmiri rebels, and possibly one of the other foreign nationals who's being held—

> *Davies:* Mr. Hutchings.

Q: Yes—were in poor health and needed medical attention. It sort of dropped off the scope. There's no more information. Do you have anything?

Davies: I don't have an update for you on Hutchings' health. We wish that we had access to him so that we would know what his health is because we're very concerned about him.

We're not going to make any deals with those holding Hutchings and the others. But I'm happy to renew our call on those individuals to release them immediately. There's no reason to be holding the hostages out there.

Q: Do you know if a doctor was able to get to them to possibly treat those that were sick?

Davies: I don't know. I saw the same reports you did about, I guess, the Indian authorities discussing getting medical help out there. I don't know if a doctor was able to get out there.

A few days later, the four hostages, disguised in Kashmiri robes (called firans), were reportedly spotted in Akingam, a village not far from Anantnag, in southern Kashmir. They appeared to be in good shape, though guarded by more than a dozen gunmen.

That same day, a man claiming to be one of the kidnappers called the British High Commission and spoke with Ambassador Nicholas Fenn. The man said he still held the hostages and wanted money for their return. He also asked that the commission pay for the call. "You know, you know, we have been treating them as our guests for the last five months plus, and you can expect that we spent lots of money." The supposed Al-Faran militant reported, in addition, that two of his men had been killed trying to defend the Brits during the December 4 encounter.

The ambassador responded: "I don't think we can be in the position to compensate you for the money you have expended. I sympathize with the loss of your colleagues. . . . I don't think we can [help.] Our position is as I describe to you. We don't think it right to accede to requests like this when our citizens are held against their will because it creates the very conditions for other citizens to be taken by some other group for similar reasons. . . . Really, I think it's in your own interest that they be released so that they could join their families for the Christmas festival. My feeling is that if they were released, this would be to your credit."

Like all unconfirmed communications, this one had to be taken seriously until it was proven to be bogus. The call did not come in the usual way, from the usual person with the usual codes to identify an Al-Faran connection. The caller could have been anyone who read the newspapers and wanted to extort money. It was not at all like the Al-Faran—not part of the profile of behavior that had been observed for five months—to nearly beg for money. When the issue of a ransom had emerged last September, the Al-Faran dropped it immediately upon public exposure, via the leak to the press. One source said they did not want the image of "mere criminals." However, they had shown in the past that they were vicious and manipulative, and now that their leader was dead, they could be desperate. They could be preparing to leave the country and to release the hostages. Perhaps they needed the money to assure safe passage back to Pakistan. The caller was given several questions and instructed to call back with the answers—a process that would confirm his connection with the Al-Faran. But he never called back.

The Indian government's current strategy was to persuade the rebels to free the hostages during the holidays on the grounds that the release would be recognized worldwide as a magnanimous gesture. Despite the lack of direct contact with the rebels and the rebels' claim of no longer holding the hostages, the government was proceeding as if nothing had changed. (In fact, everything had changed, more than anyone could know at the time.) From December 4 on, Hutchings and Mangan and Wells and Hasert slipped into a black hole. For Jane, by the end of the year, it would seem as if she had been holding on to a man dangling precipitously over the edge of a cliff. And now he had fallen into an abyss. Though she believed he was still there, she could never again be certain. The last proof-of-life had been furnished in late August.

During the week following the skirmish, the captured rebels told army interrogators that the death of their leader was a debilitating blow for Al-Faran. The militants were tired and frustrated, they said.

There was a distinct possibility, Indian officials told reporters, that without leadership, the group could fall apart. Either the hostages would be handed over to another rebel group to be released, or they would be abandoned in the mountains. Despite such reassuring scenarios, there was also the unspoken fear that the rebels might have avenged the death of their leader by harming, even killing, the hostages.

"For the last sixteen days there has been no contact, but we have not given up hope. We are still expecting that Al-Faran will talk to us and end the crisis," the government announced on December 13.

About a week later, Jane Schelly wrote in her journal: "Can it be possible that at one time so long ago that I was writing Day 25, Day 53, Day 67, Day 110 and here it is Day 167. How many more will I have to write?"

On December 24, Day 172, Jane wrote: "I'm cautiously hoping that there is at least a small chance that he will be released for Christmas; I really don't think so but I can't help but to allow some small hope."

For months now, Jane had been sending letters and cards to Don, usually addressing them to "Don Hutchings, Hostage, c/o Al-Faran, Anantnag Region, Kashmir." In early December she had mailed a Christmas box to the Srinagar post office filled with neatly wrapped parcels containing a harmonica, a soprano recorder, how-to-play books for each instrument, a sweater, socks, scarves, mittens, new toothbrushes, and sun cream. And by Christmas day, her parcels were part of a giant mound of holiday cards, presents, and taped messages sent to the Srinagar post office for the four tourists who couldn't go home. "People are thinking of you," one Christmas card read. "From the people of the village of Hurworth, England." The hostage families, friends, and even strangers sent socks, scarves, hats, gloves, all sorts of items, all addressed to the individual hostages, or sometimes just "The Hostages." Some said, "Please Forward."

Christmas night, Jane hosted a gathering of friends, who lit candles for Don and one by one wrote messages to him in her journal: "Don, we all love you and are awaiting your return." "Don, as we are all joined together here at your house, we miss you and your smile and your jokes and stories, it seems unreal that you are still not home, we hope and pray that you are safe." "Don, I look forward to the time when we can climb, bike and ski together; there is a lot of territory to explore in the Cascades in Canada. Let's go for it." "I want part of the movie rights starring Sissy Spacek and Richard Dreyfuss. Merry Christmas, Don."

Meanwhile, Indian intelligence sources, carefully positioned in numerous Kashmiri villages, continued to report that the hostages were not walking as much as before largely because of the cold. They knew almost precisely where the four tourists were being held, or so they said.

In Germany, Foreign Minister Klaus Kinkel made a special Christmas appeal to the kidnappers to free the four Western tourists and assured the hostages that they had not been forgotten.

On December 28, Tim Devlin, the member of Parliament representing the district in England where the Mangans lived, told the press: "With the mention of the word *compensation*, I think they are looking for some reasonable way out. I think they are looking for some sort of face-saving mechanism to withdraw from the situation." He confirmed that India would not release militants in Kashmir and that Britain would not pay any money for the kidnappers. "They have made their point. We understand the desire of the militants in Kashmir. They have had some world attention. If I were them, I would leave it at that." Devlin also said: "I don't think we have a reliable report of their condition. They were seen in one of the villages two to three weeks ago. They're supposed to be in reasonably good condition, looking pretty thin, but they were alive."

In the next few days, the British press carried various reports, including one that a British negotiator was talking to the kidnappers. At the same time, Keith Mangan's family was told that an intermediary had carried the parcels of warm clothing and all of the messages to the hostages sometime around Christmas.

But by the last day of the year, things looked generally bleak. It was the dreadful duty of the Foreign Office to inform the Mangans that the reports of negotiations opening up again were not true. And the parcels were still sitting in the Srinagar post office. No one knew where to deliver them. "We were so disappointed that day. I can't even describe it," said Mavis Mangan. "One minute we were all on cloud nine. Then we were simply crushed to the floor again."

That day, residents of the village of Hakura said they had spotted the hostages the day after Christmas walking with thirty or forty escorts led by an Afghan militant. They were wearing warm clothes and looking healthy, the villagers said. But the sighting was never confirmed. And many months later, Jane was told that the presents and cards sent to the hostages for Christmas had been labeled "undeliverable" and discarded as "dead letters."

⊲⊱✕⊰⊳

On New Year's Eve, Jane reread a copy of the message she had sent to Don with the Christmas parcels, hoping that he was reading the same words somewhere in the mountains of India, or Pakistan, or even Afghanistan. "Dearest Don, I will be ecstatic if this message makes it to you by Christmas time. I love you and you are rarely out of my thoughts. I pray that you are safe and in reasonable health. Be strong. And I hope that Dirk, Keith and Paul are as supportive to you as the other wives have been to me. After leaving India on Oct. 26th, I spent 10 days with my parents in Pennsylvania, then came home to Spokane and to all of our wonderful friends. They, St. Luke's Neurology Associates, the Mountaineers and so many others send their love and their prayers. I'm back at school teaching. I spent Thanksgiving with your family. My parents will come to Spokane for Christmas. The dogs are behaving perfectly. Jim Roubos [a local doctor] and [others] are handling your office and everything is going to be okay. Don, be positive. Keep your hopes up. And dream of the day when we will be together again."

PART IV

Pawns of 1996

⟨⟩⟨⟩⟨⟩

Hostage is a crucifying aloneness. It is a silent screaming slide into the bowels of ultimate despair. Hostage is a man hanging by his fingernails over the edge of chaos, feeling his fingers slowly straightening. Hostage is the humiliating stripping away of every sense and fibre of body and mind and spirit that make us what we are. Hostage is a mutant creation filled with fear, self-loathing, guilt and death-wishing. But he is a man, a rare, unique and beautiful creation of which these things are no part.

—Brian Keenan, Irish teacher, former
Beirut hostage, in the *Independent*,
a London newspaper, August 1990

24

Eighty-five miles or more from San José, ten miles from the Nicaraguan border, in the lush rain forests of Costa Rica, there lies a jungle paradise teeming with parrots, butterflies, spider monkeys, toucans, and the rare green macaw. These unspoiled forests, in the heart of the land Christopher Columbus dubbed the "Rich Coast," are veritable treasures to ecology-minded tourists, who generally regard Costa Rica as the Eden of Central America. Ten percent of the world's butterflies—more than are found on the entire African continent—flutter about this tiny country. A bridge between two continents, Costa Rica is home to plant and animal species from both the Northern and Southern Hemispheres, including 2,000 varieties of orchids and 800-plus species of birds. But by 1996, there was evidence of a new type of species—potentially very dangerous—in the northernmost region: the former contra rebel. Out of work, looking for money, they were the warriors who had fought for years against the Sandinista government in Nicaragua, and now, like animals fighting for survival, they were jumping the border in search of new, vulnerable prey—such as ecotourists.

On New Year's Day, 1996, at about 8:30 P.M., twenty or so such travelers sat on the wooden terrace of the Laguna del Lagarto Lodge, finishing their buffet dinners and looking out over a spectacular expanse of northern Costa Rican rain forests. The "Lake of the Lizard" Lodge, which offered cozy cabins, ten miles of nature trails, and a boat trip along the San Carlos River to the San Juan River to Nicaragua, was the third stop on a one-week ecotour popular with German travelers. The resort brochure boasted, "A real rain forest adventure in the paradise of the green macaw and the red and green poison dart frogs." And it included comments from previous guests: "The rainforest was great, filled with monkeys, birds and frogs. We enjoyed the canoe trips on the lovely lagoons." "Great place! Good food, birds and helpful staff." And "I fulfilled a lifetime dream by walking through your rainforest."

As the sun set and the view grew dim, the current guests at the lodge chatted among themselves by candlelight as they ate the last bites of the hearts of palm salad, the goulash, and the sweet cassava. Susana Siegfried, a Swiss-born woman known as "Susi" who worked as a tour guide in Costa Rica for a German company, remembered talking with two of the tourists about their plan that night to take a quick drive to Boca Tapada, a village four miles away, to pay a restaurant bill from the night before. Then suddenly the candles flickered as if a strong wind were gusting through the room. All conversation stopped as ten masked men carrying AK-47 automatic rifles breezed into the room through three separate entrances. The men, in their high leather boots, black gloves, and camouflage fatigues with grenades hanging from their belts, had entered "with the grace of cats," Siegfried would later recall. The room was as silent as a held breath. Though she noticed the horrified looks of the tourists at other tables, her first thought was that this must be someone's New Year's joke. Her next thought was that she, as the only one who was fluent in both Spanish and German, must be certain that all the people in that room obey the orders of the armed men. "I believe from that moment on, I acted by instinct only," she later said. "And I began to automatically translate their orders."

The kidnappers addressed each other by code names, taking the names of provinces and towns of Costa Rica, such as Quepos, Talamanca, and Limón. The first order was: "Hands up! This is an assault! It is not against you but against the government. If you do exactly what we tell you, nothing will happen to you." Next, one of the men instructed everyone, including lodge staff and Siegfried, who was still translating, to "lie on the floor, face down and hands on the back." With nearly thirty people lying on the floor, the men bound the hands and feet of the tourists, one by one. Soon, the tourists, from their prone positions, heard a sudden cacophony of tables and chairs scooting across the wooden floors and other furniture, mainly beds, crashing over the railing of the terrace. These items were taken mostly from a room where many of the people lying on the floor would soon be confined. During this time, too, the rebels forced the resort's chef to hand over his entire food supply.

After nearly three hours, one of the rebels told Siegfried to get up and follow him as he ordered the rest of tourists to stand up in groups of three. The fifty-year-old tour guide translated while walking from person to person, gently touching their feet to signal the time to rise. She reminded them, in German, "Do not resist in any way." When the last three stood up, she turned to one of the men and asked if she could go with the tourists, who were being led to the room that had been cleared of its furniture. He said no and instead took her to the bar inside the lodge, where a female tourist was standing. The rebels took that woman away because she had apparently been hysterical and they couldn't handle her. They then returned with another woman, twenty-four-year-old Nicola Fleuchaus. At the bar, Fleuchaus and Siegfried were told to change from their dress shoes to sneakers, which the rebels had brought to them. As she tied the first lace, Siegfried, a lean, muscular woman with shoulder-length straight hair and an engaging smile, knew what she and the young German woman would soon be facing: many, many miles of jungle trails and perhaps even a boat ride, but not under the amicable guidance of the Lagarto Lodge.

By midnight, the tourists and resort personnel were tied up and locked up. And, after unleashing the power of their AK-47s on the tires of the cars in the resort's parking lot, the rebels drove away in the resort owner's four-wheel-drive Toyota, taking with them the two now-blindfolded women. Jammed into the jeep were the two hostages, five of the abductors, luggage, bags of food, hammocks, backpacks, and weapons. For nearly an hour they drove across bumpy trails until they reached the San Juan River, which forms the border between Costa Rica and Nicaragua. There the rest of the abductors joined them, and the entire group, with their supplies and their hostages, boarded two boats.

Like a scene out of a Joseph Conrad novel, they moved slowly down the dark, tropical river to a smaller river called the Cano San Francisco, which led deeper and deeper into the densest jungle terrain the women would ever see. For twelve hours they floated down the Cano, feeling the brush along the banks as the river narrowed and became more difficult to navigate. Eventually, they abandoned the boats and began to walk, but only on swampy trails that would absorb their footprints.

At the first camp, the women were told they looked too conspicuous. "Niki," as her friends called her, was wearing red Bermuda shorts and a dark blue T-shirt at the time of the abduction; Siegfried, a white blouse and long black pants with a flowered pattern. The rebels gave them pants and shirts, camouflage style, so they would blend in.

For six days, the women and their captors ventured farther and farther into the swamplands, changing camps each night, until the women could no longer walk. The guerrillas, who seemed respectful of the women's needs, then set up a quasi-permanent camp. They called Siegfried "Doña Susi," an address indicating some respect, perhaps because of her age and her ability to project confidence despite the circumstances.

Back at the lodge, on the night of the abductions, the commandos had left a note on one of the tables on the dining terrace. Handwritten at gunpoint by a hotel employee, it was the rebels' list of demands for the return of the women: $1 million in unmarked hundred-dollar bills, one million colónes (Costa Rican currency equal to $5,000), an 18 percent pay raise for government workers, a freeze in utility rates, a price reduction in basic food items, and the release of four convicted kidnappers who in 1993 had abducted twenty-two Costa Rican judges. They also requested that the International Red Cross and a priest from the region should conduct the negotiation.

The next day, fourteen miles from the lodge, police found the get-away Toyota along the banks of the San Juan River. But there was no sign of Fleuchaus or Siegfried, and no word from the kidnappers. Hundreds upon hundreds of Costa Rican police trudged through the jungle in search of the missing women. At the same time, the Nicaraguan government reportedly sent troops to probe the area along the Costa Rican border.

On January 3, Germany's foreign minister, Klaus Kinkel, appealed to the Costa Rican government, as he had done to the Indian government repeatedly in recent months, to do everything possible to gain the release of the hostages, unharmed. Costa Rican president José María Figueres convened his cabinet. And his foreign minister told reporters the government was making "definite progress" in finding the women, but would not reveal the details of the investigation.

The next day someone called *La Nacion,* the big Costa Rican daily, about an envelope found in a phone booth in San José. It contained information that would prove important to the case, the caller said. The reporter dispatched to the scene found two pages of barely legible notes threatening future attacks against tourists, an assault against an unnamed American family in Costa Rica, and "terrorist attacks to destroy power lines, bridges, towers, etc.," if the kidnappers' demands were not met and if the manhunts were not called off. The government said it would try to authenticate the note while it continued efforts to communicate with the kidnappers and to find them.

The abductions caused a shudder to ripple through the National Tourism Chamber, known as CANATUR. Tourism, Costa Rica's main industry, had reaped $600 million in 1995. An average of 800,000 tourists annually visited this little country with the spectacular landscapes, spending roughly $700 million; 40,000 came from Germany. In a written statement to the press, a CANATUR official said, "We should not forget that we are faced with an isolated act, since kidnappings are exceptional cases in our country."

Costa Rica Expeditions, a highly successful firm, told a reporter that the damage to the industry would likely be commensurate with the extent of press coverage of the incident in the United States, which was Costa Rica's main source of tourists. "I may be cynical, but my reading is that unless they are tortured in a particularly spectacular way, no one gives a darn [in the U.S.]," a travel agent was quoted as saying.

Still, it appeared that this idyllic nation was in the throes of a major security crisis. In a region renowned for dictator dramas and military mayhem, Costa Rica stood alone as a peaceful, stable democracy that had even abolished its national army in 1948. In addition, as a sign of its high standard of living, it had one of the highest literacy rates in the Americas. Abductions, as the nation's tourism board stated, were certainly not common. But it was becoming apparent that displaced rebels, military personnel, and cops in Nicaragua were turning to kidnapping and extortion to make money. And Costa Rica was just over the border.

In 1993, a gang of right-wing Nicaraguan guerrillas, formerly members of the Southern Front of National Nicaraguan Opposition—part of the contra rebel movement—had attacked the Nicaraguan embassy in San José and abducted the ambassador and twenty-three other hostages. They got away with a $250,000 ransom after a thirteen-day standoff. While the identity and loyalties of the kidnappers in the Lagarto Lodge incident remained a mystery throughout the ordeal, they would later be exposed as former contra rebels who had been part of a gang headed by Eden Pastora that reportedly had operated throughout the 1980s out of the jungle along the banks of the San Juan River.

The incident at Lagarto Lodge was not the only kidnapping in Costa Rica in 1996. Before the year was over, there would be another abduction of tourists, though not at the same lodge. And in the spring of that year, the nation's police would discover a different type of guerrilla camp near the center of the famed Braulio Carrillo National Park, which was not far from the Laguna del Lagarto Lodge and numerous other ecolodges. There a Costa Rican rebel leader, mounting a fight against the government of this peaceful little nation, was training rebels. Tourism, at least from Germany, would fall nearly 40 percent by 1997.

By the end of the first week of captivity, the kidnappers and the priest who was anointed as a key negotiator had not yet made contact.

Several calls to the priest from a self-proclaimed member of the gang turned out to be hoaxes. On January 8, Fleuchaus's mother, who had flown to San José from Germany, appeared on nationwide television to beg the kidnappers for the release of her daughter.

The travel section of the *New York Times* on February 18, 1996, featured two sweeping articles about vacationing in remote, ecologically exciting regions of Costa Rica. One described a four-day package, provided by the tourism outfit Costa Rica Expeditions, to Corcovado National Park, "one of the largest, least accessible, and most biologically significant of any tropical forest park in Costa Rica and one of the last refuges in the world for such threatened species as the jaguar, the ocelot and the tapir."

The "Nuts and Bolts" column beneath the alluring photos offered advice for the reader planning such a trip. It noted airfares and accommodations such as Corcovado Lodge, operated by Costa Rica Expeditions, and information about a variety of treks as well as tips on what to bring. The article did not advise the potential visitor about safety. On the one hand, that was understandable because Corcovado National Park was in the Osa Peninsula, in the southernmost regions of the country, and the problems seemed to be contained in the nation's northernmost areas. Still, the well-written, breezy article could easily inspire interest in any part of Costa Rica, and in a country no bigger than West Virginia, the trip from the northern sector to the southern tip could be made in the time it took to drive from Washington, D.C., to New York City. It might have been helpful if the newspaper had mentioned the hint of danger in these lush, exotic lands. It could have cited, but did not, the U.S. State Department's recent advisory that provided the following information:

"Crime is on the upswing, with tourists as well as the local populace being frequent victims. Pickpocketings, muggings, house and car break-ins and thefts are common, and becoming increasingly violent in nature. Car-jackings are also on the rise and, recently, several motorists were confronted at gunpoint while stopped at traffic lights. Two U.S. citizens have been killed during robbery attempts over the past two years. *In January 1996, a foreign tourist and guide were kidnapped from their hotel in the northern border region.* Incidents of crime commonly occur in downtown San José, at beaches, at the airport, and at national parks and other tourist attractions. There have been several assaults on tourist buses as well. Travelers who keep valuables out of sight, do not wear jewelry, and travel in groups during daylight hours lessen their risk. Local law enforcement agencies have limited capabilities. Money exchangers on the street will pass off counterfeit U.S. dollars and local currency. Credit card fraud is growing. Vehicles should not be left unattended, nor any items left inside.

"Some trails in national parks have been closed because of low numbers of visitors and reported robberies of hikers in the area. Tourists may wish to check with forest rangers for current park conditions."

Nor did the article note that Costa Rica was also "one of the last refuges in the world" for that new endangered species of the post–Cold War era, the former U.S.-backed contra rebel, as well as other unemployed mercenaries, including former Sandinista soldiers, looking for ways to make money, perhaps by inciting an antigovernment crusade.

Meanwhile, somewhere in that exotic Costa Rican terrain, with all those exciting varieties of unusual wildlife, Nicola "Niki" Fleuchaus and Susana "Susi" Siegfried were spending their days and nights fearing death, either at the hands of their captors or from starvation. "When we were lucky, we got rice and beans, tuna, cooking bananas, and fish. There were times, though, when there was no food, and the Guerrilleros had to look around for some," Siegfried later recalled. "Sometimes we were hungry for days, and our diet consisted of hearts of palm, turtles, and fish. Once we had two wild hogs [boar], once a cow, and once a monkey."

At night they slept in hammocks extended between two trees and struggled with a painful mix of mental and physical torment: the anxiety of their circumstances and the sheer misery of mosquito assaults. This was a swampy area and one of the rainiest regions in all of Costa Rica. It would typically rain several times a day, almost every day, a perfect habitat for the thousands of mosquitoes swarming around them at all hours. And even when it wasn't raining, the group was so far into the jungle that they were unable to see the sun or the sky, only a canopy of treetops, which only intensified their feeling of captivity. The jungle was alive with the sights and sounds of many species of animals. At night, Siegfried, who had spent nights in the jungle with her husband, a biologist, heard sounds that were totally unfamiliar to her. There were jaguars, ocelots, tapirs, rodents, small bears, parrots, toucans with their large, canoe-shaped bills, three kinds of monkeys, snakes, lizards, poison dart frogs, turtles—always against the background chorus of crickets and cicadas. Though the sounds at night seemed louder than during the day, Siegfried was not afraid because she knew from experience that few animals attack humans. She did worry, however, that Niki's fears might heighten because of the sounds.

At one point, after deciding to move to another camp, the kidnappers took off with the women in a boat down the San Juan. Although the group traveled under the cover of night, they were on the open waterways of the big river, away from the protection of leafy canopies. Fearing their hostages could be spotted, the kidnappers wrapped the women in a stifling black plastic sheet for the three-hour journey.

On February 22, a Costa Rican television station received a threatening handwritten note, presumably from the kidnappers, warning that if their demands were not met, the "hostages will die of hunger." This came within a day or so of a statement delivered to the same station, supposedly from the hostages, saying they could not "hold on much longer."

By the end of February, a resolution to the crisis appeared to be no closer than it had been on New Year's night. The kidnappers had not moved a millimeter from their original demands. And Costa Rican authorities had yet to track the rebel hideout or to determine whether the commandos and their hostages had jumped the border into Nicaragua. The families of the hostages were understandably frantic. But this incident was particularly frustrating because there seemed to be no ongoing negotiations. The Costa Rican government flatly refused to pay the ransom, and it had been unable to make direct contact, through a negotiator, with the kidnappers. The kidnappers had asked the government to send a parish priest from the village of Pital, some forty kilometers away, or about twenty-four miles, from the site of the abduction. And the government had uttered no objections, at first. But later, in February, when the rebels asked again for the priest to come alone in a boat, with the ransom, and to follow a certain route down the big river for three days, the government objected. They did not want to endanger the life of the priest. It was about this time that the families stepped in.

The Costa Rican government had relatively little experience with hostage-taking. In recent cases, it had paid ransoms: $250,000 for the return of the twenty-four hostages in March 1993 and $100,000 in September 1992 for the return of an abducted interior minister. In another incident in 1993, which involved the abduction of nineteen Supreme Court justices, the government had paid a $150,000 ransom, but the kidnap gang was apprehended the moment they stepped onto a plane with the ransom money. Because government officials had been criticized in diplomatic and international circles for paying those ransoms, now they were apparently refusing to pay anything at all.

Time was nearly as difficult to endure for the family members as for the hostages themselves. The virtually nonexistent negotiations and the same droning demands were eating away at the families' resolve like a corroding rust. And then finally during the last week of February, Siegfried's daughter announced to the media that the families were going to wrest control of the effort to free their loved ones. They alone, sending their own representatives, would connect directly to the kidnappers.

"My family decided about the middle of February to try to negotiate themselves since the government (the crisis committee) kept making empty promises, put the families off, and didn't tell them the truth," Siegfried later recalled. "The deciding moment came when the abductors set another deadline and the government did nothing, and my family (my daughter Manuela, who played an active, important role as mediator with the government and spokesperson for [dealing with] the press) and Nicole's family decided that my husband should use this deadline [there were about four days] and should get on the river and try to meet the abductors, which he did. That he would do this was published beforehand in some important daily papers and on the radio station that had been named [as a vehicle of communications] by the abductors from the beginning. So the abductors knew about the plan. It was a hard fight with the government before they finally agreed that the families should be allowed to act and that the police and press should keep their distance."

Ekard Oehring, a longtime German friend of the Siegfried family, would travel with Siegfried's husband, Peter, east from San José to the Atlantic coast, and then in a riverboat they would venture deeper and deeper into the most remote regions of the northern Costa Rican rain forests. Oehring had lived in Switzerland for nearly ten years and before that in Costa Rica for seven. He had worked in a voluntary aid service, much like the Peace Corps, and had many connections in the country, including top-level government officials, according to Siegfried. He used these connections in the planning and negotiation of the families' involvement. Oehring and Peter Siegfried had ventured down the San Juan River twice in the past and as their vessel straddled the border between two countries—one a tourism haven with an image of tranquillity and the other, an unstable region where bandits were known to hide along the banks—they did not fear its darkness or its aura of mystery. The boat would be easily spotted with its flags of Germany, Switzerland, and Costa Rica and the white banner representing the Roman Catholic Church.

On March 1, the kidnappers, armed with their AK-47s, saw the boat and emerged from their jungle cover to convene talks with Peter and Ekard. But unknown to the two negotiators, a helicopter from Costa Rica's secret police had followed. Soon the whirring sound of a chopper's blades melded with the staccato clicking of the kidnappers' AK-47s, locking and loading, braced and ready for battle. The two men, in assuring tones, explained as calmly as possible that they did not know they had been followed. This was not part of any plan. They were victims of a betrayal as much as the rebels were. Without any gunfire, the rebel commandos vanished into the rain forest once again.

The aborted meeting took place on a Friday. Four days later, on March 5, the family issued a statement to the media saying they would try again. "We, the family of the hostages, are prepared to negotiate everything we can ourselves. Moreover, we want to do everything possible to free the two women," the statement said. They said they had nothing to do with the helicopter during the first trip. "We profoundly regret the interruption during the last trip."

The next day, the Costa Rican government announced it would not interfere in any way with the families' effort to reconnect with the commandos. "For the good and security of the relatives as well as the hostages, we have issued orders that no authority intervene in the negotiations," the vice minister of information told the press.

Two days later, the voyage was repeated, same flags waving, same determination, but this time with a guarantee that the government would not track the boat down the river. Somewhere along the banks, Peter and Ekard heard a human whistle coming out of the jungle and subsequently made contact with the kidnappers. Soon a peace was struck, not by a government, not by the FBI or Scotland Yard, not by the experienced hands of CRG, but by the impassioned determination of the people who cared the most, the families of Siegfried and Fleuchaus. In the end, the kidnappers got a small portion of what they had asked for: $200,000, raised entirely through the efforts of family members. The rebels appeared satisfied, however, and did not insist on the release of the four convicted kidnappers from jail or the freeze on utility rates or the pay raise for government workers—a fact that persuaded the authorities that their Robin Hood/rebel stance was a ruse and that money had always been their goal. And the families, after seventy-one days of waiting and praying, got all that they wanted: Niki and Susi returned alive and in relatively decent health, though Niki was ill with a high fever.

On March 13 at a press conference at the German embassy the day after she was freed, "Doña Susi" told a local TV station that the two women had not been mistreated. Their worst enemies, she said, were "tedium, isolation, and mosquitoes. It was hardest at the beginning because I didn't know if they were going to kill us."

Both women criticized the slowness of the Costa Rican government and implied that the government may have hindered efforts by other governments, mainly Germany, to resolve the crisis. In response, Alejandro Soto, the information minister, said that the government had made mistakes in the handling of the kidnapping because of "a lack of experience in cases like this."

La Nacion, the San José newspaper, also criticized the government because the guerrilla band had been operating in Costa Rica without the knowledge of the police. The incident, the paper claimed, pointed to a need for stepped-up security in a country that for so long felt immune to the violence of its neighbors. Yet it commended the government for acting "with restraint" at the appropriate time during the families' negotiations. Without such restraint and cooperation, the safe release of the hostages would likely not have occurred.

In the days ahead, there would be discrepancies in the facts released to the public regarding the payment of a ransom. There were press reports that no monetary ransom had been paid. It was a ransom of food, medical supplies, and clothing plus a few hundred dollars in pocket money and a half-page ad in Costa Rican newspapers supporting the kidnappers' views on the need for social and political reforms. Other reports, however, confirmed the $200,000 ransom. And behind the scenes, authorities sent a list of serial numbers of 2,000 one-hundred-dollar U.S. bills to Costa Rican banks. There was speculation that the disparity in reports resulted from the government's fear of the ramifications of yet another ransom being paid to terrorists or criminals or whoever the masked gunmen might be, and so perhaps, for the sake of other tourists and for Costa Rica, officials decided to edit the truth a bit. They also may have been following the lead of the family members, who at first chose to dodge the volatile subject of ransom.

Although time could not erase the event from the Costa Rican national archives nor from the family histories, it would expose the kidnappers. The leader of the kidnapping gang of former contra rebels, Julio César Vega, known as Julio Loco or "Crazy Julio," was arrested in late spring 1996 in the Nicaraguan border town of San Juan del Norte. He was carrying a neat wad of the listed hundred-dollar bills, totaling $37,600 out of the $200,000. Among his belongings, the soldiers found a Kalashnikov rifle, as expected, and some unexpected handwritten pages with a roll of undeveloped Fuji film. On the pages, Vega had expressed his anguish in separating from Fleuchaus on the day of her release. "Today, my love, I am sad because this is our last night together and you will leave me." The military had the film developed in Managua, sending the shocking pictures to police in Costa Rica, where they caused quite a stir—mainly the one showing Niki embracing and kissing Vega. Costa Rica's police chief told *Der Spiegel* magazine, in Germany, that "a romance with the blond German, who under normal circumstances would have been unobtainable to him, was a huge temptation." And psychologists were quoted everywhere on the theories of subconscious survival mechanisms that persuade hostages that they love their abductors. Known as the Stockholm Syndrome, the phenomenon can occur because of the dependence of the hostage on the captor for survival and because captor and captive often have a common enemy, such as government troops who are just as dangerous to the hostages as to the kidnappers. They bond in the face of danger. The syndrome is so-named because of an incident years ago during a bank robbery in Stockholm in which one of the hostages, stuck for days in the bank vault, fell in love with—and later married—one of the bank robbers.

The photo and all that it implied would cause a ruckus for a long time in both Germany and Costa Rica. During the trial, Fleuchaus would refuse to testify against Vega, inciting the governments of both countries. And it would indirectly cause a rift between Siegfried and Fleuchaus. The affection had clearly provoked problems for both lovers. Vega, perhaps overwhelmed with that first blush of love when the rest of the world seems like a blur, made a crucial, incriminating mistake when he had his picture taken with his wide-eyed captive: he took off his mask.

A few months later, Nicaraguan military intelligence uncovered a plot to kidnap the Costa Rican ambassador in Nicaragua. The kidnappers' plan: to demand Vega's freedom and a $200,000 ransom.

25

MARCH 1996
WORLDWIDE

While Fleuchaus and Siegfried were refreshing their memories of crisp linens, long, restful baths, and the first tasty sips of a fine red wine, businessmen and tourists and the sons and daughters of politicians and diplomats from a variety of countries from France to the Philippines to the United States were taking the first frightening steps into captivity. Throughout the first quarter of 1996, in a way eerily reminiscent of bandits robbing banks in the U.S. Wild West, gangs of criminals, rebels, and terrorists had upped the ante for kidnappings well beyond the tallies for the same period the year before.

On the day the Costa Rican hostages were released, the three granddaughters of the former head of one of Mexico's largest banks were snatched on their way to school in Cuernavaca; the kidnappers wanted $3 million for their return. A few days later, the eighteen-year-old son of a Taiwanese diplomat was abducted after a basketball game in Manila. The following week, three men seized a millionaire shipping magnate in London as he walked the twenty yards from his car to the front door of his home. The next morning, March 25, in Hamburg, an heir to the Reemtsma tobacco fortune was abducted in what would be Germany's biggest ransom kidnapping. The next day, Islamic extremists kidnapped seven French monks, ages fifty to eighty, from a farm in Algeria. On the same day, Christopher Howes, a land mine expert from England, and his interpreter were among thirty others kidnapped while clearing mines northwest of Phnom Penh, Cambodia. Also on that day, the eighteen-year-old son of a prominent Manila family was abducted at the gate of his mother's home as soon as a maid opened it. The ransom demand was $577,000.

During the first three months of the New Year, there were at least a few resolutions to incidents that began in late 1995, and some progress in ongoing cases. Twelve tourists, including four Americans, kidnapped at a lake resort in the Philippines in late December, were freed when the mayor of a nearby city promised to build a new school, a cemetery, and several homes for Muslims and to pay the expenses of caring for the hostages. The kidnappers, who were Islamic militants, demanded that the government stop oppressing the poor. The owner of one of Mexico's biggest publishing houses, in captivity for more than a month, was released after kidnappers walked away with a "sizable" ransom, authorities said. And in parts of northern California, business executives could look over their shoulders one less time each day after the March arrests of more than 100 alleged criminals in a sophisticated operation of four gangs that, among other things, had abducted high-tech executives on their way to and from work in the Bay Area.

In early March, Ulrik Schultz, a Danish engineer snatched alongside a Brit and a German in Colombia in February, was allowed to have a short-wave receiver sent to him from Denmark. Its first coded message, on the fifth of the month, went like this: "The aunt in Valby sends the warmest regards to friends and family in South America and hopes to see them again soon." This was repeated several times and followed by the Beatles song "Help." The "aunt" was the nickname for Schultz's company's headquarters in the Copenhagen suburb of Valby. The Beatles was his all-time favorite musical group. And the choice of song was meant to send the message that help was on the way.

In one of the latest stop-gap solutions that spring, Philippine tourism secretary Eduardo Pilapil had suggested that top tourist spots be cordoned off into special security zones monitored by special tourist police and private security firms.

At the same time in Yemen, where tribesmen had kidnapped a sightseeing group of seventeen elderly French tourists earlier in the year and held them for four days, government authorities barred travel agents from driving tourists to remote areas unless they had received prior approval from the interior ministry. The kidnappers had demanded the release of a fellow tribesman who was jailed for abducting an American in 1995. Meanwhile, a group of fifty French tourists had canceled their March vacations after hearing about the vacations of their compatriots—disturbing news for a country that had experienced more than a 100 percent increase in tourism from 1994 to 1995, from 30,000 visitors to 70,000.

In March, Control Risks dispatched negotiators to six new cases, one in Brazil, one in Guatemala, one in Mexico, and three in Colombia. There were now at least thirty-one foreign nationals in captivity in Colombia, where, by some accounts, kidnappings were occurring at the rate of 2.5 abductions an hour. Although the Emberlys, from Canada, were freed on October 17 the previous year, others had taken their place. That spring, too, Kroll was planning a move against its competitors: snatching several of the best freelance negotiators and placing them on permanent retainer to work exclusively on Kroll kidnap cases. Three were former CIA, and the other was former FBI agent Bob Dwyer.

Roy Ramm's schedule that spring was the very definition of stress. On March 26 when he got the call about the newest problem in Cambodia, Commander Ramm was working eighteen-hour days to find and free the abducted shipping tycoon. He had another case in Indonesia that had begun in early January. In Colombia, the case of Timothy Cowley, the bird-watching sargeant, had ended—with a rescue—but another had erupted during the first week of February. And then, unfortunately, there was still Kashmir, requiring the commander to set off for India when necessary. Later he would recall a moment that seemed almost surreal to him when he was in Kashmir on the telephone with colleague Mike Dixon. "Mike was in Colombia then. One day we were talking in offices next to one another, and the next we were talking as one was looking at the Himalayas and the other at the Andes."

On the second floor of Scotland Yard, in a room negotiators call the Control Room, there were four clocks on the wall set to the time zones of four different countries: Colombia, Cambodia, Kashmir, and Irian Jaya, the Indonesian province occupying the western half of the island of New Guinea.

"It was like the show that never stops," said Commander Ramm later. "One of the difficulties in all of this was the time difference. We had people in the field on different times, and we needed to speak to them at various times each day, while they were still awake. The days simply were endless. There was never a time when you could really say, OK, that's it now, let's pull up stumps for the evening and go out and have a beer now.

"When I looked at those clocks on the wall, I thought, If we get just one more case, how will we ever resource it? We were putting in officers from provincial forces that spring to help us as part of the overall negotiating response, and we were saying, 'My God, we've got two of these and how will we be able to handle another, if it happens,' though I can't remember exactly when that was, when we only had two. But when we did, we were attending two sets of meetings at the foreign office and had two rotation sets of negotiators going in and out of two distant countries. And then, of course, we did get more."

⤙⤞⤙⤞

Like most kidnappings in Britain and the United States, the case of George Fraghistas was brief and brutal. At 6:20 P.M. on Sunday, March 24, a balaclava-hooded man wearing an anorak and black gloves snatched the forty-three-year-old Greek shipper from a London parking lot as he was leaving his car to walk to his home in nearby Maida Vale. The man muzzled his victim with a black-gloved hand and shoved him against a car. Fraghistas struggled, even bit the finger of his abductor, but within seconds he was forced at gunpoint into the trunk of a car and driven just two miles away to a three-story house in Hogan Mews, a quaint lane in the same part of West London. There his abductor or one of the two other men stripped him naked, gagged him, blindfolded him, handcuffed him, drugged him with tranquilizers, tied him to a kitchen chair, and stuffed him into a three-by-five-foot cupboard off the kitchen. There he sat for most of every day, deaf, dumb, and barely able to breathe. Sticky tape wrapped tightly round his head held a mask and earplugs in place. For painful seconds once a day, his abductors ripped the tape from his mouth and fed him bread, rice, and water. Periodically his captors, who included a former Olympic wrestler, tortured him with threats, warning him that if the police got involved or if their mission failed, they would kill him by injection. Or, if he preferred, they would use a gun.

Thirty-six hours after the abduction, the family, now frantic about Fraghistas's disappearance, received a recorded message from him urging—even begging—his family to pay a 5-million-pound ransom (about $8 million). The kidnappers, who knew his net worth to be in the range of 100 million pounds ($150 million), warned the family not to contact Scotland Yard. But they did. One of England's most respected detectives, Laurie Vanner, organized a covert operation that included fifty officers. And Roy Ramm was put in charge.

Ramm and Vanner advised the family to stall as long as possible while their men tried to locate the hideout. The family told the abductors, who called thirty times during the captivity, that they were still trying to drum up the cash.

On the fourth day of the ordeal, Fraghistas had one of his worst scares. He was allowed to take a shower but feared for his life as his captors put fresh tape across his eyes and told him to kneel in the shower. He had overheard a conversation the night before in which two of the kidnappers had said that at 6 P.M. the next day they would "do it nicely."

Scotland Yard found the hideout on the ninth day and captured two men outside the house—one on a cellular phone talking to Fraghistas's family. Thirty minutes later, a dozen or more armed officers broke down the door of the hideout, seized two more kidnappers, and found Fraghistas. One officer gagged at the sight of the wan, fragile-looking Fraghistas. Ramm described the captive's closet cell as "the black hole of Calcutta."

"The worse thing is one moment you get some hope," Fraghistas would say later, "and you think something not disastrous might happen, and the other moment, you think the worst will happen."

With ongoing cases in Cambodia, Kashmir, and Indonesia, the commander had no time to rejoice. Bill Gent, one of Ramm's finest, was handling Cambodia—a case that had escalated when the two mediators sent into the bush to gain the release of Christopher Howes and his interpreter were themselves taken hostage. Chris Newman was still in Kashmir. And Commander Ramm would now return for a few weeks to the vexing incident in Indonesia.

26

SPRING 1996
INDONESIA

The story captivated the British press. It was a startling clash between primitivism and modernism, a classic struggle between past and present, cast in a setting straight out of Arthur Conan Doyle's *The Lost World:* Cambridge University scientists exploring the world's most remote wilderness in a quest to protect it with the modern shield of national park status. *Versus:* an archaic tribe, armed with bows and arrows and spears, kidnapping Westerners for the first time in a desperate effort to gain global attention for a hapless struggle for independence. And both sides victims of the unfinished business of colonialism.

It happened on the island of New Guinea in the Indonesian province of Irian Jaya, a region where instances of cannibalism are occasionally reported and parts of the jungle are still uncharted. The blank portions on maps of Irian Jaya note simply "Relief Data Incomplete." At the rugged center of Irian Jaya is the Grand Valley of the Baliem River, a vast highland valley nestled between the craggy peaks of two mountain ranges that was first discovered by outsiders in 1938.

"Without doubt the most remote and unknown tropical wilderness left on earth today," the four Cambridge scientists—all recent grads in their early twenties—wrote in their proposal to fund the expedition to this exotic outpost.

Prince Philip, as president of the Worldwide Fund for Nature, backed the scientists, as did the Royal Geographical Society and the charity Birdlife International. The group raised nearly $30,000 for an adventure that Colin Bibby, the director of Birdlife International, called "a biologist's fantasy . . . There are high mountains and undisturbed forests remote enough to still have human tribes and undoubtedly with biological riches still to be discovered."

Roughly the size of California with less than a thirtieth of the population, Irian Jaya is the remote, western half of New Guinea. Once a colony of the Dutch East Indies, the province shares the sprawling island with Papua, formerly an Australian colony. Although in 1949 the Dutch formally ceded sovereignty to the 3,000 islands comprising what is now Indonesia, western New Guinea remained a disputed territory. The Dutch did not want to let go and the Indonesians claimed it belonged to the new Republic of Indonesia, formed in 1950. The inhabitants of Irian Jaya wanted to be independent, like their neighbors in Papua. After years of battles and mediations over the "Irian question," the United Nations, in 1963, turned the territory over to the Indonesians; a decade later they gave the province its present name, which means "Victorious Irian." But "victorious" was hardly the sentiment of many locals, who resented the Indonesian intrusion.

The military regime in Jakarta, Indonesia's capital city, roughly 2,000 miles away from Irian Jaya, coveted a region so very rich in gold and silver, copper and petroleum. And so to assert their claim, the Indonesian government sent hundreds upon hundreds of soldiers into Irian Jaya's virgin highlands. At the sound of the first military machete cutting through the ancient brush as the first invading foot stepped onto West New Guinea soil, at the sound of the first misguided pronouncements out of Jakarta instructing the highlanders to abandon their traditional costumes, a band of rebels formed. The independence movement called itself Organisasi Papua Merdeka (OPM), the "Free Papua Movement."

Over the decades, the rebels resented more and more what they perceived to be the exploitation of their mines and their swamp forests, which comprise the world's largest freshwater swamp. Investors and developers, they claimed, ignored the traditional laws and customs of tribes that had ruled the jungle wilderness for thousands of years. Entire villages were forced to move from their sacred mountains when a huge copper and gold mine, one of Jakarta's biggest sources of revenue, expanded. Indonesian soldiers reportedly brutalized the villagers, torturing and killing those who objected to the mine's expansion.

While Irian Jaya's 16,000 species of plants, its legendary birds of paradise, and its strange assortment of mammals, including an egg-laying marsupial, are enough to lure scientists and adventure travelers, the intrigue of Irian Jaya centers on its inhabitants. From the sensationalist angle, there is the Asmat tribe in the south, once renowned for its cannibalistic rites and considered one of the possible reasons for the 1961 disappearance of Michael Rockefeller, son of Nelson. In other tribes, the women still wear grass skirts and the men, only wooden penis gourds. They pierce their noses with the tusks of pigs and their predominant weapons are bows, arrows, and spears.

But in other ways they are advanced. While only .01 percent of the world's population lives on the island of New Guinea, 15 percent of the languages known to man are spoken here. The nearly 1.6 million people in Irian Jaya speak at least 250 different languages. According to some anthropologists, the linguistic skills of some tribes border on sheer, unprecedented brilliance. George Monbiot, a Brit who has lived among certain of the tribes, has claimed that these tribesmen demonstrate "a vocabulary wider than Shakespeare's. Their ability to pick up Western languages is extraordinary." One of the favorite pastime of these "polyglot people," he told the British papers, is to create "punning poems which can last as long as two hours, with a pun at the end of every line." One British paper called the tribesmen "primitive supermen."

But despite their remarkable skills as wordsmiths, those tribesmen of Irian Jaya who had joined the OPM were unable to express to the world their desperation as that world began to smother their own.

Their quest for freedom, after two generations of fighting, was an abysmal failure. By the mid-1990s, they were at most 500-strong, with an arsenal of no more than five rifles. They could not begin to stem the flow of blood at the hands of the Indonesian troops. "Pregnant women have been bayoneted through the stomach and left to die," Monbiot told reporters. "Elders have been tied up in sacks and dropped into the sea from helicopters."

And so in 1995, after thirty years of a sporadic and virtually unrecognized insurgency, the warriors resorted to an action that they believed would place their woes in the global spotlight. In November, the OPM kidnapped two high school students from Jayapura, the capital of Irian Jaya, and demanded a ransom of 40 million rupiah ($17,500). By the beginning of 1996, while still holding the students, the rebels escalated their plan and decided to commit a much more ambitious kidnapping that would definitely give them the attention they so desired. But kidnapping, as the OPM was soon to learn, was not the way to win the hearts and minds of the world. Instead, it catapulted the group into a new category: terrorist. Worse, because of the way the case would evolve, the rebels would be viewed as savages.

On January 8, in the village of Mapanduma, near an exotic and alluring nature reserve, the rebel tribesmen attacked. Their prey: twenty-four researchers and scientists who had come to these hallowed lands to help preserve the very sacredness the tribes so desperately feared they were losing.

Among the targets were Anna McIvor, Daniel Start, Bill Oates, and Annette van der Kolk. For two years, they had planned their expedition, taking courses at Cambridge in Indonesian languages and even training with former British army officers—mainly SAS—to learn basic survival skills. But in launching their dream to explore Indonesia's heart of darkness, they had not prepared for what happened on Monday, January 8.

That day, four months into the expedition, the four Brits, a scientist from Germany, a Dutch couple (including a pregnant woman), and seventeen Indonesians (including a couple engaged to be married) had meetings and a planned lunch in the village of Mapanduma on the southwestern reaches of the Baliem Valley in the vicinity of the

Nduga tribe. In the morning, the Dutch couple and German man had spoken in one of the churches to the locals, explaining how they would be taking over the studies of the region from the four Brits and the Indonesians, who were now planning to leave. In the audience was the local OPM leader, who stomped out of the meeting in protest of the Westerners' intrusion. Shortly thereafter, while the Brits and their Indonesian colleagues were preparing lunch at the house of the church minister and the others were still in the nearby church, they all heard screams, much like war cries, coming from outside their windows. Then, just as suddenly, men with their faces covered in pig fat, their bodies smeared with war paint, wearing only the traditional penis gourds and pointing spears, bows and arrows, and at least one rifle, broke down the doors of the minister's house. The Dutch couple and German in the nearby church could hear the screaming as the tribesmen forced the people at the house into one room and tied them up. Soon the three others were moved to the minister's house. There they would spend the night and at dawn they would begin many days of marching across the landscape that had lured them to Irian Jaya.

This time the OPM did not seek a cash ransom. Among their demands in the coming weeks: that the United Nations recognize a treaty that gave Indonesia the right to develop the Netherlands New Guinea for twenty-five years and that ended in 1988; that the Indonesian military leave West Papua (the OPM's name for their land); that the national liberation struggle of the people of West Papua be recognized internationally; and that Freeport-McMoRan, an American-owned mining concern, stop its "environmentally destructive exploitation" of the province. In his first interview ever, the rebel leader Kelly Kwalik, a former Catholic seminarian and teacher whose family members reportedly had been killed by Indonesian soldiers, explained his actions to an Australian journalist: "If someone comes into your garden and steals your pig, and does not tell you or offer any compensation, then you have a right to kill him. That is tribal law."

Australian journalist Ben Bohane, who had spent two months accompanying Kwalik and other tribesmen, told reporters: "The hostages have more to fear from the Indonesian soldiers. They are a ruthless army, and my fear is they may go in and simply hunt these people down. If they go in with all guns blazing rather than trying to negotiate, the Westerners could be in danger. The kidnapping is a desperate act, a cry for help after years of oppression."

Graham Burton, Britain's ambassador to Indonesia, maintained a calm disposition and cautioned, "The essential thing is to negotiate them out slowly with no resort to military methods."

At about 3:30 A.M. that same day, the phone rang next to Roy Ramm's bed. By 10 A.M., Ramm and Mike Dixon plus 600 pounds of radio equipment and luggage were on a British Airways flight to Jakarta. And while he was racing through rush-hour traffic, traversing the sixty-seven miles between his house and Heathrow airport in a record-setting forty-four minutes, one of his two men in Kashmir was boarding a plane in Delhi, bound for Jakarta. To get from London to the village of Mapanduma would take them about two days. At Jakarta, they took a six-hour plane ride to Irian Jaya's capital city, Jayapura. From there, they traveled to Wamena, the main town in the Baliem highlands and the central post for the special surveillance teams. But because of monsoon rains, pilots were reluctant to take them on the half-hour helicopter ride to Wamena until the next day. Meanwhile, it gave the negotiators much solace to know that Burton was the diplomat in command, for Burton had attended various training exercises in London geared to crises such as kidnappings. He knew in part what to expect and, most important perhaps, what not to say and do once the rebels stated their demands.

Much like the Kashmir incident, the case in Indonesia involved a hostile army accused of human rights abuses in a harsh suppression of a long-simmering insurgency. And as in Kashmir, the government troops were as potentially dangerous to the hostages as the hostage-takers. Once again, a rugged, expansive terrain easily sequestered a rebel band and discouraged the notion of a rescue. The land was largely unknown to the outside world, filled as it was with narrow, treacherous byways, as implacable as the crime of kidnapping itself. For the hostages, there were the challenges of the terrain (as day after day they marched through dense jungle highlands) and the elements (not the formidable cold of the Himalayas but the debilitating fevers of malaria).

For Ramm and all outsiders trying to resolve the incident, it was another vexing case. Though not laden with the extra complication of numerous governments (six in Kashmir) and their mixed agendas, the Indonesian incident was burdened with issues far more subtle than a contest between good and evil. On one side was Kwalik, with his Catholic virtue and his persistent struggling band of OPM rebels. On the other were the investors, the owners of the mines, and the invading armies, possibly exploiting a land and its native dwellers. And in the middle, the innocent, curious, ideological explorers, the newest pawns in a game of chess begun by a previous generation. In the middle, too, were the negotiators, who effectively were negotiating with the military forces as much as with the rebel band.

Kidnap experts worldwide were enthralled by the case, and many of them followed it like a soap opera. They knew that maintaining the trust and confidence of the OPM while appeasing and holding back the Indonesian soldiers would be a steep challenge for the negotiators. But what seemed to fascinate them most was the odd, unprecedented mix of old and new methods and strategies. Though it could take days for messengers to reach the rebel hideouts deep in the jungles of the world's most remote wilderness, the demands of the OPM, once they were delivered to the nearest outpost, could quickly be disseminated around the world. In fact, on January 21, the OPM demands were posted on the Internet.

But from the beginning, it was clear to every expert that a resolution would be neither easy nor quick. And there were no guarantees there would even be one. Like all kidnappings, this one would hurl the participants onto a wrenching roller coaster of emotions. Two weeks into the incident, Jill van der Kolk, the mother of one of the Cambridge scientists, wrote in her diary, "For the first time today I contemplated the idea of never seeing Annette again. I don't know how to cope with the feeling of desperation."

But the scent of hope always returned. Several days after the abduction, the insurgents released nine of the Indonesian hostages, unharmed. Three days later, they freed the German scientist, with the instruction that he serve as mediator. Instead he returned to Germany.

Another Indonesian hostage was released a few weeks into the ordeal. He described the remaining captives as "safe and well." By then, the rebels were sending messages through missionary intermediaries that they agreed to the idea of freeing the hostages. Ramm, his colleague John Beadle, and other behind-the-scenes officials, including the special forces commander, so far had successfully held back the Indonesian army chiefs, who were so very eager to abandon the art of negotiation for an act of aggression.

At one point, rebel leader Kwalik had asked to meet with a Roman Catholic bishop who had been his teacher more than twenty years before. The seventy-four-year-old bishop of Jayapura, H. M. F. Munninghoff, a frail man who recently had been quite ill, flew in a light Cessna airplane into the rain forest, dropping down out of the thick cloud cover onto a grassy airstrip in the mountains near the site of the abduction. He brought battery acid for the separatists' radio and some rice. And in his heart, in addition to the courage to take the trip at all, he carried the hope that he would return with at least one more freed hostage. At the meeting, Kwalik, who did not carry a weapon, firmly and resolutely reiterated his demands and gave the bishop letters, apparently outlining the demands, for each of the governments involved: the British, the Dutch, and the German. But that was all that he offered.

The Internet carried an interview with the apparently disheartened bishop describing the reunion with his former student. "I made every effort using a number of arguments to persuade Kelly Kwalik to release the hostages. My efforts have not been successful thus far, moreover he is, rather aggressively, sticking to his original demands, that is that Irian Jaya should be given independence. . . . They said that the reason for the kidnapping was to alert the whole world to the existence of the Free Papua Movement and its demands. I said that now the whole world does know and you have achieved your aims. But they replied that the hostages were weapons, which they could use to exert pressure and that they could not release the hostages until their demands had been met. I said, now that the world knows about the OPM, it's a good time to release the hostages so that the world will also know that the OPM are of good intent. And that would mean that our journey was of use. If we return without result, then [the Indonesians] can claim that because mediation has failed, it would be better to begin military operations. [Kwalik] spoke nicely, only aggressively when speaking of his demands. He didn't want to shift. I believe he is an effective leader, as I could see that everyone there followed his orders."

Also on the Internet that day was a Dutch journalist's interview of an OPM member who now lived in the Netherlands. "Why do the OPM carry out kidnappings and kill hostages?" the journalist asked.

"Oh, that's not the case. In the current case I can say that the OPM have guaranteed the health and safety of each and every hostage. We aren't cannibals. We, the OPM, will not kill the hostages. We only want freedom."

Around this time, the press was filled with profiles of the hostages and comments about their abilities to endure a long captivity. Bibby, the Birdlife International director, told the *Independent*, "They're young, fit people. They will be used to living in fairly basic circumstances on fairly basic food and being out of doors in the tropical forest. They will be adequately equipped for that physically and mentally."

A former tutor said, of one hostage, "He is very lively. I would imagine he would cope with situations like this well. He is a hardworking lad."

But no matter how strong or diligent or fit they were, nothing could have prepared the research team for this. Eating rats, marching daily through rugged high-altitude jungles, and coping with a daily fear of death and rape had not been part of their survival tutorials.

By mid-February, there seemed to be little progress toward the release of the new hostages, though the OPM did free the high school students abducted the previous November. And another OPM band freed a French geologist and his colleague, abducted earlier in February, but only after the payment of a cash ransom. Rumor had it that Kwalik was pitching obstacles to the negotiators, a deliberate delay tactic presumably to provide more time to publicize his cause. He had broken off discussions with missionary mediators in late January and now he wanted to consult with OPM's political leaders in Papua New Guinea—a process that, given the time required to send messages in and out of his wilderness camps, could add weeks to the process.

Suddenly during the last week of February, the roller coaster ride, at least for the families, took a sharp turn, though where it was headed was still unclear. It appeared that mediators from the International Red Cross, whom Kwalik had asked to see, had persuaded the rebels to free the hostages in exchange for food, medicine, and the promise of immunity. The Indonesian military announced the news and the Associated Press, among others, picked up the story, running it on February 24. The mother of one of the Cambridge hostages wrote in her diary on February 23: "We mustn't raise our hopes too much. We've been close before and then they've been taken back to the jungle."

The appointed day came and went without any new releases. On February 25, the mother wrote: "It's been a hard day again. However much we rationalized that a release was only a small likelihood, our hopes were dashed again, to leave us wondering if it will continue to drag on. The days are long for us, but must be interminable for them."

Letters from the captives to their families revealed they were all fatigued and malnourished. A few suffered from high fevers; a few, including the Dutch woman, who was now five months pregnant, might have malaria. The Red Cross persuaded the kidnappers to allow a Red Cross doctor to examine the hostages. The doctor and mediators spent five hours with the captives and gave them fresh clothing, food, and treated them for fatigue and other conditions. There was special concern among the rebels for the pregnant captive; the rebels, who had heard the Catholic missionaries' stories of Jesus, hoped she would have the baby while in captivity because they believed it could be their messiah.

Ramm would recall later: "You don't make nationalistic distinctions in your mind; you worry about all of them. We worried about the pregnant woman's ability to move through the jungle quickly with her advancing pregnancy. It was such a worry. And the others, we were trying to relate to them, trying to think how they would be surviving. These were all exceptionally bright young people, so we were hoping that they were making all the right decisions, that they were empathizing with the hostage-takers, saying that they understood what the OPM was trying to achieve.

"There are so many issues to balance, from the macropolitical issues of the rights of the people to their land, which we as negotiators can have no impact on, right down to the micro issues, such as 'Can we have some more food because the hostages are eating more food than we've got?' You're always negotiating on several levels, trying to say to the locals we are here to help and advise, we're here as a resource for you, we're not trying to take over.

"You can very often have sympathy with the cause. It's like the converse of what Churchill said, 'I don't agree with what he says, but I defend to the last his right to say it.' The converse is true here. 'I may agree with what he says, but I don't agree with what he is doing to express it.' It cannot be right to take these young people, and one of the key negotiating lines was, 'These young people care as you do for the ecology of your region. You've got among the most eloquent voices that you could ever have to express the need to protect your region.'

"We had to be very cautious about the way we progressed [with] that case because the people who have operational control are the government troops of Indonesia, and it's no good wagging the finger at them and saying, 'Well look here, mate, if you were not plundering their bit of the countryside, they wouldn't be doing this to you.' As I said, those are the macropolitical issues that you have to leave for the politicians. You have to put blinders on; you have to stay focused, and what you have to focus on are the persons. 'I can see where you are coming from, but look at these young people. How does keeping them, harming them, do anything at all for advancing your cause? You are undermining any legitimate platform you may be building for yourself.'

"The biggest challenge here was persuading the hostage-takers that there was real political gain in releasing the hostages. And there was, as always, the personality of the rebel leadership. How charismatic is he, his ego, his level of malevolence, his level of dishonesty in the negotiations? You always have to contend with this. In the end of the day, you have to judge the honesty of what he's saying against the reality of what he's doing and how much longer you think the situation can go on. The time issue is more of a concern when there is an illness or in this case, a pregnant hostage.

"I mean she was a key issue; there's one thing about prolonged negotiations to reach a peaceful resolution, and then there's the issue of a Western woman having a baby in the jungle. You're always thinking about the tragedy that could evolve. Already she's had no prenatal care; the child could be in a breached position, a million and one things could be going on. All the time we're speaking to gynecologists trying to get an assessment on what is the window of opportunity that we have."

By mid-March, five Indonesians, the four Brits, the Dutch man, and the pregnant woman remained in captivity. Kwalik, meanwhile, had achieved little progress in obtaining his major demand: the liberation of his country. At one point, the president of the European Parliament, Klaus Hansch, had agreed to receive members of the OPM in Strasbourg and to hear about their cause. But the Indonesian government vehemently opposed such a move, saying that not only was the OPM an illegal group, it was also currently engaged in terrorist activities. The European Parliament backed off.

By April, several tactics had been tried, including one that would bring an element of humor to an otherwise tragic situation. Because the tribes had been exposed to the teachings of Catholic missionaries, there was the possibility that the rebels could be persuaded to release the hostages on the occasion of Easter. And so Easter was discussed in the back-and-forth between rebels and negotiators, which normally took several days. Letters and messengers were the main mode of exchange in this case. Phones were not an option nor were radios; the military did not want the rebels to be given any sophisticated equipment. It was suggested that the OPM would present a fine image to the world if they released the hostages on Easter. This would give them tremendous international press and enlist praise for their humanitarian gesture. But when Easter finally arrived, on April 7, nothing happened. In the next exchange, the rebels were asked why they did not observe Easter by releasing the hostages. The response was "What is Easter?"

April was a torturous month for all. Ramm and the Scotland Yard team were dividing their time among three stalled negotiations: Cambodia, Indonesia, and Kashmir. The Irian Jaya captives were losing stamina and hope. One Indonesian hostage was apparently quite ill. And there had been disturbing events that could indirectly affect the negotiations, such as riots at the Freeport copper mines and the death of an OPM hero in an Indonesian jail.

Annette van der Kolk's mother, Jill, made the following entries in her diary in April.

April 2: "No news. With the cutting back of visits by the Red Cross, this is going to be the pattern of the next week."

April 11: "We received copies of photos taken on the last medical visit. Annette looks thin. The tension is beginning to show with all the families—people are tired!"

April 18, the 100th day of captivity: "No news to report today, even though it was a milestone for us."

27

On May Day that year, the eight-year-old son of a wealthy Mexico City businessman began his twenty-nine days of captivity with a $30 million ransom demand. In Rio, early in the month, the kidnapped grandson of a prominent restaurateur was freed after spending sixteen days chained to a tree. In Germany, police apprehended the alleged kidnappers of tobacco magnate Jan Philipp Reemtsma, who was held in chains in a cellar before being released in late April after two of his friends, a pastor and a sociology professor, delivered a $20 million ransom. A Hong Kong insurance executive kidnapped while on holiday in China's Guangdong province regained his freedom after police raided the hotel where his family was told to bring the $300,000 ransom. And a German tourist cycling across Pakistan escaped from his kidnappers after three weeks in captivity, most spent traveling across the desert on camels.

The seven French monks kidnapped in March in Algeria were killed in May, their throats slit by their Islamic fundamentalist captors. That month, too, an American woman was abducted from her car by gunmen who forced her off a highway in Guatemala. Another American woman was seized by former contra rebels in Nicaragua. In Cambodia, the British mine expert and his interpreter were still alive, but, by most accounts, they had been forced into the ranks of the Khmer Rouge's slave laborers and assigned to the task of extracting explosives from artillery shells to make land mines.

In Peru, a report emerged showing a shocking reversal in expected crime stats. During the first several months of 1996, kidnappings had risen 525 percent over the previous year in Lima alone—a stunning blow to a country reputed to have nearly conquered the crime. Most were quickie incidents in which armed gangs held their prey long enough to get money out of their bank accounts or home vaults. Targets thus far had included businessmen, judges, the president of a Peruvian airline, a sports celebrity, a bank executive's secretary, and, in May, an American mining executive. He paid for his freedom with 100 kilos of gold from the inventory of his own company.

Meanwhile, on the island of New Guinea, in the dense, misty highlands of central Irian Jaya, the eleven young hostages began the month with the joyous news that their captors planned to release them on May 8 in a jungle ceremony commemorating International Red Cross Day. The OPM were assured that there would be substantial international publicity for their cause, that they would be safe from reprisals by the Indonesian military, and that a Red Cross representative would remain in the area to provide ongoing health care for their people.

"We were asked today if we wanted *the* phone call in the early hours—as if we would refuse!" wrote Mrs. van der Kolk in her diary on May 4. "I'm almost afraid to tell anyone because of tempting providence."

When the big day arrived, Kwalik marched the hostages out of the cloud-covered highlands to the small village chosen for the occasion. The atmosphere was nearly festive, with several hundred villagers coming to witness the event and the ceremonial slaughtering of the pigs. The hostages, adorned with trinkets from the OPM, sat and listened to speeches, waiting, as they had done during every second of every day of their captivity, for the moment of their freedom, for the signal and the word from Kwalik that the ordeal was finally over. The local OPM leader gave the hostages pigs and a cockerel to take home with them. But when Kwalik began his talk, for reasons that no one could ever explain, he completely reversed his plan. The hostages would not be freed that day or any other day, he exclaimed, until Irian Jaya was granted its freedom from Indonesia. Kwalik apparently believed he would get the most attention by snatching the hostages' freedom at the last minute. Stunned and inconsolable, the hostages were forced back into the wilderness once again. The next day, the Red Cross resigned from its role as intermediary. And without being told, the captives and their families knew that what they feared most was now inevitable: a military rescue.

Fear was warranted. The risks of a raid were many. A skirmish between soldiers and rebels posed an imminent danger to everyone involved, especially hostages whose hands and feet could be bound or who could be tied to a tree or to each other. What imperiled the hostages most, it seemed, was the potentially violent reaction of the rebels at the moment they would hear the whirring of the helicopters' blades and see the rescuers cascading like waterfalls down long ropes out of hovering choppers, their rifles spewing bullets as their feet hit the ground. As in cases in other countries, the soldiers could kill a hostage amid the chaos of a rescue and conveniently blame the death on the rebels.

Still, behind the scenes for months now, Ramm and other hostage experts had been working on a rescue plan with the Indonesian generals, a backup plan in case all other conciliatory efforts—from missionaries to the Red Cross—failed. After May 8, everyone knew it was impossible to hold back the military operation any longer. And so the proverbial Plan B was set into motion. Prolonged negotiations had provided all sorts of information to help mitigate the dangers of a raid, including the number of rebels involved, their daily habits, and the extent of their weaponry. The plan was not foolproof, but everyone agreed to the details. And the special forces commanders, donning heroes' mantles in the glaring spotlight of world opinion, were unlikely to betray such a plan.

The first military assault came the very next day. The hostages heard the helicopters coming and the sound of explosions nearby. The soldiers had dropped grenades onto a munitions shed, sending out sirens of explosive sounds in an attempt to distract the rebels from the hut where the hostages were staying. But the hostages, not knowing of the plan, fled into the jungle for safety. And soon they were recaptured, only to begin their ordeal anew, it seemed, walking day after day deeper into the highlands to an altitude of nearly 12,000 feet. This time, however, the soldiers were never far behind.

Less than a week later, as the hostages were hiking over and down a steep hill, one of them saw a soldiers' campsite through the brush on the other side of a loud and roaring river. The rebels, who must have seen what the hostage saw, motioned for the hostages to return up the hill, but the Dutch woman, now more than seven months pregnant, said she was too exhausted. The Dutch man stayed behind with her. But as a few of the hostages attempted the climb, they heard a terrible whacking sound. A rebel who had dropped behind had suddenly axed one of the Indonesian hostages right in front of the hostage's fiancée. The remaining hostages huddled together, with one of the Brits, Daniel Start, shielding the other Indonesians. The rebels ordered the non-Indonesians to go, but, hoping to protect the others, they wouldn't move. One more Indonesian was then dragged from the group and hacked to death with machetes. The hostages ran toward the river, only to confront the warning shots of the soldiers, who could not see their faces. They screamed that they were hostages, and the gunfire ceased. It was May 15, the 122nd day of captivity, and nine hostages had gained their freedom. Two from Indonesia were axed to death.

For hostage Adinda Saraswati, what will linger in her mind's eye forever will not be the image of eating rats or the endless fatigue or even her fractured leg. It will be the sight of a rebel driving his ax into the back of her fiancé until he died. It was that image, too, that the world would hold in its memory about the OPM and their quest, once innocent and noble, for freedom. In the end, revulsion had overtaken sympathy and the Indonesian government could feed the heinous event into their publicity machine and use it to justify far worse.

By turning to violence in the end, the rebels defeated their impassioned purpose of enlisting the world's sympathy. Instead, they killed the innocent blend of curiosity and trust that had brought the scientists to the once sacred highlands of West Papua.

And they apparently did not see futility in the act of kidnapping. A few months after the murders of the two Indonesian hostages, the U.S. State Department would issue a Consular Information Sheet for Indonesia that included the following advice: "Travelers should be aware that the U.S. Embassy has received unconfirmed information that the Free Papua Movement (OPM) may be targeting U.S. citizens or U.S. companies in Irian Jaya Province for hostage taking or for sabotage.

"Periodically, limited civil unrest resulting in violence has occurred in the province of Aceh, located in the far northern tip of Sumatra, and in the province of East Timor, located 300 miles north of Australia. In January 1996, a group of foreigners was taken hostage in the remote province of Irian Jaya. The U.S. Embassy recommends that persons traveling to the province stay in larger towns and avoid traveling to remote villages as well as contact the U.S. Embassy in advance of any travel. Travelers may also need permits from police authorities to visit certain regions in Irian Jaya province."

And while the State Department was warning Americans about the potential dangers in the outback of Indonesia, a U.S. travel magazine was telling Americans that this was one of the last bastions of great adventure and travel in the world. The August issue of *Condé Nast Traveler* ran the feature "Cannibals on Main Street," which was the diary of a traveler who had ventured into the dense wilderness of Irian Jaya with a group that included rock star Mick Jagger and his wife, the model Jerry Hall.

The path of their journey—at one point, gliding along the Lorentz River—was eerily close to the regions of danger for the biologists who became hostages. And while their trip from October 1995 to mid-November preceded the hostage incident, the publication of the article followed the abductions and deaths. Indeed, it coincided with another kidnapping in Irian Jaya: the abduction of sixteen lumberjacks, including one woman.

The article recounted the many exciting reasons to travel to Irian Jaya, including the unusual and fascinating tribes. But neither the writer nor the magazine noted the activity of the OPM, their new infatuation with the weapon of kidnapping, or even the fact that there was an insurgency movement passionately seeking freedom for Irian Jaya. The latest kidnapping, by forty armed men who called themselves the Security Disturbance Group, would later be linked to the OPM. The Mapanduma abductions, it appeared, were not aberrations.

⋖⋛⋗

On the occasion of the Cambridge scientists' return to Britain and in recognition of the loss of the two Indonesian hostages, the newspaper the *Scotsman* ran what many believed to be a brilliant editorial:

> Hostage stories make good newspaper copy, or, to be more precise, hostage stories with Western, or, more exactly, British hostages in them. There is drama, suspense and—in most cases—an eventual happy end with family reunions and British officials welcoming the returnees on the tarmac after flying home from whatever foreign parts they were being held in. For a time the media spotlight is concentrated on some remote (remote from Britain, that is) region of the world, only for it to sink back into obscurity as the crisis subsides.
>
> The one element that is usually missing from all of this, with a few exceptions in the quality press, is any real attempt to understand why the kidnapping took place in the first place. The story is the hostages, not the terrible conditions which may have led a local resistance group to adopt a strategy of hostage-taking to draw the attention of the world to its cause. Yet while the hostage crisis comes to an end—and in most cases of political hostage-taking of this kind the captives do not come to any harm apart from the physical privations which they have to suffer along with their captors—the circumstances which led to this desperate act do not.
>
> That is not to downplay the mental and physical suffering which may affect the hostages. Nor is it to condone the taking of hostages any more than negotiating with the kidnappers for their release is to approve of what they are doing. But it is to recognize that such actions are cries for help which more often than not go completely ignored by the world community. And often such situations can be traced back to messily finished colonial business.
>
> Such is the case in Irian Jaya, which Indonesia invaded and annexed with impunity after the Dutch pulled out in 1963. It now suffers from

unacceptable Indonesian human rights abuses and insensitive development by the international mining companies Freeport-McMoRan and RTZ. (East Timor is another one of those forgotten former colonial territories to suffer the unwelcome attention of the Indonesian army.) Does anybody know what is going on in Somalia, Liberia, Burma, Kashmir, the Kurdish areas in Turkey unless aid workers are kidnapped or westerners are at risk? The list is endless.

Of course, the plight of the hostages should be reported—and the happy ending. But along with that let the whole story be told, let a less narrow, Eurocentric and, indeed, Brito-centric view be adopted in the way that the media in this country observe what is happening in the world. Britain is part of a global community and when human rights and other outrages occur in another part of the world we should hear about it—and not only when a westerner is involved.

28

On the very day the hostages of Irian Jaya fled across the Papuan high-lands to freedom, a new crisis erupted in the mountains of northern India because of a man who said he knew what no one else could know: the fate of the prisoners of Al-Faran.

The man had come out of the mountains, like the first rush of the melting snows of spring, but instead of delivering the hope of a new season, he brought a flood of new fears. His name was Naser Mohammed, he told the officers who arrested him, and he was the financial chief of the Pakistan-based rebel group Harkat-ul-Ansar. Naser claimed he had spent a good deal of time at the "safe house" where the Al-Faran intermediaries talked to the government's nego-tiators and to the kidnappers. And when he told his Indian interroga-tors what he knew of the Western tourists, he reportedly wept.

The event happened in December, the thirty-one-year-old militant said, when the snows and gale-force winds howled through the moun-tain passes, humbling even the militants, who had faced the icy wall of a Himalayan winter many times before. The hostages, exhausted from months of forced marches and meager allotments of food, were slowing down the rebels' journey back to Pakistan, an escape that must be swift to elude the Indian army with its hundreds of thousands of troopers patrolling everywhere. The rebels had killed the hostages in December, Naser said, and they buried them in unmarked graves; the rebels did not want to leave a blood trail for the Indian army to follow. He did not know their exact location, Naser said, but he believed the grave site was somewhere in the vast forest of fir and birch near the village of Kokarnag in the vicinity of Anantnag.

The confession contained information that sadly fit into the chronology of events during the first several months of the ordeal. He seemed to know things that only someone well connected to the militants could have known—for example, that the rebels' original plan was to abduct foreign engineers in the Jammu area of northern India, not tourists in Pahalgam. The kidnappers had disobeyed Qari Zarar, the HUA chief in Srinagar who took his orders from "Pakistani leaders who said that HUA leaders jailed in India should be released" in exchange for the hostages.

There were surprises, too—facts that countered previously accepted notions. Naser claimed that John Childs was allowed to escape "since he had a problem with his leg" and that Ostro had been shot in the head before he was beheaded.

"Ostro was beheaded because the chief hostage-keeper got a message from Allah," Naser said in his confession. Turki, whom Naser described as "very hotheaded," gave his compatriots two reasons for the brutal death of Ostro. "He said Ostro had tried to escape several times, and in the night before the killing Turki had observed Nimam-e-Ishtekhana, after which he got a message from Allah that by killing Ostro they would achieve the goal. The Nimam-e-Ishtekhana is observed when Muslims cannot take [sic] a decision and so they leave it to Allah. Therefore, early in the morning, Turki took Ostro to Anantnag and led him to a jungle and killed him by shooting him first and then beheaded the body. Thereafter, Turki threw the body and its head separately in the jungles. We admonished Turki and told him that in the future he should not repeat such irresponsible acts. He retorted that to get Nasrullah Masur [a jailed militant] released, he would do anything."

By August, Naser said, the HUA leaders and the kidnappers were at odds. And in September, Zarar, who served as the rebel intermediary, hinted to the government that "if a sum of five crore [about $12 million] was arranged as 'security deposit,' the hostages could be released. The money would be given back to the government after the release of the jailed militants. But the news that the Al-Faran was asking for a 'ransom' was given to the media. This was not true and eroded the image of Zarar."

Toward the end of September, he said, "the HUA militants holding the hostages were jittery and fed up. Some wanted to go back to Pakistan before the onset of winter. They were being kept back by pep talk. . . . In the end of November, I was contacted and told that the HUA top leadership was under pressure from the Pakistani government to release the foreigners. I was told that Jalaluddin Akkhari [the chief commander of an Islamic group in Afghanistan] was also asking for their release and he was approached by some of his American and British friends to get the hostages freed. He said he had come to Islamabad specially for this purpose. All I could say was that the HUA was adamant not to release the hostages without getting their own leaders out of jail. And the local leaders were also not willing.

"In December 1995, I was told that Abdul Hamid Turki and four other HUA leaders had been killed in an encounter with the Rashtriya Rifles [troops] near Dabran, Anantnag. When I asked where the hostages were when the encounter took place, I was told they were in Kokarnag. On December 10, 1995, a message was sent to give a press release in Srinagar that after the encounter, the hostages had been captured by the army. On January 4, 1996, I met Parvez Ahmed Baba, a member of the HUA's Majilis-e-Amla [another militant group]. I asked Parvez about the fate of the hostages.

"He told me that after the death of Turki, the militants holding the hostages were very tense. They indicated to HUA leaders in Srinagar that the army and Rashtriya Rifles was [sic] trying to eliminate the HUA group even with the hostages, if need be. Sikandar [the field commander] was under pressure to arrive at an immediate settlement on the issue—either way. Under these circumstances, and perhaps keeping in mind the fact that the Al-Faran had already given a press note to the effect that the army had taken away the hostages, Sikandar ordered the execution of all the four remaining hostages.

"Accordingly, the foreigners were killed on December 13, 1995, in the Magam area of Kokarnag and buried in the jungles there. The exact location where they were buried was kept a secret as was desired by the group."

Mohammed, who was arrested in April, had confessed by early May. News of his confession, which hit the press on May 15, devastated the hostage families and stole some of the triumph from the resolution of the Indonesian ordeal. The May 15 stories covering the release of the nine men and women in Irian Jaya ended with a sad reminder of the Kashmir hostages who were not yet free and, in fact, could be dead.

Back in Spokane, two days before the confession was international news, Jane Schelly received her usual daily call from the State Department. Immediately, she detected a change in tone. For the past several months, Jane had been riding a wave of optimism, based largely on the frequency of the reports out of Kashmir that Don, Keith, Paul, and Dirk had been seen in various hamlets and towns. Since late December 1995, there had been at least thirteen sightings, mostly from villagers. A few had come from people in rather high political positions. And there was one in March that supposedly emanated from militant leaders who reported that the hostages were alive and even well cared for.

Fueling her optimism for those long winter months was a conversation that she had with David Mackie in December. Mackie, who now lived in San Francisco, was one of the two Brits kidnapped in Kashmir for seventeen days during the summer of 1994. For a few days of his captivity, he was held in the home of a wealthy man in the town of Anantnag. He and fellow hostage Kim Housego had beds to sleep in, access to a shower and to a TV, as well as a daily regimen of tea and biscuits. And when they emerged from the mountains, unharmed, they carried with them presents from the kidnappers; a papier-mâché serving platter and the wall clock engraved with political propaganda. This upbeat image created a picture for Jane that helped her endure the winter of 1995.

And then there was the mysterious photo of the hostages supposedly taken in March. Experts and officials staying at the military compound at Srinagar were shown a somewhat blurry photo that, by most accounts, the Indian government would not let them have. There was much speculation that someone—possibly a government informant within the HUA or the Al-Faran—would be in danger if the photo were to be published. After much urging, relatives and officials secretly received copies. Indeed the photo did depict the hostages, but to confirm that it was taken in March was difficult. The vegetation could just as easily have been present in the autumn months. Officials spent thousands of dollars running the photo by botanists in hopes of identifying one plant that would make all the difference.

Of course, if it could be determined that the photo was taken in spring, this meant the hostages were not killed in December. They could have been killed after the photo was taken, but at least the story of their deaths would be revealed as an apocryphal tale. "We had to wait six months for a copy of the photo," said Bernd Hasert, Dirk's brother. "It's a strange photo showing the prisoners dressed like the locals with machine guns hanging from their necks in victory pose." Still, despite the mystery surrounding it, the very existence of the photo had provided another hint of hope for the hostage families.

Now it was Day 311, and the first news from Jane's State Department contact was good. Two days before, there had been another sighting, this time in Bonakandwar, a village of about 600 people in the Anantnag district, roughly 7,500 feet in elevation. It was the first indication that with the coming of spring, the hostages and their guards were on the move again. In the last report, they were supposedly at about 4,000 feet, and now, with the melting of the snow, they were rising to higher elevations as they continued to dodge the ever-present threat of the hundreds of thousands of Indian troops. Just as they had moved down to lower elevations as the weather grew colder last autumn, they were now moving up the mountains. But that was only one version of reality. And, as Jane sensed, there was now a new version, sadly contradicting all that she had imagined for the past five months.

Jane wrote that day: "There is a new report that just came in that contradicts all that we have been told and they are not sure of its accuracy. The authorities are trying to reconcile the differences. The Indians have captured a high-level militant, one who has contact with Al-Faran and HUA and he has said that all the hostages were killed last December. American and British law enforcement [FBI and Scotland Yard] are now in Srinagar checking this out and they will be involved in the questioning of the militant. It is hard to believe as the last reported sighting was just two days ago. At this point it has not hit the media. But I was told that I should not be surprised if I am contacted within the next few days. There is concern, however, that if the story does come out there will be reason for the militants to go ahead and kill the four. If the media gives the story credence, it may give them cover to kill them; so I am going to say that I am aware of the rumor but regard it as unconfirmed, which it certainly is. I was really shook up when I heard this but as much as I fear them being dead, I am very very angry that we are now back to the garbage of last summer and fall. The deadlines, the threats, the reports of them being wounded. The ups and downs of the roller coaster."

On the way to work that morning, Jane stopped at Debbie Pierce's house, up a nearby hill and around the corner, to borrow her cell phone. She wanted to be within easy reach of the State Department, while not missing a minute of work. Debbie knew something was terribly wrong, but she knew also that it was best not to ask. Jane would reveal what was troubling her when she was ready. Her friends were well accustomed to the rhythm of Jane's ordeal. When Jane was upset, she would sometimes show up at the door of a friend with plants and flowers to be added to the friend's garden or perhaps a new idea for the arrangement of the plants. The McManus garden, for example, on the bluffs overlooking the Little Spokane River, had never looked so good. Gardening was therapeutic for Jane and always had been. Don used to tease her about her love for rearranging her garden. "You move the flowers around so often you ought to put them on roller skates," he used to say. On that day, May 13, one of the toughest yet, she would have spent the entire day gardening if that had been possible. But Jane's job was always a top priority. When one of the teachers told her that day that she was thinking of Jane and praying for her, the stress burst through her incredibly strong exterior and she began to sob.

On May 15, when the news broke and the reporters invaded, Jane was well prepared and her usual competent, in-control demeanor had taken over. From her journal that day: "The militant is knowledgeable and his story is consistent but both stories cannot be true. Deb called before work to tell me the story had hit the radio and as the day progressed more came out. Everybody called. At school, so many of the students wanted to know why our army just didn't go in, have a big shoot out and rescue them all. I gathered the staff together and gave them the accurate facts so they would be able to respond to the questions of students. That was a good way to handle it. The staff was very concerned, got a lot of hugs. Spent a lot of time talking. I'm so very glad that I had the lead time to prepare myself mentally. To deal with the phone calls and the emotions all in the same day would have been too much."

Among her callers was U.S. Representative Bill Richardson, a Democrat from New Mexico with a track record for helping to gain the release of hostages. Richardson, who was soon to be the new U.S. ambassador to the United Nations, had confidently traveled to Kashmir during February of that year to try to gain the tourists' freedom but obviously without success. He had shown great consideration to Jane and the other hostage families, including behind-the-scenes gestures invisible to the press; for example, he would call Jane on the eve of major holidays to wish her well and in the midst of crises such as the confession of the captured militant. Jane's answer machine recorded Richardson's message, which she later inserted into her journal.

"I'm just calling to see how you're doing. We're all working on the assumption that these reports are untrue and that all the folks are alive. We don't want to give any credence to these reports because then the hostage-takers might do something irrational. So just hang in there; I know you are sobered by this, but we are with you on this. I've called the State Department and the embassy, and you have a lot of people with you. Take care."

Officials in the four concerned countries seemed as stunned and confused as the families. None had believed the story that rebels circulated, in a written statement on December 11, about the Indian army snatching the hostages during a clash with the militants and possibly killing them. It was a story that had resurfaced several times since December. Though by most accounts apocryphal, the story now made Naser's confession seem all the more plausible. The battle had occurred on December 4, and the panicked terrorists, according to Naser, murdered the hostages around December 13. The Indian army had denied any role in such events and had said that the militants fabricated the story simply to discredit India. One theory now was that the "skirmish" story might have been a way to shuttle the blame for the hostages' deaths, in mid-December, onto the Indian army. It was possible that the rebels had been trying to hide the murders of the hostages by repeatedly planting the story about the Indian army seizing and killing them. Naser's placement of the murders in mid-December made sense also because the remaining members of the Al-Faran may indeed have panicked after the eight-hour battle on December 4, sensing the footsteps of the Indian army drawing near. Wanting to flee all the more quickly, they murdered the hostages. Or because an Al-Faran leader was killed in that December clash, one or two remaining rebels might have taken their revenge by killing the hostages.

But, of course, there were other ways of looking at Naser's version of reality. Naser was, after all, a prisoner of an army reputed to be brutal. By some accounts, he was not allowed to be questioned by Western diplomats and experts for at least two weeks after his arrest, during which time he was reportedly tortured. And the timing of his emergence was right before elections scheduled for May. To establish that the Western tourists had been killed by a group linked to the HUA helped to smear the image of the separatists.

Some skeptics, including several Indian journalists who had followed the case very carefully, believed the truth was an amalgam of several stories. If the hostages were indeed dead, they might have been killed during one of the skirmishes in early December—on the fourth or the eleventh—when Indian troops attempted to rescue them. But this was something the Indian army would never be able to confess, and so, to communicate the truth of the fates of the hostages, the captured militant was forced to tell an apocryphal story. But that was just one theory.

The Foreign Office minister in London, Jeremy Hanley, commented that there had been no proof-of-life communication since August, and that the last reliable sighting may have been December 8. But he also said the Foreign Office had certainly not given up hope and would investigate all aspects of the recent reports. After all, a captured militant might say anything to please his interrogators, especially if the rumors were true regarding the brutality of Indian military interrogations. In Delhi, a spokesman for the British High Commission told reporters: "The hostages are very much alive. We continue to work flat-out for their release."

The U.S. embassy called upon the Al-Faran to effectively discredit the militant's terrible tale by providing evidence that the hostages were still alive. Embassy officials reminded reporters that throughout the past six months there had been reports about possible killings but not an ounce of evidence of the hostages' deaths. "We continue to operate on the assumption that these guys are alive, and we are making our best efforts to get them released," an embassy spokesman said.

Indian officials, in their public pronouncements, denied that the hostages were dead. Some questioned the credibility of information from a militant. "Captured guerrillas have a tendency to say so many things," a Kashmir government spokesman said. Officials recalled, too, that villagers had reported sightings of the tourists and their abductors off and on since December, the most recent being in late February. There were also sightings of the captors buying medicine to alleviate recurring ailments of the hostages, such as snow blindness and frostbite. "All the four hostages are safe, but we do not have direct contact with them," a senior Indian army official told the London *Times* on May 16. "The London-based news of the killing is speculative. It is misinformation."

But behind the scenes, Indian authorities expressed more pessimism. They told the various foreign embassies that because the militant was a leader of the Al-Faran, he may in fact have known what he was talking about and should be taken rather seriously. Some said, too, that the sightings in recent months were far from reliable. "We couldn't trust these reports. They all spoke of 'men with their heads covered,' " an intelligence officer said.

Because no one could present proof one way or the other and the militant's tale was truly the first potentially plausible explanation of the fate of the hostages, the governments had no other choice but to search for the graves. Soon after the elections in New Delhi that May—in which Rao lost his prime minister post—hundreds of Indian policemen and paramilitary troops from the Border Security Force hiked through the dense Magam forest south of Srinagar, looking for the unmarked graves Naser had tearfully described. The hunters included intelligence experts from Scotland Yard, agents from the FBI and from the Indian Central Bureau of Investigation, and sniffer dogs flown in from Germany. Nearly fifty miles from the spot on the lush slopes where the tourists were first abducted, along the alluring expanses of forests and foothills pictured in every tourist's guidebook, they searched for the remnants of four stolen lives.

29

JUNE 1996
KASHMIR

While the men scoured the landscape searching for patches of recently turned earth, new growths of grass, a softness under their boots, or even tools for digging inadvertently left behind, and the dogs sniffed and whined, the families of the hostages replayed the events of the past six months. During the days of the hunt and the nights of fitful sleep, they tried to recall every detail of what had happened, which sightings seemed absolutely confirmed and which were not; what efforts had been made and what had not; and now what could possibly be done and what could not.

The August tapes from nearly ten months ago, everyone knew, were the last proof-of-life evidence. Using walkie-talkie radios or phones or statements delivered to Srinagar newspapers, the government and the rebels had remained in contact—that is, until November. After that, news about the plight of the hostages came from shepherds migrating through the mountains or soldiers in the Indian intelligence corps or villagers who may have provided supplies or medical assistance to the rebels and their captives. If two sources reported a sighting, it was more sound, of course, than if one did, and such was the report of December 8, considered the last truly reliable sighting. The next one, on December 23, was a boost to the families, more than usual perhaps, considering the season and the presents and clothing they had sent to Srinagar, wrapped in the abundant faith that the hostages were alive. That report had come from villagers who said they saw twenty armed men walking alongside four other men who were wearing Kashmiri serapes and who appeared to have the lighter skin of Westerners. But they later admitted they had hardly seen the skin because the faces of the four men who seemed to stand out were covered. At the end of the year, the government announced there was another sighting, in a village called Hakura. The Al-Faran issued a statement in response, on January 3, reiterating the story they had been telling since mid-December, that the hostages were no longer in their care and that after their December 4 clash with government troops, the Indian army had seized the hostages. The statement noted that "there is a large army camp in the village [of Hakura] where the Westerners are being kept hostage by the soldiers." The Indian government denied repeatedly that their soldiers had taken the hostages.

Ten days later, the hostages were seen in the Pir Panjal mountain range, near the Pakistan border. An Indian intelligence source told a local reporter that the rebels appeared to be marching the hostages— all "in good health"—one by one, over the rugged range into Pakistan. It would be nearly two months until another sighting.

January 19 was the 200th day of captivity. By then, the only fact that could be substantiated in this case was that negotiations had stalled, perhaps permanently. And though no one would express it, there was no assurance at all that the hostages were even alive to mark their 200th day in whatever way they had devised to chart the passing days. It was onto this bleak stage in January and February that several new players began to appear, hoping to assume the role of heroes.

First came U.S. Representative Gary Ackerman, a New York Democrat and former chairman of the House Subcommittee on Asia and the Pacific. Traveling to Jammu, the home of the winter capital of Kashmir, Ackerman had a new idea: to persuade the umbrella association for the thirty or more groups pushing for Kashmir's secession from India to establish contact with the captors and renew the stymied negotiations. The All Parties Hurriyat Conference agreed to try, proclaiming that the continued captivity and the behavior of the Al-Faran was damaging the image of their cause. They set up a committee to start the work, and for a while the grim days of winter seemed almost hopeful.

Still, nothing happened. On February 9, the hostage wives and girlfriends sent a new appeal to Al-Faran, calling them "honourable religious men" and asking them to please release their husbands and boyfriends after the Muslim holiday called Eid al-Fitr. (This festival marks the end of a holy month of fasting, known as the Ramadan, and falls around February 21.) Less than a week later, an intermediary for the Harkat-ul-Ansar sent a statement to the Western officials in Srinagar and to a Kashmiri newspaper saying that his group had set up mujahideen "holy warrior" squads to "rescue" the hostages from the Indian army camp where the militants had claimed for months the hostages were being held. The same day, the messenger was reportedly killed when a device he was handling blew up. Indian authorities once again denied the report. Various experts believed this might be a sign that the militants were planning to release the hostages, perhaps on the day of the holy festival, on the twenty-first.

But the twenty-first came and went without a sign of the hostages. On that day too, another U.S. congressman landed in Kashmir: Representative Bill Richardson, the Democrat from New Mexico. By now, Richardson was accustomed to the stress and uncertainty of these international crises. In 1994, he had played a part in gaining the freedom of a U.S. pilot shot down in North Korea. In July 1995, he had helped to liberate two Americans held in an Iraqi prison, and in early February, he had met with Fidel Castro and assisted in the subsequent release of three Cuban political prisoners.

Now he planned to spend two days in Kashmir speaking with pro-rebel politicians, religious leaders, and negotiators. Coming at the end of the Ramadan—a time when negotiators believed hostage releases were most probable—Richardson told reporters that he would not negotiate with the Al-Faran but would urge them, in the name of the U.S. Congress, to free the hostages. "I'm here on a humanitarian mission, not on a political mission. My objective is not to negotiate but to get a firsthand assessment," he told the press. While everyone seemed to expect him to speak with the captors, as he had done in other incidents, this time there was simply no one to talk to.

On February 23, Richardson informed the press that although he could not reveal why, he did know that the hostages were alive and that they "will be released soon." And he said, "My plans are to continue working on this issue. I will be going to Pakistan this evening to talk to authorities about this issue."

At the same time as the Richardson visit, two other hopeful rescuers of a different sort gathered reporters and announced their goodwill and laudable intentions in resolving this crisis. They were Peter von Zschinsky and Jurgen Sick, both Germans claiming to be human rights workers.

In late January, von Zschinsky had unveiled his intention to forge his way through the snowbound Himalayan foothills with his cameraman, Sick, at his side, to find the hostages and to reason with the militants. The plan was outlined in a letter "to my friends," published in a German newspaper. To accomplish a task that five governments had been unable to achieve in seven months, the Germans were equipped with three items: a satellite telephone, a film camera, and a contract between von Zschinsky and the mother of the German hostage, Dirk Hasert.

The contract, which referred to von Zschinsky as a baron living in a castle on the Danube River, stated [in German] that, "By doing extensive research, von Zschinsky has laid the foundation for direct contact with the abductors and the hostages. Since the Federal Government [of Germany] has not made any progress in the liberation of the hostages for lack of engagement, this has to be tried through private engagement."

Mrs. Christa Hasert, Dirk's mother, agreed to speak only to von Zschinsky regarding her son and the ongoing ordeal, giving him exclusive rights to her photographs and background information. Von Zschinsky also had an exclusive arrangement with the respected German magazine *Focus* to report the details of his mission to free Dirk.

What happened to von Zschinsky in Kashmir is a matter of some debate: mainly between von Zschinsky and the negotiators, diplomats, and government authorities. Those who had been working the case worried about the intrusion and what it would do to the efforts to reconnect with the Al-Faran. From late January through the February holiday, there was a sense of hope, though it was based on a fragile mix of real and potential events. The situation was extremely delicate and caution was the word of the day. The death-defying German duo could easily be the proverbial bull in the china shop. Among other acts, von Zschinsky distributed medical supplies valued at 25,000 deutsche marks (about $18,000) to Kashmiri separatist groups on the Pakistani side. While it was a generous gesture that could reap the reward of something in return, its effectiveness depended on what was happening behind the scenes. If, for example, von Zschinsky gave money or supplies to a group that was on the verge of cooperating with authorities in exchange for such supplies, then the deal with authorities could be upstaged and doomed.

At one point, in a public fanfare of bravery and self-sacrifice, von Zschinsky offered himself in exchange for the release of the hostages. He had the offer and his satellite phone number published in the Kashmiri press, appealing to the militants to free the hostages in the name of Allah. At a press conference on February 21, he announced that the kidnappers had phoned in and asked him to wait a while. The next day, after engaging in a fistfight with pro-Indian extremists, von Zschinsky called another press conference, saying that since his arrival in Kashmir in late January, he and his cameraman had filmed fourteen hours of material, including interviews with the Al-Faran. Security experts later said it was utterly impossible that the German men had conducted such interviews and that no one in authority—no negotiator, no official, no journalist—ever saw any film.

Von Zschinsky never accomplished what he set out to do and while he and his cameraman were in India, the German media exposed them as con artists suspected of criminal activity by the BKA (Germany's version of the FBI). Sadly, von Zschinsky had gained the trust of Hasert's mother, telling her what every captive's family wants to hear: that he could free her son.

"He approached us, showed us his references to prove that he already had been in Afghanistan, where he had had contact with freedom fighters," Dirk's brother Bernd Hasert said later. "He told my mother, 'I have legitimate hope that I can bring your son home.' And, wanting this so very much, she believed it. In January 1996, they signed a contract, which gave him the right to market everything after Dirk came home."

The Haserts soon learned more about their would-be hero as the German press became intrigued with the story. One German newspaper wrote that von Zschinsky had tried to enlist corporate sponsors for his Kashmir quest, saying that he would use their logo on his equipment, which would then be seen on television worldwide. In another campaign, in 1992, according to the newspaper *Süddeutsche Zeitung,* von Zschinsky and an Iraqi with German citizenship told a Prague printing company that they had permission from the Iraqi State Bank to create Iraqi money for a humanitarian mission to help the Kurds in northern Iraq. When the document they supplied from the bank turned out to be a forgery, Czech police arrested them. The case against von Zschinsky, who spent several months in jail, was eventually dropped. While incarcerated, the same newspaper said, he met his cameraman. Regarding Kashmir, the newspaper commented, the duo had sullied the image of Western negotiators in the eyes of the kidnappers, thus potentially jeopardizing the welfare of the hostages.

Said Bernd Hasert: "On March 4, I read in our local newspaper that, according to the *Frankfurter Allgemeine Zeitung* [a newspaper], von Zschinsky had received an advance of 50,000 deutsche marks from *Focus* [about $33,000 at the time] and that most of the money had gone to my mother and some for his travel expenses. The article said that *Focus* denied this and had severed ties with him. And my mother did not receive any money. This was the first time we learned anything about money. Because of this article and because *Focus* had terminated their agreement with him, and also because we had heard that he has a questionable past, my mother canceled the contract with him on March 13."

Von Zschinsky's version of his Kashmir expedition was intriguing. In a 1997 letter (to this author), he claimed that he had met with the Al-Faran and that an exchange for the hostages "had been agreed upon." What botched the deal, he said, was the media. The magazines that did not have an exclusive contract with him wanted him to fail, he said, so they published "false statements" about him to besmirch his image. One magazine, *Der Spiegel,* he claimed, stated that he was "trying to stage a rescue operation with a German group of mercenaries." This provoked the Al-Faran, according to von Zschinsky, to believe he was a spy for India and for the United States and to cut off their contact with him.

"I was on the road in this mission from January 21 through March 8, with much engagement and patience," he wrote in his letter (in German). "It was my investment to build trust, friendship and understanding on the part of the Al-Faran, which I partially achieved. But this was finally destroyed by jealous conflicts of interest on the part of the media in Germany. This was especially bitter for me when I was so close to a successful mission."

The hostages, von Zschinsky wrote, were killed near Anantnag on February 21, partly in reaction to what the militants perceived as his betrayal of them. They were looking for an "out," a way to end it, as they wanted to return to Pakistan and Afghanistan, he claimed, adding: "I had been the last neutral possibility for the Al-Faran to distance themselves from the hostages."

In early March, von Zschinsky returned to Germany to begin a new enterprise, a book. "It's about my life as a war correspondent in Uganda, Romania, Somalia, Ruanda, Angola, Bosnia, Serbia, Croatia, Afghanistan, Indochina, Chile, Czechoslovakia, and other war territories," he explained in his letter.

In the closed circles of those handling the case, little was said about von Zschinsky after March that year. "If he had revealed his film, given some concrete evidence, some proof of what he said, it would have been a different story," said one individual close to the case. "As it was, what could anyone do about it? His credibility was not exactly strong."

Several weeks later, like a lone flower popping up from the hard earth of a winter of despair, good news suddenly came out of Kashmir. In the small town of Baramulla, northwest of Srinagar, on March 10, the Kashmiri chief of police, M. N. Sabharwal, told the local PTI

(Press Trust of India) that the state government had received information that the hostages were alive and safe. The message was short and without details, but it was clearly what everyone wanted to hear. Still, by April the rebels were not communicating, nor was there any solid evidence that the hostages were indeed safe or even alive.

The new month did bring a new potential hero, however, one who ironically came out of Islamabad, Pakistan's capital and the very seat of support, allegedly, for the Al-Faran. His name was Allah Baksh Sabir, and he was the father of Masood Azari, a devout Muslim who once edited two right-wing religious publications that, among other things, recruited able-bodied men for the Islamic holy wars. Azari was number one on the list of militants that the Al-Faran wanted released from India's prisons in exchange for the hostages. And it was this that made it difficult for his father to speak. He choked back tears at the press conference arranged by the U.S. embassy in April in Islamabad.

"I know how the families of the hostages must be hurting. I feel the same for my son. I know their agony," he said. He then begged the Al-Faran to drop their demands for the release of the militants, though he knew that, considering the Indian government and its policies, the demands of the Al-Faran were perhaps the only hope for his twenty-eight-year-old son. Azari, he said, was a journalist and did not do anything wrong. Still, he urged the rebel group to forget the demands and move on. "One hundred times I appeal to the Al-Faran to release the hostages."

In April, too, the Al-Faran sent a message to the India news agency PTI, reiterating their claim that the tourists were no longer their hostages, but rather in the captivity of the Indian security forces. And Indian authorities once again denied the claim.

Then, on April 24, only a few weeks before Naser Mohammed marched out of the Himalayan foothills with his tale of terror and before the May 15 headlines told the world that the hostages might be dead, Jane Schelly traveled to Washington, D.C., at the behest of President Clinton to watch him sign a bill allocating $1 billion of additional funding to fight terrorism at home and abroad. At the ceremony on the South Lawn of the White House, Jane sat with at least a dozen victims of terrorism, including Joseph Cicippio, a former hostage held for five years in Beirut in the 1980s. Jane's brother-in-law Don Snyder, a state representative from Pennsylvania, accompanied her and stood nearby as Jane faced a media invasion. Jane, still believing in the power of governments, was more than pleased that the president was aware of her husband's plight and was equally impressed with the help she was getting to bring her husband home. On this special day, she broke her silence with the press.

"I think they [government officials] have done everything that they can do, and continue to do that," she told a swarm of reporters. "They've done a very, very good job of staying in touch with me. The most difficult thing about this situation is just waiting and finding the one thing that will bring him home. I don't set my heart for any particular day. I just feel comfortable enough that some day he's going to be returned to us, and I hope it's safe and soon.

"The thing that really hit me here today is that, in our world today, terrorism is touching so many people, whether by . . . kidnapping or whatever. It used to be that those things were unheard of. But more and more you know somebody else who's a victim. Sooner or later, that becomes your neighbor or your husband. Terrorism is affecting all of us."

The same day, Day 292 of Don's captivity, she wrote in her journal: "We were ushered into the Blue Room, where we were introduced to many people and served great home-squeezed orange juice. I couldn't help but think of how ironic it was that here I am sipping fresh-squeezed orange juice at the White House while Don is probably eating lentils and rice in some shepherd's hut. . . . President Clinton and Vice President Al Gore came into the room and made the rounds, shaking hands and having a word for each of us. I expressed my appreciation for all that has been done and Clinton commented that they would keep working on it until he was home safe."

⊲⊱⊰⊳

At the State Department on May 20, reporters beseeched Nick Burns to inform them about the situation in Kashmir. "This is a very sad story," Burns began, and then recounted some of the facts of the case before taking questions.

Burns: We are following this case very closely. We're working with the Indian government very closely on this case. We know that the hostages have been held in a mountainous area, which is very hard to reach, where these militants operate with great freedom. We are continuing to operate on the assumption that the hostages are alive. We are working closely with the Indian government, with other governments, and with some international organizations to secure their release. At the same time, we're trying to keep the family of Donald Hutchings apprised of everything that we know about this case. Every time we have any new information, we let them know.

Obviously, our hearts go out to his family. It's a terrible, very hard ordeal for the Hutchings family. We're doing everything we can to secure his release. We shouldn't forget that there are German and British hostages held with him. We're working with those governments, and we shouldn't forget Hans Christian Ostro of Norway, who was murdered by the Al-Faran group, who was part of this group that was taken hostage last July fourth.

Q: The latest reports were, at the end of last week, that there is a project that did get under way for remains possibly in that region. Can you speak to that? What would you advise his family here? Is that to be disregarded at this point? Is that search—

Burns (interrupting): I can't speak to that. I cannot speak to that. Again, I would just direct you to one thing that I said. We continue to operate under the assumption that Mr. Hutchings, the German and British hostages, are alive. We are continuing our very intense diplomatic efforts from our embassy in New Delhi under the capable leadership of our senior diplomat, Frank Wisner, who has been working on this case very hard since last July fourth. It's a difficult case because this Al-Faran group has not been, by and large, communicative. It certainly hasn't respected the wishes of all of us in the international community that it not seek its own political objectives through the abduction of innocent people.

Q: As a follow-up, what is the Indian government—I mean, they're the people on the scene, relatively speaking, there. What, specifically, are they telling the embassy in New

Delhi—that they have no information, that reports are just rumors? Is there anything of substance as to what allegedly happened this weekend? Can they give the guys any hard information at all?

Burns: The Indian government has been in constant contact with our embassy in New Delhi. Obviously, for a variety of reasons, which you will understand, having to do with the security of the hostages themselves, I can't tell you publicly everything that the Indian government has relayed to us. I can tell you, it's been a considerable amount of information. We believe the Indian government has done everything it can to try to identify where the hostages are being held and to do something about it, to convince this Al-Faran group to give them up.

Unfortunately, those efforts have been unsuccessful. We believe the Indian government will continue its efforts. It has all the support from the United States, from Britain, and from Germany, all the support it needs to continue to monitor the situation and try to see it through to a positive ending. But there really hasn't been any good news on this particular case since July 4.

As the one-year anniversary drew near, the Kashmir incident was stuck once again in a mire of misinformation, propaganda, and fear. In June, the search through the alpine forests ended without a scintilla of evidence to back up Naser's story or to reveal the fate of the hostages. India was still blaming Pakistan, and vice versa. In a statement that month, the Pakistani embassy in Bonn stressed, "It is regrettable that these young men became innocent victims of a conspiracy which was initiated to discredit the legitimate fight for self-determination and human rights by the people of occupied Jammu and Kashmir." There were individuals close to the case who admitted that they didn't know beyond a doubt who was holding the hostages. But there was no Western country that would dare to endanger its relationship with India.

Meanwhile, the Al-Faran, despite international publicity in recent weeks, had not broken the silence. And authorities were responding to questions in the same way that they had for nearly a year. They were doing all that they could do, they said in droning, all-too-familiar tones of assurance.

But there *was* a change. The families, after months of following suggestions from their governments and others to maintain low-profile images, launched an aggressive campaign, inspired and largely led by Jane Schelly. Soon the State Department, the diplomats of the G4, the FBI, Scotland Yard, the governments of Pakistan and India, Islamic leaders, and high-powered militants would witness the determination, tenacity, and courage of the schoolteacher from Spokane.

30

⊲≷⊳

KASHMIR

On June 26, 1996, Jane Schelly faced the man who claimed her husband was dead. Naser Mohammed, the captured militant, sat cross-legged, as if to meditate, on the floor adjacent to the American woman and her interpreter. When she introduced herself, he was quick to respond, "I am sorry. I am sorry." Looking well-groomed with his black hair and beard neatly trimmed, the young Islamic militant calmly and politely answered her numerous questions, though rarely looking her straight in the eye.

This was one of many meetings for Jane in India that summer, all part of her eight-week crusade to find Don Hutchings. She had kicked off the campaign in Spokane with a press conference and her first in-depth interviews with reporters. "I have felt I've had good cooperation from the government. But the year has not produced anything," she told reporters. "Something has to change. The time has come."

It had been nearly one year since Jane and Don had been sitting serenely along the banks of the Lidder River. And Don was still missing. That heinous fact in combination with the news of Mohammed's confession had infused Jane with determination and drive. She was simply unstoppable. Sometimes she even surprised herself. Her list of requested interviews was long. "I thought it would be a huge long shot," she said later, "that I could meet with these people."

Jane's theory was that the more people she could talk to, at all levels from villagers to Pakistan's Prime Minister Bhutto, the greater her chances of getting a lead to solving the mystery of the hostages' fates. It wasn't a brilliant theory, but to enact it took a good deal of courage. Her list included the militant Naser Mohammed, the top three jailed militants on Al-Faran's list of demands—one of whom had a reputation for being dangerous—heads of the Pakistani intelligence corps known as ISI, the chiefs of the notorious Pakistani-based group Harkat ul-Ansar, the most powerful Islamic leader in Pakistan, whose tapes were carried by followers throughout the Kashmir Valley, the All Parties Hurriyat Conference (the umbrella group for the thirty or so Kashmiri rebel bands), Indian government leaders, Kashmiri police officers, and, of course, Bhutto. These were her goals, she explained to embassy officials in Delhi. And, with the exception of the ISI, which she would reach on a subsequent trip, the combination of Jane's drive and the embassy's clout allowed her to reach her goals. On some of the interviews she went alone, and sometimes members of the other hostage families accompanied her. A week or so after her arrival in New Delhi that June, Julie Mangan joined her as well as Bernd Hasert, Dirk's devoted brother, who was accompanied by representatives of Germany's Christian Democrat Party, the Socialist Party, and the Green Party.

But facing Naser that hot June day in the sitting room at the government offices of an Indian prison, Jane was alone, except, of course, for her interpreter. In later years, she would look back on this interview and those with the three imprisoned militants as immense challenges. Though she had scaled Mount Rainier and other daunting summits, she was not accustomed to prisons or rebels or the world of hidden agendas that enveloped her every move in both India and Pakistan. Her passage to India was not an easy one, and certainly these interviews were the toughest part. Still, Jane not only endured this most difficult of landscapes but performed as if she had spent most of her life touring the world to build bridges between cultures. Teaching children had certainly eased the comfort of speaking in front of large groups and especially in articulating her thoughts as clearly as possible. It had also given her patience, which she needed in abundance in places such as Pakistan and India where the phones didn't always work and bureaucracies stalled the simplest of tasks.

Jane and her interpreter sat on a sofa facing Naser, who was dressed in the traditional Kashmiri kurta pajama consisting of a tunic worn over baggy pants. She wore the traditional dress for women, including the dupata, a scarflike stole draped across the shoulders with tails falling down the back. Perched on the edge of her seat, Jane leaned forward to speak to Naser. She spoke slowly just in case he understood some English words and because she wanted him to feel comfortable with her voice and her expressions. Jane explained that she had returned to India to find out what had happened to her husband. She asked him to paint a picture for her of Don's life as a hostage.

He told her that the hostages had had a "free life." It was only for the drama of the staged photographs, sent to the press and families, that they were ever tied up. They had had adequate food, he said, mostly meat and rice. And, to his knowledge, they had never suffered from frostbite nor from snow blindness, though they had had colds and coughs. Reports of illnesses were pressure tactics and nothing more.

Jane inquired about relations between the hostages and the Al-Faran. Relations had been good, Naser said. Why was Don chosen to speak on the radio in late August of 1995? she asked. Naser told her he believed that Tikoo (the government negotiator) and Turki (the Al-Faran leader) had decided this largely based on the fact that he was the only American. Jane surmised that an American was selected because the United States was perceived as the country with the greatest power in general and the most diplomatic power in particular.

She asked if he could shed light on the reasons for Ostro's murder. He repeated what he had said in his confession, that Turki had prayed for guidance and had a dream saying that if one hostage was killed the group would achieve its goal of getting the militants free from Indian jails. And he added that when Ostro was first abducted, he had attacked the rebels with a knife and tried to escape, the implication being that he had alienated them.

"Why couldn't the Al-Faran simply release the hostages and disappear?" Jane asked.

"The snow was there," he explained, "and they were scared."

Had Al-Faran wanted anything other than the release of the jailed militants? she asked. He said that a member of Al-Faran had asked the government to pay a "guarantee" of RS. five crore, or 50 million rupees, or about $12 million. But then the proposal was leaked to the newspapers in New Delhi, and so the deal fell apart.

She asked if there was any hope that her husband was alive. He had heard, Naser said, from "two responsible people" that he had been killed.

Later she would recall: "Neatly dressed and respectful, I thought he looked sincere. But so many people seemed sincere, and considering the difference in cultures, I have no idea whether they were. Still, my instincts told me that Naser was in fact sincere."

A week after her interview with Naser, Jane was back in New Delhi at the German embassy for a meeting that would be just as memorable as that bleak August day in 1995 when after a splendid luncheon Ambassador Elbe had announced the tragic news of the unidentified fair-skinned dead man near Anantnag. This time, Elbe had invited her to the embassy a few days ahead of Bernd Hasert and the three Bundestag politicians, who were coming to scrutinize the progress of the diplomats' efforts to find Dirk. Jane was not certain why she was called to the meeting. The embassy had been very helpful in the past, and they seemed to want to inform her about what would take place in the coming days. The German press and individuals close to the Hasert family had been critical of the German embassy in Delhi, and so perhaps, Jane thought, they wanted to know whether she was friend or foe. As with many of the diplomats, she surmised, the Germans wanted to know what she knew, especially if she knew something they didn't know.

The criticism in Germany focused on Dirk's status as an East German, rather than a West German. Some newspaper commentary had implied that had he been from the old West Germany, greater efforts might have been made from the beginning of the case. Others claimed it was simply a matter of economic status. "Unfortunately, Dirk Hasert happens to be a simple man without influence, power or fortune. If he were a diplomat or a manager of a corporation the matter would be dealt with differently," wrote a German man to the mayor of Dirk's hometown, Bad Langensalza. And now Bernd and the German politicians representing Dirk's district wanted to be certain that the diplomatic community was doing everything it possibly could to bring the young man home. The ambassador had plenty of proof that the diplomats involved were making an effort that some characterized as nearly a "mission," and he and others would explain this effort to the German emissaries at the briefing on July 3.

But now, a few days before that presentation, Elbe met with Jane, sharing with her his recent experiences and concerns. He told her how he had gone to Srinagar to talk with some of the militants, and he said he had been in Magam during the search. He believed, based on his exchanges during both of these trips, that "we certainly have to take Naser's story seriously," Jane recalled him saying.

Ambassador Elbe was the first person on that trip with whom Jane had discussed the subject of Naser's confession. Why hadn't they found the bodies if Naser was telling the truth? she wanted to know. No one, not even Elbe, could answer that question. Still, she knew that what Naser had confessed and had told her was indeed believable. And Elbe strengthened that belief. "Elbe did not say that he believed the confession was true," she said later, "but certainly I came away with the feeling, with the realization that there was a strong possibility that this report was plausible and had to be very seriously considered."

Before the back-to-back meetings with the militant and the ambassador, Jane had told herself that she would not believe anything until the facts were confirmed. "It's just another one of those things that puts you on the roller coaster of emotions," she told herself. But the combined effect of Naser's words and a high-level diplomat admitting that the militant could be telling the truth forced Jane for the very first time to face the possibility that Don could be dead.

"The hard part for me was leaving the embassy that day," Jane later recalled. "I had to go back and deal with this. And that is when I felt so very very alone. For several days, though I told no one, of course, I walked around with a big knot of tension. It took me back to the summer of 1995 to the reports that summer that Don had been killed, could be killed any day, would be killed unless . . . I didn't have anyone to talk to about it. Couldn't talk to a diplomat, and my family and friends didn't have the background. Julie was not there yet. It was the most traumatic event of the summer."

⊲≻≺⊳

The State Department briefing on the morning of July 3, 1996, included the following interchange between a reporter and Nicholas Burns:

> *Q:* Tomorrow, I believe, is the first anniversary of the capture of Westerners by militants in Kashmir. Do you have any reaction, any statement? Is there any progress on this?
>
> *Burns:* July 4, 1995, six people were taken hostage by the Al-Faran organization in Kashmir. Among them, Donald Hutchings, an American citizen from the state of Washington; Keith Mangan and Paul Wells, British citizens; Dirk Hasert, a German citizen; Hans Christian Ostro of Norway, who was later murdered by the Al-Faran organization. A sixth hostage, an American, escaped, fortunately, several days after he was abducted. This is a truly tragic situation. We continue to operate under the assumption that these hostages are alive, and we continue to work with the Indian government in an effort to find them and to have them released.
>
> Mrs. Jane Schelly, who is the wife of Donald Hutchings, is currently in Kashmir. She has been meeting with a variety of people in an attempt to gain some information about her husband's whereabouts and his well-being. I think as tomorrow is the one-year anniversary of their abduction, we should call again today for their release and for information as to what happened to them. We are doing everything possible to find them. We will be releasing, about twelve hours from now, a joint statement with other governments about this. But since you've asked, I think it's appropriate for us to call again for their release and to hope very much that this despicable act of terrorism will end. There can be no gain from taking six people

hostage. Terry Waite spoke out today from Britain. Terry Waite, who spent so many years in prison, spoke out and called upon this group to release these hostages.

⊲≋⊳

Hundreds of people gathered at Riverfront Park in Spokane on July 4, 1995, for a candlelight vigil in honor of their stellar citizen and friend Don Hutchings. A giant banner "Welcome Home Soon" stretched across the top front of a bandshell tent. One by one, friends of Don and Jane and the town's VIPs stepped onto the stage under the tent and spoke into the microphone, expressing their appreciation for Don's dedication to patients and friends and his sorely missed sense of humor. The daughter of the chaplain who married Don and Jane came forward to ring the Tibetan bells Don had once given the family. Her father had noticed in recent months that she was periodically picking up the bells and carrying them around the house. When he asked her why she was ringing those bells, she told her father, "I'm ringing them for Don." That night, she rang the bells as the candles were lit. And across the grassy slope, from the bandstand to the river, there were numerous posters on pickets stuck in the ground.

WE MISS YOU, DON. COME HOME SOON.

DON, YOUR VACATION TIME HAS
BEEN USED UP. COME HOME.

HOMER TO GRADUATE FROM DOG OBEDIENCE SCHOOL.
HOPE YOU CAN MAKE THE COMMENCEMENT.

CLIMB ON, CLIMB OUT, CLIMB HOME.

IF YOU CAN CLIMB MT. MCKINLEY,
YOU CAN GET OUT OF INDIA.

In India, the insanity continued. On July 6, another captured militant claimed that Don, Keith, Dirk, and Paul were "alive and safe" and that he indeed had spent a day with them in June. This man told his interrogators that he had done construction work at one of the Al-Faran jungle hideouts south of Kashmir in the Wadwun Valley, a vast forested region known to be almost entirely free of Indian troops. Was he telling the truth, or was the word out among militants that if they were captured they should tell a story about the four hostages to improve their treatment at the hands of the Indian security forces?

Later that July, halfway around the world, a new kidnap drama involving an American tourist was beginning to unfold, this time in the voluptuous jungles of northern Ecuador.

31

AUGUST–DECEMBER 1996
ECUADOR AND WORLDWIDE

Nothing in John Heidema's past nor in his long hours of research that summer could have prepared him for Ecuador. He read books and brochures about the famed Galápagos Islands, and, as an avid bird-watcher, he consulted travel agents and sites on the Internet about the best tours to Ecuador's Cuyabeno Wildlife Preserve, a rain forest in the northeast known for its hundreds of avian species. But neither book nor agent nor Web site informed him about what he really needed to know, what he must know to ensure that he and his eighteen-year-old daughter would enjoy—and survive—their trip. No one told him that kidnappings were on the rise in Ecuador, especially in the north near the Colombian border. Ecuador, the fifty-four-year-old computer scientist was told, was one of the safest places in all of Latin America.

Throughout Latin America that year, kidnappings were on the rise, and crime along the border regions of some countries, including Ecuador, Venezuela, and Panama, was increasing. The northeastern corner of Ecuador, home to 540 species of birds, was now also the roosting place for itinerant Colombian guerrillas as well as roving gangs of local bandits and even bandits posing as politically motivated rebels. But Heidema didn't know. He also didn't know that an American working as the treasurer of the Protestant Nazarene Church in northern Ecuador had been abducted in early December of 1995 and rescued several weeks later, or that two American oil workers were kidnapped the year before and released for cash ransoms. He did know about the dangers of malaria and yellow fever in Ecuador and about the kidnapping problem in Colombia. And had he known that the threat of abductions had spread to Ecuador, had he sensed the slightest hint of trouble, he would have taken his daughter to a different country for the trip that was her high school graduation present. But that didn't happen.

And so it was that on July 29, as the bird-watcher from Little Silver, New Jersey, was peering through binoculars at a golden-tailed sapphire hummingbird, three armed men suddenly appeared at his side. Heidema and his daughter were part of a group of ten tourists that day, plus a tour guide and a machete man whose job was to clear a path through the remote jungle outback. After a week in the Galápagos, the Heidemas had decided to take a three-day tour of the Cuyabeno rain forests and this was their first morning hike. Sarah was at the front of the group with the tour guide and a fifteen-year-old girl from California, while Heidema was about 100 yards away at the very back. He was wearing a T-shirt with the message: "Have an out of car experience: Walk and bike, feel the wind, meet friends, see wildlife, and be part of nature."

It was about 11:30 A.M. when the three armed strangers, bare-chested with dark brown trousers, surprised the tourists. The first to see them was Heidema, who believed they must be hunters or poachers. Two of the men carried 22-caliber rifles with wooden stocks; the other, a 38-caliber pistol. One stayed at the back, while the other two walked up the line of hikers, as if to announce their arrival. Sarah rushed to her father's side while the men began to frisk the hikers, one by one, looking for weapons and anything else of value. They took penknives and cash as well as earrings, necklaces, and rings, including wedding bands. They ransacked backpacks and camera bags, taking more cash, one video camera, and several flashlights. Then, nearly an hour later, much to the shock of the tourists, who believed the strangers were bandits only—hell-bent on fleeing after the pillage—the men set about the serious business of selecting hostages.

The guide, Pablo Reyes, soon came to Heidema to explain that the men wanted to take his blue-eyed daughter Sarah, a slim, agile girl who appeared capable of enduring the rigorous daily marches that the rebels would be undertaking. The other prospective hostage, the young girl from California, was bilingual—a fact that was clearly important to the rebels, who knew they would need to communicate with their other English-speaking hostage. Most important, however, was their perception of an American girl as a valuable hostage. "They were thinking $5 million, while a guy in his fifties, like me, had the image of bringing a ransom somewhere in the range of fifty-five cents," Heidema later said.

But the kidnappers underestimated the intelligence and quickness of the American girl from New Jersey. Suddenly, after it was clear that she had been targeted, Sarah began to choke as if she couldn't breathe, as if she were suffering an acute attack of asthma. She appeared ill enough for the guide to tell the kidnappers that she would not be able to walk much farther than the next tree, much less fifteen miles a day. At the same time, Reyes, who was bilingual, explained that he would take the place of the California girl. There was still the problem of a second hostage. The kidnappers told Reyes they wanted an American, and Heidema told Reyes that he would go. At first, Reyes declined the offer. He looked to the other tourists—some of whom were younger than Heidema—for volunteers. There was only silence.

Sarah knew and feared that her father would insist on going. She knew that socially responsible side of his. He was the one guy in the neighborhood back home who took the time to pick up the cans and other litter from the creek across the street from their home. He was recycling cans and paper long before it was mandatory to do so, carefully bundling the papers and cleaning the cans, then taking them in the trunk of the car to a recycling center miles away. She had watched him many times as he graciously gave up his place in line at a store or a movie theater to an elderly man or woman. He was just that way. And now, fearing the inevitable good deed, she pleaded with him to stay. There were others in better condition than he was, and younger;

they should go, she reasoned. But Heidema was certain the kidnappers would take one of the women. A good candidate was a forty-four-year-old woman from Texas who was in excellent condition. Worried about the consequences of a woman traveling with the rebel band, he insisted on going. Reyes communicated the request to the rebels. Heidema knew by the looks on their faces that he and Reyes were now the official hostages. What crossed his mind as he turned to his daughter to assure her that he would be fine was that he could endure whatever the kidnappers had in mind. But he was certain he would not emerge unscathed. There would be malaria, he thought, or perhaps a broken leg.

Heidema stood five feet ten inches and weighed 175 pounds. He was in decent shape, though he did not exercise regularly. When he did, he typically bicycled. A few summers before, he had ridden 250 miles along the eastern seaboard, from New Jersey to Washington, D.C., in four days. Years before, he had circled Lake Michigan on a 1,300-mile ride. But the most he had ever hiked was eighteen miles along the Appalachian Trail with Sarah in 1994. Now in the captivity of men who claimed they were Colombian guerrillas—but whom Heidema later believed to be common criminals—he would be walking from two to eighteen miles a day across rugged, sometimes swampy terrain. "It was what I call water-up-to-your-thighs jungle," Heidema later recalled.

At first, he tried to think positively; perhaps he could take advantage of the situation, and at the very least, as he walked through terrain where tourists certainly had rarely ventured, he could look for new species of toucans or magpies or swallows. But on the fourth day, a few miles into an eighteen-mile march, he lost his glasses. He was trying to gain his balance on a log that served as the makeshift bridge across a muddy river when he began to fall. As if in slow motion, he watched as the glasses fell into four feet of murky water. Retrieval was impossible. From then on, his vision was blurred beyond ten feet, which ruined his plan to distract himself through bird-watching and added to the anxiety of his captivity.

On the sixth day, Heidema's fellow hostage, Reyes, talked his way to freedom by promising to serve as a liaison between the kidnappers and the authorities. While Heidema was sad to see Reyes leave, he was pleased that his family would know now that he was alive. He gave Reyes a two-paragraph note for his wife saying that he was surviving and that he loved her. From then on, for nearly a month, no one knew whether Heidema was alive or dead.

From the start, the kidnappers wanted money, starting at $30 million, for the release of their American prey. Even before they left the tour group, Reyes had managed to persuade the captors to come down from $30 million to $5 million, and later, to $3 million. After Reyes's departure, Heidema, using a combination of elementary Spanish and hand gestures to communicate, continued the job, bargaining the bandits down to $1.5 million. Just because he was an American, he told his captors, did not mean he was rich.

A few days after Reyes got out, Heidema wrote the demand note for the rebels, some of whom were illiterate. He tried to persuade them that $1.5 million was still much too high, and that if they were lucky they would get $1 million. "They waved a pistol in my face and said, 'Write the note and make it say $1.5 million.' And of course I did. I wrote that $1.5 million must be paid or I would be killed," Heidema said. But that note would never emerge from the jungle, for reasons Heidema would never understand. More than a week later, he wrote the note again, though authorities would not see it until the end of August.

For a week after Reyes had left, Heidema and his captors continued moving through the jungle—until August 12. It was then, exactly two weeks after his abduction, that Heidema tried to escape. Since the first moments of his captivity, Heidema had been as cooperative a hostage as he could be. He helped set up the campsite at the end of each day, hanging the hammocks from tree to tree. He helped with the meals, boiling the water or cleaning the fish. Once he plucked the feathers off a dead partridge. He knew his behavior would be key to his survival and the more trust he could inspire, the less vigilant his captors would be. While his first thought was always survival, his second was escape. Besides men with guns—there were more of them now—one big inhibiting factor was the terrain. The brush was so thick that every leaf-crunching footstep could be heard unless, of course, it rained.

And so the timing of the escape had to be perfect. He must take flight during a tropical downpour or in the minutes following one, and it must be when his captors were not watching him.

This rare moment occurred late in the day of the twelfth as the group was hiking to a new hideout for the night. Heidema knew that about half a mile back he had passed a trail that headed south. When the torrents of rain began to fall and his guards were distracted by the task of pushing ahead, Heidema, his feet covered with blisters, slipped into the jungle thicket, quickly and quietly crawling on all fours. He ran and ran, and within an hour or so he came upon two men from a nearby village, who said they would help him by bringing a car to him by dusk. But as the trio was making the arrangements, two of his captors suddenly appeared to reclaim their prey. They threw him into a car, forced him onto the floorboards, blindfolded him, and told him they were taking him to Colombia. That never happened. Instead, Heidema soon found himself sitting in a shoebox-like shack perched on stilts behind the residence of the parents of one of the kidnappers—a fourteen-year-old boy clearly apprenticing with the others, who ranged in age from early twenties to midthirties. Here, in a town alternately called Lago Agrio and Nueva Loja, he would be confined for the remainder of his captivity, with a Berlitz Spanish phrase book and a copy of the novel *The Fan* by Peter Abrahams. "I don't know where they got the books, maybe out of a backpack of a previous captive," Heidema said later. "*The Fan* had a Borders bookstore price tag on the back."

And while Heidema was reading and rereading *The Fan* and learning Spanish, his wife, Karen Karl, was doing everything possible to gain his release. It was a crusade with a wobbly start. When Heidema was abducted, there was no U.S. ambassador in Quito, the capital of Ecuador. The post had been recently filled, and the newly appointed ambassador had not yet arrived, nor had the second in command, the deputy chief of mission (DCM). Heidema was kidnapped on a Monday. It was not until the following Friday that the DCM and the new ambassador arrived in Quito. For the first week of Heidema's captivity, his wife had stayed in the States and worked the phones, trying to get some action from her government, while her brother had flown to

Quito to help Sarah and to represent the family. Karl had no idea what to expect or how such cases typically were handled. The Embassy had assured her that the staff was doing everything in its power to gain her husband's release. Still, Karl had worried that first week that things weren't happening quickly enough.

A few days after the abduction, Karl phoned her congressman, Representative Richard A. Zimmer, who was on the road campaigning. The next day, she was able to reach him, and after hearing her concerns, Zimmer called FBI director Louis Freeh, who contacted the State Department. "It was clear that Freeh shook the trees for us," Heidema said later. Within the next twelve hours, the FBI had deployed several negotiators out of Miami to Quito. Later, Karl would reflect that the vacancies at the embassy were in some respects a blessing in disguise. Once she became acquainted with the ambassador and the DCM, she was glad to have such skillful and compassionate officials aboard. But if the ambassador had been at his post at the time of the abduction, there would have been the question of whether he would have invited the FBI's negotiators to assist in the case. Red tape and interagency squabbles might have bogged down the case. She would learn much later that there indeed had been power struggles but that both agencies had done everything within their power to resolve the case. And by the time the ambassador had arrived on the scene, the FBI was firmly ensconced in the case. When Karl arrived in Quito, a week after Heidema's abduction, she launched a networking campaign among the locals that brought her praise from Quito to Miami to Washington. She effectively became the case coordinator, monitoring who was doing what and when. If there was a ransom to be paid, for example, she would know the best and most trustworthy people to deliver it.

"I was horrified to realize that there was no central place to go and no one agency to oversee all the many details that go into coordinating this type of thing. There's no policy or set procedure because basically the government doesn't want to be doing this. So the FBI basically does the best it can do, but someone has to be coordinating all the details," Karl said later, adding that she was willing from the start to pay a ransom and whatever it took to get her husband out alive. "I mean, what do you do when something like this happens, when the government really doesn't have a clear policy in place? These guys have to reinvent their ways every time. My job was overview. Just keep things going, make sure something is happening toward the goal at all times. I did a lot of networking in the town. Got to know a lot of people. At one point, I went to church one Sunday, and there in the congregation was just about every person I had been talking with over the past week. I was even introduced to the congregation. Everyone I had been sort of secretly talking with all week was there. It was like an Agatha Christie novel. Even the deacon, well, he was from the private firm, Control Risks. A memorable experience.

"When I first called the State Department, I was told that they don't deal with this, well, with negotiating this type of thing. 'Well, guess what, your policy has changed,' I told them. 'Do you want me to take this to the papers and tell them that my government is stonewalling me? Geraldo [Rivera] lives in my neighborhood,' I told them, which is true. I was incensed. Then, I just went into high gear, and I did as much as a Little Silver housewife could do."

It was Karl's networking that helped the FBI to zero in on the town of Lago Agrio, where Heidema was held. Her contacts cut through the local red tape involved in leasing an apartment and in placing a tap-and-trace system on a telephone. With this in place, the negotiators established phone contact with the kidnappers, keeping them on the line long enough to locate a phone bank in Lago Agrio. With the phones, the FBI was able to ask proof-of-life questions for the first time since Reyes had emerged from the jungle nearly a month before with the note proving Heidema was still alive. What were the names of the Heidema family cats? How old were they that summer? What was the name of their dog? One of Heidema's guards called with the answers: Seal and Shadow, four and eight years old, and Raven.

On September 3, around 3 P.M., Heidema looked out the tiny window of his room and noticed that down the road a bit there was a jeep-like vehicle cruising very slowly toward the property in front of his shack. It was an image that had little meaning until shortly before dawn the next day when he was suddenly awakened by a cacophony of shouts and gunfire. For moments, he didn't know whether the heavily armed men outfitted in black who had just killed four of his captors were going to kill him. But when one of them used his body to shield Heidema from a bullet, he knew he was being rescued. The men in black belonged to the highly secretive and reputedly very effective Ecuadoran SWAT team known as UNASE. The four men who were killed—two from Colombia and two from Ecuador—were part of a group of about eleven kidnappers.

By the time the frail, enervated Heidema had returned home to Little Silver, New Jersey, he had learned just how lucky he was. While any captivity is, indeed, long, his thirty-eight-day stint was far shorter than the average in most Latin American cases, which is about ten months. Part of the reason the ordeal was curtailed was that he was rescued. But rescues are not always successful; in many cases, one or more hostages are killed.

Still, Heidema was frustrated that the abduction had occurred at all, and a few days after his return, he began to complain about what he believed to be a State Department shortcoming: insufficient warnings about Ecuador.

It wasn't just his experience as a hostage that provoked his concerns. During his captivity, Heidema had overheard conversations among his captors about plans for more kidnappings. Reading through travel brochures and making maps, they were conducting what Heidema later called "market research" for future abductions. Tourists were the "in" prey now in Ecuador, Heidema believed. And so he took his worries to Zimmer, who then sent a letter to Secretary of State Warren Christopher urging the government to enhance its warning about travel in Ecuador. "I am concerned that this kidnapping will be treated as an isolated incident," wrote Zimmer. "Mr. Heidema's family advises me that other abductions of foreign travelers have recently taken place in Ecuador and that American tourists are increasingly at risk."

The State Department responded by saying it would review its current travel advisory to decide whether to make a change. A spokesperson for the department said that the government had warned of kidnappings in Ecuador, referring to its most recent Consular Information Sheet on Ecuador, issued in March 1996, which said, "Kidnappings of wealthy Ecuadorans and foreign residents for ransom are on the rise." But because of the Heidema case, the agency would consider the possibility of revising the language. A full-fledged advisory, however, would be issued only if the entire country was dangerous, and in this case, it had been determined that only a portion of Ecuador, near the Colombian border, was worrisome.

At a press conference, Zimmer said, "I applaud the State Department and the FBI for helping free John from a horrible ordeal, but we must do more to inform American travelers of potential dangers."

In October, the State Department changed its Ecuador advisory, adding warnings for certain regions along the Colombian border and noting the Heidema incident.

In the months following Heidema's rescue, the New Jersey couple were very outspoken about their experience. And they began to network with other families that were in the midst of hostage ordeals or had already survived one. "We are concerned that travel agencies continue to send people to areas that are dangerous," Karl told reporters. "Nor are State Department travel bulletins always adequate."

⋖⋗⋖⋗

During the August of Heidema's captivity, there were other kidnappings in Ecuador, including the abduction on August 1 of an executive of the Swiss firm Nestlé. And there were numerous kidnappings worldwide. A Hong Kong businessman was taken in Shenzhen, China, and released after the payment of a $1 million ransom. A wealthy rice-mill owner in Manila was snatched while jogging and released two days later after his family paid $15,380—down from a $192,000 ransom request. In Guatemala, the kidnap wave hit an all-time low on the morality scale. After church one day, the eighty-four-year-old wife of a cement factory magnate was abducted. In what was a well-organized abduction, the kidnappers posed as police blocking the highway. They even brought a wheelchair for the elderly woman, who was unable to walk because of a recent operation.

In Irian Jaya, in the same area where the Brits had been abducted in January, at least forty armed men calling themselves the Security Disturbance Group—later linked to the OPM—ambushed a camp of timber workers and abducted fifteen men and one woman. Two escaped and two were released to deliver a letter with a ransom demand to authorities. In Costa Rica, former contra rebels were blamed for another kidnapping near the Nicaraguan border. This time, the victims were two Dutch citizens, both fifty years old and both employees of a Dutch company allegedly exploiting the forests of northern Costa Rica; the ransom request was $1.5 million.

But the most high-profile kidnapping that month was in Mexico, on August 10, only a few miles from the U.S. border. Mamoru Konno, the fifty-six-year-old president of Sanyo Video Component Corporation, USA, was playing baseball at a company barbeque in Tijuana, the locale of the Sanyo division's plant. For eight years Konno had commuted from his home in Chula Vista, California, south of San Diego, to the plant eleven or so miles away, fearlessly crossing the border twice a day. But this day would be different. At about 7 P.M., four men brandishing automatic weapons snatched Konno and two of the company cheerleaders. The young women were released the next morning, but Konno was held, with the warning that the company had until August 17 to pay the $2 million ransom for his release.

Kidnappings were hardly unusual in Mexico that year, though most incidents were unreported because of victims' suspicions of police involvement or their lack of confidence in police capabilities. Mexico City's *El Economist* newspaper had recently reported 2,000 kidnaps for 1995, a 100 percent increase over the previous year. And so far, 1996 had been a record year. The reasons were varied: Mexico's economic problems were not improving, nor was the law enforcement infrastructure stabilizing anytime soon. Expelling police officers for orchestrating kidnappings and other corrupt practices didn't mitigate the problem because the ex-cops often formed or joined criminal kidnap gangs. In June of that year, another problem had surfaced in the form of a new rebel group that was either a "subsidiary" of a Colombian group or simply modeled after one, and which was building its financial strength in the kidnap racket. The band, known as the Popular Revolutionary Army or EPR, was fairly sophisticated in its approaches, and there was much speculation that it would continue its marauding ways for a long time to come. This was unpleasant news for a nation that was already a breeding ground for kidnappings. Victims ranged from wealthy Mexicans, to middle-class Mexicans, to Americans who lived in Mexico or spent long periods of time there, and to Japanese businessmen who, since the signing of NAFTA—the North American Free Trade Agreement—had invested more than $800 million in Mexico.

Konno was not the first Japanese national to be abducted in Mexico. And he was hardly the first Japanese businessman to be kidnapped abroad. The Japanese had a reputation for paying, and paying fast. Among other Latin American cases, one in Panama in 1992 had commanded a $750,000 ransom; Colombian guerrillas were the chief suspects. The man's body turned up twelve days after the snatch.

Konno was, however, the first Japanese hostage to gain international attention. One editorial commented that as kidnappings got closer to the U.S. border, they would get more press coverage. And indeed, the glare of the media spotlight was suddenly revealing what everyone in Mexico, in the states that hugged the Mexican border, and in cities such as Los Angeles, San Diego, and Tucson had known for more than two years: Mexico's deep economic crisis was spawning kidnappers at an unprecedented rate, though until now foreigners had rarely been targeted.

Konno's kidnappers warned officials at his company that if they reported the crime to the police or the media, they would kill their captive. Two days later, the story made headlines all over the world. A vice president of Sanyo North America told several papers, "We're willing to cooperate and do whatever we can to get our president back." And they did. They paid the $2 million—not a penny less—and delivered it on August 17, as requested, in new, unmarked hundred-dollar bills, without a guarantee of Konno's release. One official involved in the case said he wasn't sure at all whether this would gain Konno's release. Luckily it did. And when he was back and the ordeal was over, the company announced the happy ending and the amount of the ransom payment.

Kidnap experts all over the world shuddered as they read the headline. It was a green light for more abductions. And there were at least 8,000 foreigners crossing the U.S.-Mexican border to operate factories called maquillas in northern Mexico, not to mention the thou-sands of foreigners flying in every day, especially to Mexico City, to do business.

By the end of August, violence in several Mexican states had bro-ken out, mainly in the form of assaults against police stations, military posts, and public buildings. More than a dozen people were killed and many more injured. Among the dead were members of the rebel group that had surfaced in June. Because its operating expenses were likely funded through kidnappings, some experts surmised that the assaults late that month had been funded by the Konno ransom.

But the State Department's advisory for Mexico didn't reflect the reality of dangers there. The latest advisory, dated May 29, 1996, informed the traveler that crime was increasing, especially in urban areas. The robberies occurring in Volkswagen-style roving taxis were noted, as were the heavy seasonal rains in Baja and the rebel presence in the state of Chiapas. But the word *kidnapping* did not appear. And by the end of the month, the advisory had still not been updated to include mention of the recent violence in three Mexican states.

At the State Department, the last briefing of the month went like this:

> *Q:* Do you have any reactions to the violent events in three different Mexican states in the last forty-eight hours, and have you issued a travel advisory or [are you] planning to do something like that?
>
> *Briefer Glyn Davies:* We have not issued any kind of travel advisory at this state. . . . We condemn these attacks. There can be no justification for violence in pursuit of political ends in Mexico. However, it's important to underscore that the U.S. does not consider these actions threatening to Mexican political or economic stability.

At the same time, the private security firms that compiled risk assessments for their clients were busy re-evaluating Mexico from the moment the Konno headlines appeared. On August 22, Pinkerton's lead story for the day in its risk assessment newsletter was its new analysis of the risk to investors and travelers in Mexico: "Based on a review of all available information, including valuable insight from

Pinkerton colleagues in Mexico, the risk level is raised from 'low' to 'moderate.' A 'moderate risk' level exists in countries where political or economic turmoil is evident and/or terrorist/guerrilla groups are regularly active, but have not become strong enough to threaten government stability. Also, nations involved in potentially violent regional disputes or with high rates of crime. Upgraded security precautions are warranted for travel or investment. Pinkerton believes current conditions in Mexico meet all these criteria except for 'regional disputes' and security precautions must be upgraded accordingly."

Two weeks later, on September 3, the State Department issued a new Consular Information Sheet regarding Mexico. It included the attacks by the new Popular Revolutionary Army in August. And it said, "The Embassy suggests that American citizens traveling in Mexico exercise caution." The word *kidnapping* did not appear in the information sheet, nor was there any mention of the successful abduction of the Japanese businessman and the subsequent $2 million ransom payment.

⋘⋙

In September that year, in the weeks following Heidema's release from the Ecuadoran jungle, the two Dutch citizens abducted in Costa Rica were released, after the payment of a ransom reported to be $600,000. In Irian Jaya, bodies of two of the twelve remaining hostages abducted from the logging camp in August were found; another of the hostages had escaped in early September; and Indonesian troops had rescued nine others held by the group, which was later identified as part of the OPM.

In Colombia, two engineers—a Brit and a Dane—walked out of the Andes Mountains after seven months in captivity. The governor of northwestern Antioquia province, where they were snatched, angrily accused the German government of paying $2 million for the release of the two men plus a third man, a German, released earlier, and railed against the practice of paying ransoms as nothing more than the funding of terrorism. "With the payment of the ransom, the German government and foreign firms become sponsors of the guerrillas. They should tell the truth about their pacts with the subversives." The German embassy fired off a response: "In accordance with its principles and general practice, the German government does not pay ransoms. As far as the embassy is aware, neither at the moment when the German was freed nor in the release of the other men [the Brit and Dane] a few days ago was any ransom paid." And Colombia's antikidnap czar, Alberto Villamizar, tried to mediate. He said publicly that he condemned companies for caving in to ransom demands, implying that the engineers' company had paid, but that it was not illegal to do so. This controversy would erupt again before the end of the year when two Germans would be exposed, and arrested, for their role in facilitating the release of a German hostage.

⋘⋙

On October 1, in Germany, six months after the Reemtsma kidnapping in which the family paid the largest ransom ever in German history, Jakub Fiszmann, a wealthy Frankfurt businessman, was kidnapped in front of his office around 10:30 P.M. Ten days later, his brother dropped a ransom of 4 million deutsche marks ($2.62 million) at a designated spot in a field along a motorway north of Frankfurt. But Fiszmann, whose wealth was estimated at $250 million, was not released. Even after the kidnappers were apprehended and the ransom was recovered, there was no sign of the forty-year-old Fiszmann. After hundreds of sniffer dogs searched the dense woodland outside Frankfurt and fighter planes equipped with infrared cameras scanned the area, the body, partly covered by the leaves of a fallen tree, was finally found on October 19. Fiszmann, who needed medication for his food allergies, was already dead when the ransom was paid.

That same day, a Muslim guerrilla chief who was now a regional governor in the Philippines railed against former Muslim guerrillas who were now kidnapping for a living. Nur Misuari, the leader of the Moro National Liberation Front (MNLF), which began fighting for a separate Muslim state in the southern Philippines in 1974, had signed a peace agreement with Manila on September 2. Former Muslim rebels had already begun to kidnap for a living as the settlement drew near, and now the fear was that their activities, especially after they formed a new breakaway group called the Moro Islamic Liberation Front (MILF), would escalate. Calling them "a social menace that draws away investors," Misuari said he wanted to "neutralize them." President Fidel Ramos assured Misuari that the national police and the armed forces would help him fight the war against kidnappers. A few days later, Muslim rebels threatened to mount their own campaign: to kidnap teachers and public officials.

Around the same time, to protest kidnappings and the inability of the police and the military to stop the crime, residents in the central Mindanao region of the Philippines staged a two-day strike. Gas stations and banks closed, and public transportation shut down. "We want everyone to know, including the international community, that kidnappings can no longer be controlled by the government," a Catholic priest told local newspapers.

In Brazil, São Paulo was struck with an unexpected wave of "minikidnappings," or "fast-food kidnaps," as they were called in other countries. In this hold-up style abduction, the kidnapper holds the victim in a car and drives along crowded urban streets until the family pays a ransom anywhere from $500 to $5,000. Meanwhile, the Guajajara Indians abducted eighty people from cars and buses on a roadway in northeastern Brazil and demanded that the Brazilian government pave and repair roads in the areas where they live. The government agreed, and a week later all the hostages were released unharmed. In Brazil now, there were an estimated 500,000 private security guards compared with 200,000 or so civil and military police.

In Bangkok, the police arrested a kidnap gang that preyed on tourists, mostly Chinese; in sixteen reported cases, they had yielded an average ransom of $10,000. In Yemen, a French diplomat, who had been kidnapped in mid-October, was released a week later, but as he was returning to the capital and his home, he was abducted again by different members of the same Toaiman tribe.

Toward the end of the month, the eighty-four-year-old wheelchair-bound woman was released in Guatemala after two months in captivity. An unconfirmed $6 million ransom was reportedly paid. And, as leftist rebels and government negotiators neared agreement on a treaty to end Guatemala's thirty-six-year-old civil war, citizens were more and more worried about kidnappers, who in the last half of 1996 had frequently targeted women, children, and the elderly.

And in Colombia, the latest quick-hit solution was a revenge campaign against insurgents by paramilitary groups with links to the military. One tactic used in the campaign had been tried earlier that year in Brazil: to kidnap the relatives of kidnappers. In October, gunmen posing as judicial investigators abducted the mother and sister of a high-ranking guerrilla leader. They called themselves the "Peasant Self-Defense" group and said their goal was to gain the release of all hostages held by rebels of the Armed Revolutionary Forces, or FARC.

⊲≫≼⊳

In November, for the first time since Guatemala had instituted the death penalty for kidnapping, three people were sentenced to death for a $17,000 ransom kidnapping the year before. In China that month, three men were executed for kidnapping a Hong Kong businessman and demanding a $646,830 ransom. In the Philippines, in response to the strike the previous month, President Ramos ordered 300 marines to help local police crack down on the quickly escalating kidnap industry. He also set up the Task Force Tabang, a special antikidnapping group consisting of the military, police, local government units, civilians, and former members of the Moro National Liberation Front. Utilizing the skills and intelligence of the former rebels, and more important, giving them something to do, this task force was considered a brilliant move by analysts of the problem worldwide.

In Mexico, police in the northern state of Sonora captured five members of a kidnap ring that was targeting wealthy businessmen in the northernmost states, including Baja California; one of them had participated in the kidnapping of Konno. And in the United States, a well-known San Francisco philanthropist, Marshall Wais, who was eighty years old, was abducted from his bed at gunpoint early one morning. Federal agents negotiated with the kidnappers to pick up a $500,000 ransom near Golden Gate Park, which they did; after giving Wais $20 and sending him on his way, they were captured.

In Colombia, abductions of children were on the rise, a trend highlighted that month when a thirteen-year-old national BMX cycling champion was snatched off a school bus by a guerrilla band in the northwestern city of Medellín. Police rescued him the next day.

But the most startling news out of Colombia was the November 17 arrest of a German man and woman as they were boarding a plane to Venezuela with Brigitte Schoene, a German who had been abducted months before and was held for a $6 million ransom. This was the latest installment in the ongoing conflict between the Colombian government and German diplomats and business executives over their alleged clandestine payments to kidnappers, which the Colombians claimed were financing the rebel movements. The German embassy in Bogotá released a letter on November 21 saying that the German couple indeed had been on a mission from the German government to negotiate Schoene's release. Colombian officials accused the couple of being supporters of the National Liberation Army.

There was no denying the good fortune of Schoene, the wife of a former BASF chemicals executive, to be freed from the hands of her guerrilla captors. The problem was that her rescuers, a former German secret agent and his wife, were allegedly ransom brokers who had struck their own private deal with the rebels: they would take over the kidnap negotiations, but instead of striving for a lower ransom, they allegedly would guarantee a high ransom for the rebels if they could get a cut. The Germans apparently undercut Control Risks Group, whose negotiators were in the midst of dealing with the rebels when suddenly the captive disappeared, "abducted" by the so-called brokers.

When German officials admitted on November 21 that the couple had been sent by the German government on secret missions to smuggle German hostages out of Colombia, the family and friends of Dirk Hasert were stung by the news. The German student was still missing, along with Don Hutchings and the Brits, in Kashmir. The juxtaposition of the two cases gave some credence to the criticisms that if Dirk had been more than an ordinary citizen, a student from a small formerly East German town, then perhaps more would have been done to rescue him.

In Cambodia, a drama was unraveling in November that gripped every negotiator who had ever worked a case, especially at Scotland Yard. Around the twentieth of the month, newspapers bannered the triumphant headlines announcing the freedom of Christopher Howes, the thirty-seven-year-old British mine expert who had been in captivity since late March. Howes, a former British soldier with service in Northern Ireland and the Falklands, had been one of thirty or so men clearing land mines in a village in northwest Cambodia near the twelfth-century Angkor Wat temple—Cambodia's main tourist attraction—on March 26 when a band of thirty Khmer Rouge guerrillas snatched them all. Most were released just as quickly because of an act of heroism on the part of Howes. When the guerrillas asked Howes to act as a ransom courier for the other men, he refused. The kidnappers then released the rest of the men and kept Howes and his assistant, Huon Hourth. For most of their captivity, they had been held in Cambodia about six miles from the Thai border. In August, an unnamed officer of the Khmer Rouge told the government that Howes had been killed and his partner had died of malaria. Later, a Khmer Rouge radio broadcast denied that, and with the denial came their admission, if it was to be believed, that the men were indeed alive.

By November, it appeared that Howes and his assistant were going to be rescued by a Khmer Rouge rebel who planned to trade them for the right to defect to the government without a penalty. Behind the scenes, the Mines Advisory Group, a British charity, reportedly had paid a ransom of 75,000 pounds ($120,000), without the knowledge of the British government, to a Cambodian who said he would deliver the cash to the defecting rebel. But just as the news of Howes's imminent liberation was released, he and his assistant disappeared into the jungle without a word to anyone. By the end of November, the word was that they were fleeing some 300 hard-line guerrillas with orders to kill.

In Kashmir, the month ended with an observance of the one-year anniversary of the last communication with the Al-Faran. Mohammad Amin Shah, head of a special investigating team, told reporters, "We are desperately looking for clues that can help us in reaching conclusions."

⋘⋙

December began with a peoples' march against kidnapping in Colombia. At least 15,000 citizens waved poster-size pictures of their missing loved ones as they paraded through downtown Bogotá. The protest followed the discovery of the corpse of a seven-year-old boy who had been abducted on his way to school on November 23. The family could not afford the ransom request of $10,000. At the same time, the rebel group FARC was holding sixty Colombian soldiers hostage in the mountains, and the sister of a FARC leader was released by her captors in the "Peasant Self-Defense" group after three months of captivity. On December 10, five heavily armed men snatched American Frank Pescatori, Jr., who was working for an Alabama-based coal company called Geomet. The forty-year-old geologist from Birmingham, Alabama, whose parents lived only a few miles from the Heidemas in New Jersey, was driving a company car in northern Colombia at the moment of the ambush.

In Cambodia, seventeen tourists were kidnapped that month. After a week in captivity, the tourists stabbed to death one of their abductors, beat up another, and then escaped. And in Yemen that month, as plans were under way for a big tourism push in 1997, tribesmen snatched five tourists.

32

◁≥X≥▷

While the revolving door of kidnapping continued to turn through-out December, most incidents paled in comparison to what happened in Peru.

By the end of 1996, the motivation for perhaps as many as 80 per-cent of the kidnappings worldwide was money, though so many inci-dents were still unreported that it was tough to confirm such a number. Depending on the region, the perpetrators were career crim-inals, rebels-turned-criminals, former military or police officers, or terrorist bands seeking funds for their war chests. The rest were polit-ically motivated kidnappers wanting anything from the release of jailed compatriots, to an end to poverty, to compensation for the dissipation of their lands and resources. Colombia, where guerrilla bands were responsible for roughly 40 percent of the cases, still led the world with 1,439 reported kidnappings in 1996—a 35 percent increase over 1995. And the typical targets across the globe continued to be busi-nessmen, though tourists were highly favored. Until the night of December 17, the year had unfolded much like 1995, though the revolving door was turning many more times.

On that night, in Lima, Peru, more than 500 people gathered at the grand residence of the Japanese ambassador to celebrate Emperor Akihito's sixty-third birthday. It was an annual gala that drew a prominent and well-connected crowd. This year, the guest list showed representatives of twenty-eight different countries, including the ambassadors of a dozen European, Latin American, and Asian countries, high-level Peruvian officials, generals, and Lima's wealthiest citizenry. There were, as always, hundreds of flowers and festive decorations everywhere; food included international delicacies and Christmas cakes. But this year would be different as many guests would remain together far longer than one glittery night—3,019 hours to be exact. Hidden among the flowers and in the cakes were the clips of automatic weapons. And some of the waiters were not really waiters.

At about 8:30 P.M., the guests heard a sudden blast coming from the direction of the garden. The guerrilla waiters were quickly joined by their comrades, who blew a hole in an outside wall to get into the residence. Then came the sound of breaking glass and the loud shouts of men waving automatic weapons: "Heads down! Keep your faces down, and don't look at us!" The twenty men and women invading the sprawling residence were Marxist rebels in the Tupac Amaru Revolutionary Movement (MRTA), one of Peru's two rebel bands. The other group was the more notorious and more violent Shining Path, a Maoist group. And both groups were inactive—or so it was thought until that night. Peru's get-tough President Alberto Fujimori supposedly had blotted them out by capturing 90 percent of their top leaders and offering amnesty to others. In fact, the decline of terrorism in Peru was one of Fujimori's claims to fame since taking office in 1990.

After fighting against insurgents for two decades, the Peruvian leaders were lauded for their apparent success in smashing the rebels. But there was one very large problem. The government had done little to mitigate the root cause for the existence of the groups: poverty. In 1995, 49 percent of Peru's population lived in poverty compared to 46 percent the year before, and, among other statistics, 85 percent of the people did not have full-time jobs.

Not only was the Tupac Amaru resurfacing, but also the Shining Path was reportedly recruiting new members. (In August of 1997, the

Shining Path would kidnap thirty oil workers in Peru.) Some analysts believed that the recent upsurge in kidnappings, beginning in late 1995 in Peru, was in part due to the rebels' financial needs in their crusade to revive. Bolivian intelligence sources confirmed that the MRTA funded its takeover of the Japanese ambassador's residence out of the $1.2 million ransom they obtained in the November 1995 kidnapping of Bolivian newspaper magnate Samuel Doria Medina. Intelligence reports indicate that it cost about $600,000 to train and equip the insurgents for the seige, including a $5,000 fee paid to each rebel who participated.

By midnight that December night, the rebels had released the women, including President Fujimori's mother and sister. The next morning they threatened to kill the remaining hostages unless the government released 400 to 500 jailed comrades. The same day, they released ambassadors from Germany, Canada, and Greece, as well as one Peruvian diplomat. In the next several days, more than 250 hostages were released, including ambassadors from Austria, Venezuela, Panama, Spain, Cuba, and the United States. After two Tupac Amaru rebels were released from an Uruguayan prison, Uruguay's ambassador was released. And by New Year's Day, nearly thirty more hostages would be released. Eighty of the guests from the mid-December gala would usher in the New Year together. On New Year's Day, eight more would be released. Among those who remained were a dozen or so Japanese businessmen and diplomats, Fujimori's younger brother, as well as his agriculture and foreign ministers, the Bolivian ambassador, and the past and present chiefs of Peru's antiterrorist police. To distract themselves from the imminent danger of their new lives as hostages and from such concerns as the limited water supply, they would while away the hours reading back issues of the *Economist* magazine, Tom Clancy novels, and works from the ambassador's library.

The *New York Times* called the incident a throwback to another time, to the late 1970s and early 1980s when taking over embassies was the rage among revolutionaries. And, to be sure, the MRTA's attack was a rerun of several past shows, particularly the takeover of the Dominican Republic's embassy in Bogotá in 1980 by Colombia's

M-19, a nationalist, non-Marxist group, and the 1993 takeover of the Nicaraguan embassy in San José, Costa Rica, by right-wing Nicaraguan guerrillas. But while targeting diplomats and holding hundreds of people at an ambassador's residence was a relatively outdated strategy—"Revolution as a Relic Come to Life," read the *New York Times* headline—the tactic of taking and holding hostages was clearly in vogue.

The international community, including negotiators in both the private and public sectors and the families of hostages, as well as former captives, in other recent incidents, would watch the Peruvian incident very carefully. In the era of CNN and the Internet, the crisis in Peru had the potential for being an international Waco. Instead, it would be a showcase for the efficacy of negotiation and for the ability of negotiators and military rescuers to cooperate.

33

❖❖❖

The families of the Kashmir hostages watched the crisis in Peru with
intense interest. Though the incident was contained in one known
locale, and the Kashmir kidnapping was not, observing the behavior of
nations in the midst of this new crisis might help in understanding
what had happened in India. Jane Schelly and others wondered, for
example, whether it would be handled differently from Kashmir
because of the sharp glare of daily media coverage and the VIP status
of some of the hostages. Like Kashmir, the case highlighted the inconsistencies in how governments handled hostage-takings. Japan was
averse to using violence or military force to solve international conflicts, and Japanese corporations had a reputation, within the secret
confines of kidnap negotiations, of paying ransoms. In the not-so-
secret case in Mexico earlier that year, Sanyo had paid a $2 million ran-
som. In another case in Panama, a $750,000 ransom was paid for a
Japanese businessman, who was later found dead. While Peru had a
tough, very real "no-concessions" policy, the incident had occurred
technically on Japanese "soil," so it was really Japan's call. Yet to

achieve resolution, Japan must work closely with Peru, whose policies were at polar ends of the planet. Analysts said it was the most serious challenge to Japanese diplomacy since World War II.

For the Kashmir hostage families, the Peruvian incident was a slight distraction from their own troubles, though nothing could sway their thoughts from Kashmir on the afternoon of December 23. It was only two days before Christmas when the families received phone calls from the press asking for comments on the latest episode in their cruel ordeal. This time, a respected English-language newspaper, the *Indian Express,* had received portions of the 120-page report on the interrogation of Naser Mohammed, and it published, for the first time, those parts of Naser's confession regarding the fate of Hutchings, Mangan, Wells, and Hasert.

The article appeared in the Indian daily on Sunday, December 22, and by Monday the hostage families were hounded once again by reporters asking for comments on the "news" about the possible deaths of their sons, husbands, brothers, and boyfriends. Once again, the families told the world that they believed the hostages to be alive. Besides, they said, this confession was hardly news. The militant's allegedly teary account of the deaths of the hostages and how they had been buried in the Magam area of Kokarnag district had been told and retold the previous summer. It seemed the height of cruelty to replay the drama only a few days before Christmas, and especially to reprint parts of the confession. Some reporters even read to members of the hostage families the part of the confession pertaining to the deaths of the hostages: "Accordingly, the foreigners were killed on December 13, 1995, in the Magam area of Kokarnag and buried in the jungles there. The exact location where they were buried was kept a secret as was desired by the group."

The circus had begun again as government officials, militants, religious leaders, and families were compelled to issue statements, initiate press conferences, and respond to very emotional, personal questions from strangers on the other end of a phone. The responses were the same as before: the spot where the jailed militant leader had said the hostages were killed had been thoroughly searched, and there was no evidence of the bodies, no trace of their remains. There was simply no firm evidence to support a claim that they were murdered.

For Jane, the timing couldn't have been worse. Suffering from giardia, an internal parasite she picked up in Pakistan that year, she answered the press calls between bouts of vomiting and extreme nausea. She had come to terms with the fact that again Don would not be home for Christmas, but the reminder that he could be dead was not what Jane needed to hear. As always, she toughed it out. She told the press, with her usual poise, that it was important to remember that the militant said he was not in fact present at the time of the supposed murders. His information, she explained again, was second- or third-hand. Without a witness to her husband's death, without the remains of his body, such a death could not be confirmed. "The longer we go with no information and no demands [from the rebels], the more puzzling it becomes," she told reporters.

In looking back over the previous year, Jane saw the meeting with Naser in June followed by her conversation with Ambassador Elbe as a significant turning point. From then on, her quest was as much about determining whether Don was alive as it was about finding him. And though she had spent nearly ten out of the past eighteen months in India and Pakistan working hard to find that truth, she could not be satisfied that she had done enough. There were moments now when she had regrets.

Perhaps she should have been more aggressive during July of 1995, she thought, or more insistent that the United States apply diplomatic pressure to Pakistan or India or both during those early stages of the case. "I understand that we didn't necessarily have power over Pakistan because of the weapons situation and the diminishing power of Bhutto," she said, "and that from the American government's point of view we didn't have power over India because we were trying to get along."

But she couldn't help wondering whether increased press coverage might have applied more pressure on the U.S. government or on the Indian and Pakistani governments "to create a possibility for a release." Jane knew that David Housego, the father of one of the

Kashmir hostages in 1994, had kept the incident in the press every day of his son's captivity. Should she have done the same, though doing so would have defied the advice she had been given at the time?

For several months in 1995, she had considered putting on her hiking boots and venturing into the mountains herself to talk with the rebels. Who could be more persuasive than the wife of one of the hostages? During that time, she had asked to speak with the rebel intermediaries at least once. And she was told that it would be too emotional to speak with them. They could be threatening, saying things like, "If you do not do such and such for us, it will jeopardize the lives of the hostages." It would not be helpful, she was told, for her to personally connect with the rebels. But now, nearly eighteen months later, she thought perhaps she should have been more forceful. And then there was the issue of the "ransom" that first September. Was that a missed opportunity? What if she had taken a ransom payment into the Kashmir Valley herself or hired a mercenary with such experience?

In addition to worrying about all the things she could have done but didn't, Jane considered whether the government could have done more. Worst of all, perhaps, was the nagging question: if Don had been more than an ordinary civilian, would her government have risked more and pushed harder to gain his release?

Jane, like her husband, was a person who played by the rules. And, accordingly, throughout most of the first year of the crisis, she felt very strongly that a no-concessions policy was the right one. Negotiating with terrorists, making any sort of deal, only instigates more incidents, she believed. Although she and Don had never had a reason to discuss how one should deal with kidnappers, she was certain, during that first year, that Don would have agreed with such a policy.

But at some point—she couldn't pin it down precisely—Jane's thinking had changed. She could no longer listen to the audiotape sent out in July 1995, in which Don says, "We just want to be free." She began to believe that his ordeal in Kashmir had probably changed his perspective. The more Jane thought about the matter, the more she felt that *something* had to be exchanged in these crises, especially if a rescue was out of the question. There had to be some sort of bargain, a face-saving concession that would not encourage the crime.

Jane knew that what law enforcement called "substantive concessions," meaning prisoners, weapons, and foreign policy changes, could never be considered. But there was a wide gap between such huge concessions and no concessions. She recalled the rebels' request, back in September 1995, for a "guarantee" of money to be put in escrow until they were safely over the border into Pakistan. Although the idea was flawed, maybe it was on the right track. Jane now realized that if she got a call tomorrow with a ransom demand, she would round up the money, perhaps with the help of the Mountaineers and a nationwide campaign. Later, she would wonder: "Should I have offered money? What good is savings if you can't save someone's life?"

Jane's guilt, though a normal response to the ordeal, was unfounded. Everyone who knew the case well knew how complex it was. Jane had done the very best with the information that she had. Still, to such a determined and capable woman, her efforts never seemed to be enough. She wrote in her journal one day during that difficult month of December 1996: "As long as this continues, I will feel that there is always something more to do. The case will never leave me. I will get one thing done, regroup, then launch another plan."

After returning from India the previous summer, Jane had started a new campaign, this time to persuade the U.S. government to initiate a reward program in India and in Pakistan for information regarding the four missing men. An individual who was empathetic to Jane's cause—and who requested anonymity—informed her that the State Department had a cache of money (then totaling $2 million) earmarked for rewards in relation to terrorist acts. The fund was legislated into existence in the 1984 Act to Combat International Terrorism and had been used in various cases since then to encourage informants to come forward. The director of the Diplomatic Security Service, a division of the State Department, chaired an interagency committee that picked reward candidates and made recommendations to the secretary of state. The committee consisted of representatives from the FBI, the State Department, the National Security Council, the CIA, the Drug Enforcement Agency, the U.S. Marshals Service, the Witness Security Program, the Federal Aviation Administration, the Department of Justice, the Immigration and Naturalization Service, and the Department of Energy. More than $5 million had been paid out through the years in twenty cases, ranging from the World Trade Center bombing to the murder of the CIA officials in 1993. It was a laudible program, but to administer rewards required a good deal of work. Every scintilla of information had to be checked out, and every source thoroughly investigated.

The FBI, which was busy launching a task force in India to try to end the crisis in Kashmir, at first questioned the practicality of a reward program in connection with the case. The agents worried they would be chasing a plethora of new leads, many of which could be bogus, when there were still substantial leads they hadn't yet had the time to track down. Still, Jane felt a certain urgency in setting up and publicizing the reward program before the coming of the winter snows. In winter, the shepherds, who were excellent conduits of information through the vast hill country, migrated to other, warmer regions. And once they were out of the area, they would be unable to spread the news of the reward until spring. Jane feared this would be another missed opportunity. Her persistence, in combination with the influence of those within the government who supported her cause, helped her over this first hurdle. The next obstacle was Great Britain.

Government officials as well as the hostage families in Britain viewed rewards as synonymous with ransoms. Reward money could be construed as an incentive to the rebels, just like a ransom. And of course it was possible that the rebels would be the ones collecting the reward because, after all, they knew the most about the case. Although the contact person would likely have an indirect, indiscernible link to the Al-Faran, the reward money might end up in the coffers of the terrorists, again just like a ransom payment. There was also the fear that if the hostages were indeed still alive, the reward could endanger them. Someone could kill the hostages just to have the information about what had happened to them and to lead authorities to the exact location of their remains, as the all-important proof. It took weeks for the Brits to endorse the program.

Next on the list of entities that must agree to the rewards was the central government in India. Throughout the process of putting the reward program together, Jane, who had spent nearly all of October and November of 1996 in India, could not help but think that she was encountering a microcosm of the bureaucracies and conflicting agendas that had bogged down the resolution of the crisis during the summer of 1995. Certainly, the issue of India clinging to its sovereignty and objecting to the intrusion of Western experts was central. India seemed to have a chip on its shoulder—a problem that had delayed the involvement of professional negotiators at the front lines of the case back in July 1995, and that now was becoming the boulder on the road to a smooth-running reward system. Officials of the central government, who had decided to prohibit the FBI from opening a task force office to investigate the Kashmir incident, claimed that the rewards were OK with them but that the Kashmiri government would not allow an office in Srinagar to oversee the program. In the end, India would not approve the American rewards program. "It was plain and simple a matter of sovereignty. That's India. India did not want U.S. investigators to be given free reign. It was partly a pride issue; I mean, can you imagine the U.S. allowing Indian investigators to set up shop here? But it was also a bit of paranoia, not wanting U.S. experts snooping around Kashmir," said a government official knowledgeable about the case.

Pakistan, however, allowed the United States to set up a $2 million reward program in Islamabad beginning November 21. It was the first time the United States had ever offered a reward for information regarding a kidnapped American. The government would pay on a case-by-case basis, depending on the value of the information, and if necessary, it would help informants to relocate at U.S. expense to assure their safety.

India eventually, in December, cooperated in its own way by offering a reward of 1 million rupees, or $28,000, in a program staffed and promoted by the Indian government. Both programs began with a shared handicap: by the time they were publicized, the shepherds were already gone. And the Indian program had an additional problem: few Kashmiris who had information pertaining to the kidnapped tourists would want to draw the attention of the Indian government to themselves and their families. The villagers feared and hated the Indian government. Knowledge about the actions of the Al-Faran could easily cast a long shadow of suspicion over their lives. Would they face retaliation? And would they ever even see a single rupee? Worse still, would they be killed by the militants for coming forward?

That Christmas, as Jane reflected on the past year, she realized that the most peaceful and memorable moments were those spent with Frances Waite, the wife of former Beirut hostage Terry Waite, and Jill Morrell, the girlfriend of journalist John McCarthy, also a Beirut hostage. On her way home from India in November, Jane had stopped in London, where she and Julie Mangan spent an afternoon and evening with Frances and Jill. There was a lot of hugging and commiserating. Jane felt very reassured, especially when she realized that Don's captivity to date was only one-fourth as long as John McCarthy's 1,943 days and close to one-third the length of Terry's 1,763 days. Still, that was Lebanon, not India, and the incidents occurred during the 1980s, which seemed to Jane to be an entirely different era in terms of kidnappings. The comparison she tried not to dwell on was the one in Kashmir itself. Don had now been held thirty times longer than David Mackie and Kim Housego, two of Kashmir's tourist hostages of 1994.

On Christmas Day, Jane didn't write in her journal, as she was in the habit of doing. But a few days later she wrote:

Christmas Day was a real downer for me. I was alone. I had giardia. I was extremely nauseated, very, very dizzy. I didn't even get out of bed until after 10 A.M. I did the usual routine of the past few days, first reading the newspaper, then opening a few gifts, this time from my sister and brother-in-law. They sent me a gourmet cookbook with CD tape music to go with it and I thought: for whom am I going to gourmet cook? Me? I spent a lot of time thinking about how last year at this time I was optimistic and how we all really believed that Don would be back with us soon. We lit candles for him. We wrote in my journal for him and we were certain that he would be reading it at some time in the future. I thought he might be here through that winter [of 1995]. But I really didn't think that he could ever be killed. It was starting to look grim last year; I remember last year sitting on the sofa crying with Mom, though I still thought he would be back. And Mom took me into her arms and was hugging me and we were all hoping for the best. This year I really don't think so; as a matter of fact I feel almost certain. In my heart, I don't believe he's alive but I've been wrong so many other times that I have no faith in gut feelings now. I wish now I were wrong but I don't think so.

Still, how can I ever give up when I remember looking into the eyes of Terry Waite and hearing him say, "Never give up until you have proof positive." So how can I ever be certain? How can I ever give up? Until I have some conclusion, I can never stop looking. I remember so many of the wonderful times we've had together. Don and I really got along so well together. We were keepers. We had planned on growing old together. I just can't imagine finding someone as good as Don. Don loved me and treated me so well. A very gentle and sensitive person; I love you sweetheart.

The year ended with the Peruvian case in a standoff. In Latin America, the big news was that the Guatemalan government and the leftist guerrillas known as the Guatemalan National Revolutionary Unity signed a final armistice ending thirty-six years of civil war, on December 29. But behind the jubilant scenes of celebration, there were suspicions that the peace wouldn't hold. Those who understood kidnappings and the needs of demobilized warriors braced for the new year.

But there was no news out of Kashmir. In England, songwriter James Bowman, who was Keith Mangan's uncle, wrote a ballad about Mangan and his fellow hostages, which was widely played on radio stations throughout England.

> *Spare a thought for the hostages this Christmas.*
> *Spare a thought for their wives and families,*
> *Spare a thought for their lovers, their sisters and their brothers.*
> *It may help to set them free.*

34

At the State Department briefing on January 6, 1997, official briefer Nick Burns talked about the hostages in Kashmir: "That is a very serious issue. Mr. Donald Hutchings is on our mind as are his three colleagues who were abducted on July 4, 1995. We are working closely with the Indian authorities and have been for a very long time. Ambassador Frank Wisner has been centrally involved in this in Delhi. We are hoping and praying for the release of all the hostages, including our American, Donald Hutchings."

The next day's briefing, at which Glyn Davies presided, went like this:

> *Q:* Nick said yesterday that Ambassador Frank Wisner was still on top of the Kashmir hostage situation. Last month, you said you are still operating on the assumption that the hostages are alive.

> *Davies:* That's right.

> *Q:* Is that still the assumption that you're operating from?

Davies: It is.

> *Q:* Have you all been reassured by the Indian authorities that they are alive?

Davies: We don't have any assurances really one way or the other, but we are operating on the assumption that they are still alive. That's one of the reasons why we put out some months ago a reward for information leading to finding them. Mr. Hutchings has now been missing for quite a while and we will assume he is alive until we get information to the contrary.

> *Q:* In his only failure, then-Congressman Bill Richardson and now current designate to the UN went out to Kashmir early last year and failed to get the hostage back, and then he had a press conference. He said during the summer there has to be some serious action taken. Have you thought about any serious action in terms of some concerted activity or some rescue mission or anything of the sort?

Davies: We're working with the other governments concerned but especially the Indian government on a daily basis, and Frank Wisner, our ambassador in India, has been up to Kashmir on at least one occasion to look into this directly. I, myself, have spoken with one of the officers who deals with this, and we continue to work with the Indian government on a daily basis.

> *Q:* But you've sort of laid back the effort where you all are just waiting for the information to come in, or how—

Davies: No, I wouldn't describe it as a laid-back effort. The problem is, absent specific information about where Mr. Hutchins [sic] and the others might be, it's very difficult to do anything Rambo-like in a situation like this. We have to operate based on what information we can gather. We're doing what we can to gather that information, including offering a rather substantial reward for information leading to their whereabouts.

PART V

The New Year

⊰⧓⊱

Kidnapping in Yemen is part of tourism; it's an adventure for the tourist because the tourist will end up learning about the customs of the tribes as well as their good hospitality.

> —Abdullah Ahmar, speaker of the
> Yemeni parliament and leader of
> Yemen's largest tribe, the Hashid, 1997

We were locked in the dark and, under threat of arms, we were stopped from going out even for hygiene purposes.

> —A tourist/hostage in Yemen, 1997

35

FEBRUARY 1997
ECUADOR

Professor James Thurber was a man with connections, though he never flaunted them and never pondered the question of their power—that is, until the week of February 17, 1997.

On the afternoon of the fifteenth, his son, Mark Thurber, a thirty-two-year-old environmental geologist and the coauthor of *Hiking and Climbing in Ecuador*, became a hostage in the Amazonian jungles of Ecuador. It was shocking enough that his son had been abducted, but the fact that during the early days of the ordeal he was unable to reach the U.S. ambassador in Quito or to break through the bureaucracy of the U.S. embassy transformed an already frustrating and frightening experience into a Kafka-esque drama rendering Thurber's arsenal of contacts indispensable.

"We felt like we were in the middle of the movie *Missing*," Thurber said later, in an interview. "No matter what I said I could not get beyond the low-level people to find out what was really happening. I can't describe the frustration."

By February 15, Mark Thurber had been working in Ecuador's remote backcountry, about 100 miles southeast of Quito, for nearly twenty days. He headed a team of specialists, including a botanist, a zoologist, and an anthropologist, contracted to conduct an environmental study of the area for Walsh Environmental Scientists and Engineers Company, out of Boulder, Colorado. Walsh, in turn, had been retained by Compania General de Combustibles (CGC), an Argentine petroleum firm that had purchased the rights at public auction to Ecuador's Block 23 oil reserve deep in the Ecuadoran jungle. The team spent its days taking water and soil samples, as well as plant specimens, to evaluate which sectors of Block 23 could be drilled and which should be left untouched, or "environmentally pristine," as they called it.

To procure the all-important permission to work in the region, Mark had negotiated with the Ecuadoran government, the Ecuadoran military, and the leaders of several indigenous communities, most notably the Achuar group. After four months of intermittent talks, he had finally obtained the green light, in writing. But that didn't seem to matter on the afternoon of February 15 when several Achuar men abducted Mark and his team in Shaimi, a village in an isolated pocket of southeastern Ecuador, about 100 kilometers, or 62 miles, from the Peruvian border.

For years, Ecuador's indigenous communities had resisted the invasion of foreign explorers. Oil was the treasured resource now, but before oil, it was timber, and before timber, it was rubber. Conflicts between the Amazonian natives and the outside world had been ongoing since the days when Amazon gold was first discovered centuries ago. In recent years, they had even resorted to lawsuits to stave off what they perceived as the exploitation of their homeland. More than 100 Amazon communities—roughly 30,000 plaintiffs—filed a class action against Texaco in 1992 alleging the company had perpetrated irreparable social and environmental harm against their land and their people. To compensate, they wanted $8 million in legal damages. But the case was stalled when the Ecuadoran government declined to join the plaintiffs' cause. Perhaps the slowness of the courts had become as irritating to the native tribes as the foreign intrusions. Whatever the motive, by 1997, some indigenous leaders clearly had decided to test the power of a tactic that might deliver quicker results: kidnapping. It was indeed ironic that the team of workers the Achuar chose to abduct in Shaimi that February day was probing the land to be certain that any future explorations would not ruin the environment. Mark Thurber was, after all, an environmental geologist, not a pillager of the land.

Later on that first day, February 15, the kidnappers released two of their hostages: the sixty-five-year-old anthropologist, likely because of his age, and Walsh's legal representative Peter Ayarza, to communicate their demands to the outside world. They wanted $1 million, as well as all scientific data from the Walsh study of Block 23, a public apology for conducting such a study in Achuar territory, and a commitment from CGC to cease its oil exploration in the block. Peter, whose father was Ecuadoran and whose mother was American, assumed the role of negotiator. Before Peter left, Mark entrusted him with his carefully compiled field notes, which chronicled the kidnapping, related his healthy state— "in good spirits"—and cautioned authorities to "do nothing rash." The notes also revealed the intriguing fact that one of the kidnappers' leaders was Luis Vargas, who worked at a well-known ecotourism camp called Kapawi Lodge on the Pastaza River, forty minutes by air from the site of the kidnappers' hideout and reportedly a favorite vacation spot among ecology-minded North Americans. It was Peter who informed Mark's fiancée, Jane Letham, that Mark had been abducted.

At approximately 10:45 P.M. on the night of February 17, Jane rang up the Thurbers at their home on a quiet, leafy street in northwest Washington, D.C. She told them the grim news and what few details she could relate at that time. The Thurbers, their minds racing faster than the world around them, shifted into high gear.

James Thurber—no relation to the comedic writer—is the director of the Center for Congressional and Presidential Studies at American University and his wife, Claudia, is a lawyer for the U.S. Department of Labor, specializing in OSHA cases (Occupational Safety and Health Administration). Though naturally distraught at the news of their son's abduction, both Thurbers, from the start, were well aware of the realities of the situation. "The thing we decided from the very beginning was that no one would be on Mark's side," Professor Thurber recalled later. "The State Department was mainly interested in U.S. foreign policy; the CGC, in their profits and their own position; and the CIA would reinforce what the embassy wanted. Who would care about Mark? We were later surprised to learn that one government agency really did care, and that agency was the FBI."

The first person Thurber called, early in the morning of February 18, was Louis Goodman, the dean of the School of International Service at American University. Thurber knew that the esteemed dean was working on a study of relations between the military and civilians in Ecuador and that he had attended Yale University with the current minister of defense in Ecuador, General Paco Moncayo. After listening carefully to Thurber's concerns, Goodman called Moncayo to alert him to the case. Moncayo assured his American friend that nothing irrational would happen to jeopardize the safety of the hostages and that indeed he would personally monitor the case, putting all the necessary resources into a swift resolution. This was the first successful intervention into the case—and one that would later prove meaningful.

The second person Thurber called was the U.S. ambassador in Quito. But he could not reach him. Nor could he reach the second in command, the DCM. Thurber wondered, How was it that the father of a hostage in a foreign country could not speak to the authorities at his own country's embassy?

Meanwhile, an intelligence bulletin was circulating through Washington offices, spreading the word about the abduction to agencies such as the FBI and the United States Information Agency (USIA) and landing on the desks of some high-powered individuals, including the head of USIA, Joe Duffy. Duffy was a former president of American University, a good friend of the Thurbers, and a longtime friend of Bill Clinton.

"I just got the report of your son," Duffy said when he called the Thurbers that Tuesday night. "From father to father, if there's anything I can do for you, just let me know."

Thurber thanked him, and then, after recalling some of the frustrations of his first day on the case, he decided that indeed he must call on Duffy to help. "I do need a favor," he told Duffy Wednesday morning. "I can't get through to the ambassador in Quito, nor can I reach the DCM."

Duffy immediately rang up the U.S. undersecretary of state, and within minutes the undersecretary called the assistant secretary for Latin American affairs, Jeff Davidow, who asked the former ambassador to Ecuador, Peter Romaro, to join him in his office as he called Thurber. Davidow, of course, asked Thurber what he could do for him.

"Well, first thing, I'd like to be able to speak with the ambassador," Thurber said firmly.

"You haven't spoken with the ambassador?" a surprised Davidow responded.

"No," said Thurber. Davidow politely, though quickly, ended the conversation. Only minutes after he had hung up, the phone rang at the Thurbers'. It was the DCM in Quito.

"Dr. Thurber," he said. "What can we do for you? We put three good men on this."

Thurber explained that he wanted effectively to be wired to the embassy—nothing less. He wanted to know their every move, including what the negotiators were doing and what the native leaders were demanding or threatening. But as he hung up the phone, Thurber, like all hostage family members, felt he still was not doing enough to gain the freedom of his son.

The next move came from Louis Goodman, who connected Thurber to Mitchell Hammer, a professor at American University who is an expert in negotiation and teaches at the FBI Academy in Quantico. Hammer recently had worked as a consultant in Lima on the Peruvian hostage case. This day he advised Thurber on basic strategies of negotiation: time is on your side; show that you understand the kidnappers' needs; reduce the number of people at the negotiating table; narrow the agenda, and so on. Thurber listened carefully and took detailed notes that he immediately faxed to Ecuador to Peter Ayarza, who was facing daily talks with as many as twenty highly emotional indigenous leaders. It was Hammer who introduced the Thurbers to the FBI's hostage negotiators on the Critical Incident Negotiation Team (CINT), including CINT's leader, Gary Noessner, who had been working international kidnappings since 1985. In retrospect, the Thurbers felt that the connection with Noessner and with the FBI in general was the turning point in the case.

"Gary made us feel comfortable that there was an institution in the U.S. government that cared about what was happening to us and to Mark," Claudia Thurber said later. From that point on, the Thurbers wanted Noessner's men on the case. But there was another bureaucratic maze to conquer. Noessner explained that FBI negotiators could not assist in a case abroad unless the U.S. ambassador invited them. Thus far they had received no invitation to Quito to assist in gaining young Thurber's freedom.

Professor Thurber later recalled: "At that point Gary asked me, 'Who do you know?' and I gave him a list of people I knew in Washington politics. Gary said, 'Well, that seems like enough,' and then I said, 'Look, I'll just call the ambassador directly because he told me to call if I wanted something.' And so I did." Their conversation went like this:

Ambassador: Oh, I thought they [the FBI] had been called.

Thurber: Mr. Ambassador, I want the FBI in immediately, and I want to know why they aren't in.

A (after a pause): Oh, I think they have been invited.

T: No, sir, they haven't.

A: Well, let me check on this.

T: Mr. Ambassador, I've been talking to Gary Noessner and—

A: You've been talking to Gary? [He knew Gary from the Heidema kidnapping the previous year.]

T: Mr. Ambassador, as soon as I get off the phone, I am going to call Gary and say that you have invited him in, right?

A: Well, give me a little while.

T: No, I am not going to give you a little while. Thank you.

And at that point, Thurber hung up and called Noessner. " 'The ambassador says that he thinks he has invited you,' " said Thurber. "Gary said that he didn't believe that was the case. Then, within the ten minutes that I was talking to Gary, he got a call from the State Department saying that the FBI had been officially invited. For us, things began to change the minute the FBI was on board."

While Thurber was enlisting the FBI's assistance, the embassy in Quito had picked up the rumor that the kidnappers were threatening to kill their hostages within the next couple of days. Meanwhile, the story of the American and his fellow hostage, a Brit, in captivity in Ecuador had leaked out to the Ecuadoran press. And shortly after the first stories had hit the wires, the rebels had upped the ransom from $1 million to $2 million. Within twenty minutes of hearing the rumor, on Thursday night, the Thurbers had booked a flight to Quito, for the next day, February 21, with a stopover in Miami to meet up with two FBI negotiators who would be accompanying them on the Quito flight. Understandably, the death threat had heightened their anxiety, which only exacerbated their frustration when their plane was delayed for more than an hour on the Washington runway. Every second that separated the Thurbers from Ecuador and from their son was unbearable at this point, and the idea of missing the flight to Quito was torturous. The next flight was hours later, and the FBI was meeting them with the intention of spending the flight time briefing them. They must delay the departure of the flight in Miami, and, to do this, they called their daughter, Kathryn Thurber-Smith, who had just flown into D.C. from Lawrence, Kansas, that day, with her four-month-old baby, to manage a quasi-communication center out of the Thurber home. Her first duty: to relay a message to the FBI, telling them of the need to delay the Quito flight. By the time they boarded the plane in Washington, American Airlines was fully aware of the Thurbers' distressful saga and upgraded the couple's seats to first class. The pilot also took it upon himself to request an international gate for the Miami landing of his domestic flight, a gate right next to the Thurbers' Quito flight. When they arrived in Miami, the FBI agents were standing at the gate to whisk them away to the waiting plane.

On the flight to Quito, the agents, one-on-one, each with a
Thurber, explained that the ordeal could be prolonged. One worked
with Mrs. Thurber to develop a personality profile of Mark, asking questions, much like a doctor, to determine the young man's strengths as a
captive, the judgment calls he might make, and what role he might be
able to play in the effort to gain his release. He also wanted details about
Mark's life that could be used in proof-of-life questions. The agent with
Professor Thurber wanted to know the chronology of events.

By the twenty-first, Vargas and his fellow kidnappers were holding
Mark and one other team member, British biologist Victor Morley
Read, in a dirt-floored palm hut deep in the jungle thicket, at least
100 kilometers, or 62 miles, from the nearest road. The hostages were
not restrained by chains, nor were their hands and legs bound by
ropes. They were free to move around. But the idea of an escape,
though never far from their thoughts, was daunting. The terrain was
dense and rugged, an unmapped and shifting domain as potentially
unnerving as darkness itself. And always there was the possibility of
one or more of Vargas's men, their guns propped in readiness at their
sides, hiding in the brush. Mark was a strong-willed, healthy young
man with a sturdy six-foot-two physique. He had experience in high-
altitude climbing and more than a casual acquaintance with Ecuador's
jungle terrain. Armed with a compass and topographic maps, he
believed he could eventually find his way to the road and to freedom.
But he was not entirely confident that Read could, or wanted to,
undertake such a journey. And Mark felt he could not walk out and
leave a fellow hostage behind.

When the Thurbers arrived in Quito, the DCM greeted them with
a handshake and good news. A deal had been struck. Although the
Thurbers would never know all the details of the agreement, it
appeared that the hostages would be released if CGC agreed to cover
the expenses of the abduction and to reconsider the exploration of
Block 23. The Thurbers would never know the exact amount of cash
exchanged, though it clearly exceeded $10,000. Behind the scenes,
the Thurbers would later learn that someone in General Moncayo's
strike force—the same highly trained team that had rescued John Heidema in 1996—had sent a message to the kidnappers advising them

that what they were doing was not a good idea, and that if they did not release the American and the Brit, the force would "wipe them out." It was nothing the Thurbers could ever confirm, though they believed that Moncayo was one of the reasons their son and Read were released, unharmed and quickly.

Whether it was the threat or the money that had resolved the kidnapping, the men were set free on Sunday, February 23. Still, the Thurbers could not breathe easily. The weather was so stormy that day and the cloud cover so dense that the helicopter deployed to retrieve Thurber and Read was barely able to fly into Shaimi to pick them up. Mark Thurber would always remember the sound of the helicopter's approach—"like the fluttering wings of angels," he later said. And though the clouds rolled back enough to allow the helicopter to shuttle them from the jungle village of Shaimi to the modern town of Shell, they were unable to continue to Quito. And so the hostages and several security guards drove, in two four-wheel-drive vehicles, along rain-drenched, muddy roads to Quito. It was a ten-hour drive through dark jungle terrain. Besides the threat of mudslides at every turn, washed-out bridges, and flash floods, there was still the possibility that the kidnappers would try to retrieve their valuable prey, bursting through the curtain of rain and beginning the insanity all over again.

Luckily, that didn't happen. At 3 A.M., the elevator doors of the Radisson Hotel in Quito opened on the fifth floor to the sight of a smiling young man wearing rubber boots and covered in mud. The Thurbers had been up all night waiting. To say it was the happiest day of their lives was clearly an understatement.

Upon their return to the States, the Thurbers wrote to FBI Director Louis Freeh and to the U.S. secretary of state, Madeleine Albright, commending them equally for the fine work of their staffs. They even wrote to the staffers themselves, some of whom wrote back. One FBI agent wrote: "The entire experience that I shared with you during that last week of February 1997 will forever be engraved in my heart and mind as one of the highlights of my Bureau career and as one of the special times of my life. To know that I was a small part of helping someone in need was very special for me. And the fact that things turned out so well made it even more so."

Indeed, the Thurber story had a happy ending. When it was over, positive thoughts, like mists across a field, blanketed the events of the week. It seemed appropriate to thank everyone equally for their help. After all, once Professor Thurber had broken through the barrier of the embassy bureaucracy—albeit with the help of his Washington contacts—the U.S. ambassador had been very helpful. But the Thurbers knew in their hearts that connecting with their own embassy should not have been so difficult. And what if they had not known Goodman or Duffy or Davidow? Would their son be free? Would he even be alive?

Meanwhile, the FBI and the State Department would continue to slug it out over the issue of how to resolve kidnappings abroad. In some embassies, the FBI's negotiators were always welcome; in others, they were not. There was no consistency in what families were told, nor in how the FBI's presence was handled, if at all. Later in the year, a case in Venezuela would come to a standstill because of a classic catch-22 syndrome in which the State Department refused to invite the FBI to help with the case unless the agents promised not to negotiate or bargain with the kidnappers. Because this was indeed what the agents intended to do, they declined the invitation. And the hostage all the while remained in captivity, with his family hanging by an emotional thread. By summer, one congressman would call for hearings regarding the agencies' differences on the issue, quietly, out of the public view, in nondescript rooms on Capitol Hill where the scent of controversy was beginning to seep through closed doors.

As for the Ecuadoran tribes, they would score a minor, though hopeful, victory in the U.S. courts that year when the Ecuadoran government decided at long last to support their cause in the class action suit against Texaco. But they would continue to use kidnapping to force foreign invaders to the bargaining table. In a case that June, for example, an Ecuadoran oil company postponed seismic studies in a province 240 kilometers, roughly 150 miles, northeast of Quito after the Organization of Indigenous Peoples kidnapped an employee of a U.S. company retained to do the studies.

36

As the Thurbers embraced their son on a drizzly morning in Quito, another American family had just begun a kidnapping ordeal in Latin America that would last many months, and yet another was within days of facing a tragic resolution.

In February, around the time Thurber was snatched in southeastern Ecuador, Colombian guerrillas from the National Liberation Army (ELN) crossed the border into Venezuela to abduct Jerel Shaffer, a 48-year-old oil engineer from Texas, and his airplane pilot. Shaffer, who was the general manager of the Venezuelan branch of Houston-based Production Operators, had just arrived for a weekend of fishing at a camp along a tributary of the Orinoco River in western Venezuela, roughly 40 miles from the Colombian border, 100 miles from the nearest town, and 430 miles west of Caracas. But his vacation never began. As the six-seater Cessna, on which Shaffer was a passenger, landed in Venezuela, armed guerrillas were waiting on the airstrip. Forcing a stunned Shaffer to turn around and board the plane once again, they instructed the pilot to fly over the border to

Colombia. The pilot, who was quickly released, later revealed that the guerrillas had snatched Shaffer because they believed he was a wealthy American oil executive. In fact, he was a technician who had simply accepted an invitation to go fishing with several other businessmen. Colombia's antikidnap coordinator, Dr. Alberto Villamizar, said that the guerrillas' main interest may have been the aircraft, a white Cessna 310.

Shaffer and his fellow fishermen apparently had not been warned that for the past year, at least, abductions had been increasing in Venezuela near the Colombian border. Two days before Shaffer's abduction, two oil engineers from the state-owned Petroleos de Venezuela had been kidnapped about 500 miles southwest of Caracas, close to the border. In fact, during the week before Schaffer and his pilot were taken, a total of seven people had been abducted near the Colombian border.

The 1,400-mile border was very difficult to police, partly because of the terrain. And for years the ranches nestled in the remote valleys surrounded by nearly impenetrable jungles and mountains had been the targets of kidnappers. Venezuelan ranchers frequently paid protection money to guerrilla groups to discourage kidnappings. Now the problem was spreading to foreigners as their numbers increased due to the privatization of Venezuela's oil industry. Giving up its monopoly, the government welcomed competition and the infusion of foreign money to develop its expansive oil fields. Consequently, more and more foreigners were venturing to Venezuela. Colombian guerrillas knew this, and as in Ecuador, the guerrillas appeared to be retaining local criminals to pluck unwary targets. Shaffer was one.

Back at the State Department on February 18, spokesman Glyn Davies responded to reporters' questions about Shaffer, "This is an act the U.S. government deplores and we call for the release of an innocent American citizen." No one asked about Frank Pescatori, Jr., the forty-year-old geologist from New Jersey who worked for an Alabama-based mining concern. Perhaps they didn't know. A week or so later, that crisis came to a tragic end. Eleven weeks after his abduction, Pescatori's body was found in a guerrilla stronghold in northern Colombia.

That same week, FARC guerrillas in Colombia released a French engineer after holding him for more than three months, and ELN guerrillas released an Italian businessman held for six months. Neither the governments nor the families would comment on whether ransoms were paid. The week ended with FARC's latest abduction: a Norwegian foreman of a Swedish hydroelectric power project, followed a week later by the FARC kidnapping of Frank Skee, a forty-four-year-old American geologist from Philadelphia, who was working on a gold-mining project in southern Colombia.

Among other early 1997 incidents, an American oil engineer from Houston-based Halliburton Energy Services was abducted while jogging in eastern Yemen. And in Colombia, four backpackers, between the ages of twenty-five and thirty and all from Germany, were snatched as they hiked from Panama over the border into Colombia. The twenty or so kidnappers were FARC guerrillas who apparently spotted the tourists in a lush yet remote area called the Darien Gap, in Colombia, just over the border. They demanded a $15 million ransom. Nearly a month later, a small battalion of government soldiers stumbled upon the rebel camp, and as two of the tourists bathed in a nearby river, the other two were shot to death in a skirmish between the guerrillas and the soldiers.

In early March, shortly after a Yemeni mountain tribe released the American jogger taken the month before, fifty other tribesmen in Yemen, armed with AK-47s, ambushed seven German tourists as they were cycling across a mountain pass. Taking them hostage, the tribesmen demanded $12 million in ransom. Nine days later, the tourists were released, though it was unclear whether any part of the ransom was paid; no one would comment one way or the other. Later that same month, tribesmen snatched four more German tourists, who were freed after a military rescue. It was the first time that the government of this conservative Islamic country had resorted to military force to gain the release of hostages. Worried about the impact of kidnapping on the burgeoning tourism trade in Yemen, the government was losing patience with its indigenous tribes, whose kidnapping escapades had been escalating each year since 1993. The tribes had never harmed a hostage, though the intrusion of the military could increase the danger of a kidnapping in Yemen. Kidnappings of foreigners had become so common in Yemen that a local columnist suggested changing the name of the Ministry of Tourism to the Ministry of Kidnapping.

Throughout the early months of the new year, unusual stories continued to fill the annals of kidnapping. In Hong Kong, for instance, plumbers were called to a public lavatory early one morning to inspect four clogged toilets. The problem: dozens of $1,000 bills (Hong Kong dollars) later linked to a $2.5 million ($323,400 in U.S. dollars) ransom paid for the return of the son of a Chinese businessman. With gloved hands and pinched noses, police officers spent the next few days rummaging through refuse at two waste treatment plants to recover the ransom's remains. On the darker side, also in Hong Kong, parts of the dismembered body of a thirty-four-year old female insurance agent were found in garbage bags on a hillside. The kidnappers had demanded a $300,000 ransom for the agent, and though they stole a total of $5,000 from the woman, via her bankcard, while she was still alive, they could not wait for the ransom. They panicked, apparently because she caught a glimpse of their faces. She could identify them, and so they had to kill her, according to trial testimony.

Back in Latin America, where kidnappers were targeting more and more children—frequently at shopping malls or parks—a Colombian gang struck a new moral low when its members snatched a baby that was not yet a day old. Colombia continued to be the number one nation on the kidnapping global hit parade, with some new reports showing that in 1995 and 1996 kidnappers there had raked in more than $1 billion in ransoms. Though most victims were Colombian nationals, abductions of foreigners were rising, with energy company officials high on the list of preferred targets. In other parts of Latin America, foreigners were increasingly at risk, in places like Venezuela, as the Schaffer case and others that year would demonstrate. Honduras was a relative newcomer to the problem, attributed in part to spillover from Guatemala. CRG reported that sixty businessmen were abducted between December 1996 and May 1997 in Honduras, including a few foreigners. Ecuador continued to have problems along its Colombian border, as did Panama. Only Rio could report good news on the kidnapping front; the number of kidnappings so far in 1997 was below the rate for the previous year.

In an in-depth analysis of political violence for 1996, released in the spring of 1997, Pinkerton's reported that "incidents motivated by ideological considerations continued their decline of recent years and narcoterrorism remained less a threat than in the past. Economic, ethnic, religious, tribal, racial and xenophobic tensions again dominated as the grounds for political violence in most parts of the world as extremists of all varieties sought to obtain their objectives through the use of force. The economic consequences of political violence, measured in terms of damage inflicted, ransoms demanded and amounts robbed, rose 530% to $278.9 million from $47.2 million in 1995. Ransom demands accounted for $70.4 million of the 1996 total, well above the $41.2 million of 1995 but just over a third of the 1994 record total of $200 million. There continue to be cogent reasons for ransoms both demanded and paid to be underreported and the true totals are certainly higher than those reported. Whether politically or profit-motivated, kidnapping-for-ransom remains a 'growth industry' in such countries as Colombia, Cambodia, Mexico, the Philippines, and Guatemala, which collectively accounted for 53.3 percent of the year's kidnappings."

A large percentage of the ransoms paid that year went to kidnappers in Mexico and Colombia, the report went on. German criminals reaped roughly one-fifth of the ransom totals. "Given the reluctance of many kidnapping victims and their families to notify authorities or acknowledge ransom demands and payments, these figures [in the report] understate the true dimensions of the kidnapping problem worldwide," the report said.

"Even when ample information is available, as it was regarding the March 1994 kidnapping-for-ransom of Mexican bank executive Alfredo Harp Helu, the motive of the kidnappers, whether political or purely criminal, usually is unclear. To illustrate the disparity between what can be recorded based on available facts and informed estimates, Pinkerton's added 14 kidnapping incidents in Mexico to its data base in 1996. Local media [in Mexico following the abduction of the Japanese executive in August that year] referred to unofficial totals of as many as 3,000 kidnappings a year in Mexico. Daniel F. Donahue, CPP, a managing partner of the Miami-based Incident Management Group and a recognized authority on kidnappings, cites estimates running from 3,000 to 6,000 incidents a year in Colombia, 1,500 in Mexico, 1,000 in Brazil and 1,000 in the Philippines."

At the annual conference of the Risk and Insurance Management Society, in Atlanta that spring, one speaker noted the high-risk countries in Latin America as Colombia, Mexico, Brazil, and Costa Rica. Another speaker, a Pinkerton executive, said that recent studies showed that 90 percent of kidnappings take place in the morning, often as the target drives to work.

"The success rate for negotiated release of kidnapping victims is over 95 percent," the Pinkerton executive said. "The real danger in kidnappings is in the first few minutes of the thing going down, something happening that even the kidnappers do not want to happen."

In Washington, D.C., in March, Ambassador Philip Wilcox, Jr., coordinator for counterterrorism in the U.S. State Department, delivered a speech about international terrorism to the House Appropriations Subcommittee on Commerce, Justice, and State. "The picture is mixed," he said, "and a clear trend is difficult to discern. Statistics suggest that international terrorism is declining, since the number of incidents had dropped from a high of 665 in 1987 to less than 300 in the past year. One explanation for this drop is the end of the Cold War and the sharp decline in revolutionary Marxism."

Still, he said, U.S. interests abroad were being targeted "disproportionately" by terrorists and criminals. In some cases the groups were out of the control of any governments. They were funded in mysterious ways, he said. "Freelance Islamic elements are a much tougher target for intelligence and law enforcement than state-sponsored terrorism and previously known organized groups. Their sources of funding are difficult to trace." Those who followed the kidnapping trends worldwide and who read or heard Wilcox's speech suspected immediately that kidnapping was one of those "difficult-to-trace" sources. At the same time, the very same forces that Wilcox mentioned as mitigating the threat of political terrorism, "the end of the Cold War and the decline in revolutionary Marxism," had clearly enhanced the kidnapping threat. And while there were fewer terrorists perpetrating the crime, there were more former terrorists and other displaced warriors utilizing its implacable powers.

By spring, businessmen on the islands of Trinidad and Tobago were suddenly targets of kidnappers in a new trend that perplexed both government and police officials. In Taiwan, too, a spate of kidnappings was spreading fear through communities, especially among business executives. The abduction of a well-known actress's daughter was drawing attention to a problem that had been slowly increasing behind the scenes in the past few years. When the kidnappers sent the seventeen-year-old girl's finger through the mail to her mother, the local presses dredged up all sorts of kidnap stories, many previously unreported. The press played up the angle that Taiwan could soon overtake the Philippines as the Asian kidnap capital. Some said that executives of foreign companies were targets. One article quoted the Ministry of Justice saying that in 1996, 216 people had been prosecuted for kidnappings, a 52 percent rise over 1992. One American executive of a top U.S. company told *Business Times,* "It is becoming more like Manila every day. My company is now guarding the homes of executives around the clock."

One of the newest hot spots was Russia, where kidnapping, as well as other crimes, had been slowly escalating throughout the 1990s. "Many experts fear that the former Soviet Union will become a breeding ground for acts of corporate terrorism including kidnapping and commercial extortion. . . . The possibility that organized crime could turn to abduction and ransom to raise hard currency is frightening, to say the least," *Risk Management* magazine reported in 1994. By 1997, the threat had become a reality, especially for foreign businessmen. And the problem was particularly acute in Chechnya.

After fighting a twenty-month war for independence from Russia, the republic, which considered itself an independent state, was more dangerous than ever, with rogue bands of armed fighters operating out of the control of Chechen authorities. The *Moscow Times* quoted a Russian official as saying, "The problem is that in the wake of the war too many criminal groups are looking for a profitable line of business." In the impoverished, war-torn land, some kidnappers were seeking money just to survive. Others were trying to raise funds to resume their war against Russia; the same groups were demanding billions of dollars in war reparations from Russia. It was believed, too, that some kidnappers emanated from Russia with the goal of ruining the reputation of the new separatist government.

"Kidnapping has become an epidemic in Russia, soon perhaps to rival Colombia," said Guy Dunn, the Russia specialist at CRG. "It's affecting Russians, but also foreigners. Since mid-1996, there have been sixty-three foreigners abducted there. The demands are small, relative to other parts of the world, an average perhaps of $100,000 to $500,000."

The problem for the rest of the world, said Dunn, is that Chechnya could be one of the routes used to transport oil out of the Caspian Sea region. At the same time, there are huge projects to rebuild Chechnya, and foreign companies are winning the contracts. And there is always the threat that the heavily armed bandits could easily move over the border into Turkey.

"It's really the most dramatic kidnapping story of 1997 so far," said Dunn, late that spring. "And although it seems very far away, it's an example of what we see now in the world, the internationalization of a local conflict."

An early 1997 intelligence report issued by the London office of Kroll speculated about kidnappings in the year ahead. "There are serious concerns for the future. Where peace breaks out, foreign businesses and agencies are keen to make the most of business opportunities, whether they be diamond mining in Angola or oil transit in Chechnya. In Nicaragua, El Salvador, Honduras, Angola, Sierra Leone, and Chechnya—to name just a few—peace agreements between rebel groups and governments have left thousands of youths, skilled only in violence, without any means of supporting themselves. Many will become involved in drug trafficking and related criminal activity; others will take to kidnap and ransom as a relatively lucrative means of income.

"Two big emerging markets—Russia and India—are not only offering opportunities to legitimate investors. Crime syndicates flourish in both countries. Ransoms to the tune of 1.1 million pounds

[$1.87 million] are nothing out of the ordinary in India. With more than 1,000 kidnappings in Russia in 1996, expatriates will increasingly be exposed to the risk of abduction and ransom."

Meanwhile, crime-stopping efforts trudged onward. In the Philippines, where kidnappings were occurring at a rate of one every forty-eight hours, a judge sentenced three men to death for kidnapping a fourteen-year-old boy and killing him after collecting a ransom of 1.5 million pesos ($57,700). "Kidnap Watch," a joint project of the Movement for the Restoration of Peace and Order and the Citizens Action Against Crime (CAAC), reported fifty kidnap victims in the Philippines during the first two months of 1997, in which at least 31 million pesos (about $1.6 million) in ransoms had been paid. The problem was escalating faster than anyone had predicted. At least 199 people—some at beach resorts on the southern Philippine island of Mindanao—were seized in 1996, with kidnappers reaping approximately $3.8 million for the year. The CAAC and the local Chamber of Commerce implored the national police to take more steps against the crime, including public executions of kidnappers and the creation of an emergency police hot line devoted exclusively to kidnapping incidents. At the same time, on Mindanao, the government admitted that the police had lost the war against kidnappers and that the problem had become a matter of national security demanding the aid of armed forces. Despite a truce between the government and the Moro National Liberation Front in 1996, kidnap gangs led by renegade guerrillas were ravaging the land.

In China, fifteen convicted kidnappers, who collectively had extorted 440,000 yuan, or $53,000, in ransoms in 1995 and 1996—and had killed one hostage—were executed before a crowd of more than 10,000 people. In Colombia, based on the theory that arrests and prosecutions were the best deterrents, there were now 2,000 Colombian government agents focusing on the kidnapping problem.

In Costa Rica, on March 21, in a rather high-profile trial, the former contra rebel who kidnapped Susana Siegfried and Nicole Fleuchaus in 1996 was sentenced to thirty years in prison. At the trial, the defense made the claim that the kidnapper, Julio César Vega, and one hostage, Fleuchaus, were in collusion. To support the argument, photos of the rebel and Fleuchaus kissing were submitted as evidence. But the three-judge tribunal dismissed the photos as proof of nothing more than the well-known Stockholm Syndrome.

In London, on March 26, George Fraghistas, the Greek shipping heir abducted the year before, wept as he listened to Judge Simon Goldstein announce the terms of prison for the four men who had imprisoned him in a cupboard for nine horrific days. The judge described the lead kidnapper who had devised the abduction scheme as "the most evil and dangerous man" he had ever met. The kidnapper had continued his scheming in the courtroom by twisting the incident into a diabolical plot instigated by the victim himself. Fraghistas, the kidnapper claimed throughout the trial, had faked the kidnapping to pay off gambling debts. The judge clearly didn't buy this theory, nor did the jury, which convicted the four men on all counts. Outside the court, Fraghistas told reporters: "The worst part was having to go through it a second time in court. I am so emotional now because of the stress of all of it. Now I can get used to the idea that they will be away for twenty-five years and I can live my life again."

In April, during the last two weeks, two resolutions, a rescue in Peru and a swap in Texas, sent mixed messages to the world at large about the best ways to gain the release of hostages—though both effectively were victories for those who championed the psychological weapon of negotiation.

On April 22, a highly trained SWAT team—140 strong—closed in on the fourteen guerrillas of the Tupac Amaru Revolutionary Movement, and in exactly sixteen minutes, the team rescued seventy-one of the seventy-two hostages held for four months at the residence of the Japanese ambassador in Lima. In one of the most successful rescues in the history of kidnappings, only one hostage died: Supreme Court Justice Carlos Giusti, of a heart attack after being shot in the leg during the raid. The rebels were all shot to death. Some were even decapitated. It was hard to control the zeal of rescue teams, one official said later. No one had instructed the team to brutally kill the rebels, but such violent images of the demise of those who dare to kidnap might be an effective deterrent to future kidnappings, some officials said at the time. Others feared the ramifications of such violence. Still, for a moment, President Alberto Fujimori, Peru's get-tough leader who firmly believed that poverty did not lead to terrorism, but rather terrorism was a cause of poverty, looked like a hero. Here was a man who had been patient enough to wait until 140 men were expertly trained for a nearly perfect rescue, and he had been decisive when it was time for the team to attack. But while the spotlight kept a narrow focus on the decisive and patient Fujimori and on the power of a rescue mission to end a hostage ordeal, people behind the scenes knew that negotiation had played a considerable role in delivering a successful outcome.

From the start of the Peruvian crisis, which began on December 17 of the previous year, dozens of kidnap negotiators, from both the private and public sectors, had flown into Lima to advise their clients and governments. The private sector experts were there representing numerous businessmen taken hostage. Both Kroll and Control Risks had their representatives. CRG began with six negotiators, one assigned to each of six clients with employees in captivity. With several of the hostages freed by the early part of the year, two negotiators departed. The remaining four rotated in and out of Lima until the April resolution.

"It was a veritable convention of kidnap consultants," said one negotiator who attended. Every company with an employee in captivity had at least one consultant or negotiator. And those who gained their freedom early were swapped for ransoms. And then there were the government agencies' hostage experts, from such places as the FBI and Scotland Yard.

But the crucial importance of negotiators was the role they played in advising the Peruvian government and the headstrong Fujimori, cautioning him to be patient above all. It was the power of negotiation that had kept the seventy-two hostages alive long enough to plan a rescue involving such intense projects as the construction of a model residence to allow the troops to practice over and over until their approach was indeed nearly perfect. Negotiation slowly, tediously, and effectively wore down the rebels, making them more and more vulnerable to a tactical move. At the same time, during the months leading up to the rescue, the government, from the intelligence gained throughout the negotiations, learned the daily habits of the rebels, their psychological states, and such useful details as the rooms where the hostages were typically kept at various times each day. "We learned a great deal from charting the times of day the rebels wanted to talk, where they were when they talked, where their buddies were when they talked, where the phones were located, when they ate," said one negotiator who was there. "Things like this helped a lot in the long-term planning for the rescue. Because of continued talks with the MRTA, it was possible, for example, to detect the fact that they were beginning to get a bit slack in their habits. There was a break after the rebels determined that there were tunnels being constructed beneath the residence. But they never found the tunnels, so the building of the tunnels continued and the talks resumed. All this, you see, allowed for this mirror facility, a compound duplicated on the model of the real one, to be built. What negotiation allows is time for whatever authorities want to do: investigate, plan a rescue, build a model, whatever can be done behind the scenes to effect a successful release. It also provides up-to-date reassurances and proof that the hostages are still alive.

"Negotiation just doesn't have that sexy, action-movie drama that rescues have. But it's the backbone of a solid rescue, believe me on that, for one very simple reason: the longer you have to prepare a rescue the more successful it will be. If they had stormed the residence in December, it was possible that three-quarters of the hostages would have been killed."

The headlines and news stories, for the most part, ignored the negotiations behind the scenes. Fujimori was the man of the moment, and military aggression had reigned supreme as the way to deal with terrorists, in this case hostage-takers. However, the *Washington Post,* in an editorial on April 24 entitled "Amazing Feat in Peru," took notice: "In hostage takings, it is always tempting to speculate on alternative strategies and their likely consequences. In this case President Fujimori prepared two courses, negotiation and attack. He gave the first a reasonable chance including an offer to the guerrillas of safe passage outside Peru. Having used the time to make meticulous preparations, he then moved to the second."

While Peru was still commanding attention in the world press, in the mountains of West Texas, another hostage incident came to an end in quite a different way. On Sunday April 27, in Fort Davis, Texas, members of the Republic of Texas separatists, a group claiming Texas is still an independent nation because its annexation was illegal, burst into the home of a Texas couple, firing guns, wounding the husband, and taking the couple into captivity. The separatists were locked in a land dispute with the couple, whom they accused of reporting their activities to law enforcement officials. Their demand: the release of a jailed member of their group. The next day, officials did indeed swap the jailed separatist for the hostages. The community of no-negotiations/no-concessions purists was stunned, but several voices of reason came forward to explain why this was an intelligent move. For one, Clint Van Zandt, the FBI's former chief hostage negotiator, told the *New York Times* on April 29, "It's not normally done but in this particular case, knowing what I do about what they're dealing with out there, it's not a bad decision."

The incident was a lesson in why flexibility in formulating ways to deal with terrorist incidents was crucial. The swap freed the hostages unharmed, while depriving the militants of the one thing that drew the attention of the press and gave them power. Jerrold Post, the director of the political psychology department at George Washington University, told the *New York Times*, in the same piece: "You can look at these kinds of groups as conducting psychological warfare, with their major goal being to gain prominence and recognition. One really needs to counter such groups not with Delta Forces and military might, which just proves to them that we really are out to destroy them, but to counter psychological warfare with psychological warfare."

Eventually, the hostage-takers were arrested, convicted on various charges, and sentenced to very long prison terms, ranging from fifty to ninety-nine years. In both cases, in Peru and in Texas, the impact of the resolution strategies remained unknown. It was unclear whether the violent murders of the MRTA would compel the few remnants of the group—very few, and mostly in Europe—to regroup and exact revenge. And in Texas, experts were watching to see if the swap would inspire more domestic militants to take hostages.

Toward the end of May, another American hostage, this time along the central Pacific coast of Mexico, took the risk that few hostages have dared to take—that incredible plunge into the unknown. He escaped.

37

MAY 1997
ON THE PACIFIC COAST
OF MEXICO

Stuart Havenstrite was resting near the banks of a reservoir in one of Mexico's most popular resort regions, the central Pacific coast of the state of Michoacán. It was about 10 P.M., and a full moon shone above him as bright as a lantern's beam. Roughly twelve miles away (twenty kilometers), was the town where Havenstrite was staying, Lazaro Cardenas, situated between the two beach resort towns of Playa Azul and Ixtapa. About fifty feet away, at the shore of the reservoir, called the Presa de los Infiernillos, or "Gateway to Hell," were Havenstrite's kidnappers. Alone for the first time in thirty-six hours of captivity, Havenstrite was contemplating escape.

Thus far, the sixty-five-year-old American from Salt Lake City had been an ideal hostage. He never moved without permission. He walked when his captors said walk. And he agreed to call home and arrange for ransom money to be sent. In less than two days, good behavior had compelled his kidnappers to change the way they addressed him: from "hombre" to "amigo." Now it appeared they were trusting their new "amigo," leaving him alone above the reservoir banks, where he lay on his back, as he often had done to ease the pain of a sore hip after walking with his captors along miles of roads and trails. He had three kidnapper-guards, not counting the leader, who appeared periodically to check on the progress of the case. Perhaps the leader had other kidnappers to supervise, thought Havenstrite.

For the past several hours, Havenstrite and the three armed men had climbed out of a small valley that cradled the reservoir to follow trails in search of a road they were told would lead them to Lazaro Cardenas. There they planned to find a phone to call Havenstrite's wife. They would assure her that he was alive, and then arrange some sort of deal for the ransom money. But so far they had been wandering along roads that led only into more roads or tangled, unwieldy thickets of brush. Their hostage was tired, and although they were far younger than he, the series of dead-end roads was wearing them down. Besides their heavy guns, they had been taking turns carrying Havenstrite's heavy briefcase, which resembled a doctor's satchel and contained his wallet with $400, credit cards, driver's license, passport, work visa, Spanish-English dictionary, and many papers relevant to the work that had led him to this very beautiful part of Mexico.

Havenstrite runs a geological consulting business, HMS, out of Salt Lake City, and he is a director of Nevada Star Resource Corporation, a Vancouver-based Canadian mining company. He and two other men from Nevada Star were conducting a core-drilling project at La Virgen Copper Mine ten kilometers (seven miles) outside Lazaro Cardenas. They had been working at the site for a week when the kidnapping occurred—at about 9 A.M. on May 20. While the other fellows typically arrived at the site between 7 A.M. and 8 A.M., riding together in a pickup truck owned by the company president, Havenstrite was in the habit of driving alone, in his rented car, and arriving at about 9.

Havenstrite would say later: "I opened the trunk of the car to extract my field gear and was immediately set upon by two screaming young Mexican men armed with pistols. They attempted to force me into the small trunk of the car; however, in the hot climate at La Virgen I would have been literally cooked within a half hour, and so I resisted. Thinking that their objective was to steal the car, I took the keys from my pocket and threw them on the ground while I continued to struggle with the men. This did not deter them. Then a third man joined the first two, also armed with a pistol, and the three of them forced me into the back seat of the car."

After driving about two miles, the young men abandoned the car to walk the rest of the way to the reservoir, where they waited for a boat to take them to their hideout. At that time, the lead captor, who spoke *some* English, and Havenstrite, who spoke *some* Spanish, tried to converse. "Muerto?" Havenstrite asked the leader, meaning, Were they going to murder him? "No," the kidnapper said. "Dinero," meaning they wanted money. And then he used his hands to communicate that if Havenstrite tried to escape, he would be shot.

It was after this conversation that Havenstrite realized he was not the victim of a robbery, nor would he necessarily be killed. It was abundantly clear now that he had been kidnapped. Now it made sense that the men didn't shoot him when he so ardently resisted their plan to stuff him in the trunk of his small rental car. Later, in his report to the FBI, Havenstrite wrote: "I did not have two facts which I would learn later: that kidnappings were common in the area and that white men are usually not harmed if the ransom is paid."

What he also did not know was that the Popular Revolutionary Army (EPR), which had first surfaced in June 1996 in Michoacán's neighbor state, Guerrero, was moving into the western and northern parts of the country, particularly in the states of Michoacán and Nayarit. While Havenstrite's captors appeared to be common bandits, they easily could have been working for the EPR, helping to fill the rebels' war chests with ransom funds.

In 1997, there had already been numerous kidnappings in nearby Guadalajara. Most were Mexican targets, though a few had been foreigners, including an Israeli businessman and the daughter of an American couple. Held for thirty-nine days in a ramshackle house in a Guadalajara suburb, the Israeli man was freed by a mercenary "troubleshooter" from New York City. The police were not called into the case, which was not uncommon. The five-year-old American girl, kidnapped about twenty-five miles outside of Guadalajara, was still in captivity that May. Abductions of foreigners were clearly rising throughout Mexico, though the tally was far, far less than the kidnappings of Mexicans. Americans had rarely been targeted prior to 1994; the first American to be snatched that year was likely in October when a businessman was taken outside his picture frame factory near Tijuana and returned two days later after the payment of a six-figure ransom.

Two hours after Havenstrite's abduction, at about 11 A.M., on May 21, he and his captors arrived, by boat, at their campsite. Based on the sounds, Havenstrite knew that the small, rock-strewn clearing had to be near a railroad and a trail frequently used by either wild horses or people on horseback. He was not blindfolded, but he dared not look at his captors, a habit that he knew could save his life. At the camp, he asked the lead captor how long they would be there, and the answer was "a long time." The man then asked him if he was rich. Havenstrite replied, "Mi familia non rico." But he assured the kidnapper that he had ample credit cards and that if they took him to the bank in Lazaro, he could retrieve 3,000 pesos, or $400, out of the ATM. The kidnapper seemed uninterested.

By late afternoon, a new man appeared on the scene, with a pistol and a semiautomatic rifle, just like the others. But this one had a confident swagger that the others lacked. Slightly older than the others, who were in their teens and early twenties, this man was their leader. Havenstrite asked him if this was a "sequestrada," and the man said yes. He was asking $500,000 for Havenstrite's safe return, he said. The Utah man, who had five children and eight grandchildren, paused for a moment, shook his head, and said that he was not a wealthy man. He had only $15,000, though perhaps he could borrow $10,000 more. The leader asked Havenstrite for his Utah phone numbers, and then he left.

Later, Havenstrite would learn that the leader had called his home and had spoken with his wife, who wisely said she would not negotiate with her husband's captors until she had proof that he was alive.

The static-filled conversation between Georgia Havenstrite and the Mexican kidnapper, who was calling from a roadside telephone booth, had proceeded as follows:

Kidnapper: Hello.

Georgia: Hello.

K: Who, who is this?

G: Who is this?

K: Oh, you are the wife of Havenstrite?

G: Yes.

K: Do you know what happened?

G: No, what happened?

K: I got your husband.

G: What are you doing with him?

K: I want riscote [ransom] 500,000.

G: 500,000 what?

K: Yes.

G: I'm sorry I can't hear you.

K: 500,000.

G: 500,000 dollars? Pesos?

K: Yes.

G: Who are you?

K: Somebody.

G: How do I know how to get a hold of you?

K: You got the money?

G: Do I *have* the money?

K: Yes.

G: I will get the money.

K: Okay. Do you know where he is working?

G: No, I do not know where he is working.

K: He is working in Michoacán.

G: Mich-o-wa-cán.

K: Yes.

G: Where is that? In Mexico?

K: Yes.

G: All right.

K: When you get the money, you come to Michoacán.

G: How do I get it to you?

K: Oh, okay. Hold on, okay?

G: How do I know that you have him?

K: Oh, that's another problem.

G: I need to talk to him.

K: To who?

G: To my husband.

K: He can't talk to you.

G: Why not?

K: Because I got him.

G: You what?

K: Don't worry. I got him. I got your husband, so hold on, okay?

G: What is my husband's boat's name?

K: Huh?

G: Ask my husband what his boat's name is.

K: What?

G: What is the name of his boat?

K: I got your telephone number. He gave it to me.

G: Tell me the name of his boat.

K: Salt Lake City, Utah.

G: No, the name of my husband's boat. I need to know the name of his boat.

K: Okay, hold on. I'm going to get it on the paper, have him sign a paper, and put it in the mile [mail] for you. Okay?

G: No, it isn't okay. What is your name?

K: Okay, I'll call you back later. He's going to mile [mail] to you.

G: And I want you to call back later and give me the name of our boat.

K: Okay.

G: And you call back later.

After the call, the leader returned to the camp, and this time brought Havenstrite his watch, which one of the captors had ripped from him in the early moments of the abduction. Havenstrite fastened the watch around the lean trunk of a tiny tree, as a gesture of generosity so that the rebels too could check the time.

Toward dusk, the lead captor smoothed out a place on the ground, where Havenstrite spent his first night in captivity. The next morning, the same man asked Havenstrite if he could possibly get that $15,000 over the phone. And of course, knowing that any exposure outside the camp would be beneficial, the hostage said yes. But nothing happened on this slower-than-slow day. At 7 P.M., a boat pulled up to the dock near the campsite and the captors stuffed Havenstrite into the bottom, this time blindfolding him. After an hour or so, they deboarded to begin their quest to find the road to Lazaro Cardenas.

Now, as he lay alone along the "Gateway to Hell" reservoir, Havenstrite thought it had been just about three hours since they had left the campsite. He had left his watch on the little tree, but he surmised that it must be nearly 10 P.M. He looked up at the rocky hillside that he and his captors had just descended. He was certain that his captors were confident that their hostage, whose sciatica condition seemed to be worsening the longer they walked, would never even consider climbing back up the trails. These were, after all, trails that seemed to lead to nowhere.

Havenstrite pondered the idea of escaping for no more than a minute. Then he bolted. He ran as fast as he could up the hill, the path seeming to unroll beneath his stride. At an overview that he had spotted on the way down, he stopped and hid. From there, he could hear a boat's motor and then the sound of men coming toward the hill. They called for him and shouted at each other as they poked through the thicket in search of their valuable prey—a man whose courage they had clearly underestimated. Eventually, they returned to the boat.

After it appeared safe to move, Havenstrite decided he would try again to find the trail to the road and to the town or at least to a phone. And so he climbed farther up the trail than he had gone with his captors. But the higher he climbed, the more obstructive the vegetation became and the more he suffered from dehydration. Still unable to find the trail, he began to climb down again. By 3 A.M., he was back at the reservoir, where he was able to at least quench his thirst with the tepid, impure Gatesway to Hell water. He would later be able to pinpoint the event with a time because at 2:53 A.M. as he walked down the trail, there was an earthquake in the area (registering 6.5 on the Richter scale).

At this point, Havenstrite believed he had four choices: (1) to flag down a train and ride out of the area of danger (the section of rail nearby was between two tunnels and so the train would be moving at a slower than usual pace); (2) to search for the still-elusive road to Lazaro Cardenas; (3) to find a boat and pilot willing to take him to Lazaro Cardenas; (4) to walk down the track to Lazaro Cardenas.

His first choice was to flag a train. Using materials from his briefcase, which he had painfully carried since the escape, he made a sign on the back of a geological map with black magic marker. "Yo soy Americano sequestra," he wrote. (I am a kidnapped American.) And then he waited by the tracks, like a hobo waiting for a ride. At about 5 A.M., the train chugged toward the exhausted, anxious Utah grandfather. He waved his sign, but the train, moving at about twenty-five miles per hour, did not slow down. As it rounded the curve toward the tunnel and its roar began to fade, Havenstrite heard the motor of a boat. His first thought was that it was the kidnappers. And it was. He darted again into the hills, this time leaving his briefcase near the tracks.

Havenstrite hid in the brush-covered hills until first light and then ran to one of the houses along the ravine leading to the reservoir. He awakened a family, all of whom appeared to be afraid of him. But after he explained his plight, the man of the house agreed to show him the road to Lazaro Cardenas. For two hours, he climbed along the trail the man had so carefully described, only to discover a hub of many more trails. He had no idea which one to choose and was too exhausted to risk taking another road leading nowhere. And so he headed back along the same trails, trying to think as he fought the now-extreme fatigue.

As he neared the base of the hill, he noticed a man, woman, and child watching him. Now *he* was afraid. But the man approached him and politely invited him to luncheon with his family. Freshly caught perch was the fare. The man had just returned from a morning fishing expedition in his boat. Havenstrite was very pleased with the invitation, the graciousness of the family, and, most of all perhaps, the fact that the family owned a boat. He decided he must trust them and proceeded to tell them of his plight. He explained that he would be very grateful if the man would take him to Lazaro Cardenas in his boat but warned that it was very dangerous. Havenstrite offered him $300 for his trouble.

The man agreed to take him, but only after what turned out to be a long, stressful luncheon. While they were eating the perch, the man left the table to speak with another man, who then quickly departed in the boat, supposedly to fish for a while. Havenstrite feared that the fisherman and his family were somehow associated with his captors. Perhaps he had sent the other man to bargain with them, to "sell" Havenstrite back to them. But he was wrong. The fisherman, sensing Havenstrite's tension and his despair, showed him his driver's license and voter registration card as if to demonstrate his credibility. His name was Gilberto, and he was not in any way related to the bandidos. His friend was indeed borrowing the boat to fish for an hour or so. They did this every day of the week.

After lunch, with Havenstrite sequestered at the bottom of the boat, Gilberto motored thirty minutes along the western shore of the reservoir to a dam. There he and Havenstrite met up with a friend of Gilberto's, a woman who knew the way to Guacamayas, a town where there would be a phone. She agreed to take the two men in her pickup truck to this, the nearest town. On the way, Havenstrite decided it was much wiser to drive the extra miles into Lazaro Cardenas right to his hotel. There he would be able to get money to pay Gilberto, and his ordeal would be over, he hoped. The woman agreed, but the ride to his hotel was nearly as frightening as the ordeal itself. The brakes of her truck barely worked. On many a curve, Havenstrite could see his life flashing before him and a cross erected over the edge of a cliff at the site of a car crash, as he had so often seen in the hills and along the switchbacks of Mexico.

At 11 A.M. on May 22, the truck arrived at the entrance to the Jacaranda Hotel. Fifty hours after the kidnapping, Havenstrite at long last saw a familiar face: Jim Sanders, one of his Nevada Star colleagues. Havenstrite paid Gilberto $400 for his help and gave the woman $100 for new brakes. He immediately filed a police report, then flew to Mexico City, where two FBI agents briefed him. After spending the night at the Aeropuerto Hotel, he flew to Salt Lake City. His wife, five children, and five of his eight grandchildren welcomed him home. At that time he learned that about twenty FBI agents were on the case, out of Salt Lake City, Miami, and Mexico City. And later Havenstrite would discover that a close friend of the family, who was in the mining business in Mexico and had some knowledge of kidnappings and negotiations, had phoned a Control Risks consultant to seek preliminary advice, which he had passed along to Havenstrite's wife.

Two of the kidnappers were later arrested. The leader was never found. As for Havenstrite, although his body was covered with cuts and abrasions from climbing and hiking, he recovered quickly, with the immense satisfaction that he had indeed escaped. Gilberto eventually found the briefcase along the railroad tracks and sent it to Havenstrite. And so, like a tale out of O. Henry, the kidnappers gained nothing—not even his watch, which may still be dangling from the branches of a small tree, moving in the gentle breezes of Mexico's famed Pacific coast.

38

The advent of summer inspired a fresh batch of alluring travel articles and ads, some flashing a bright light on parts of the world where there were still corners of darkness. Travel to Turkey was widely advertised in major U.S. newspapers by mid-June, though the month had begun with a widely disseminated statement from the Kurdistan Workers' Party (PKK) saying that the PKK was planning to attack tourist centers in Turkey. A spokesman for the group warned potential travelers of the dangers of vacationing in Turkey. On the Internet, on June 2, Pinkerton's Global Risk Assessment printed the PKK statement, adding that "according to Reuters, the group plans to attack US and Israeli targets in Istanbul, Turkey's largest city, and elsewhere in Turkey."

The PKK separatists had been fighting a war for autonomy for almost thirteen years. While the warning, coming as it did from the separatists themselves, clearly was a tactic to drive away tourism dollars from the coffers of the Turkish government, the threat was, nonetheless, a real one—as real as the threat to travelers in war-torn Kashmir. One State Department staffer said that June: "Is there a Jane and Don couple preparing for a trekking trip to Turkey this summer? Probably. Will they get kidnapped? It's a game of Russian roulette, as it was in Kashmir that summer. Probably not. But then, the probability of Jane and Don getting kidnapped was low, too. Many people had hiked in Kashmir that summer and the summer before, but few visitors were kidnapped. The problem is that the threat exists, and everyone should be aware of it. You can't censor destinations, unless of course they are terribly dangerous overall, like Algeria, for example. But somehow, and the State Department tries to do this, people must know that there are dangers and that in the world today the areas of danger can change very, very quickly.

"In Kashmir, for example, the likelihood of an American getting kidnapped was much greater in 1995 than in, say, 1992 or 1993, largely because of the influx of Afghani mercenaries who were trained to do this sort of thing and who were trying to escalate the war and transform it into a fight for the unification of Kashmir with Pakistan, rather than the local fight headed by Kashmiris for autonomy alone.

"Yes, Turkey is dangerous. No, Turkey is not dangerous. It all depends on what month you are talking about and what region you are going to. If you go to Beirut, will you have a problem? No. If you go to southern Lebanon? Yes. The problem is that if you are traveling today, you check and recheck, just to be sure. The government tries to keep up."

Venezuela was another popular destination that summer, if ads and articles were any indication of popularity. An article in the travel section of the *New York Times* in June began: "These days the environmentally friendly style of travel called eco-tourism is all the rage, especially in Venezuela." The article described a ranch in northern Venezuela, which has hosted the visits of biologists, naturalists, and students from all over the world for more than a decade. To be sure, that particular ranch and its 300 square miles could offer dazzling spectacles of wildlife without a single incident of crime to ruin its stellar reputation. But there were other ranches slightly to the west of this one that were close to points of danger, too close perhaps to the Colombian border to be considered safe, or dangerous enough to merit a note of caution. And with the privatization of Venezuela's oil industry luring more foreigners as well as more Colombian guerrillas to Venezuela by the summer of 1997, the nation was not exactly a worry-free zone for travelers.

By that summer, Control Risks Group's tally of kidnappings that the firm could confirm in Venezuela for the first half of 1997 was sixteen, as compared with five the year before. Of the captives, a third were foreigners, and all but two were abducted in the northern and western sectors, mostly on ranches and farms. On February 20 that year, the *El Globo* newspaper in Venezuela announced that in the previous seven weeks there had been eighteen abductions. This was not a huge problem, but it could become one. And right next door, in Colombia, there had been at least 317 kidnappings in the first half of 1997, CRG's records showed.

Guatemala was also on the hit parade of ecotourism destinations. With the country officially at peace, as of December 29, 1996, the Mayan ruins under the canopy of many square miles of rain forests— off limits during the war—were suddenly accessible once again. By spring, new hotels were under construction, and government officials were anticipating at least a 20 percent annual increase in foreign visitors. Bird-watchers, anthropologists, Mayan aficionados—of which there are many—and trekkers alike were booking flights to return after many years or to venture there for the first time. One tourism company offered a package that included a trekking trip from Honduras to Guatemala, hiking through remote jungle areas and crossing the border overland into rain forests previously inaccessible to trekkers because of the war. And by summer, just about every travel magazine and newspaper travel section in the United States had done a feature about the "new" Guatemala. "Back from the Dead: Mayan Guatemala Rises Again," read one headline.

But as everyone who knew anything about the aftermath of civil wars knew, Guatemala was not yet the perfect vacation spot. "The armed conflicts left behind psychological scars and violent attitudes," Frank La Rue, a Guatemalan political analyst, told the *Financial Times*. "They also left large numbers of unemployed people carrying guns."

Travel pieces in two publications that summer, the *New York Times* and *Escape* magazine, gave the reader a hint of problems that might exist in a country releasing thousands upon thousands of soldiers from duty. Two, sometimes three, generations in the same family had fought this war. "The rebels are handing in their guns. The government is mothballing death squads," began the *Escape* article. "But will there be peace?" the author asked later, as if to warn the reader that all was not perfect yet in Guatemala. The *Times* piece bore the headline "At Peace, Guatemala Is Ready for Visitors." But it also warned: "Though the danger of getting caught in the crossfire between guerrillas and army troops no longer exists, Guatemalan Army forces are being withdrawn from some areas of the countryside where they have traditionally constituted the only public security force. As a result, criminals have moved to fill the vacuum."

⋖≥×≼⋗

By summer, CRG was working six cases: two in Brazil, one in Panama, one in Colombia, one in Guatemala, and one in the Philippines. It had begun the year with five new cases: one in China, two in Colombia, and two in Mexico, in addition to four ongoing cases in Colombia and Mexico. This was in contrast to a total of two ongoing cases and no new cases in a comparable period in 1996. Bob Dwyer was on permanent retainer at Kroll, which by summer's end was planning to merge with an armored-car manufacturer. The legal dispute between Tom Hargrove and the people hired to gain his release was settled out of court, for an undisclosed amount. And there was no new word on Christopher Howes, Jerel Shaffer, the three American missionaries missing since 1993, the geologist from Philadelphia, Frank Skee, or Hutchings, Wells, Mangan, and Hasert, not to mention dozens of other hostages in captivity worldwide.

Roy Ramm, meanwhile, had resigned his post at Scotland Yard, an utter shock to many with whom he had worked. After twenty-seven years as a cop—a top cop—it was not an easy decision. But Ramm could see where his life was heading. His skills and age were leading him onto that irreversible track as an administrator, which meant little time for fieldwork. With all his responsibilities, with all the hats he wore, it was increasingly difficult for him to spend time in the field. And if he did, he paid the price when he returned to an office full of papers and people requiring attention. He knew himself well enough to recognize that if he denied himself the satisfaction of working cases, he would envy the very people who reported to him. It was time to move on.

He would now be a director for London Clubs International, PLC, a job that ironically would take him back to former war zones and other locales where he had traveled as a cop. Now he would promote the interests of his company, which, like so many others, was trying to compete in the emerging international markets of the 1990s. He would utilize that diplomacy that had served him so well as a hostage negotiator to arrange deals in foreign lands, devising strategies in contract negotiations to keep his company within the laws of Great Britain while giving it enough of an edge to win the contract. In other words, he would make deals without partaking in the sometimes bribe-filled atmosphere of international competition.

But in his heart, he was still a cop, a seasoned, thick-skinned, high-level cop with a sardonic wit and a penchant for storytelling. For a very long time, Ramm would carry with him the images of Cambodia, of Kashmir, of the men who had not walked free. There was the unfinished business of Christopher Howes, which would nibble and nag at the edges of his mind. And by the second anniversary of the hostage-taking in Kashmir, there was still a photo in his wallet, tucked between the various identification cards that revealed his new career. A remnant of his old life, it was a color photo of four men: the prisoners of Al-Faran.

39

One May night in 1997, Jane had just climbed the winding redwood stairs from her garden to the sunroom. As she stood at the expanse of windows looking out at the work she had just completed, the flowers, luminous under the light of a full moon, seemed like dozens of twinkling lights. Suddenly, she heard a rustling in the front of the house. Remembering that she had not locked the front door, she ran toward it, with Bodhi and Homer barking at her side. There, struggling with a heavily loaded backpack and looking very tired, was a thin, unshaven man with very scraggly hair and that unforgettable smile.

"Don," she said, as she tried to wipe the dirt from her hands and clothes.

"I'm sorry I'm late," he said, still smiling. "But I ate the burned meat and it made me very sick."

"It's OK," she said, as she embraced him.

A dream. Only a dream. But it was the first dream Jane had had in which Don had come to her alive and well. It was far better than the one in which a parcel came through the mail from Kashmir and she opened it only to find his frozen, amputated foot. Certainly it was more pleasant than the one in which she was sitting on a staircase with a terrorist who was holding a knife to her throat. This was a dream that seemed so very real in the few moments preceding wakefulness when life seems dreamlike and dreams seem lifelike. But it was only a dream.

In Spokane that spring, the friends of Jane and Don spoke of hope. Conversations about their faraway friend always began in the present tense. "Don likes to say . . ." "His favorite joke *is* . . ." "He *is* so smart, so fit . . ." But then, engrossed in thought as they recalled events and told favorite "Don" stories, they lapsed unconsciously into the past tense, into the language of eulogies. While everyone hoped, few truly believed. But Buddy McManus was a true believer.

"Don is alive. I know it. I feel it," the Spokane pediatrician said in early summer 1997. "I believe he is in Pakistan somewhere, living in a house perhaps, but still in captivity. They are waiting to use him to get something they want, something in the pursuit of Kashmir. After such a long time, and such a buildup, imagine the power in still holding even one of the hostages. There was no point in killing them, but there is a point in keeping him or them alive. I have a very strong instinct that I will see him walk through this door someday. I just hope his psychological recovery is not too difficult; I hope he hasn't changed too much."

The case itself had changed very little, if at all, by 1997. The late August conversation with Don in 1995 was still the last official proof-of-life, and since the end of November that year there had been no confirmed contacts with the elusive Al-Faran. A steady rhythm of ups and downs continued, though less jolting perhaps and certainly slower moving than during the first six months of the ordeal. A roller coaster on low speed. But a ride that seemed neverending.

Sightings still trickled out of the Kashmir Valley, some informants eliciting elaborate details about the hostages and their daily lives. A local police officer came forward in early 1997 with an account about a Kashmiri man who, during the summer of 1996, had come to him to report that Don, Paul, Keith, and Dirk had stayed at his house for six days in May that year. The man, who lived in the village of Kuzuz, in a small wooden house with a stone foundation, said that the captives and captors appeared to have a good working relationship and that everyone was healthy. When asked why he had taken so long to report this potentially important event, the policeman said that among other reasons he had been assigned to a post and an area that had nothing to do with the "hostage-tracking operation" and that it took him a while to persuade the owner of the house to allow the story to be released. The owner had feared reprisals from the rebels, the policeman added. But authorities were never able to confirm or negate the tale.

"The Hostages in Kashmir Campaign," based in Middlesbrough, England, now had a Web site that displayed a compassionate message from former Beirut hostage Terry Waite, as well as updates on the case, lyrics to a 1996 song about the hostages, and details about a prayer vigil.

Though still afflicted with nightmares, Julie Mangan had become an inveterate campaigner in her efforts to keep the memory of the hostages stirring in the hearts and minds of Britons. Since her husband's abduction, she had returned to Kashmir three times and now in late spring she was preparing to meet Jane in India for the second anniversary of the incident.

Just before her second trip back to India, in November of 1996, Julie had moved from Middlesbrough down to the Tooting section of London to rent the apartment she and Keith had shared before their 1995 tour. She had learned that it was vacant again, and so, renewing the lease, she moved in and fixed it up in great expectation of Keith's homecoming—by Christmas, she hoped. It was indeed the power of hope that motivated her as she instructed a painter on the colors for the kitchen and the spare room, refurbished the small garden the couple had shared, and neatly arranged their ninety-six videotapes of *Star Trek* episodes in chronological order on a bookshelf in the living room.

On her trip to India that fall, she was accompanied by a BBC camera crew to film the documentary *The Big Story: Search for the Forgotten Hostages* and the hostage families—this time including Charlie and Mavis Mangan, the upbeat and forever courageous parents of Keith. It was no small effort for the working-class couple from the middle of England to be venturing halfway around the world and then to be driving through war-torn Kashmir in search of their son. No one could predict what they might find. At one point, the BBC cameras filmed Mavis and Charlie as they gazed across a rich landscape of mountain peaks and misty clouds. "It's just so vast. Keith could be anywhere, couldn't he?" Mavis said. "I'd walk every inch if I could. I would." Julie tried to protect the couple from as much stress as she could, an effort that distracted her from her own troubles. It was not an easy trip that fall.

Their expectations had been as high as the snow-capped peaks, making the disappointments seem lower than low. They had planned, for example, to mingle with the villagers, some of whom, they believed, must know shards of the truth. But the Indian troops insisted on protecting them *and* escorting them, in intimidating caravans of armored cars. When the families came upon a village rumored to be home to the hostages for the winter of 1995, they were shocked to find the men of the village, with pained looks on their faces, lined up, like a long row of hedges, at the edge of the road. Troops had arrived hours before to order the men out of their houses to wait by the road for the caravan. The BBC caught the scene on camera as Bob Wells, the father of Paul, approached the line of angry and scared men. Equally pained, he tried to apologize, "We did not know this would happen." But clearly no one in that village would dare to reveal even knowing the existence of any Western hostages. One villager said: "We have never seen them. Kashmir is very big."

It was strange the things that gave her strength, Julie would sometimes think, such as the little silver pen that was part of a set Keith had won when he was sixteen years old—the "Best Achiever" award at the school they both had attended and where they had met at the age of thirteen. "Haines Prize 1978" was engraved on the side of the pen. Julie always kept it with her, sometimes clutching it in those anxious seconds that came more frequently now, when she felt hope suddenly slipping away.

In the spring of 1997, Julie booked yet another passage to India. Paul Wells's father, Bob, and Paul's girlfriend, Cath Moseley, accompanied her again as well as Keith's uncle, James Bowman, the songwriter and lyricist. But this time, Keith's parents were unable to come. Mavis had suffered a heart attack that winter. This trip, everyone believed, might be different, especially because relations between India and Pakistan were supposedly improving. In early April, the foreign ministers from both nations had talked at meetings characterized in the press as the most hopeful summit of the past seven years. And the trip was timed to coincide with a religious holiday that could perhaps be the occasion for the Al-Faran to release the men.

"All we want to know is the truth," Julie told the press upon their arrival in New Delhi on April 14. "Let us not be in the dark any longer. Even if they are dead, please let us know."

It was a whirlwind trip during which they met again with government officials, Islamic militant leaders, police officers, and others. They distributed pamphlets, gave speeches, held press conferences. But nothing they learned was ever confirmed. In the midst of the tour, the militant captured the year before, the one with the elaborate confession describing when and approximately where the hostages had been killed, recanted his story. But he didn't replace it with anything enlightening. No one did. "The whole hostage event does not seem to have any sense in it," Sabir Shah, a moderate pro-independence leader told the Associated Press during the Brits' visit. "It has not and is not going to benefit anyone."

In late April, a few days after their return to England, without the information they so needed, an Israeli psychic named Uri Geller joined the crusade. Geller, best known for his touted ability to bend spoons with the strength of his willpower alone, announced that he was willing to pay a $50,000 reward for information about the Kashmir hostages and to offer himself as an intermediary to speak with the insurgents about terms for the tourists' release.

"The families approached me and asked me if I could help. Obviously, I agreed, as what you are talking about here is human life," Geller told Reuters. "I think they had come to a dead end. They had exhausted all their avenues. They believe in mind power. . . . Remember I am from Israel and the militants are Moslems. But that is why I think they [the militants] are going to respond."

For the mission, Geller created two special pages at his Internet Web site. At the top of the first was the beginning of a message: "Touch this orange disc and pray to." Then came the rest of the message—"Release the hostages"—contained in a big orange disc that filled most of the page. Beneath the disc were the hostages' names and this instruction: "Please try to do this every morning at 11:11 A.M. your time. Your mind power is strong enough to stop the Big Ben at 11:11." The second page read: "To the Al-Faran Group from Uri Geller, In the name of God, we all ask you to please release your hostages. Their parents, relatives and friends are desperate. The people you hold are innocent and have done nothing to hurt you. We are willing to listen to you and hear your side. I would be willing to take a message to any world leader. I undertake personally to give $75,000 [sic] for their safe return. If they are not alive, please allow us to collect their bodies for an honourable burial."

Also at his Web site, which was called "The Geller Edge," Geller offered promotional information about himself. "Best known for his skills as a television entertainer and psychic clairvoyant, Uri Geller has now set up a business consultancy, specialising in helping multinational corporations take [sic] better decisions. By using his insights and forecasting skills, Uri Geller can help you predict the major events that can affect your business, such as the actions of competitors, rapid changes in prices or unpredicted changes in customer needs. Conventional business advisors can offer limited assistance on these types of issues—no one can match Uri Geller's ability to see clearly beyond the obvious. Uri Geller uses a unique combination of both substantial conventional knowledge and psychic powers. In an increasingly turbulent world, your business needs the Geller edge."

But "the Geller edge" was not enough to find the truth about the Kashmir hostages.

Jane Schelly was unable to join the spring expedition to Kashmir. School was in session. And, as always, she felt strongly about her responsibilities to her students and to an employer that had been compassionate and yielding during her times of need. But also, a storm of uncontrollable events had swept through her life, again. For such an organized person, always striving to control her well-ordered world, Jane was facing the emotional equivalent of a twister that spring. First, in March, Don's father, who lived in nearby Coeur d'Alene, passed away in his sleep. Ill with Alzheimer's, the 87-year-old man never knew of his son's misfortune. Jane was thankful for that, though it wouldn't be easy telling Don that while he was in captivity his father had slipped away forever. Don had so enjoyed regaling friends with stories about his father's years as a cowboy. She could almost hear his chuckle each time she looked at one of the canes his father had carved, the one with a handle made from the calcified penis of a bull, neatly stowed with the others in the corner of his office.

A few weeks later, Jane's mother called with the news that her father had an inoperable brain tumor. The doctors gave him six weeks to two months. In April, Jane flew home to Allentown, Pennsylvania, to spend time with her father and to give her mother as much support as she could. Her father died on May 22. If anyone had ever doubted the strength of Jane Schelly, they learned quickly that spring how wrong they had been.

Throughout the spring, Jane chronicled every new event in Kashmir, rarely missing a daily entry in her nearly two-year-old journal. She also monitored other ongoing cases. She watched as the Peru hostages were rescued and the couple in Texas won their freedom through a swap for a jailed militant. And while she could never deny anyone else their happiness and relief, she could not help but envy the families of the hostages who had walked free.

Jane's 1997 trip to India was scheduled to begin in late June and would last eight weeks. It would be different from all the others. For one thing, Jane was different. Though her friends said she had always been strong and assertive, those who knew her best detected a change. "She's beyond Spokane now," one friend said. Perhaps it was because her mind was so often in two places at once, that her very being was divided in half: the life in Spokane with friends and students and the life in India with the State Department, the foreign officials, the reporters, the other hostage families—and with Don. There were experiences she couldn't always relate to friends in Spokane. So very much had happened to her away from them. How could she describe the bruising course of her emotions along the ups and downs of the ordeal, or explain the feeling when the life of a loved one is reduced to the status of an American interest? How could she express the contradictions in her feelings about her own government, the conflict between her intense gratitude for all the people with whom she had worked and her nearly unbearable frustration with the lack of resolution? When friends said she should be angry at her government, she could only think of the people who had cared so much and whose eyes could not lie in their message of compassion. And, as she well knew, the U.S. government had allocated hundreds of thousands of dollars, perhaps millions, in resources and staff to resolve the case. But then the doubts would begin. Had her government done all that it could? If the United States cared more about the war in Kashmir, if the conflict in Kashmir were as prominent as the one in the Middle East, would the U.S. government have been more aggressive?

You could see the change in the way she walked, and in the way, almost like a politician, she would pause before answering a question or smile at the appropriate moment. She had an air of sophistication that had grown with each new trip to India, as she met with the heads of state, Islamic leaders, and the international media. Her hair was a little longer; the tight curls were now waves. And that orderly world Jane had always tried to hold together was so much bigger now. To control it was impossible. To embrace it was the only option. She had learned more about living in the present from this ordeal than from any mountain trek she had ever taken. "If you want something, you must grab it now. That's what I know," she said in May. "You must not hesitate, because life can elude you so very quickly."

On the trip that summer, Jane planned to do things that she had not done during those first several weeks after the abduction, when she would stare at her hiking boots each morning, tempted to lace them up and venture into the hills alone with only a guide to reclaim her husband's life herself. A Kashmiri-American who spoke Urdu and who was part of the freedom movement—someone who had contacted her in the States and offered his help—volunteered to accompany her. He believed that Don might be living in a militant training camp in Pakistan. Now, one by one, she would visit the villages where her husband had supposedly been seen in the nearly two years since the abduction. Without the imposing convoy of Indian troops that had accompanied the hostage families on their autumn 1996 trip, villagers might be more forthcoming. Jane would hike now to hamlets as high as 12,000 feet. And wearing the traditional Kurta pajama attire, she would mix with the locals. The women, she thought, might be forthcoming; they would be the most compassionate. The woodcutters, too, she had been told, might know. She would stay in the huts of the villages and walk the rock-strewn roads. Someone would tell her. Someone had to know.

It was a plan that worried her friends *and* the State Department. Friends felt that her guilt about Don's captivity could be unconsciously driving her into a dangerous situation. Although she had not expressed much guilt, she had spoken on occasion about being more aggressive during the early stages of the incident. At the State Department, one official, who had followed the case very closely and knew Jane, worried that somewhere deeply buried in her unconscious was the desire to be kidnapped just like Don. Then perhaps she would learn what had happened to him or even find him. At least she might be free of guilt. But one Spokane friend said that it was not as deep as all that. Jane was thorough, organized, and determined. She simply didn't want to miss a single opportunity to find Don. While the State Department seemed to think that this was her last trip, Jane's friends knew that she would not stop going to India until she got what she wanted: the truth. Only then would she be free to return to her life again.

A few days after her father's funeral, Jane received the news that, based on a tip from a captured militant, the police had mounted yet another search—just like the one the previous year in the forests of Magam—for the remains of the four tourists. The location was in the same region as the 1996 confessor had identified, though in a different area within the region. The problem was that most of the details in this, the most recent confession, had been available to the public for many months, especially after the 1996 confession was published in the *Indian Express* in December that year. Claiming to know what had happened to the prisoners of the Al-Faran was becoming a cottage industry. Perhaps the word was out among militants: if you get captured, tell a story about the four Western hostages, just use what you have read in the newspapers as a basis. Was that what was happening?

These confessions were like the sightings, Jane thought. Nothing could be confirmed. And to be sure, like the perfect workings of a clock, after a confession there would come a new sighting, spinning the gears of uncertainty once again, and keeping the story alive. After the May 1996 confession, villagers supposedly spotted the hostages north of Anantnag, "looking healthy," an Indian official told the press at the time.

Though always hopeful, Jane had developed a theory about the sightings. Throughout the ordeal, the Indian troops had been told to clear away from the villages and the mountain hideaways where the hostages were believed to be. This was a strategy, of course, to prevent the hostages from being killed in a skirmish between troops and ter-rorists. Jane believed it was indeed possible that the sightings were fabricated by the militants to clear a path for themselves free of the threat of Indian soldiers. Wherever it was that they wanted or needed to be, there would then be a sighting to allow them safe passage to their destination. It was only a theory, but an intelligent one. At the same time, she believed that the media could also be fostering the sightings. Newspapers and other media paid for tips about the four tourists from shepherds, villagers, freelance writers, even police. And as long as the story was kept alive, there was money to be made.

At first, it looked as though Jane's timing for the 1997 trip was perfect. While nuclear nonproliferation and trade with India had been the top priorities in India during Clinton's first term, during the first month or so of the new administration it appeared that stability in Kashmir—clearly a requirement for developing the region economi-cally—might now be a central concern in Washington. In February of 1997, Ambassador Wisner had advised India that the time was "ripe to resolve the conflict that has gripped this state [Kashmir] for so long." In late May, the new U.S. secretary of state, Madeleine Albright, was telling the press of her interest in the resolution of "the Kashmir problem." She even had a personal connection. Her father, Josef Korbel, the former chairman of the 1948 United Nations Com-mission on India and Pakistan, had written a book about it: *Danger in Kashmir*, published in 1954 by Princeton University Press. "I think from what we've heard, there seems to be some potential progress,"

Albright told the press before beginning a May 21 meeting with the Pakistani foreign minister. "We would consider it very important, and a dialogue between India and Pakistan about the subject would be very useful, and it would be terrific to resolve it."

In the meeting that May, Albright urged Pakistan to ratify the Chemical Weapons Convention and to provide a full accounting for what had happened to Donald Hutchings. But the meeting did not turn out as well as planned. The Pakistani foreign minister seemed stuck on the problem with the F-16s. If the United States did not return the money Pakistan had paid for the weapons by February 1999, the nation would take legal action. By June, relations between the two nations would only worsen.

In early June, two U.S. congressmen submitted an amendment to Congress calling for the release of the hostages from captivity, the continued use of the State Department reward program to solicit information, and the cooperation of six governments to share all information in the pursuit of the truth. Known as the Nethercutt-Pallone Amendment, it was the creation of George Nethercutt, a Democrat from Washington state, and Frank Pallone, a Democrat from New Jersey. The amendment began with Congress's findings in the case: "1) Al-Faran, a militant organization that seeks to merge Kashmir with Pakistan, has waged a war against the Government of India. 2) During the week of July 2, 1995, Al-Faran abducted Donald Hutchings of the State of Washington, another American, John Childs, and four Western Europeans in the State of Kashmir. John Childs has since escaped. 3) Al-Faran has executed one hostage and threatened to kill Donald Hutchings and the remaining hostages unless the Government of India agrees to release suspected guerrillas from its jails. 4) Several militants have been captured by the Indian Government and have given conflicting and unconfirmed reports about the hostages. 5) Donald Hutchings and the three remaining Western European hostages have been held against their will by Al-Faran for nearly two years."

In presenting the bill on June 6, Representative Pallone said, "Before my trip to India this year, I had the opportunity to meet with Jane Schelly. Obviously, she was upset and would like the safe return of her husband, and although the safe return of her husband does not look promising, she continues to hope. In her heart, she believes her husband is alive. Mr. Chairman, we cannot lose hope."

During the week before Jane's trip began, American agents captured a Pakistani man wanted for the 1993 killing of two CIA employees. The Pakistanis were fuming. Editorials raged about the Pakistan government allowing a Pakistani national to be plucked from his homeland by U.S. officials and then swept away on a U.S. military jet. Normal extradition had been waived, and the Pakistani people were livid. The United States "rarely acts to circumvent its own laws, but expects others to waive and ignore theirs," said one editorial. "Pakistanis Irked that U.S. Seized Fugitive in Killings," the *New York Times* headline read on June 23. The prospect of Pakistan giving up information now about Donald Hutchings was looking less and less likely.

At the same time, the war in Kashmir appeared to be intensifying, perhaps because the fiftieth anniversary of India's independence from Britain—and the beginning of Kashmir's problems in modern times—was drawing near, on August 15. By the time Jane had arrived in New Delhi, embassy officials worried that her expedition into the remote reaches of the Kashmir Valley—where she was certain she would find the truth—was too dangerous. Very reluctantly, she changed her plans.

She would stick to Srinagar and the main towns of Kashmir and pass out leaflets explaining the U.S. $2 million reward program for information regarding the hostages. This would be helpful, she knew, because India had not allowed the United States to set up the program there. She felt that many people in Kashmir had likely not been informed about the prospect of a cash reward in exchange for information. This could account for the failure of the program to unearth any useful information, though the main reason was, of course, the villagers' fear of Indian authorities. She would also talk with officials in New Delhi and Islamabad, once again. This time, she would be educating some of them about the case. The turnover had been so great in the past two years that there were now few left who were as informed as she was.

During the first week of her trip, Julie Mangan and Birgit Hasert, Dirk Hasert's sister, flew to New Delhi to join Jane in the latest campaign. "Somewhere, somebody knows," Jane said at a press conference. "You cannot keep secrets in the Kashmir Valley. People know things. If they were killed, somebody would know. And likewise if the hostages are alive, people would also know that."

Her quest was so clear to her now. She must keep the memory of the incident alive, and she must continue shining a bright light into the dark corners where the truth could be hidden, hoping to discover a clue about the fates of the four men. But on some days that summer, the light seemed to fade, like the wavering light of a drowning candle.

By July 4, 1997, the story of the prisoners of the Al-Faran had reached mythical proportions in the vale of Kashmir, like a tale out of Rudyard Kipling or the lyrics in a traveling minstrel's song. Everyone had a theory, but no one was willing to reveal the truth. And it was possible by then that whatever so-called truths seeped out of the Kashmiri hills, they would be very hard to prove or disprove. This person might have heard it from that person, who might have read the details in the press or heard it from someone who claimed to know what happened but who had only read about it. Long after the women of the village of Prazmulla could gather their willow branches without the fear of once again facing the specter of violence at the edge of the grove, villagers would be telling stories of their nation's half-century struggle for independence, of the loved ones who had lost their lives, of the ones who were tortured, the ones who were maimed, and the ones who disappeared in the night. And some would remember the five Western tourists who never returned home.

That July, Jane had a new dream.

It is raining in the hills above the Spokane River. Jane and her friend Debbie Pierce are riding bicycles. Debbie tells her that Don and Bill (Pierce) will certainly come to get them soon. Jane nods her head, but in her heart she is thinking that they will not come. She and Debbie will wait and watch for the men, but they will not come. The rain worsens. She calms herself by watching the rain and how it falls on the road, which, in the dream, is a rugged, rock-strewn path. Then, suddenly, through the haze of wind-swept rain, she sees a vehicle approaching them, perhaps a jeep. It is Don and Bill. She is so very glad to see Don. She doesn't care about the rain, she tells him. She is just glad to be with him. He apologizes for not getting there when the rain began.

Notes

⬦⬦⬦

This book is based on hundreds of interviews with sources that include former captives, the families of former and current captives, government agents and officials, academicians, former kidnappers, public and private sector negotiators, law enforcement officials, travel agents, and counterterrorists. The author also consulted the books noted in the bibliography, and studies, reports, and documents from governments worldwide and from private industry groups that study issues such as political terrorism, international patterns of crime, tribal clashes, risks in developing nations, and the impact of peace in nations long at war. Clips were periodically referred to, mainly to enhance the narrative flow by providing timely quotes dealing with relevant events. The notes section includes published information used in the book. If there is nothing listed for a particular chapter, this simply means that the chapter was based entirely on interviews. The section also cites some articles and studies that the author read but did not use directly in the text. These, as well as quotes that were not included in the text but contribute to an understanding of the topic, are included for the further edification of the reader.

Ransom covers two years in the world of kidnapping, from July 4, 1995, to July 4, 1997, beginning with the abduction of Hutchings, Mangan, Wells, and Childs. The other cases mentioned throughout the narrative and back-ground chapters of the book comprise a reliable composite of worldwide kid-nappings that were reported for this two-year period. To chart reported kidnaps worldwide requires consulting with numerous organizations, which fall into the following categories: crisis management companies whose clients are multinational corporations; local law enforcement agencies in various countries afflicted with the crime; insurance companies; government agen-cies, such as the FBI and the State Department; advocacy groups working for human rights, citizen safety, and other causes; and former captives and their families, who often develop networks of people with similar experiences or are simply interested in keeping track of other cases. Another source is the Internet. Each day for two years, my trusty Internet researcher Sari Levin scanned the world for new kidnapping cases, looking at clips and press com-mentary as well as visiting online chat groups and even Web sites of rebel groups. The combination of the traditional information-gathering practices and Levin's high-tech assistance have made the book's chronicle of two years as close to the truth as possible. Still, the reader must be advised that there were likely numerous cases we could not find. So many kidnappings are unreported.

PART I

Chapters 1–4

Quote from Hans Christian Ostro: From audiotape recorded during his captivity in July 1997.

Facts in chapters 1–4: Culled from extensive interviews; the files, letters, and journals of hostage families; and interagency government memos on the Kashmir case.

Where and how Ostro's body was found: Details in chapter 1 from inter-views and from the local Kashmiri press on the day the body was discovered. Accounts in the international press as well as government reports and inter-views show discrepancies about how many women found the body, where they were walking, and even in what village the incident occurred. Some say it was the village of Seer and six women; others say one woman fetching water from a nearby irrigation ditch in the village of South Ashumuquam. Some reports, repeated in many accounts, said the head was found on top of the body though it was found forty yards away. I chose, of course, what I believed to be the most reliable information.

PART II

Chapter 5

One of the earliest recorded kidnappings in history was in 94 B.C., when a descendant of the first king of Armenia Major was released for a ransom of seventy valleys; he deposed the king of Armenia Minor and united the two kingdoms, making Armenia the greatest power in western Asia. While the Bible, the Talmud, and other religious books refer to the act of kidnapping, the first use of the word *kidnap* in the English language may have been as late as the seventeenth century.

My sources for statistics on kidnapping include intelligence reports and country-specific risk assessments prepared by Control Risks Group, Kroll Associates, and Pinkerton's for their clients; government studies within various countries; as well as human rights groups, citizen watch groups, and church groups. In all instances, it must be remembered that the percentage of kidnappings that are reported varies from country to country, with roughly 30 percent of kidnappings reported worldwide. In some countries, the reporting rate is as low as 10 percent.

To deter any possibility of sensationalizing the problem, the statistics in this book tend to be conservative. For example, some newspapers in early 1997 reported that there had been 3,000 kidnappings in Mexico in 1996. My interviews and reports indicated a rather broad range, from about 700 to 1,500 to 2,000. I used the 1,500 figure in the text, largely because of the credibility of the sources. There was a wide discrepancy, too, regarding the kidnapping of foreigners in Mexico. After looking carefully at the stats, the sources of the stats, and the definitions of the kidnappings—some being detainments during robberies, for example—I concluded that foreigners by 1997 were indeed more at risk in Mexico than in past years, especially in western Mexico along the central Pacific coast, and even in Guadalajara. But the problem was far less intense than in other Latin American countries, such as Colombia and even Venezuela. And among the cases involving Americans, most were American expatriates—not business travelers or tourists. Thus, in the book I've stressed that kidnapping in Mexico is not yet a problem for foreigners, though it is clearly a threat to all.

A word of caution about kidnap statistics. Because it is so difficult to obtain exact numbers, the kidnap figures, like all statistics, can be manipulated to serve particular agendas. Some governments hoping to lure tourists to their shores will diminish the numbers; in those same countries, various advocacy groups will embellish the tallies, intending to draw attention to their particular cause.

But it's important to note that the statistics, in fact, are not the issue. The issue, as chapter 5 discusses, is that numerous groups—former rebels, criminals, guerrilla groups, tribes—are using the crime of kidnapping for various purposes, mostly to raise money via ransoms; thus, tourists and business travelers are at risk far more than they usually realize. This is an era during which caution must be exercised when traveling. One of the most important points perhaps in chapter 5 is that peace does not necessarily follow a peace treaty, and tourists, especially, must be alerted to this fact because after the wars end, the travel ads begin.

Between 1968 and 1982, 951 hostages in seventy-three countries: From *International Terrorism: Hostage Seizures,* U.S. Department of State, March 1983.

At least 6,500 kidnappings in Latin America in 1995: From the *Economist,* October 19, 1996; verified by a number of analysts in my interviews with them.

List of countries most afflicted: From Control Risks Group.

Another finding comes from Alexander and Alexander, a U.K. risk consultant and insurance broker, which reported in a newsletter in the summer of 1996 that since 1989, in Colombia, Brazil, and Mexico, respectively, there had been 7,500, 4,500, and 2,300 kidnappings. Each of these figures is quite feasible. In Mexico, considering that kidnappings intensified dramatically from 1994 on, the Alexander and Alexander figure is sensible. To lessen confusion and an overload effect, however, I did not include it in the text.

Sources consulted for specific countries are provided in the following paragraphs.

For Brazil: The government's Divisão Anti-Secuestro (antikidnapping division), the Getulio Vargas Foundation (FGV), the Rio police, and articles including "Kidnappings: New Boom Industry in Big Cities: Drug Gangs May Be Moving into Profitable New Business," *Latin America Weekly Report,* June 8, 1995; "Ransom Country," *Brazil,* January 18, 1996; "New Latin American Kidnappings Going for the Gold," by Laney Salisbury, Reuters, February 21, 1996.

For Colombia: The National Police Statistics report for 1996, the Anti-Kidnapping Agency, and Fundacion Pais Libre (a group for victims of kidnappings, translation: Free Country Foundation). The stats on ransoms come from *Los Costos Economics del Conflicto Armado en Colombia: 1990–1994,* a report by the Colombian Departamento Nacional de Planeacion, Unidad de

Justicia y Seguridad, in December 1995. Translated into English for me by Marianne Siegmund, a translator and librarian in Provo, Utah.

For Ecuador: Ministry of Defense, and Control Risks Group, which furnished police statistics obtained from a former director of intelligence of the Joint Command of the Armed Forces.

For Guatemala: Grupo de Apoyo Mutuo (human rights group), Neighborhood Guardians (local anticrime group).

For Ireland: "Owen Is Challenged on Reported Kidnaps," by Dermot Kelly and Michael O'Regan, *Irish Times,* May 11, 1995.

For Mexico: *El Economist* (newspaper in Mexico City), Centro de Investigacion y Seguridad Nacional, Pinkerton's risk assessment reports, and CRG analysts.

For Nicaragua: Bob Dwyer, who got his information from government contacts in Managua.

For Panama: The Technical Judicial Police.

For the Philippines: Citizens Action Against Crime, and the Movement for Restoration of Peace and Order (a citizens group monitoring kidnap cases). See also "Kidnap Corp.," by John Kohut, *Asia Inc.,* April 1996.

For the United States: The FBI, local newspapers, and private industry groups. See also references to Silicon Valley abductions in part III, and "Kidnapping Is a Criminal Growth Industry in Baja," by Gregory Gross, *San Diego Union-Tribune,* January 8, 1994.

For Venezuela: *El National* newspaper, and *El Globo* newspaper.

Americans in captivity: *Significant Incidents of Political Violence Against Americans, 1995,* U.S. Department of State, Bureau of Diplomatic Security, July 1996. Also, "Reported Kidnappings of Foreigners in Colombia, 1995–96," *Jane's Intelligence Review,* May 20, 1996.

Other sources consulted for this chapter: Various books listed in the bibliography; the U.S. Department of State's *Patterns in Global Terrorism* for the years 1994, 1995, and 1996; an article in the *Economist* on rising instances of piracy (August 9, 1997); reports by terrorist expert Brian Jenkins, before and during his employment at Kroll, including "Kidnapping and Extortion: An Essay," in Kroll's *Risk Issues Quarterly,* vol. 1994, no. 4; CRG's *Kidnap for Ransom: Worldwide Statistics (1989–1995);* and *The Hallcrest Report II: Private Security Trends (1970–2000).*

Also helpful were various articles throughout the 1990s in trade magazines, such as *National Underwriter, Risk Management, Business Insurance, Business Horizons,* and *Security Management.* Two noteworthy articles were

"Industry Responds to Rising Kidnapping Threat," by Christopher Dauer, *National Underwriter,* January 16, 1995; and "Protecting a Target," by Marcy Mason, *Security Management,* June 1991. The latter begins: "It's a subject no one wants to talk about. Crimes committed against executives in North America are unreported; no one keeps statistics, not even the FBI. As a rule, when companies are queried about their executive protection policies, mum's the word—the boardroom doors are firmly shut."

Among the useful articles in the mainstream press: "Hostage-Taking Is a Weapon of War Whose Time Is Now," by Stephen Engelberg, *New York Times,* June 25, 1995; "K&R Policy Boom Reflects Rising Risk of Abduction: Stepped Up Business Travel Has Meant More Opportunities for Terrorists and Industrial Spies," by Carol Smith, *Los Angeles Times,* November 24, 1995; "Lost Horizons: The Kashmir Kidnappings Highlight an Increasing Threat," by David Wickers, (London) *Times,* November 6, 1995; and "Travel Firms Admit Tourists Are Prime Terrorism Targets," by Harvey Elliott, (London) *Times,* July 13, 1993.

Individuals especially helpful in piecing together the facts for this chapter were Robert Dwyer, Guy Dunn, John Bray, Justine Barrett, Eleni Jakub, David Lattin, Hugh Barber, Russ Ross, Frank Johns, Richard Clutterbuck, Bill Ilsley, and Mike Ackerman.

The "$170 billion" figure for the amount of private capital invested in developing nations in 1995, 200 percent over 1990, comes from an impressive *Washington Post* series on the gap between rich and poor worldwide, four articles beginning January 1, 1997.

Quote from the United Nations study: From the *1996 Annual Human Development Report of the United Nations Development Program* as outlined by the UNDP chief administrator James Gustave Speth in *New Perspectives Quarterly,* vol. 13, no. 4 (fall 1996).

Five-year study on outcomes of reported kidnappings: From Control Risks Group.

Chapter 8

Childs's quote to the *Boston Globe:* From "Escaped Hostage Recalls Ordeal," a 477-word piece in the *Boston Globe,* August 16, 1995.

Chapter 9

"Nothing in a guerrilla's repertoire compares": From "Danger Zones," by Simon Calder, in *Independent,* July 22, 1995.

"What is so sinister about today's terrorists": From "Tourists Caught in the Terrorists' Sights," by Michael Binyon, (London) *Times,* June 24, 1995.

Stats on American citizens residing abroad: From the U.S. Department of State, Bureau of Consular Affairs, as of January 1997. Stats on Americans traveling abroad: From the Tourism Industries, International Trade Administration, as of September 3, 1996. Stats on tourism: From World Tourism Organization.

Cambodia piece: "Angkor Emerges from the Jungle," by Barbara Crossette, in New York Times, Jan. 28, 1996, p. 17.

Myanmar piece: "Seeing Myanmar at a Stately Pace," by Margaret Erhart, *New York Times,* December 15, 1996. Companion piece: "Weighing the Ethics of a Trip," by Seth Mydans, same day.

Travel advisory for India: Pinkerton Weekly Risk Assessment, April 2, 1993. Travel advisory for the Philippines: "U.S. Travel Advisory Miffs Philippines," by Evelyn Tan, December 30, 1994, *USA Today;* and U.S. Consular Information Sheet, August 12, 1994.

The 1991 government study on travel advisories: *Travel Advisories: State Needs Better Practices for Informing Americans of Dangers Overseas,* report to the chairman, Legislation and National Security Subcommittee, Committee on Government Operations, House of Representatives, U.S. General Accounting Office, August 1991 (GAO/NSIAD-91-249).

To quote extensively from the GAO study would have bogged down the text, but there are more noteworthy examples in the study. The Kenya advisory, for example, had problems of its own. The advisory encouraged Americans to travel in tour groups with a guide from a respected safari firm. The problem was that the American who had been murdered was in a tour group that had even employed an armed guard. Over the following year, the attacks continued in Kenya, where another American tourist was killed—in a Safari tour group, according to government records. The GAO study also exposed inconsistencies in the dissemination of travel notices and advisories. Though such information was available on airline reservation systems, only 10 percent of the travel agencies investigated had regularly advised clients of the current advisories. Travel industry representatives informed the investigative committee that there was no question that travel agents should inform travelers of pending advisories just as they would any other travel information.

In response to the study, one article of interest: "The Federal Page: Helpfulness of Travel Alerts Questioned. Critics Say State Department Stresses

Policy Agenda over Information," by Brent Mitchell, *Washington Post,* August 23, 1991. It includes a noteworthy example of policy overriding reality—this time resulting in too harsh an advisory: "During the Persian Gulf War, the government issued an advisory for Tanzania after learning that terrorists might try to assassinate the U.S. ambassador in Dar es Salaam. The alert covered the entire country and emphasized the danger in the major cities. Cord D. Hansen-Sturm, a former Foreign Service officer who is now a travel industry consultant, said the warning bankrupted a U.S. company that ran tours of Tanzanian game parks, even though tourists enter the parks through Kenya. 'You will not see a travel advisory in downtown London, no matter how many IRA bombs blast how many tourists,' Hansen-Sturm said."

About Overseas Security Advisory Council: Details from the *U.S. State Department Bulletin,* October 1986.

About adventure travel: Of interest, see the interview with Robert Young Pelton, the author of the Fielding guide to the world's most dangerous places, in *Outside* magazine, May 1996. In this interview, he describes the audience for his book: "Dual income, no kids, highly educated. Eastern or Western seaboard."

Details about Cambodia: Among other sources, a piece about the 1994 Cambodia kidnappings entitled "Death in the Ruins," by Philip Gourevitch, *Outside* magazine, September 1995. Of interest, Gourevitch quotes the Cambodian correspondent for the *Far Eastern Economic Review* as saying that his take "on the 'hostage thing,' as the serial kidnappings of Westerners had come to be called, was that anyone who had ever imagined that tourists were immune to the violence and predation of Cambodia had simply been deluding himself."

Tourists as easy targets: "Targeting the Tourists," by Bruce Wallace, *Maclean's* magazine, September 4, 1995, vol. 108, no. 36; "Ticket to Trouble in Holiday Hot-Spots," by William Russell, (Glasgow) *Herald,* January 13, 1996.

Tourists lured to Kashmir: "Travel: Innocents Lured into Kashmir Despite Growing Risk of Violence," by Cathy Urquhart, *Daily Telegraph,* September 9, 1995. The quote "full of government tourist offices, most of which were unofficial": From a later article by the same writer, "Travel: Con Men Lure Innocents to Kashmir," *Daily Telegraph,* May 18, 1996.

"There are still hundreds of people going to Kashmir": The British official quoted here was Mike Foord, first secretary consular at the British High Commission in New Delhi.

Chapters 10–14

Anette Ostro's eulogy to her brother: Provided by Hans Gustav Ostro and translated from the Norwegian by Richard Hacken, translator and librarian in Provo, Utah.

Abductions in India and Kashmir: From India High Commission in London and from a Reuters piece, "Kashmir Has Long List of Abductions," Reuters World Service, August 17, 1995.

Transcripts of actual negotiation talks between Tikoo and rebel intermediary and the details of that first week in September: Partly from sources and partly from *India Today,* September 30, 1995.

Details about leaked "ransom" stories: From interviews. The news reports of the leaks were in the Indian press on September 18, 1995, as well as AP international wire: "India Negotiating Ransom with Kidnappers, Official Says," by Dilip Ganguly; and in Reuters, "India Tight-Lipped on Hostage Ransom Reports," by Hari Ramachandran. News reports of ransom discussions earlier than this, in July and August, were inaccurate, according to sources who were on the scene at the time. And there are news reports later in the year (mostly in December 1995) with comments attributed to Indian officials saying that three of the Western nations (United States, Britain, and Germany) "may have paid ransom money" to free the hostages. This could never be confirmed, and so was not used in the text. One such article: "Hostages: Western Nations May Have Paid Ransom Money in Kashmir," *Deutsche Presse-Agentur,* December 27, 1995.

PART III

Chapters 15–17

Temperatures in Kashmir: From AccuWeather, Inc., State College, Pennsylvania.

Quote about the identity of the Al-Faran: "Fate of Four Kashmir Hostages Is Lost in the Himalayan Mists," by John F. Burns, *New York Times,* May 27, 1996.

President's Directive regarding United States and Pakistan, noted also in "How the FBI Got Its Man, Half the World Away," by David Johnston, in *New York Times,* June 19, 1997.

On U.S. relations with India, early Clinton years, up to summer of 1995: Historical discussion based on recently unclassified materials in reports by the U.S. State Department (*Foreign Relations of the U.S., 1961–1963,* vol. 19,

South Asia, includes documentation on U.S. policy toward India, Pakistan, and Afghanistan, gives perspective on the dilemma in Kashmir), numerous editorials in the international and U.S. press in 1994. See "U.S. Policy on Kashmir Stands," by Aziz Haniffa, *India Abroad,* March 1994; "U.S. Role as Catalyst on Kashmir," by Aziz Haniffa, *India Abroad,* April 1994; "Rao Tries to Build Bridge to Washington: But India and US Still Find It Hard to Make Progress on Links," by Stefan Wagstyl, *Financial Times,* May 13, 1994; "A New Light on India. U.S. Reassesses That Nation as It Transforms Its Economy in the Post–Cold War Era," *Los Angeles Times,* May 29, 1994; "Hostage Killing and After," by Inder Malhotra, *Hindu,* August 8, 1995; and "Himalayan Time Bomb: The World Needs to Come to Grips with the Kashmir Problem," *AsiaWeek,* September 15, 1995.

Foreign policy in the new era: "America's Foreign Policy Priorities in a New World," highlights from a conference at the U.S. Department of State, November 24, 1992.

On role of U.S. State Department: "Promoting U.S. Economic Interests and the FY97 International Affairs Budget Request," Joan Spero, undersecretary for economic, business, and agricultural affairs, prepared statements before the House Appropriations Committee's Subcommittee on Commerce, Justice, State, and Judiciary, May 8, 1996. Also, Warren Christopher's Statement before the same committee, May 15, 1996.

Quote from Warren Christopher: From speech to the American Chamber of Commerce in Jakarta, Indonesia, on July 25, 1996.

About commercial investment in India: *1996 India Country Commercial Guide,* Office of the Coordinator for Business Affairs, U.S. Department of State.

Details about Enron contribution to Democratic National Convention, in "The Scoop," *Time,* September 1, 1997.

Background of Kashmir elections, partly from book *Kashmir in the Crossfire* by Victoria Schofield, chapter 15.

Local coverage of Ambassador Wisner's 1995 trip to Kashmir: *Kashmir Times,* June 25, June 27, July 4, 1995. Local editorials about July 4 abductions: "Abductions in Pahalgam," *Kashmir Times,* July 4, 1995, and "Urgency of a Political Settlement in Kashmir," by Nikhil Chakravartty, *Kashmir Times,* same day. Press comments from "A Trek Too Far," by Tim McGirk, *Independent,* July 6, 1995.

Later that summer, while the world appeared to be waiting for the United States to make a move, one individual knowledgeable about the case commented, "The truth is its hands were tied. It was caught, like the hostages, between Pakistan and India. What did it show? Basically the whole episode showed how helpless governments could be in the face of these crises."

The quote "There is much speculation now about an imminent release," as well as the details of a swap of two militants for the hostages on the 100th day of captivity: From "Britain Denies Reports of Offering Payment to Kashmir Militants," *Deutsche Presse-Agentur,* October 12, 1995, and "Fate of Four Western Hostages Still Unknown in Indian Kashmir," *Deutsche Presse-Agentur,* later on the same day. More about the release of militants, moving them out of their prison cells to an area closer to the Pakistani-controlled portion of Kashmir: "National Briefs," *Hindu,* October 11, 1995.

Study of Algerian kidnapping: "Algeria's Lessons for French Intelligence," from *Jane's Intelligence Review,* no. 291, April 7, 1996.

"Hostages Languish as Public Interest Wanes: Kidnappings: Captives of the 1990s Are Forgotten as Terrorism Has Become Part of the Political Landscape," by Robin Wright, *Los Angeles Times,* June 6, 1996.

"State Department's Hostage Efforts," letter in response to above article, written by Mary A. Ryan, assistant secretary for Consular Affairs, U.S. Department of State, *Los Angeles Times,* June 21, 1996.

Historical information: Sources include Russell Buhite's compelling book *Lives at Risk* (especially for John Lamb, Charles Dickenson, and Ellen Stone), old *New York Times* clips dating back to the incidents, Richard Clutterbuck's books, a congressional report on the Ellen Stone case (cited in bibliography), and, for the recent incidents—for example, during the Reagan years—interviews with current and former government officials.

Quote from Ronald Reagan, "America will never make concessions": From *New York Times,* June 15, 1985.

Quote from Teddy Roosevelt, "If a man goes out as a missionary, he has no kind of business": From Buhite, who found it in *The Letters of Theodore Roosevelt,* vol. 1, edited by Elting E. Morison (Cambridge, Mass.: Harvard University Press, 1951–1954).

Detail about CIA hiring psychic in Dozier case: from a former government agent and a former Italian law enforcement official.

Chapter 18

Hargrove's lawsuit: *Thomas R. Hargrove, Susan Hargrove, et al. vs. Underwriters at Lloyd's, London; Professional Indemnity Agency, Inc.; Corporate Risk International; Centro Internacional de Agricultura Tropical dba*

CIAT; and Fritz Kramer. In Galveston Federal Court (the U.S. District Court for the Southern District of Texas), G-95-674, filed October 13, 1995. (Settled out of court in May 1997.)

Ransoms as tax-deductible: From U.S. Tax Code, noted in several articles, including "Strange But True Income Tax Laws," by Arthur M. Louis, *San Francisco Chronicle,* February 27, 1995.

On negotiation within the FBI during the Waco incident, and changes after Waco: U.S. House of Representatives, *Events Surrounding the Branch Davidian Cult Standoff in Waco, Texas, Hearing before the Committee on the Judiciary,* 103rd Congress, first session, April 28, 1993; *Report and Recommendations Concerning the Handling of Incidents Such as the Branch Davidian Standoff in Waco, Texas,* submitted to Deputy Attorney General Philip Heymann, by panelist Alan A. Stone, M.D., professor of psychiatry and law, Faculty of Law and Faculty of Medicine, Harvard University, November 10, 1993; *Recommendations of Experts for Improvements in Federal Law Enforcement after Waco,* letters to Philip B. Heymann, deputy attorney general, from Dr. Nancy Ammerman, Colin Birt, Dr. Robert Cancro, Dr. Alan A. Stone, Dr. Lawrence E. Sullivan, William H. Webster, Dr. Ariel Merari, Ronald M. McCarthy, Robert J. Louden, and Richard J. Davis; *Report to the Deputy Attorney General on the Events at Waco, Texas, Feb. 28 to April 19, 1993,* October 8, 1993; *Evaluation of the Handling of the Branch Davidian Stand-Off in Waco, Texas, by the U.S. Department of Justice and the FBI,* by Edward S. G. Dennis, Jr., October 8, 1993.

On the international role of the FBI: U.S. Senate, Committee on Appropriations, *Appropriations Hearing before the Subcommittee on the Departments of Commerce, Justice and State, the Judiciary, and Related Agency,* March 16, 1995; U.S. Senate, Committee on the Judiciary, *Legislative Initiatives to Curb Domestic and International Terrorism, Hearings before the Subcommittee on Security and Terrorism,* 98th Congress, June 5, 6, and 13, 1984; and, among others, *The FBI's Presence Overseas: The Need for FBI Agents Abroad to Better Protect the US from International Crime and Terrorism,* a 1996 FBI report backing budgetary requests.

Quote from Louis B. Freeh, taken from a speech on October 25, 1995, before the National Jewish Appeal's International Leadership Reunion, in Washington, D.C.

Three other quotes of interest:

From Robin Montgomery, the head of CIRG, which oversees CINT: "It's all about what negotiators and everyone can bring to the table, a more thorough understanding of the resources available so that good decisions can be made and so we're not reinventing the wheel with every new crisis. We're talking about communication and not being afraid of talking to people outside of the FBI. Part of our philosophy now is to be more outreaching and much less insular."

From Steven Romano, a CINT negotiator who was part of the FBI team in Kashmir: "Law enforcement people are trained to come on the incident and to take charge. Resolve it. Fix it. But when you deal with a crisis situation, you have to take a step back and this goes against the grain. The grain is traditionally tactical, that is, the sheriff in town confronting a situation. And it's hard to shift gears, to tell them, let's take a step back and see what we're dealing with. But this is what must happen, and now it is happening; there is respect for the process, the negotiation process."

From Freeh, submitted to Congress in *The FBI's Presence Overseas: The Need for FBI Agents Abroad to Better Protect the United States from International Crime and Terrorism:* "The Federal Bureau of Investigation believes that it is essential to station more of its highly-skilled Special Agents in other countries to prevent foreign terrorism and foreign crime from reaching into the U.S. to kill and harm Americans in their own workplaces, streets, homes, and houses of worship. . . . For better or for worse, the Global Village is now a late-20th century reality. . . . The dangers posed to the U.S. by international terrorism and crime are grave indeed. . . . Some of the worst crimes and crime threats have become multinational and international in scope. And that requires that we set up our first lines of defense—in part, a distant early warning system—in many nations where some of the most dangerous crimes and crime rings originate or flourish. . . . With conditions changing so rapidly in so many parts of the world, the FBI has to improve its anti-crime efforts to meet the grim realities of the decade of the 1990s. We are refining and shifting certain of our anti-crime priorities in a determined effort to make certain that we protect the U.S. and its people against new disasters while working harder than ever to solve long-standing problems of crime and violence."

Chapters 19–23

Basic facts about the Curtis case and the details of actual negotiations: From the extensive public record on the case, mainly, Gustavo G. Curtis and Vera Curtis, plaintiff, vs. Beatrice Foods Co., defendant, U.S. District Court for the Southern District of New York, 78CIV1316.

Quote from Mrs. Guinness: From "An Irish Heroine Stands Her Ground," *Financial Times,* April 19, 1986.

The ransom figure in the Ben Dunne case: From *The Financing of Terror,* James Adams, chapter 8.

Campaign to outlaw K&R and to prosecute CRG: (London) *Times,* April 17, 1986; *Daily Telegraph,* April 15, 1986; *Review,* February 13, 1988. *Post* magazine quotes and some details of the controversy over K&R: From its issues of May 1, 2, 16, and 23, 1986. New firms: "Look Out Control Risks, Securicor, and Other Commercial Combatants of Kidnap, Terrorism, and Ransom," *Sunday Telegraph,* November 30, 1986.

Quote "For every penny": From *The Financing of Terror,* James Adams, chapter 8.

Out of the more than 5,000 kidnaps recorded by CRG, only 109 have been insured: from CRG records.

Information about various agencies: From interviews with employees and from their own brochures. Details on American cases: From analysts' reports and interviews as well as the following clips about the kidnappings of high-tech executives in California: "Thieves Abduct Ceos to Steal High-Tech Gear," by Dennis Akizuki, *San José Mercury News,* January 27, 1996; "Massive Chip-Theft Raids Sweeps: Nearly 100 Arrested in High-Tech Thefts, Terrorism," by Raoul V. Mowatt and Bill Romano, *San José Mercury News,* February 29, 1996; "High-Tech Robbers Get Bolder," by Raoul V. Mowatt, Dean Takahashi, and Brandon Bailey, *San José Mercury News,* May 20, 1996; "Steal Gold? That's Old," by Michael S. Malone with Virginia Christian, *Forbes,* February 26, 1996; "Chip Thefts, A Silicon Gold Rush," by Richard C. Paddock and Julie Pitta, *Los Angeles Times,* February 23, 1996. And quote from Piiceon executive: From "Under the Gun: High-Tech Robberies Bring Fear to Silicon Valley," by Raoul V. Mowatt, Dean Takahashi, and Brandon Baily, *Austin American-Statesman,* June 17, 1996.

For Dwyer profile: Interviews with Dwyer, friends, and colleagues; also, some details from his *Anatomy of a Kidnapping: Management Considerations in Addressing the Kidnapping Threat,* which includes an account of a debriefing of a kidnap victim in Colombia; and his *The Kidnapping of Sergio Lobo: November 5–11, 1992: Rio de Janeiro, Brazil.*

References to the Talmud: From Rabbi Amy Ehrlich, Temple Emmanuel, New York City.

Solutions to the kidnapping problem: "Extraterritorial Jurisdiction under International Law: The Yunis Decision as a Model for the Prosecution of Terrorists in U.S. Courts," *Law and Policy in International Business,* vol. 22, 1991.

Ransom policy in the United States: Several sources told me that President Reagan initiated the no-pay policy in cases of political kidnappings. I decided to track down the news stories chronicling that event, but there was nothing in the 1980s. Still, I was determined to find the story announcing the policy; I wanted to read about the hearings and commentary surrounding the event. I finally found it in 1971. A *New York Times* article, March 9, 1971, page 14, ran the headline "Nonransom Policy Adopted."

Quote about Ecuador, "We need to pay more attention to groups that have been marginalized": The source was Rodrigo de la Cruz, a consultant at the Coordinated Indigenous Organizations of the Amazonian Watershed.

The $240 million figure for the Monteneros ransoms: From *The Financing of Terror,* James Adams, chapter 8.

The details of the Exxon and Born cases in Argentina: From *Kidnap, Hijack and Extortion,* Richard Clutterbuck, chapter 14.

Most up-to-date information about Italy and the ransom law: From interviews with individuals, including journalists, in Italy who have followed the issue carefully in recent years. Information on the Colombian law: From an official there, from professional negotiators, and from the Supreme Court decision in the spring of 1996.

The Heimdal story: From *Chicago Tribune* and Peoria's *Journal Star* for May and June, 1990.

PART IV

Chapter 24

Costa Rica: From interviews, correspondence with principals, though Nicola Fleuchaus declined. Anita Verschoth translated all correspondence from the German. Quote from *New York Times* article, as noted in text, "Life at the Top in Costa Rica," by Francesca Lyman, February 18, 1996. Criticism of the case: "Costa Rica: Kidnap Victims Returned to Safety, But Questions Remain about Government's Handling of Crisis," *NotiSur,* Latin American Political Affairs, Latin American Institute, University of New Mexico, March 15, 1996, which also referred to an editorial in *La Nacion* newspaper, March 12, 1996. Concerns over tourism: "Costa Rica: Government Baffled and Tourist Industry Worried by Kidnap Case," *NotiSur,* Latin American Political Affairs, Latin American Institute, University of New Mexico, March 1, 1996.

Chapters 26–27

Indonesia: From interviews with various individuals, including the negotiators. The principals sold their story exclusively to the *Mail on Sunday,* May 26, 1996. A few details in my account are culled from this 1,000-word story entitled "Exclusive in Their Own Words, 'We Had to Stay Alive, We Needed Each Other,' The British Hostages' Incredible Story; So Young, So Brave." Quote from George Monbiot: *Guardian,* January 12, 1996.

The editorial on hostage coverage and the unfinished business of colonialism: From the *Scotsman,* May 20, 1996.

Chapters 28–34

Confession of captured militant: "Confessions of a Terrorist," the transcript of the confession, reported by Ritu Sarin, *Indian Express,* December 22, 1996.

Among responses to the confession, not included in text: On May 15, adding kindling to the already explosive news was a report issued by the Indian news agency PTI that the Jammu and Kashmir Liberation Front, known as the Amanullah Group, expressed "sorrow and anger" at the reported killings of the hostages by "Pakistani mercenaries." The killings were "an inhuman act of violence," a group leader said in a written statement to the PTI. "The perpetrators of the outrageous act cannot be considered to be working for the cause of Kashmir."

Richardson announcement that Kashmir hostages "will be released soon": From "Western Hostages May Be Freed Soon," *Los Angeles Times,* February 23, 1996; and "Hostage Release Predicted," by Kenneth J. Cooper, *Washington Post,* February 23, 1996, among other news reports.

Story of the German "rescuers": Partly from sources and partly from *Der Spiegel* magazine and *Süddentsche Zeitung,* March 4, 1996. Translated by Anita Verschoth. Comments from Baron von Zschinsky also translated by Verschoth.

About Allah Baksh Sabir: "Weeping Father Pleads for Release of Western Hostages," by Kathy Gannon, Associated Press, April 5, 1996.

Kidnapping in Peru, 1996–97: Detail about what the hostages were doing, from The *Economist,* January 4, 1997; see also "Taking Hostages in Peru: Revolution as a Relic Come to Life," by Clifford Kraus, *New York Times,* December 29, 1996.

PART V

Quote about Yemen: In "Kidnapping in Yemen Is Hospitality," by John Lancaster, *Washington Post,* May 16, 1997.

Chapter 36

Story of ransom found in Hong Kong sewage: "Public Toilets Flush with Kidnap Cash," by Clifford Lo and Wanda Szeto, *South China Morning Post*, January 31, 1997.

Honduras statistics: From CRG specialists, and an Associated Press article that reported two businessmen were killed (out of sixty abducted) for the year 1996.

Reports: Risk and Insurance Management Society report, 1997; Kroll Associates intelligence report, *Future Trends in Kidnapping*, 1997; Pinkerton's *Annual Risk Assessment, 1996.*

Quoted Pinkerton executive: Andrew J. Duffin, managing director of the Crisis Management Services Group of Pinkerton Consulting and Investigation Services in Miami.

About Taiwan: "Taiwan: New Kidnap Spot?" by Bruce Cheesman, *Business Times* (Singapore Press Holdings, Ltd.), February 1997.

About Russia: From Pinkerton's report, from CRG's Guy Dunn. Also, "Russia's Mafiyas: The New Revolution," by Tom Hunter, in *Jane's Intelligence Review*, June 1, 1997; and the earlier story predicting increase in kidnapping, "Target: CEO; Kidnappings and Other Acts of Corporate Terrorism," by Dean O'Hare, *Risk Management*, July 1994.

About the Philippines: The National Statistical Board, in Manila, and the Philippine National Police who quoted kidnap statistics for 1995 as 62 and for 1996, 179.

Swap of Texas Couple for jailed separatist: "Swap to Free Two Hostages Was Right, Experts Say," by Michael Wines, *New York Times*, April 29, 1997.

Chapters 37–38

Story of Havenstrite: From the man himself and the FBI report. The conversation between Georgia Havenstrite and the kidnapper, translated from the actual tape from the family.

Quote on Venezuela: From "In Venezuela, A Refuge On a Ranch," by Florence Fabricant, *New York Times*, June 15, 1997.

About Guatemala problem: Arias Foundation for Peace and Democracy; quote from "Central American Criminals Take Up Soldiers' Guns," by Johanna Tuckman, *Financial Times*, October 1, 1996; quote from "After Midnight," by Jeff Salz, *Escape*, July 1997.

Chapter 39

About sightings, example of sighting after the 1996 confession of the captured militant: "Western Hostages in Kashmir Said Sighted Last Week," in Reuters, May 15, 1996.

Quote from Uri Geller: From Reuters, April 25, 1997.

About U.S. secretary of state and the Kashmir issue, in 1997: "U.S. Rules Out Intervention in Kashmir," by Seema Sirohi, in "The Telegraph," May 22, 1997. More about Clinton administration and Kashmir, in "White House Puts Focus on Kashmir Policy," by Tom Carte, *Washington Times,* February 22, 1997.

New York Times headline: From story by John Burns, June 23, 1997.

Quote from Jane Schelly, in India, at press conference: From Reuters, June 26, 1997.

Bibliography

Adams, James. *The Financing of Terror*. New York: Simon and Schuster, 1986.
———. *Trading in Death*. London: Century Hutchinson, 1990.
Alexander, Bevin. *The Future of Warfare*. New York: Norton, 1995.
Alix, Ernest Kahlar. *Ransom Kidnapping in America, 1874–1974: The Creation of a Capital Crime*. Carbondale: Southern Illinois University Press, 1978.
Allison, Graham, and Gregory Treverton, eds. *Rethinking America's Security: Beyond the Cold War to New World Order*. New York: Norton, 1992.
Anderson, Terry. *Den of Lions*. New York: Ballantine Books, 1993.
Barnby, H. G. *The Prisoners of Algiers*. London: Oxford University Press, 1966.
Bryan, Lowell, and Diana Farrell. *Market Unbound: Unleashing Global Capitalism*. New York: John Wiley, 1996.
Buhite, Russell D. *Lives at Risk: Hostages and Victims in American Foreign Policy*. Wilmington, Del.: Scholarly Resources, 1995.
Chandler, Ann Howell. "Kidnapping in the United States: Characteristics and Offenders." Ph.D. dissertation, Temple University, May 1975.
Clutterbuck, Richard. *Kidnap and Ransom: The Response*. London: Faber and Faber, 1978.

————. *Kidnap, Hijack, and Extortion: The Response.* Foreword by Sir Robert Mark. London: Macmillan, 1987.

Danziger, Sheldon, and Peter Gottschalk. *America Unequal.* New York: Russell Sage Foundation, 1995.

Economist magazine, such as the October 19, 1996, and August 9, 1997, issues.

Farrell, William R. *The U.S. Government Response to Terrorism, 1972–1980.* Boulder: Westview Press, 1982.

Follett, Ken. *On Wings of Eagles.* New York: William Morrow, 1983.

Foreign Affairs magazine. Of particular interest: "Postmodern Terrorism: New Rules for an Old Game," by Walter Laqueur. September–October 1996.

Forsyth, Frederick. *The Negotiator.* New York: Bantam Books, 1989.

Francis, Dick. *The Danger.* New York: Ballantine Books, 1984.

Frank, Robert H., and Philip J. Cook. *The Winner-Take-All Society.* New York: Free Press, 1995.

García Márquez, Gabriel. *News of a Kidnapping.* Translated by Edith Grossman. New York: Alfred A. Knopf, 1997.

Guehenno, Jean-Marie. *The End of the Nation-State.* Translated by Victoria Elliott. Minneapolis, Minn.: University of Minnesota Press, 1995.

Hargrove, Thomas R. *Long March to Freedom: Tom Hargrove's Own Story of His Kidnapping by Colombian Narco-guerrillas.* New York: Ballantine Books, 1995.

Head, William Bruce. "The Hostage Response: An Examination of U.S. Law Enforcement Practices Concerning Hostage Incidents." Ph.D. dissertation, School of Criminal Justice, State University of New York at Albany, April 1988.

Hobsbawm, E. J. *Nations and Nationalism since 1780: Programme, Myth, Reality.* New York and London: Cambridge University Press, 1990.

————. *Primitive Rebels: Studies in Archaic Forms of Social Movement in the 19th and 20th Centuries.* New York and London: Norton, 1965. (Originally published under the title *Social Bandits and Primitive Rebels,* 1959.)

Hostage Negotiation: A Matter of Life and Death. International Security and Terrorism Series, no. 2. Defense Information Access Network (DIANE). Rancocas, N.J.: DIANE Publishing, 1987.

Huntington, Samuel P. *The Clash of Civilizations and the Remaking of World Order.* New York: Simon and Schuster, 1996.

Jackson, Geoffrey. *People's Prison.* London: Faber and Faber, 1973.

Jenkins, Brian. Various pamphlets published by the Rand Corporation between 1974 and 1984, in Santa Monica, Calif. *Should Corporations be Prevented from Paying Ransoms?* (1974). *Hostage Survival: Some Preliminary Observations* (1976). *Talking to Terrorists* (1982).

Keenan, Brian. *An Evil Cradling: The Five-Year Ordeal of a Hostage.* London, Random House, 1992.

Keenan, Brigid. *Travels in Kashmir.* Oxford: Oxford University Press, 1989.

Kessler, Ronald. *The FBI: Inside the World's Most Powerful Law Enforcement Agency.* New York: Simon and Schuster, 1993.

Krotz, Larry, *Tourists: How Our Fastest Growing Industry Is Changing the World.* London: Faber and Faber, 1997.

McCarthy, John and Jill Morrell. *Some Other Rainbow.* London: Corgi, 1994.

Mirow, Kurt Rudolf, and Harry Maurer. *Webs of Power: International Cartels and the World Economy.* Boston: Houghton Mifflin, 1982.

Muller, Kal. *Irian Jaya: Indonesian New Guinea.* Hong Kong: Periplus Editions, 1996.

Naipaul, V. S. *A Bend in the River.* New York: Alfred A. Knopf, 1979.

New Perspectives Quarterly. Of particular interest: "Third Wave Terrorism," vol. 12, no. 3 (summer 1995). Includes excellent articles by L. Paul Bremer III, the former head of the State Department's counterterrorism unit during the Reagan years; author Alvin Toffler; Robert S. McNamara, former U.S. secretary of defense and president of the World Bank; and the intriguing article "Breaking Up the Nuclear Family" with contributors Madeleine Albright (then U.S. ambassador to the United Nations), Narasimha Rao (India's prime minister during the Kashmir hostage crisis), and Benazir Bhutto (former prime minister of Pakistan). And "After the End of History," vol. 13, no. 4 (fall 1996).

Ohmae, Kenichi. *The End of the Nation State.* New York: Free Press, 1995.

Pelton, Robert Young, and Coskun Aral, *Fielding's The World's Most Dangerous Places.* Redondo Beach, Calif.: Fielding Worldwide, 1995.

Pizam, Abraham, and Yoel Mansfeld, eds. *Tourism, Crime, and International Security Issues.* West Sussex, England: John Wiley, 1996.

Schlossberg, Harvey. *Police Response to Hostage Situations.* New York: Maxwell House, 1979.

Schofield, Victoria. *Kashmir: In the Crossfire.* London: I. B. Tauris, 1996.

Schwartz, Peter. *The Art of the Long View.* New York: Currency and Doubleday, 1995.

Slater, Stephanie. *Beyond Fear: My Will to Survive.* With Pat Lancaster. London: Fourth Estate, 1995.

Sterling, Claire. *The Terror Network: The Secret War of International Terrorism*. New York: Holt, Rinehart, and Winston, 1981.

Thurow, Lester C. *The Future of Capitalism: How Today's Economic Forces Shape Tomorrow's World*. New York: William Morrow, 1996.

Toffler, Alvin. *Power Shift: Knowledge, Wealth, and Violence at the Edge of the 21st Century*. New York: Bantam Books, 1990.

Toffler, Alvin, and Heidi Toffler, *War and Anti-War*. New York: Little Brown, 1993.

U.S. Senate Committee on Foreign Relations. *Ransom of Miss Ellen M. Stone*. 63rd Congress, May 14, 1913, Doc. 29.

Waite, Terry. *Taken on Trust*. London: Hodder and Stoughton, 1993.

Wroe, Ann. *Lives, Lies, and the Iran-Contra Affair*. London: I. B. Tauris, 1991.

Acknowledgments

⋘⋙

To write a book is to embark on a journey that is full of discovery and illumination yet littered with moments of loneliness and even occasional despair. But it is always a journey that leads to a new place for the mind and soul, so that all challenges and pain endemic to the process are endurable. This book was challenging on several levels and for this reason there are many people to acknowledge for their support.

I must first thank the former hostages and the families of former and current hostages who gave me so much of their time, sharing details and describing scenes that must have resurrected feelings they were trying to forget. I learned a good deal about courage from them all. One afternoon in Oslo in the tea room at the GabelsHus Hotell, as I was interviewing Hans Gustav Ostro, the translator began to stumble over words and to pause for long moments. I stopped the interview when I realized she was crying. She had been friends with Hans Christian and hearing the story from the point of view of his father had overwhelmed her. Hans Gustav gently placed his hand on hers, saying that he understood her tears and thanked her for caring. He closed his eyes, took a deep breath, and went on. I thank Hans Gustav for his time and his gracious spirit. In England, Keith Mangan's parents spent an entire afternoon with me only two days before their big trip to India, and at dusk they escorted me to the train station to be certain I didn't lose my way. Julie Mangan was always ready to drop anything to answer a question, to clarify a detail. And then there was Jane Schelly. Don Hutchings would be proud if he could witness the way Jane juggles the many duties of a hostage wife, honoring the requests of journalists, planning the trips to bring him home, maintaining her job, working with government officials, keeping her friends informed. Her courage, generosity, and endless energy are a marvel to all who know her. Thanks, too, to Buddy and Jackie McManus, Cindy and Bill Erler, Debbie Pierce, Emily Gordon, George Neal, and Dr. Jim Roubos.

I also thank Stu, Georgia, and Cindy Havenstrite, who kindly sent me the tape of that fascinating conversation between Georgia and her husband's kidnapper in Mexico. Jim, Claudia, and Mark Thurber respected my tedious concerns for accuracy and granted me the honor of being the only journalist to whom they told their story. John Heidema and Karen Karl were simply terrific, always offering to go many extra miles in helping me. I thank also Terry Waite for sharing time and wisdom on a subject he knows only too well. Susana Siegfried, in Costa Rica, spent many hours answering my questions and I am grateful to her. Though not included in the book, Robert de Cruz, a Brit who spent five months in captivity in Sierra Leone in early 1995 (months before the book's chronology begins), drove two hours on his motorbike to meet me at my London hotel and to share the intriguing details of his experience, including the rebels' dinner delicacy of barbecued termites.

In the course of seeking sources for the book, I faced numerous obstacles. So many aspects of the story of kidnapping are secretive. Negotiators are often reluctant to reveal who they are, what they do, and where they do it. Families worry about the impact of publicity, especially in an ongoing case. Corporations don't want to talk about it. And victims are not always willing to discuss their ordeal, sometimes advised by lawyers or employers to keep a low profile. Consequently, there were numerous people who asked to remain in the background. And some chose not to speak to me at all. I understand the reluctance to talk to journalists. And I harbor no resentments for those who did not wish to be interviewed. I want the people I interview to be comfortable with their choice. I do, however, find fault with those who asked to be paid for interviews. This happened to me several times during this book; it's a sorry trend.

Among those who asked for anonymity are individuals at the International Committee for the Red Cross, an organization whose heroic efforts during kidnap incidents are so discreet, diplomatic, and behind-the-scenes as to be unknown and unheralded. Perhaps I can acknowledge them best by quoting Daniel Start, one of the British hostages in Irian Jaya in 1996, who upon his release told the press:

"Especially I would like to thank the International Committee for the Red Cross. Since February, they've been coming into the area almost on a daily basis in helicopters to very remote villages up in the mountains—sometimes in very dangerous and difficult weather—to hold negotiations and talks with, really, a bunch of very tricky people indeed who were armed and generally quite threatening and frightening."

Among those who declined to be interviewed for this book, some expressed concerns that the book would encourage more kidnappings by revealing the locations of incidents and the ways families and victims had responded, and by offering a glimpse into the world of kidnap negotiation. My response was and is that kidnappers don't need this book to be motivated to ply their trade. Further, the importance of informing the general public that the problem exists—not only in Colombia—and that the social and economic conditions fostering the crime are intrinsic to the post–Cold War landscape and the globalization era far outweighs the potential threat of provoking more kidnappings. In response to the same sort of skepticism, Richard Clutterbuck noted in the preface to his book *Kidnap & Ransom:* "If for fear of telling criminals and terrorists what they already know, we were to insulate ourselves from the means of acquiring this understanding [of the crime], the balance would be negative."

Some sources too were hesitant because they believed that to shed light on the kidnap problem would be tantamount to sensationalizing it. What must be understood, some individuals reminded me, is that the problem has reached epidemic levels in only a few parts of the globe. And the likelihood of getting kidnapped is, of course, small relative to getting in a car accident. That is true. But the odds of being in an airplane wreck are small too. Still, passengers are warned about the possibility and are even told how to react in the event of a crash. My purpose here has been neither to sensationalize kidnapping nor to discourage travel. The purpose is simply to give people fair warning, which will inspire them to be informed before taking a trip. Traveling to Costa Rica is not a problem but, depending on current conditions, it is wise to stay away from the Nicaraguan border. There are dangers, too, in traveling and living in New York City, but if one takes certain precautions then New York is a fine place to be. The key is to be aware. I have only sought to raise the consciousness of travelers in the age of globalization. Though

Clutterbuck's 1978 book is about a different era in the kidnap saga, it once again offers some wisdom. In the foreword, Sir Robert Mark, an ex-commissioner of London's Metropolitan Police, wrote: "Read superficially, it [the book] is rather alarming; considered objectively it is a useful and timely warning of the need to be prepared for, but not daunted by, the unpleasant prospects it unfolds."

The refusal of some sources and the expressed reluctance of others only underscores the generosity of those who did choose to spend time with me. These include Bob Dwyer, whose enthusiasm and energy have always been a delight. From the start, New Scotland Yard was especially helpful. There, I must thank Jane Watts for her patience and hard work and Roy Ramm for his many hours of assistance and his exquisite sense of humor; also, John Beadle, Chris Newman, Lorne Johnson, and Nicky Benwell, among others. At Control Risks, I'd like to thank David Lattin and Edward Grubb above all. They were cursed with the time-consuming and unpopular job of "dealing with the journalist"—something the firm was not thrilled about. And they handled their plight with grace, intelligence, and wit. Also, at Control Risks, thanks to Guy Dunn, Eleni Jakub, John Bray, Sandy Markwick, Justine Barrett, and Richard Fenning. I am grateful also to Richard Clutterbuck, Russ Ross, Bill Ilsley, Frank Johns, Hugh Barber, Mark Hansen, Benito Romano, Bart Schwartz, Al La Porta, Geoffrey Potter, Richard Carlson, Alison Jamieson, Jim Camden, Steve Mann, John Morrison, Rabbi Amy Ehrlich, and Jan Euden. At the FBI, though it took several frustrating months of letter-writing, I was able to work my way into the inner sanctum of the agency's team of crisis negotiators. My apologies to Director Louis Freeh for the strident letter I sent to him in early 1996. And my abundant thanks to Gary Noessner and Leon Schenck, among others.

I'm indebted to my readers: John and Phil Auerbach, Sarah Byers, Sari Levin, William L. Nack, Rorie Sherman. I could not have done the book without the individuals who translated letters, reports, and interviews for me: Anita Verschoth, Marianne Siegmund, Richard Hacken, Bob Dwyer, Tora Mellbye. My special thanks to Anita, who helped me to track down some rather elusive individuals in Europe. Thanks also to Einar Sjoblom at the GabelsHut Hotell in Oslo, to Demir Gonc at the Diplomat Hotel in London, and to the staff at the Marriott Courtyard in Spokane for repeatedly providing wonderful rooms and accommodating my needs for interviewing sources in quiet, private spaces. While on the subject of hotels I must also note those tolerant folks at the Sheraton Belgravia in London, whose lobby I used as a quasi office, organizing notes, indexing interviews, and even writing parts of the book. I am also indebted, as always, to the *Wall Street Journal,* whose editors taught me the importance of structure in the art of storytelling.

This book was originally meant to cover one year in the world of kidnapping, using one case for the narrative, weaving in other cases and background to tell the full story. During the summer of 1995, in the early stages of the book, I was still undecided about which case might best provide that narrative. As incidents occurred, I would open a new case file and my researcher Sari Levin would stick a pin in her world map noting the location: red pins for ongoing cases and white pins for resolved ones. As the months wore on, many red pins were happily replaced with white, but the red pin in northern India remained. My concern for the hostages, my interest in the issues surrounding the case, and my curiosity about what was blocking a resolution compelled me to focus on Kashmir for the narrative. I always believed, however, that by the summer of 1996, Hutchings, Mangan, Wells, and Hasert would walk out of the mountains. And I had planned to fly to India, chronicle the event, and end the book. But that didn't happen. And so I expanded the book to two years, knowing that this would provide a much more realistic view of the crime and hoping, of course, that the case in Kashmir would be resolved.

Extending the book and trying to come close to the original deadline meant many added hours of work for everyone involved and the need for much support from family and friends. It is these people to whom I am the most indebted. Sari Levin, my incredibly bright, resourceful, and enthusiastic researcher and friend, listened patiently to my plans for the book's structure and to my complaints about the obstacles I encountered. And she tolerated my endless requests in the pursuit of accuracy and originality. William L. Nack, one of the best friends a person could have, listened well to my theories and themes as they evolved, reassuring me during bouts of self-doubt and always believing in me as a writer. My agent, Alice Martell, is a saint by nature. I have known her for more than a decade now and my respect for her intelligence and her sound instincts continues to grow. Ruth Schubert, now a writer at the *Seattle Post-Intelligencer,* worked for me in the early stages of the book, always offering her excellent insight and clarity. And, of course, I am indebted to Henry Holt and Company—also the publisher of my previous book *Wild Ride*—and my two wonderful editors there, the former editor-in-chief, Bill Strachan, and senior editor Allen Peacock, both so very bright, sensitive, and talented.

Last, and far, far from least, there is my family. My husband, John Auerbach, also a writer, understood my devotion to the book and never complained about the many hours I spent in my office and on the road. John saw the book potential in the subject matter long before I was confident I could pull it together; his enthusiasm and patience were invaluable. And I'm indebted, as always, to my mother, Elizabeth; my sister, Sarah; my nephew, Scott; and to the Auerbachs, Phil, Gloria, Marcie, Alan, Jason, and Philip, who were all wonderfully supportive throughout the project.

Index

❖❖❖